Feminist Trouble

Feminist Trouble

Intersectional Politics in Postsecular Times

ÉLÉONORE LÉPINARD

Oxford University Press is a department of the University of Oxford. It furthers
the University's objective of excellence in research, scholarship, and education
by publishing worldwide. Oxford is a registered trade mark of Oxford University
Press in the UK and certain other countries.

Published in the United States of America by Oxford University Press
198 Madison Avenue, New York, NY 10016, United States of America.

© Oxford University Press 2020

Some rights reserved. No part of this publication may be reproduced,
stored in a retrieval system, or transmitted, in any form or by any means,
for commercial purposes, without the prior permission in writing of
Oxford University Press, or as expressly permitted by law, by licence or under terms
agreed with the appropriate reprographics rights organization.

The pre-press of this publication was supported by the Swiss National Science Foundation.

This is an open access publication, available online and distributed under
the terms of a Creative Commons Attribution – Non Commercial – No Derivatives
4.0 International licence (CC BY-NC-ND 4.0), a copy of which is available at
http://creativecommons.org/licenses/by-nc-nd/4.0/.

You must not circulate this work in any other form
and you must impose this same condition on any acquirer.

Library of Congress Cataloging-in-Publication Data
Names: Lépinard, Éléonore, author.
Title: Feminist trouble : intersectional politics in postsecular times / Éléonore Lépinard.
Description: New York, NY : Oxford University Press, [2020] |
Includes bibliographical references and index. |
Identifiers: LCCN 2019034419 (print) | LCCN 2019034420 (ebook) |
ISBN 9780190077150 (hardback) | ISBN 9780190077167 (paperback) |
ISBN 9780190077174 (updf) | ISBN 9780190077198 (online) |
ISBN 9780190077181 (epub)
Subjects: LCSH: Feminism.
Classification: LCC HQ1155 .L466 2020 (print) |
LCC HQ1155 (ebook) | DDC 305.42—dc23
LC record available at https://lccn.loc.gov/2019034419
LC ebook record available at https://lccn.loc.gov/2019034420

Contents

Acknowledgments vii

1 Introduction 1
2 Theorizing Feminism: Politics, Morals, and Emotions 23
3 Race, Religion, and Gender: Feminist Intersectional Politics in "Postsecular" Times 45
4 Feminist Whiteness 81
5 Resisting Whiteness, Claiming Feminism: Racialized Feminists' Moral Addresses 127
6 Toward a Feminist Ethic of Responsibility 179
7 Conclusion: Revisiting the "We" of Feminism 234

Appendix on Methodology 251
Notes 257
Bibliography 295
Index 317

Acknowledgments

This book is dedicated to all the feminists who gave some of their time to answer my questions, who shared their thoughts, analyses, despairs, and hopes, and enabled me, not to adopt their perspectives and standpoints, but to enter in *relation*, to understand what is important for them, and for us.

For many reasons writing this book has been an experience in the strong sense of something that gave me a voice, shared with many of my interviewees, an encounter with the unpredictable, and a descent into myself to understand my own attachment to feminism. I hope this book conveys to readers the pleasure of giving some intelligibility to one's own experiences of feminism. It certainly provided me with the pleasure of deploying my own thoughts with freedom—a rare chance, and an addictive experience. I want to thank especially my editor at Oxford University Press, James Cook, who believed in this book and in its unusual interdisciplinarity and style.

This experience has been made possible by various institutional supports; the grant I received from the Fond Québécois de la Recherche sur la Société et la Culture, which allowed me to conduct the fieldwork; and the support of the two universities I was a faculty member of during the time of research and then writing, the Université de Montréal and the Université de Lausanne. In both those places I found among my colleagues good friends, with the dose of humor that is necessary to sail through academic life with pleasure. I am very grateful for their friendship. At the Université de Lausanne I have been lucky to join a Center on Gender Studies that has allowed me to focus on feminist theory and provided me with fantastic doctoral students with whom to exchange ideas on feminism and feminist theory. Support also came in the form of assistance from Marie Laperrière, for interviews in the fieldwork; from Muriel Bruttin, for formatting the manuscript and dealing with software bugs; and from Madeleine Arenivar, for copy-editing. The three did a wonderful job, and I thank them deeply for their skillful work.

During the course of writing, I was lucky to receive feedback on this project and invitations to present my work from several colleagues, whom I thank here for their generosity and their insights: Amélie Barras, Pascale Dufour, Elizabeth Evans, Delphine Gardey, Matteo Gianni, Leslie McCall, Noémi

Michel, Marylène Lieber, Sabrina Marchetti, Sarah Mazouz, Bruno Perreau, Anne Phillips, and Gloria Wekker. I am also very grateful to Pascale Molinier, who introduced me years ago to the work of Teresa de Lauretis and of care theorists. It took me a while to act upon this invitation to explore beyond the boundaries of my discipline, sociology, but the journey has been enlivening. Finally, the title of this book is indebted of course to Judith Butler's *Gender Trouble*, a book that starts by looking directly into the trouble within feminism and that profoundly marked my own political subjectivation when I read it and discussed it with young fellow French feminists in search of new political and feminist horizons two decades ago.

More than support, my partner in life and parenting, Grégoire Mallard, read the whole manuscript, encouraged me to break disciplinary shackles, and never doubted that this manuscript would see the light of day. His kindness, generosity, and humor compose the music of our life together.

1
Introduction

Feminism is in trouble. Antagonisms, conflicts, and disputes abound in many liberal democratic countries around pop culture, neoliberalism, and postfeminism, around sex work and pornography (yes, still), around trans* politics, around race and postcolonialism. They seem to concentrate, with an ever-escalating force, around religion, in particular Islam. In many corners of Europe and North America, it has been not a small irony of history that women's rights have been presented by right-wing movements as a new national treasure against which to judge immigrants' claims to be included in the political community, and claims by Muslim citizens to equal treatment in the face of the perpetuation of racial exclusion and discrimination in Western postcolonial societies. Even if voices rising from within feminist movements have denounced hegemonic whiteness,[1] racism, colonial aphasia,[2] and Islamophobia when they are associated with feminist claims, they have remained, in many contexts, marginal and marginalized. For many, the collusion of feminist ideals with right-wing populism and xenophobic political agendas puts in peril the future of feminism as a political utopia. The feminist collective project thus seems to be once again fragmented and disintegrated and in urgent need of reinventing itself.

The increasingly heated disputes about the place of Islam in liberal democracies may not be surprising, considering the broader geopolitical landscape that the liberal democracies in Europe and North America have inherited since the terrorist attacks of 9/11. Nationwide debates questioning the compatibility of Islam with European or "Western" culture and its conception of secularism have focused on gender relations,[3] and have therefore moved to the center of the feminist agenda. Veils, niqabs, forced and arranged marriages, polygamy and sharia rules concerning women have all been the object of intense public scrutiny and legal regulations in many Western countries since the 1990s, and these policy debates have split the women's movements into various positions with regard to the status of gendered symbols and gender relations associated with the practice of Islam.[4] With a particular intensity in Europe, the feminist concern about gender

Feminist Trouble. Éléonore Lépinard, Oxford University Press (2020). © Oxford University Press.
DOI: 10.1093/oso/9780190077150.001.0001

inequalities in "minority cultures" has become closely intertwined with national anxieties about the boundaries of the political community, its heterogeneity, and the necessity to integrate groups perceived as embodying different cultural and religious values.[5]

Few European states have been left untouched by these political dynamics, which have led to the imposition of more restrictions on Islamic practices. Between 2003 and 2019, bans on forms of Islamic veiling (in public service, public schools, or public space) have been adopted in France, Germany, Belgium, Switzerland, Bulgaria, Austria, Denmark, the Netherlands, Turkey, and Quebec, as well as in Italian and Spanish municipalities, and have been fiercely debated in Norway, Latvia, and Finland.[6] Gender equality has suddenly gained a new visibility and a new status. In each country where these debates have emerged, gender equality has been presented as a national achievement, a Western cultural specificity, and a new norm, which determines who will be able to assimilate and what practices are or are not politically desirable. The concept of "femonationalism," coined by Sara Farris, following the term "homonationalism," forged by Jasbir Puar,[7] refers to the ways in which political parties and government institutions have used women's rights to bolster nationalist identities and pass repressive policies against immigrants and Islam.[8] As Farris writes: "The mobilization, or rather instrumentalization, of the notion of women's equality both by nationalist and xenophobic parties and by neoliberal governments constitutes one of the most important characteristics of the current political conjuncture, particularly in Europe."[9]

One should add that xenophobic parties and right- or left-wing governments are not the only players in this game. Indeed, women's rights organizations themselves participate in this trend, whether fueling it or resisting it. While they do not have the power to shape public policies as political parties and governments do, they have appeared as experts and legitimating voices, in particular when they have stood side by side with power-holders.[10] As gender equality has become associated with secularism[11] and anti-Islamic, xenophobic, and racist policies, feminism has been enrolled in nationalist projects[12] and lost its critical edge in public discourse. While these debates have incentivized many feminist scholars to reflect on the articulation between colonialism, gender, race, and Islam in contemporary Europe,[13] this perilous context asks for a renewed theoretical feminist imagination that can dissociate feminism from nationalist and racist policies.

Critical feminist work has been engaged in this task, documenting resistance to these discourses by women and feminists of color,[14] unveiling epistemic violence perpetrated in the name of feminism and ideologies of racelessness in Europe,[15] and analyzing collusion between feminism and neoliberal logics.[16] I argue in this book that we also need to elaborate a feminist critique that can revive feminist imagination and that can put feminist ideals at work not to support nationalist and racist agendas but to dismantle them. To do so demands, I contend, we start from the experience and discourses of feminists engaged in these debates and, what is more, engaged in daily feminist work and activism. Indeed, despite numerous sophisticated analyses of the ways in which these policy debates have rearticulated feminist public claims in the language of nationalism, anti-immigrant sentiment, and Islamophobia, we lack an account from the point of view of those who are primarily concerned with this political project and its future: activists who self-identify as feminists.[17] Only if we understand their attachment to nationalist and secular ideals, or on the contrary their ability to remain critical, can we envision a feminist project that will appeal to feminists' political imagination.

So far, few studies have investigated the actual impact that these policy debates about the regulation of Islamic religious practices have had on feminist movements, especially in European contexts. Few have documented how, beyond a set of limited public discourses made in the name of feminism by prominent public figures, feminist activists themselves have energetically participated on both sides—in favor of prohibition and in favor of accommodation.[18] Because we lack many narratives from feminist activists involved in Islamic veiling debates, we are still at pains to explain why these debates have triggered such powerful and opposite emotional reactions from feminists, and why these controversies have shattered feminist movements, creating new divisions, performing exclusions and nurturing long-lasting rancor, while in other contexts, feminist organizations have found ways to maintain coalitions. In other words, we are still missing an understanding of the extent to which these debates have empirically transformed a variety of feminist subjectivities and have altered feminism as a normative political project. Why are Islamic veiling debates troubling feminism? What is the exact nature of this trouble? How does this trouble engage us to rethink feminism?

Ultimately, the participation of feminist voices in these public debates that have crystalized around religion and race in Europe reflects controversies within feminism about what is true emancipation and who can be a feminist subject. France is a case in point. Many French feminist organizations identifying with secularism have supported policies prohibiting forms of Islamic veiling, such as the 2010 ban on full veiling in public spaces, in the name of enforcing gender equality and protecting Muslim women from their patriarchal religion and beliefs. The list of prohibitions begins with the ban on veiling in public schools in 2004, leading up to the most recent ban passed by municipalities against burkinis—the full-body covering used by devout Muslim women to swim on French beaches—in the summer of 2016, which was subsequently overturned in court. Still, as municipal decrees against burkinis were multiplying on French beaches, an open letter signed by a number of French feminists was published to encourage mayors from the cities in question to annul these bans.[19] The petition pointed to the rampant Islamophobia in the French public sphere and society that these decrees revealed and fueled, and to the incompatibility of these measures with a true conception of feminism. But its authors dramatically failed to obtain the support of the most important national French women's organizations. The episode of the 2016 burkini controversy showed that questions of religious differences and postcolonialism remained highly divisive among French feminists. It proved that what is a true feminist politics—and a good feminist subject—in France is still the object of much controversy and contention.

Debates about Islamic veiling have therefore struck at the heart of the desirable definitions of the feminist subject—of the *emancipated* proper feminist subject. As European feminists have fought over if and how Muslim veiled women should be considered emancipated and potential feminist subjects, or instead as subjects to be educated by or excluded from the feminist project, their debates have exposed the limits of the Western, dominant strand of feminism as profoundly liberal and, despite protests to the contrary, exclusive of female subjectivities that do not suit the liberal political and moral imaginary.[20] These debates waged in the name of feminism have also revealed the perpetuating equation between liberalism and whiteness that suffuses many feminist discourses. As authors of the petition against the 2016 antiburkini French laws have contended, using the language of postcolonialism, racism, and feminism to analyze the political issues at stake, the language of feminism can become the vehicle for racist policies that delegitimize the public presence of nonwhite bodies.[21] Hence, debates about Islamic veiling have fueled a critical theoretical discussion within feminism on the meaning of agency and autonomy, on the relationship between subjectivity and subjection, that has called into question basic premises of (liberal) feminism. In doing so, these debates seem to have imperiled feminism as a modern political project of emancipation.[22] For this reason, Islamic veiling debates cast a much larger shadow on feminism as a political project of emancipation than have previous debates over "differences" within feminism.

Feminist Agency in Postsecular Times

What type of challenge do female pious religious identities and subjectivities pose for feminism? And why do they do so? As Rosi Braidotti aptly put it: "The postsecular turn challenges European feminism because it makes manifest the notion that agency, or political subjectivity, can actually be conveyed through and supported by religious piety, and may even involve significant amounts of spirituality."[23] Feminist theory has been preoccupied for several decades with the identity/freedom paradox, as Allison Weir recaptures it, that is, the paradox that what makes us subjects, our social identities, is also what subjects us. Identities are "both sources and ends of freedom, and identities are the shackles that imprison us."[24] However, the postsecular context offers a new paradox and challenge, not so much one that is preoccupied with how identities might foster or restrain freedom, as one that questions the value and meaning of freedom per se, and for feminism in particular.

In this context, religious women's agency has become a focal point of interest for feminist theorists, and a growing literature has explored and complicated feminist understandings of agency and freedom.[25] Various strands of feminist theory—liberal, multiculturalist, and postcolonial—have struggled with the challenge of reconceptualizing women's autonomy in a way that can account for practices, emotions, and desires that fall outside the scope of the Western liberal conception of autonomy. While liberal feminists such as Marylin Friedman propose a minimalist conception of autonomy, one in which the procedures through which women reach a decision—rather than the substantive content of this decision—matter in determining individual moral autonomy,[26] multiculturalist feminists such as Monique Deveaux and Anne Phillips also insist on the deliberative procedures within cultural and religious communities that can ensure that women are participants in the decisions that concern them.[27] Postcolonial feminist Uma Narayan shares the concern of multiculturalist feminists to avoid the twin pitfalls of ethnocentricity and cultural relativism in judging religious women's agency, and argues that the only proper way to describe both religious and Western women's relationship to patriarchy is the concept of *bargaining* with internal and external constraints shaped by political, economic, and moral factors.[28]

These various redefinitions of agency remain, however, within the scope of the traditional liberal feminist conception of subjectivity and freedom—albeit at its margins. Indeed, while their efforts to pluralize conceptions of freedom and autonomy in order to recuperate religious subjects within the feminist project are important, they fall short of accounting for desires other than the desire for freedom, and therefore of accurately describing the ethical dispositions of religious women.

In contrast, studies of female religious agency have tried to disentangle the deep relationship between Western feminism and its biased conception of agency as subversion, its conception of freedom, and its enduring ethnocentrism. Drawing on her fieldwork with pious Muslim women participating in the mosque movement in Egypt, Saba Mahmood takes on this very task in order to propose an alternative to the feminist conception of agency and freedom. She notes, with others,[29] that dominant conceptions of feminist agency always associate it with individual political and moral autonomy, with a desire for freedom and the subsequent subversion of norms rather than their acceptance. She argues that this dominant conception of agency imposes on conservative and religious women who decide to abide by norms perceived as oppressive by Western women a gaze that constructs them as eternal and absolute victims, victims of false consciousness or complicit with their oppression.

To "speak back" to these liberal-secular assumptions,[30] Mahmood proposes to reformulate the concept of agency via a focus on ethical dispositions. Indeed, mobilizing Judith Butler's definition of agency, which locates agency within structures of power rather than in the individual subject, Mahmood suggests that agency can be traced not only, as she claims Butler argues, in practices of resignification and subversion of gendered norms, but also in the way one inhabits and experiences these norms. Here Mahmood departs from a strictly political account of agency and power to turn to the process of ethical formation and modes of subjectivation. She departs from the association of agency with resistance to domination while she also displaces the location of agency from the self to a nexus of social relations that permeate and shape the self. Doing so, Mahmood radically decouples agency from its (liberal) feminist roots in individual moral and political autonomy and resistance to oppression. Following Foucault's insight that ethics is a positive modality of power, Mahmood interprets the processes of ethical formation to which women participating in the mosque movement are subjected—through authoritative discursive traditions interpreting religious norms, conduct, and imperatives—as processes that create forms of ethical agency, which are tightly interwoven with political agency in that ethical agency enables, for instance, the political actions of the mosque movement. Expanding the realm of ethical agency to moral actions such as submission to God, docility, and humility, Mahmood asserts that ethical agency "does not belong to the women themselves, but is a product of the historically contingent discursive traditions in which they are located."[31] She effectively breaks with the dominant liberal feminist conception of autonomy and emancipation, as agency can mean chosen submission to God, inhabiting conservative gender norms and engaging, through reading and other religious interpretative practices, in a self-fashioning as a devout Muslim.

The literature on religious agency has unveiled implicit liberal beliefs at the heart of feminism, but this critique has left us with some degree of political powerlessness: Mahmood's careful theoretical and anthropological account of the formation of the ethical agency of women participating in the mosque movement[32] leads her to argue that "the question of how the hierarchical system of gender relations that the mosque movement upholds should be *practically* transformed is, on the one hand, impossible to answer and, on the other hand, not ours to ask."[33] Her work has struck at the heart of both the moral individual subject of feminism and the viability of the collective political subject of feminism, but has not provided many indications about which routes we might want to explore to reclaim this project.[34] If one can agree with Mahmood's warning that the feminist notion of agency should be critically scrutinized in order to avoid the pitfall of global sisterhood, and agree that there is some analytical payoff in her choice to decouple the notion of agency from progressive politics, her position raises a thorny issue for feminist politics and theory.[35] Her critical reappraisal of agency implies that one should shy away from the temptation to elaborate a collective feminist imagination and avoid thinking through modalities of solidarities across different contexts and subjectivities (liberal and nonliberal). From this perspective, both the transnational feminist imagination some have called for[36] and the very possibility of feminist coalitions across religious identities in Western countries seem impossible to achieve, even undesirable to pursue.

Speaking back to liberal feminist assumptions from the vantage point of ethical religious agency, Mahmood therefore leaves us with a major question regarding our feminist beliefs—what do we mean when we as feminists say that gender equality is the central principle of our analysis and politics? or in other words, can a feminist project exist without liberal and therefore exclusive premises?—and a very modest proposal to address it. While she does not abandon a critical stance toward practices we find unjust, she suggests that we should be open to the possibility of having our political and analytical certainties "transformed in the process."[37] I wish to take on this task—suggested but not carried out by Mahmood—following some of her insights but also displacing the question. Indeed, while Mahmood's anthropological account expands the meaning of agency and reveals both the complexity of nonliberal ethical practices of self-fashioning and how they differ from what has been considered as feminist agency, feminism, as a normative political project, also demands that we engage with the moral and political questions raised by these differences. At this critical juncture, we have to thus ask ourselves: Does Mahmood's understanding of agency provide us with a new and more inclusive agenda for feminism? This was, after all, the question that feminist theorization of agency meant to address in the first place. Framed in the terms posed by Mahmood, the breadth of the challenge to liberal feminism as a political project is daunting, and an indication that, indeed, questions regarding religious difference appear today as different as can be from previous questions of differences with which feminist theory and practices have struggled before.[38] If autonomy or equality, understood in their liberal sense, are performing inacceptable exclusions of nonliberal subjects from the feminist project, then what is the future of feminism? For those unhappy with liberal feminism—not only because its conception of ethical agency is restrictive and inadequate but also because its politics perpetuates exclusions—what is the alternative?

Beyond the Religious Agency Debate: Exploring Feminists' Political Subjectivations

I argue that our theoretical energy must not be consumed by attempts to redefine agency as a way to salvage the feminist project. We do not need to engage in debates about what counts as autonomous behavior or free action in order to address questions such as Islamic veiling, or more broadly to address the question posed by Mahmood about the possibility of feminism beyond its roots in liberal visions of emancipation. Indeed, what we need is an understanding of how hierarchies between feminist subjects, through discourses about agency and emancipation, are created and sustained, and a normative proposal to undo them. Theoretical conceptions of agency and freedom are only a part of the story of femonationalism and Islamic veiling debates. As I will argue, we need to focus our analytical energy on our moral and political attachments to these conceptions, which are rooted in hierarchies and power and which should be the focus of our critical inquiry.

While accounts of "solidarity" and gender equality imposed by Western feminists and international organizations from the top down have provided us with cautionary tales, in Europe and other Western countries the possibility of elaborating a feminist project that cuts across racial and religious differences is a matter of political survival for feminism itself, because it is about finding and building what we have in common. I argue that in order to go beyond the negativity of critique,[39] we must redirect our inquiry. Rather than focus on those who have been labeled as "improper" feminist subjects—illiberal or not-liberal-enough devout women supposedly impossible to *theoretically* or *morally* accommodate within the (liberal) feminist project—I argue that a productive way to think about feminism is to look at how feminists themselves grapple with the recurrent crises and conflicts over racial and religious differences, and to explore their moral and political agency. If we are looking for an understanding of the current feminist predicament, then shouldn't we explore how self-defined feminists address these issues, the limits they erect, and the alliances they imagine? We must ask them and ourselves, to paraphrase Mahmood, "What do *they (and we)* mean when they/we say gender equality is, or isn't, the central principle of *their (our)* analysis and politics?" We must take seriously their moral dispositions and scrutinize their modes of political subjectivation as liberal, or radical, or socialist, or intersectional, or Black, or Afro, or Muslim feminists.

Beyond the theoretical grammar of liberal feminism, many feminist practices address the challenge that perceived illiberal religious practices pose to feminism, and thereby trace the contours of feminist praxis that might well define feminism outside, or at the margins of, the liberal grammar. What is more, many feminists are also well aware of how the liberal grammar of feminism reproduces exclusions and hierarchies between feminist subjects. As gender equality has become heralded by conservative pundits as a new fundamental value, and as Western feminists and their organizations struggle to find common denominators and elaborate positions in recurring disputes over sharia law, arranged marriages, or veiling practices, we must investigate their (and our own) ethical dispositions, in order to reconceptualize both the values at the center of this political project and our and their relationship to these values. Hence, I suggest a practical and normative investigation into the ethical dispositions of feminism and feminists.

As I will develop, this is not an instance of an ethical turn away from politics. Like many, I conceive of ethics as intimately articulated with politics, in particular when scrutinizing feminist ethics.[40] Indeed, what I propose to explore is how feminist ethical dispositions sustain—or undermine—the political community that is feminism. Mine is not a call to disregard power within feminism, but rather to examine how power shapes feminists' ethical dispositions and, thereby, the orientation of the future of the feminist project. Power shapes relations, those very relations that sustain the feminist project in its various instantiations, and thus also shape the distribution of responsibility among feminists, an important political issue. I contend that exploring the various modes of subjectivation that inform feminist commitments, conflicts, and desires offers new insights on the ways in which hierarchies of power might be rejected, and differences included, within a feminist political project.

What can the moral and political subjectivation of feminists tell us about the future of their political project? Exploring the moral dispositions formed by a diverse array of feminists in different contexts provides an access point to understand the conflicts that characterize the political project they claim to embody and to make happen. Why do some white and racialized feminists react in such potent emotional ways to the issue of Islamic veiling, while others do not? What values seem to be at stake for some white feminists that make coalitions with Muslim or Afro-feminists impossible to imagine? On the contrary, how do some practices of inclusion emerge in other contexts, practices that challenge the whiteness of the feminist movement and provide a political and moral vocabulary to prevent exclusions along the lines of race or religion? How are we to understand the resentment that some racialized feminists express and their strategy to resist the hegemony of whiteness within feminism?

I argue that only by understanding why feminists do what they do can we begin to explore the ways in which practices and norms can be carefully reimagined to build bridges, to bring transformative political change, and to experience a freedom to transform the world and be transformed in the process. To do so, we must examine the moral dispositions that feminists from various strands adhere to and develop, and we must explore how they *respond* to the political and moral challenges they identify. Only then may we understand what is at stake—politically and morally—what is being lost, and what might be found.

Feminism as a Moral and Political Project

Feminist Trouble offers such an account by focusing on the moral and political dimensions of the feminist project, and on its articulation with feminist politics. Indeed, feminism presents itself as a political project: a project that creates a political community that shares political ideals and goals. However, how feminists define the content of those goals—equality, emancipation, freedom—varies. For some, veiling practices and religious beliefs impede female autonomy, and gender equality requires banning Islamic veiling practices, and for others, on the contrary, true feminism implies accommodating these practices and granting agency to pious Muslim women. The political community that feminism creates is therefore divided by conflicts over what these values mean, and which value must take precedence over the others.

Conflicts about good and bad feminist subjects, about the type of political community feminism is about, are not new. The history of feminism abounds with episodes of feminist troubles. These have included conflicts over the importance and political significance of race,[41] class, sexuality,[42] attitudes toward pleasure,[43] sex work, and the definition of femininity heralded by popular culture.[44] While these conflicts are expressed and explained as political disputes, the claim I make in this book is that they also entail a moral appeal. The trouble within and with feminism is not only a political conflict about the *feminist project* and its future—that is, a conflict over the content of shared values such as equality, agency, or emancipation—but also a moral one, that is, a crisis that calls into question the *feminist subject* as an ethical, moral subject. Indeed, feminism must be understood as not only a political project of social transformation, but also a promise that feminists make to build the world in a certain way. Feminists are emotionally invested in their own promise, and their promise creates moral and political relations with others: a promise is always made *to* someone. As feminists, we make promises first and foremost to other feminists, promises to share a vision, promises to act together and in a common name, that of *feminism*. The relations our feminist commitment creates are not only political—sharing a vision for social transformation, sharing a critique of power relations—they are also moral: keeping a promise made to each other. Hence, moral relations are at the heart of the collective feminist project. They define who is to participate and how feminists engage with each other.

Teresa de Lauretis captured this dimension, calling it the *ethical drive* within feminism, a drive toward community and accountability.[45] It is no surprise, then, why Islamic veiling debates have elicited such affective and disturbing responses. They have revolved around figures of desirable or abject feminist subjects, discussing the moral dispositions that pious Muslim women should display if they are to be incorporated in a project of emancipation that pretends to be universal but nonetheless rests upon what Judith Butler has termed "excluded domains."[46] By discursively casting out or recuperating pious Muslim women in the feminist project, feminists create specific moral bonds—or enact abandonment—with them. Hence, the underlying question that haunts Islamic veiling debates is that of the nature of the moral bonds feminism can and should create, across racial hierarchies and in the context of rising racism and Islamophobia, if it is to live up to its own promise of inclusion and community. Because feminism is not only a *political* horizon that feminists wish to see realized, but also implies a moral subject we wish to embody ourselves, as feminists, and that we want to see others adopt and personify as well, it is a deeply moral project that defines moral relations between us, actual or potential feminist subjects.

To understand how the current crisis is reconfiguring the feminist project and producing new—and reproducing old—feminist subjects, we therefore need to analyze jointly the various dimensions of these feminist disputes—political, affective, and moral—and their reciprocal relations. To explore feminism as a moral and political project means that we must be attentive to the *connection* between feminist morals and politics. Indeed, understanding feminism as a moral project, and thus turning our attention to feminists' ethical responsibilities, is not a turn away from politics and from a critical focus on power relations within feminism and among feminist subjects, as some would argue.[47] Relational conceptions of ethics stress how our becoming a subject is enmeshed with our encounter with and dependence on the Other,[48] and they therefore interrogate our responsibilities toward distant and concrete others. Understanding feminism as a moral project entails asking the question of feminist responsibility: to whom are feminists accountable? What types of hierarchies distribute responsibilities and power among feminists? These are highly political questions. They ask what type of political community feminism is, and they interrogate the social and political conditions for the moral responsiveness of feminists. How are vulnerability and privilege distributed among feminists, with what consequences for feminism as a moral project?

A first way to capture this connection between ethics and politics is to keep in our analysis the political and social context in which moral arguments are made.[49] Joan Tronto reminds us that we must recognize that "all moral arguments are made in a political context, and feminists ignore the political setting of their moral arguments at their peril."[50] Indeed, moral arguments about "good" and "bad" feminist subjects are deeply embedded in specific political contexts, marked in Europe and beyond by rising Islamophobia, heightened racism, and xenophobia. What is more, feminist moral arguments about who can be part of the feminist project have obvious political consequences for the racialized women they discursively include as equals or, on the contrary, regulate as improper subjects, as well as political consequences for white feminists whose privilege they may contribute to securing or to dismantling. Feminist involvements and attachments to opposing sides of the current moral debates on the *good* feminist subject therefore produce contrasting political consequences for feminist movements and beyond for democratic politics. *Feminist Trouble* thus explores in depth the social and political context in which moral arguments about who can be a "good" feminist subject are being made, to identify those relations of power that shape asymmetries within feminism.

Another way to analyze the connection between feminist morals and politics is to acknowledge that feminist politics implies and is based on moral relations. To cite again Joan Tronto, "No feminist theory that cannot address questions of distance and of otherness will be adequate."[51] That is to say, under any type of feminist politics and discourse lies a moral address toward distant or concrete others. We must therefore ask how feminists relate morally to others, especially feminist others. Ethics here is not opposed to politics but articulated with it: to think about ethical responsibilities among feminists is to think about the boundaries of the political community that feminism creates, and about the hierarchies that structure it. There is an underlying current of disagreements running through the debates about Islamic veiling that has to do with how feminists propose to treat distant or proximate others. When reasoning about the reasons to ban or accommodate, for example, Islamic headscarves, whose situation and welfare are put at the center of our attention and care? While many white feminists voice their concern or care for other women, these are often distant others, abstract figures who secure white feminists' privilege to universalize their experiences as women and define who may be considered a "good" or a "bad" feminist subject. If caring is to be equated with treating the other well, it must be grounded in a concrete relationship. Following Tronto's proposal of an ethic of care, we must be attentive to the ways in which we pretend to care when others are distant, and how we actually care when they are close.

To analyze feminism as a political and a moral project, *Feminist Trouble* describes and analyzes the moral dispositions displayed by a variety of feminists in order to map how these moral dispositions sustain forms of feminist politics and include or exclude other feminist subjects. *Feminist Trouble* also engages in a normative endeavor, that of defining the contours and content of what I call a *feminist ethic of responsibility*; that is, a set of moral dispositions that, I argue, can foster and sustain equal relations within the feminist project, and help to dismantle hierarchies of privilege, especially those based on race and religion. The normative endeavor proposed in this book is not an abstract one: it is grounded in the social and power relations that shape feminist communities. This endeavor is not about solving the crisis of the feminist subject or about reconciling differences. This would be an impossible and undesirable task since, as Teresa de Lauretis argues, feminism's essential difference lies in the paradoxes and contradictions of its history and thought.[52] There will always be trouble within and with feminism. The normative endeavor that *Feminist Trouble* proposes is rather about rearticulating politics and morals; it is about redeploying feminist imagination in new directions, and thinking through what is a *feminist* responsibility to others—especially fellow feminists—that recognizes privilege and power, with the aim of dismantling hierarchies.

Critical Feminist Theory and Ethics of Care

To achieve its normative ambition, *Feminist Trouble* situates itself in the tradition of critical theory, following which normative inquiry must emerge from a sociologically realist analysis of power.[53] However, feminism is not only about power; it is also, as this book argues, about care and moral relations. Hence *Feminist Trouble* also draws on a rich tradition of ethics and philosophical inquiries of care, which are also empirically grounded in experiences and also explore subjective emotions as important clues about the moral nature of relations and about the forms of responsibility—which can be both moral and political—they entail. This book argues that only if we can capture the concrete and lived meanings that the troubles I document have for feminists can we understand the impact they have had on feminism as a political project, and how they may imperil its future or open new venues for activism. *Feminist Trouble* is a normative reflection on existing feminist practices, looking for those "possibilities glimmering" in actual experiences, as Iris Young suggests, and being attentive to feelings of dissatisfaction that orient us toward normative principles.[54] Hence, in this book, I approach feminism both as a collective political project—with its historical and sociological thickness—that triggers tremendous emotional responses from its participants,[55] and as an individual process of political subjectivation, which involves emotions and moral dispositions, and which I capture through empirical fieldwork with feminist activists. As Didier Fassin reminds us, "The boundaries between the moral or the ethical and the political are empirically more confused than what one usually believes."[56] *Feminist Trouble* proposes an empirical and contextual investigation of how feminists' political subjectivations are shaped, and how they might be transformed. Through an investigation of how Islamic veiling debates have transformed feminist coalitions and feminists' political subjectivities, *Feminist Trouble* traces how postcolonial racial relations of privilege and disadvantage shape feminist discourses, regulating their subjects and the political projects they aspire to realize, as well as the moral relations they wish to forge with other feminist subjects.

While the focus of *Feminist Trouble* is on feminist movements and the feminist project, the approach it proposes could be extended to other emancipatory identity/postidentity movements that are also structured by relations of relative privilege and disadvantage. Indeed, the question of how to resist the sirens of nationalism in populist times—how to forge a political project of emancipation that does not use tropes that can be recuperated for xenophobic agendas—cuts across the field of contemporary social justice movements. The development, and critique of, homonationalism is a likely candidate for such a task. As feminist and queer movements struggle in many contexts to put into practice their ideological commitment to intersectionality,[57] conceiving these social justice projects as embedded in political *and* moral relations among their members may help decipher and counter dynamics of exclusion and inclusion along lines of race, sexuality, disability, age, or religion.

Researching feminism and feminist subjectivities is a tricky methodological exercise. Indeed, the boundaries of "the" feminist "movement" are famously hard to draw. To borrow Jo Reger's metaphor, feminism is "everywhere and nowhere" at the same time,[58] and it is also often difficult to neatly separate women's movements from feminist movements.[59] Delimiting who belongs and who can legitimately be recognized as such is an exercise in categorization, and therefore power. Conflicts over who rightly belongs to this category and can embody the "good" feminist subject remind us that the category is highly politically and morally charged. My focus on feminists' discourses and experiences in the context of feminist conflicts along lines of religious, racial, and immigrant identities has determined the methodological design of the study. Because I wanted to capture feminists' political subjectivations, I selected interviewees in two national contexts, France and Quebec, working in organizations or groups that *self-identified as feminist*, and interviewed fifty individuals, both feminists who self-identified as racialized feminists (twenty), and feminists who did not identify racially and were predominantly white (thirty).[60] These activists perform their commitment to feminism in their day-to-day activities, and are immersed in feminist organizations, which shape their worldviews, their identities, and the politics of everyday life that comes with their "becoming" a feminist.[61] As I detail in the next chapter, I use the concept of political subjectivation to capture both the shaping of one's political identity and its inherent moral dimension, in particular as it plays out in the *concrete* confrontation or encounter with differences within the movement. It was thus important to interview feminists who were active members—volunteers, officers, and employees—in more or less organized settings.

Through this fieldwork, my goal was to shed light on, and identify, processes of political subjectivation in order to describe and analyze forms of attachment to the feminist project, attachments that are emotionally and morally invested. These attachments and forms of political subjectivation are historical ones, shaped by a specific social context, as well as by my own positionality. Feminist epistemologies have taught us to carefully assess our own positionality when making knowledge claims and that there is no "outside" position to which we can abstract ourselves from the world we analyze.[62] I argue that our positionality also entails a moral dimension: the moral position that the theorist or sociologist occupies implies that she engages, in different modes, with the moral issues at stake for those she encounters in the field.⁶³ Because the values that underpin the feminist project are inextricably political and moral, and the relations we, as feminists, want to create with other feminists are at the heart of this project, as a feminist scholar studying the moral and political project that is feminism, I cannot *not* attempt to propose ways in which, as a feminist, I should be accountable to other feminists. I must respond to the claims being made about feminism; to do otherwise would be to renounce the idea that I share a common political space and a common form of life with the feminists I have engaged with during my fieldwork.

The method and approach I propose in this book, as well as my standpoint as a feminist, are thus shaped by my disciplinary trajectory within academia, my feminist encounters in the field as an academic and as an activist, and of course my social positioning as a white, privileged academic in the global North. This positioning has given me many resources with which to carry on my research and thinking. It has also led me to many migrations between France, the United States, and Canada/Quebec that have influenced me as much as my point of departure. However, my standpoint remains always partial and limited, and I am indebted to the many feminists I interviewed for their insights and their agreement to my borrowing from their variegated experiences to gain a deeper knowledge of the issues at stake and to decenter my gaze. In return, as Joan Tronto suggests, I offer to place their perspectives, interests, and concerns as "a more central concern than the starting point from which (I) otherwise might have begun."⁶⁴ Nevertheless, I have been keenly aware of the risk of not being able to convey the complexity of the reasonings, moral issues, and emotional charges I have encountered and experienced. The feminist literature on care was a helpful guide in taking on the daunting task of describing in adequate terms what the reality has felt like.⁶⁵ Hence, the standpoint from which this book has been written is also a moral one, that of my own moral relationship to feminism and to other feminists. Both aspects, my positionality and my own moral standpoint, limit my possible perception and understanding of the subjective positions of others, especially those less privileged.⁶⁶ But both aspects also constitute the inescapable ground upon which I can pretend to give meaning to my own experience as a feminist attached to the collective feminist project, a feminist that feels uncertain about the viability of this project, and who wishes to respond to the moral and political claims laid upon her by fellow feminists.

Outline of the Book

In the next chapter, I introduce the theoretical framework I use to analyze feminism as a moral and a political project, with a focus on what I call feminists' political subjectivations. To understand current feminist theoretical and political debates about Islamic veiling, it is important to first situate them within a broader theoretical history of feminist theory's engagement with the question of "difference." I argue that theorizing feminism is often an effort to theorize differences between feminists. Reflecting on this political and moral urge to theorize difference, I argue that feminist debates on Islamic veiling, with their ambition to define proper and improper feminist subjects, and to rethink and critique core moral and political values of the feminist project, bring a renewed attention to its moral dimension. To make sense of the deeply moral nature of these feminist debates and the challenge they pose to feminist theory, I focus on feminists' political subjectivations. Indeed, I argue that the theoretical focus on pious Muslim women's agency, as the site of tension and challenge to the feminist project, diverts our gaze from feminist political subjectivations and how they shape feminists' responses to Islamic veiling debates. If we are to reimagine feminism, I argue, feminists' political subjectivation is a good place from which to start investigating what type of moral dispositions sustain feminism as a moral and political project of equal relations. To do so I draw on a genealogy of intersectionality theory that has been interested in exploring how emotions, affects, and moral dispositions shape identities and relations among feminists.

Chapter 3 maps the politics of intersectionality with respect to race and religion in feminist movements in two contexts, France and Quebec, that present striking features and therefore opportunities to investigate the effects of Islamic veiling debates on feminist movements and their ability to remain critical in the face of rising femonationalism. The chapter retraces the headscarf debates and how feminist organizations and public voices engaged in them on both sides of the Atlantic. While these histories are specific to each context, they certainly echo the political dynamics that played out in other liberal democracies, especially in Europe. This chapter draws the contours of feminist activism in each country and underlines the variety of positions, conflicts, and coalitions that these debates sparked. It also argues that intersectional conflicts over race and over respect to religion, specifically Islam, both overlap and differ, and that we must be attentive to these differences if we are to understand the complexity of intersectionality in both contexts.[67]

The chapter thus provides the reader with the historical and sociological context of feminist activism and its transformation in the wake of a rising femonationalism. In particular, I demonstrate why intersectional coalitions and discourses in the context of heated debates over secularism and hijab and niqab proved possible in Quebec while they failed in France. Hence the chapter focuses on a crucial issue for feminist scholars and scholars of social movements, exploring how some feminist coalitions managed to remain inclusive and critical of femonationalist discourses, while others have not resisted this new hegemonic discourse. This chapter thus sets the stage for the next two chapters, which further explore how feminists' political subjectivations have been transformed by Islamic veiling debates.

Chapter 4 focuses on feminist whiteness, a concept the chapter introduces and defines as the product of a process of political subjectivation as a white feminist. The concept captures the various repertoires that white feminists elaborate to talk about—or rather actively ignore[68]—race relations of power and their own privileged positions in this racial order. Chapter 4 documents how whiteness informs white feminists' political subjectivation as feminists, and how it has changed over time. It traces how white feminists are constituted as political subjects through their relationship to nonwhite feminists, and to those whom they perceive and label as "bad" feminist subjects. Tracing the construction of *feminist whiteness* means documenting how feminism is made white, how it marks nonwhite feminist subjects as others, as racialized and improper subjects to be excluded from the feminist collective project. This chapter shows that debates on Islamic veiling have effected a shift in feminist whiteness, from feminist whiteness as *ignorance* to feminist whiteness as active participation in *national identity* and femonationalist discourses.

While it charts a general evolution in feminist whiteness, chapter 4 also shows that feminist whiteness is multiple and varies across contexts. In France and Quebec, white feminists use different repertoires to address race and racism. Some work around or evade race, while others recognize its political salience. These different repertoires therefore point to different ways in (and extents to) which feminism is made white and the location of white feminist privilege is made invisible or acknowledged. The chapter introduces a distinction between feminist practice as a *social* project—that of responding to the need of vulnerable, "othered" women—and feminism as a *political* collective project of transformation that bonds women together. While in the first instance, feminist whiteness translates into specific feminist moral dispositions, such as the suspension of judgment, self-improvement, benevolence, and ignorance of white privilege, in the second case, religious and racial differences are highly politicized and used to define improper feminist subjects. Feminist whiteness then entails moral dispositions such as disapproval, indignation, and self-righteousness, and emotions such as melancholy, fear, and anger.

Chapter 5 turns to racialized feminists' activism and their political subjectivations. It analyzes how racialized feminists have forged specific political vocabularies to name and politicize their relationships with white feminists in the context of the headscarf debates. As for white feminists, these political vocabularies are articulated with a set of emotions and moral dispositions. This chapter thus attempts to capture the formation of (collectively produced) moral, political, and ethical dispositions that are intimately linked to and shaped by the context of postcolonialism and (post) secularism in France and Quebec. In particular, it asks: How do nonwhite feminists address their political and moral relationship to the mainly white feminist movement in both contexts? What are the moral dispositions and emotions that the encounter, conflict, or alliance with white feminists elicits for racialized feminists? How do they resist racism and the exclusions from white feminist spaces it performs? This chapter argues that racialized feminists occupy a minority position, in the Deleuzian sense—that is, not an identity or a sociological "object," but a position of endogenous conflictuality within a hegemonic normative system[69]—from which they seek to create a new language, and from which they articulate specific moral addresses. Thus, racialized feminists' forms of political subjectivation are relationally connected to white/mainstream/hegemonic forms of feminist discourse. This relationship is both political and moral. The chapter explores the political emotions, such as indignation, frustration, pain, unease, anger, or lassitude, that sustain racialized feminists' relationship to white feminists, and the forms of moral address they convey to white feminists through both resistance and resentment. This chapter analyzes, in particular, resentment as an attempt to fashion new relations.

Chapter 6 brings the insights of the previous chapters to bear on a normative endeavor that seeks to center the feminist project on a *feminist ethic of responsibility*. Indeed, while feminism is often understood as a political project of representing women, or advancing their social situation, I propose to conceive of feminism as a political project that creates relations between feminists, comprising both those who claim to be part of this project, and those who are claimed by this project. I argue that such a conception of feminism orients our normative endeavor not so much toward theorizing inclusive coalitions, reflecting on the conditions under which coalitions might be sustained while acknowledging a differential of power, but rather toward defining the nature of the moral relationships created between feminist subjects by feminism. Taking seriously the moral dimension of the feminist project and drawing on moral theories of care, *Feminist Trouble* argues that we need a feminist ethics of responsibility at the center of this political project. Such an ethics aims at treating the other equally and treating her well, at creating a space of possibility for the "others" of feminism within the feminist project. Such an ethics is resolutely pragmatist: it considers that the *concrete consequences* of our actions define our moral responsibility, rather than the values we wish to uphold, and that an ethical responsibility entails *responding* to others[70]—which often means finding *compromise* and *translating* demands. Hence feminists need to accept that values we hold dear—such as gender equality—must always be put in *relation* to other values, because feminists are attached to a multiplicity of values: freedom, inclusivity, respect, dignity, and so on. Heralding only one value over all others as deserving of our attachment is morally unproductive and politically ill fated. It is bound to misrecognize other feminists' attachment to other values. The conception of feminism deployed in chapter 6 and centered on a feminist ethics of responsibility is a salutary plea to turn our attention to *relations* between feminists—rather than to supposed common identity as "women" or to not-so-liberal subjectivities supposedly embodied by pious Muslim women—and to "the world in between us," as Hannah Arendt would say,[71] which endows us with a political and moral responsibility toward others. It is not, however a plea to return to a nurturing feminist community or sorority. Rather, by elaborating a feminist ethic of responsibility, I propose feminists work to disestablish hierarchies within feminism, a work transformative for feminism but also, evidently, for society at large.

The conclusion of the book assesses what it means for feminism and feminist theory to revisit its "we" along the lines I suggest, that is, to conceive feminism as a project focused on the ethical and political relations between feminists and between subjects enrolled in the feminist project, rather than focused on "we" women or as oriented toward shared values such as equality. I argue that such a displacement of our drive to theorize enables us to revisit the theoretical debate on the "foundations" of feminism. It also encourages us not to get trapped in the agency debate that has concerned much feminist theorizing. Indeed, while these theoretical discussions have proved tremendously important in articulating a critical feminism, they have also fueled a legitimate suspicion about the viability of the feminist project. Redirecting our theoretical and political energies from scrutinizing the agency of subjects perceived as not so liberal and not recoverable for the feminist project, to examining our own ethical practices as feminists, may prove to be, this book argues, a potent way to move beyond the negativity of critique. As Elizabeth Grosz aptly reminds us: "Theory is never about us, about who we are. It affirms only what we can become."[72]

2
Theorizing Feminism
Politics, Morals, and Emotions

What does it mean to theorize feminism as a political and moral project in the context of public debates that, in the name of gender equality, have fueled nationalism, anti-immigrant sentiment, and Islamophobia? These policy debates have led, in many contexts in Europe, to the dismantling of former alliances and solidarities among some women's rights organizations, as well as spurred new configurations of antagonistic feminist politics.[1] The development and consolidation of what Sara Farris has termed femonationalism[2] has restructured the political landscape and imposed new grammars to voice women's rights claims. This is not the only development transforming feminist mobilizations in Europe,[3] but it is a worrying one. This context urges us to develop a critical discourse on feminism and its claims, a critical discourse that must recapture feminism's promise. To do so, I argue, we must be attentive to the morality, or the ethical drive, that characterizes feminism. Finding ways forward to forge critical discourses to dismantle femonationalism demands that we consider jointly the political and moral dimensions of the feminist project.

In this chapter, I argue that to capture both the political and the moral dimensions of feminism we must explore feminists' political subjectivations. Such an approach places at the center of its inquiry the moral dispositions that feminists cultivate toward other feminists, taking into account the power inequalities—particularly, but not only, along axes of race and religion—that shape these relations between feminists. This perspective is indebted to specific genealogies of intersectional feminist theory that have insisted that social locations and hierarchies of power shape feminist subjectivities through emotions, affects, and moral sentiments. I argue that such a perspective, taking into account both hierarchies of power and the ethical drive that characterizes feminism, can provide a new and productive way to rethink the "question of differences" that has animated feminist theory. Theorizing feminism in this way also offers important insights on intersectionality theory

Feminist Trouble. Éléonore Lépinard, Oxford University Press (2020). © Oxford University Press.
DOI: 10.1093/oso/9780190077150.001.0001

when it comes to analyzing feminist movements and how they address power hierarchies of race and religion.

In a first section, I argue that the recent history of theorizing feminism is a history of theorizing differences within feminism and between feminists. I elaborate on this insight about the centrality of differences to feminist theorizing to approach the nature of feminism as a political project to create a political community, that of feminists, sustained by relationships of equality between feminists. These relationships of equality also have a moral dimension, as treating the other equally is also treating her well. I develop this understanding of feminism as a project to create such a political community in the second section. To explore the politics of difference within feminism in the "postsecular" context, articulating both the political and the moral dimensions of the feminist project, I argue in the following section that we can draw on intersectionality theory. I then nuance this account in the fourth section, in which I situate my approach in an alternative genealogy of intersectionality, less focused on identity and more attentive to how experiences and emotions shape relations between feminists. I argue that such an approach captures both the moral and the political dimensions of the feminist project and, crucially, how power hierarchies structure both dimensions. In this vein, I propose in a last section the concept of *feminist political subjectivation* as a framework to understand how feminist subjectivities are produced, in a specific historical and political context, by a set of moral discourses about the "good" feminist subject, sustained by specific emotions. This concept helps tease out the relationship between ethics, emotions, and politics that shapes feminist practices and discourses. I argue that such an approach can help us understand the dynamics of feminist intersectional politics in "postsecular" times, in which some feminist subjects are heralded as "good" or to be saved, while others are cast out and denigrated.

Theorizing Feminism / Theorizing Differences between Women

Exploring the nature of the trouble within feminism is an exercise in theorizing feminism. No normative investigation of feminist conflicts can evade theorizing feminism. However, this is no small task. Feminism is historically and contextually variegated, as many sociological works on feminist movements have underscored. For scholars of feminist movements, the challenge has long been to delimit the borders of such a protean practice and identity: who counts as a feminist?[4] Interestingly, for feminists who theorize feminism, the question of who may or may not count as a feminist seems much less problematic: the desire to be freed from sexism and patriarchy, the desire to "end sexism, sexist exploitation and oppression," to use bell hooks's encompassing definition, will make one a feminist.[5] Being a feminist is often presented as a set of dispositions that one has adopted and is attached to—"We are moved to become feminists," as Sara Ahmed insists[6]—without having to adhere to or define a specific set of values or to practice certain types of action. However, this does not mean that theorizing what feminism is is easy. This apparent lack of need for a normative foundation to define *who* can be a feminist is matched by an intense preoccupation with the differences among those who claim to be feminists. While the subject of feminism need not be predefined or confined to a specific foundation, its conflictual nature, its heterogeneity, and the power asymmetries it harbors have been causes for feminist theorists' concerns.

Theorizing feminism has thus been equated to some extent with theorizing differences within feminism or, more to the point, theorizing differences— marked by power hierarchies—among feminist subjects and among women. Much of the most challenging and productive feminist theorizing of the past decades shares a common impulse and a common conundrum: thinking through the impossibility of a unified feminist subject while continuing to theorize and practice some kind of feminist politics, the very possibility of this thing called feminism.[7] This tension has unfolded in distinctive ways as feminist theorists with diverse locations, immersed in different political struggles and deploying singular feminist imaginations, have tried to address the "difference" question within feminism. Judith Butler's immensely influential *Gender Trouble* starts with the very question of the (im)possible unity of the feminist collective subject[8] and proposes to rethink the subject itself as a way to escape what Linda Zerilli has presented as an unending dilemma for feminist theorists: "We nod to the importance of acknowledging difference among women, yet we persistently return to the idea that feminism demands a unified subject. Alternatively, we vigorously refuse such a subject, but are at a loss about how to say or claim anything beyond the particular case."[9]

This long history of feminist theorizing that engages with the "difference" question suggests that how feminists address issues of power and how they construe it is in fact central to defining the nature of feminism. The "difference" question has taken hold of feminist theory in different ways since the second wave of the feminist movement, and various genealogies of the difference question can be traced and imagined. To name a few, and to chart the contours of this foundational dilemma, we can invoke black/Chicana feminist thought from Maria Stewart's and Sojourner Truth's initial formulation up to the development of intersectionality,[10] which provided both a trenchant analysis of the political question of differences and power differentials among women and inside feminist movements, and a profound reflection on the relationship between political identity and subjectivity that debunked white feminists' pretension to represent feminism both as a political movement and as a form of subjectivity.

The unfolding of the subject question within feminist theory at the beginning of the 1990s, be it through the work of Judith Butler, Teresa de Lauretis, or Drucilla Cornell, also provided new articulations of subjectivity, sexual difference, and sexuality and attempted, often through theoretical use of Freud, of Wittgenstein, and of Jacques Derrida's *différance*, to rethink the relationship between sameness and difference in the formation of subjectivity in a way that could untie gender identity—and feminist subjectivity—from sexual difference, and therefore open up the subject to transformation and differences.[11] The poststructuralist theoretical turn in feminist theory and the debate on the "category of women"[12] attempted to use the deconstruction of the gender dichotomy as an avenue to also address differences of race and sexuality.[13] In doing so, it provided much of the fuel for the deconstruction of the feminist subject, individual and collective.[14]

At the same moment, postcolonial feminist theorists provided a powerful critique of the feminist Western gaze on Third World women—motivated by her difference and by the status ascribed to her of an eternal victim in need of saving[15]—a critique that would be revived and expanded a decade later during the multiculturalism versus feminism debate launched by Susan Moller Okin.[16] Interestingly, differences were no longer located within feminism, among feminists, but within "women," and attention was focused on the "Other" woman, her agency or complicity in her own oppression and how she might be recuperated, or not, for the feminist project.[17] Finally, the success of the concept of intersectionality at the turn of the twenty-first century also testifies to the continuing need to think about differences among women. Indeed, as Kathy Davis has summarized, "'intersectionality' addresses the most central theoretical and normative concern within feminist scholarship: namely, the acknowledgement of differences among women," and this is, in her opinion, the main reason for its academic success.[18] These theoretical debates that question the nature and boundaries of the feminist subject "have proved to be among the most bitter and enduring within feminism."[19]

In all these instances of debates about differences and feminism, feminism as a collective project of emancipation and as a political subjectivity has been questioned, deconstructed, and sometimes revived in the name of acknowledging "differences"[20] to the point that, despite their richness, these debates have also appeared to some as dangerously vexing for feminist theory because of their tendency to reify feminism(s), including black feminism, as identity politics.[21]

Feminism and the Constitution of Political and Moral Relations

Why is theorizing differences so central to theorizing feminism? Why do feminist theorists focus their theoretical energies on the question of how to adequately acknowledge and act upon differences of power among them and among women? What does this centrality of differences tells us about the very nature of feminism that feminist theorists have tried to capture? The insistence on theorizing differences reveals, I claim, a political and ethical drive to account for differences that is central to the feminist project. It informs us about the nature of feminism itself, as a project that requires that inequalities among its participants be acknowledged and addressed, both as a political endeavor and as a moral responsibility. Feminism therefore constitutes relationships between feminists that are based on recognizing other participants in this project as equals.

Linda Zerilli's theorization of feminism as a political project that constitutes a political community directs our attention precisely to this dimension of feminism, as creating relationships. Indeed, Zerilli theorizes feminism following Hannah Arendt's conception of political action, as a practice of freedom that creates a political "we."[22] To sustain this "we," what we have are promises we make to other participants, and the recognition of the "world between us," to use Arendt's words.[23] That is, the recognition that we share the world, but also that we are all positioned differently toward it. This world is therefore defined by plurality. Zerilli's conception of feminism thus emphasizes the political nature of the feminist project that creates a "we" not based on a shared identity but rather, for Zerilli, on the project of creating free relationships between its participants. Zerilli focuses her analysis of feminism as a practice of freedom, understood in its Arendtian dimension—that is, in relation to world-building activities such as founding, promising, judging—as a way to refute any foundationalist account of feminism based on identity.[24] Her insistence on freedom also shuns the tendency to focus on individual subjectivities—considering the self as the locus of politics and transformation—that she associates with poststructuralist accounts of feminism, which she argues are misguided in their concern with the self.

While Zerilli's account of feminism as a project of creating free relations between women is inspiring, my argument in this book is slightly different. I take from Zerilli the important notion that feminism creates relationships that are political (as in world-building), but I depart from her analysis when I state that the relationships that feminists create by calling themselves feminists and appropriating feminism are also—and may be chiefly—about treating the other equally, which is also treating the other well. Hence, while she focuses on freedom, I argue that equality, in both its political and its moral dimensions, is also central to feminism. What is more, as I will argue in this book, Zerilli's claim that feminism creates free relations among *women* is, I contend, too broad. Rather, I argue that feminists' ethical drive is primarily directed toward other feminists, or other subjects enrolled in the feminist project.

To consider the ethical drive and the moral dimension of the feminist subject is not a way to divert attention away from politics and power. Theoretical reflections on the formation of an ethical self (and of the self) as relational, dependent on the other, which characterize, for example, authors in the perspective of the ethics of care but also the work of Judith Butler, are deeply political. Indeed, they interrogate in various ways how moral boundaries are drawn within political communities and with others. Butler's reflections on ethical violence as it is displayed when some lives are considered not worthy of being grieved[25] is clearly articulated with a critique of nationalism as a way to delimit the political community, and to calls for a global ethics.[26] Tenants of an ethics of care have also ventured into proposal for a global ethics that address asymmetries of power between global South and North, and ecofeminist political proposals.[27] In a similar vein, I argue here that we must scrutinize our feminist ethical drive and its affective grounds if we are to reimagine the feminist political community and address issues of difference and power that are at the heart of its political project.

But how are we to keep our promise as feminists while recognizing the differences that characterize the world and "we" feminists? Because her focus is on freedom, the question of differences for Zerilli is resolved by a normative proposal about differences that is indebted to Hannah Arendt. Indeed, for Zerilli, what matters are not social or identity differences, but rather plurality. Plurality, a concept introduced by Arendt, refers to differences in perspectives, differences in judgments, in our points of views on the world. Plurality is, like uncertainty, inherent to political life and to the world, and is what makes freedom so central as a political practice of world-building. Because we share the world between us, and because it is a world marked by plurality, the way to create a political community is to exercise one's freedom by judging the world, expressing one's point of view—and putting oneself in the place of others.[28] This perspective reminds us that differences that cut across the political community that feminism seeks to create are not only differences linked to identities and power asymmetries, but also differences in judgment and values. However, if we consider, as I do, that feminism is also and mainly about treating other feminists well and equally, we must engage with the question of differences with other theoretical insights, to address the question of what it means to treat the other well in a context of power asymmetries. This question, I think, is to be solved empirically and normatively by reflecting on feminists' practical engagements with differences of power.

Feminist theories offer much thought about these issues. In the next section I review two bodies of literature that have addressed differences within feminism, and I explain how they can be put to use to analyze current feminist disputes about Islamic veiling debates. The first one refers to the dominant understanding of intersectionality theory, and the second one is an alternative genealogy of intersectionality that focuses on the moral and emotional dimensions of feminism.

Theorizing Difference in Feminism: Identity and Intersectionality

With its long history of theoretical engagement with the question of differences within feminism, the concept of intersectionality has become a favored tool to approach conflicts within feminism and to address power asymmetries related to race and class in particular. Intersectionality, defined as the theoretical approach and political critique that aims at making visible the identities and interests of women of color who have been marginalized, has been a tremendously important conceptual tool to analyze divides, make visible power relations, and challenge white hegemony within feminism in various Western contexts.[29] I explore here what this specific approach can bring to a theorization of feminism in the context of Islamic veiling debates and femonationalism, and its limits.

A prominent field of studies of intersectionality in feminist movements focuses on the relationship between unequal power relations and racial/ethnic identity and divisions in women's movements. This approach is epitomized by Kimberlé Crenshaw's analysis showing that single-identity movements sideline and render invisible the interests and identities of women situated at the intersection of other axes of domination than gender alone.[30] Indeed, Crenshaw proposed two different meanings of the term intersectionality.[31] First, intersectionality is *structural*. This term refers to the intersection of two axes of domination such as race and gender, which constitutes a social category with a specific experience of social life. This first understanding stresses the unique experience that characterizes the subjectivity and the social positioning of individuals situated at the intersection of multiple axes of power relations. The second meaning is *political*. It refers, for Crenshaw, to the fact that the political interests of intersectional groups, such as Black women, will most likely differ from the political interests of nonintersectional groups, such as Black men or white women, and that consequently these interests are being misrepresented or ignored by some social movement organizations: Black women are "sometimes excluded from feminist theory and antiracist policy discourse because both are predicated upon a discrete set of experiences" that does not accurately describe their intersectional experience.[32] For Crenshaw, there is an intimate connection between structural and political intersectionality: structural relations of oppression, domination, and marginalization constitute intersectional, multiply-marginalized groups that have a specific social experience, and its theoretical and political misrecognition leads to the political marginalization of the group.

The underlining logic is, of course, that the specific *social experience* of intersectional groups implies necessarily specific *political interests*, which happen to be denied, underrepresented, or misrepresented by current theories and policies. Intersectional theory hence offers a new semantic and political platform to represent and promote those interests that have been misrecognized and those experiences that have been inadequately represented. The political answer to this situation is *more* identity politics; that is, the recognition that Black women have specific interests that they should be able to voice and have recognized by the single-issue movements. At the heart of Crenshaw's theorization of intersectionality is an analysis of power and its intimate link with identities and political interests. There is also the conviction that identity politics is the right—and most efficient—way to promote black women's interests and that recognition of their specific needs is required to tackle their political and social marginalization.[33]

This approach, rooted in the genealogy of black feminism and the theorization of the "double oppression" or the "triple jeopardy" that women of color face in the context of the US second-wave women's movement,[34] has inspired several important studies of intersectionality in women's movements that stress how unequal power relations between women based on racial/ethnic identities structure women's mobilization in various contexts. Studies on the US context have shown that women from minoritized ethnic/racial groups have followed "different roads to feminism," to borrow the illustrative wording of Benita Roth, both on account of structural racism and unequal power relations with white women,[35] and on account of their desire to "organize one's own" on the basis of their shared identity and experience.[36] The tendency for most privileged subgroups in a constituency based on a shared identity (such as gender, race, or class) to impose their agendas and define their interests as "universal" for their whole group has been documented beyond feminism.[37] Because the privilege of whiteness includes the ability to see oneself as "unmarked" by race,[38] and to understand one's interests as universal, studies have shown that coalitions or daily work across racial boundaries in US women's organizations have met with resistance and obstacles.[39] While white women may acknowledge the pervasiveness of racism in society, they are often unwilling to apply this analysis to their own organization and their own behavior. Similar findings have been found for women's movements in locations as diverse as Uruguay,[40] Norway, Spain, the United Kingdom,[41] Belgium,[42] and France.[43]

This important body of work focuses on how social relations of power structure inequalities, marginalization, and identities within women's movements. It shows how power asymmetries fuel identity politics within feminism, and the need for more identity politics in order to place women of color's interests at the center of analysis and at the center of policymaking processes, thereby redressing the epistemic erasure of women of color.[44] Thanks to their emphasis on power and inequalities, these studies contribute to explaining the pervasive divides among women's organizations along racial and ethnic identities. They also document how coalitions might emerge and how "strategic sisterhood" may at times build bridges across these divides.[45] Intersectionality in that sense brings to the fore the conditions under which coalitions across racial differences, for example, may be envisioned and sustained; among these conditions, the politics of representation—who can speak for whom—is of particular importance.[46]

Interestingly, while the politics of difference and representation is potentially an issue for any social movement, since, as studies on social movements have shown, identity is an important element of movement politics and of the ability to coalesce individuals around a cause,[47] it has been particularly divisive and conflictual in the feminist movement.[48] This is due in no small part to the forceful focus on the collective dimension of the feminist subject and of feminist politics. The insistence on collective rather than individual emancipation in recent Western (white majority) feminist movements fuels a suspicion about diversity, because differences are intrinsically perceived as divisive if they are not overcome by a common political project that, more often than not, implies a unitary vision of identity.[49]

Debates on Islamic forms of veiling show that race, class, coloniality, and sexuality—to name a few—continue to delineate tensions, fractures, and alliances within feminist movements—in France and Quebec and beyond. Logically, intersectionality must be put to use to critically assess the claims by liberal, secular, or multicultural feminists regarding the headscarf debates to unveil the racialization, erasure, and hypervisibilization of women of color that they convey.[50] In this perspective, while the public debates, and some feminist theorists, frame the issues as pertaining to religion, culture, and gender, they are in fact new instances of the "haunting of Europe's silent racializations and ethnicizations," to borrow Fatima El-Tayeb's illustrative metaphor.[51] The concept of intersectionality is therefore crucial to analyze current disputes in the sense that it provides an account of the operations of power that structure relationships between feminists: it makes manifest the continuities between colonial racial politics and current prohibitive political and legal regulations of Muslim religious practices, especially in France but also in Belgium, Denmark, the Netherlands, and Switzerland, where the presence of racialized migrant/Muslim women within the nation is continuously questioned and their identities and interests are excluded from mainstream/dominant feminist agendas.[52]

This book is thus indebted to intersectionality methodologically[53] and theoretically, and situates itself within this wide field of research and political project by making visible in the analysis the experiences and discourses of women of color.[54] However, I also argue that the political critique that is leveraged by intersectionality must cast a wider net, looking beyond identity politics. Indeed, there is a risk in this approach of conflating identities and interests, or identities and values and judgments. If we draw on Zerilli's account of feminism and her focus on freedom, we are reminded that differences may also be differences in judgments, and not only in identities and power. What is more, and as critiques of this approach to intersectionality have underscored, it provides a trenchant critique of power asymmetries and marginalization, but less exploration of relations between feminists based on other grounds than identity, such as solidarity, shared ideals, recognition, or even love.[55]

We are reminded by Sara Ahmed of the complexity of how power shapes feminist practices and ideals when she writes: "We need to take care not to install feminist ideals as ideals that others must embody if they are to pass into feminism. Such a reification of political ideals would position some feminists as 'hosts,' who would decide which others would receive the hospitality of love and recognition, and would hence remain predicated on a differentiation between natives and strangers."[56] Hence, while a strand of intersectionality research on feminist movements focuses on marginalization and invisibility, and associates closely identities and interests, Ahmed's reflection suggests that feminism is also about moral relations of hospitality and foreignness, about love, recognition and distance, and indifference, and that power expresses itself through the dynamic process of hosting or being hosted.[57] Feminism is thus also about relationships that engage our moral responsibilities to treat the other well, relationships that are therefore also grounded in affects.

In this vein, I argue that theorizing feminism, in general and in particular in the context of the "post-secular condition"[58] that characterizes most Western liberal democracies, demands that we complexify our understanding of the politics of identity, exclusion, and visibility within feminism with an account of how emotions and moral dispositions support those dynamics of marginalization, and of how they may also support other political and moral relations based on equality. As religious difference has emerged alongside race and migration as a ground for difference politics and a topic for antagonism within feminism, we must reflect on whether the conflicts around Islamic veiling are only conflicts about power asymmetries along racial identities. In the 1980s, migrant women and women of migrant descent were seen in countries such as France as a legitimate concern for feminist action and as potential feminist subjects, and dominant strands of French feminism defined themselves as antiracist, as they still do today.[59] Once veiled, however, the same girls and women became an impossible or ambivalent subject for many of the same white French feminists.[60] From subjects of care, even though distant and marginalized, Muslim women and girls became subjects of conflict and of exclusion as these feminists claimed to save pious Muslim women from their religion for their own good. Racial and religious identities have thus not been perceived in similar ways by many white, and some nonwhite, feminists.

Another important nuance to bring to an intersectional analysis based on postcolonial and racialized identities is that it tends to underestimate the differences within each group and the plurality of positions and identities that characterize these public discussions.[61] An intersectional approach reveals how these debates perform processes of racialization, political marginalization, and the preserving of white privilege. Nevertheless, as I detail in the next chapters, in both contexts I study closely, France and Quebec, not all women's organizations representing racialized women agree; far from it. Different types of racialized feminists voice their claims in various national contexts, and while they might all be critical of the dominantly white women's rights organizations, they do not all advocate the same policies when it comes to veiling, although they aim at representing the same constituency. While some women who identify as Muslim and feminist have politicized the veil as an issue of racial and postcolonial politics, others have criticized the veil as potentially oppressive, and others have stated that it should not be the focus of their politics.[62]

Islamic veiling debates bring to the fore feminists' moral claims to save subjects, to establish moral relations between feminist subjects, and to define "good" and "bad" feminist subjects, drawing moral boundaries between those deserving of feminists' attention and care, and those who must be cast away or reformed for the sake of feminism's endeavor to transform the world. Hence, the deep moral overtones of feminist debates about the regulation of forms of Islamic veiling remind us of the deeply moral nature of feminism. This realization urges us to complexify accounts of intersectionality focused on identity politics within feminism to also recapture other dimensions of the feminist project and its conflictual nature that revolve around morality, emotions, and relations. Debates on Islamic forms of veiling thus make apparent how the contentious feminist politics of racialization, marginalization, deprivation, and silencing of the voices of women living at the intersection of several axes of domination, which include religion, race, and citizenship status,[63] is articulated with moral ambitions to define and patrol the borders of "good" feminist subjects, worthy of feminists' care and attention. Reciprocally, a feminist politics that fights racialization and marginalization of women of color and pious Muslim women also expands and challenges moral ideas about the feminist subject, thriving not only for epistemic justice,[64] but, I argue, also for the moral duty to keep a promise: a promise to create relationships that are more equal, a promise "to find ways to support those who are not supported," to borrow Sara Ahmed's formulation.[65] To capture these complexities of the moral and emotional stakes of the politics of difference within feminism, I suggest we turn to an alternative genealogy of intersectionality, one that has problematized identities and feminism's emotional dimension.

Theorizing Feminism: Experience and Affective Politics

An alternative genealogy of intersectionality, not always included under the label of intersectionality despite its kinship and simultaneity with the first,[66] looks at differences and power within feminism in conjunction with the emotional and psychic dynamics they trigger.[67] Rather than theorizing identity politics within feminist movements, this body of work is more interested in theorizing affective politics and the delicate invocation of solidarity and crafting of relationship between feminists. This approach considers that identities are being constructed in the very process of alliancing, coalescing, or separating. They are not a given that would predetermine possibilities of coalitions or conflicts between opposite interests. This approach is illustrated by Chandra Mohanty's theorization of the politics of location within feminism and its critical take on identities and identifications.[68] For Mohanty, a politics of location implies more than a geographical or historical location, although it starts from there. It also implies "psychic and imaginative boundaries,"[69] and it involves a conception of experience as shaped by politics, rather than only the reverse. In other words, while of course any project of feminist coalition should necessarily recognize differences and inequalities based on ethnic, racial, sexuality, or class inequalities, Mohanty underlines that feminist politics also construct gender, sexual, and racial identities: "It is the kind of interpretive frame we use to analyze experiences anchored in gender, race, class, and sexual oppression that matters."[70] Political consciousness and praxis shape experiences and identities; thus, in the words of Mohanty, "We cannot avoid the challenge of theorizing experience."[71]

While it may be tempting to read feminist movements' intersectional politics as the pure product of identity politics based on "experiences" produced by social structures of power, I suggest with others that we need to approach the processes that lead to intersectional conflicts, divisions, and coalitions with more caution toward "experience" and "identity." To borrow Chandra Mohanty and Biddy Martin's words, we must question "the all too common conflation of experience, identity and political perspective."[72] Joan Scott has similarly emphasized that we must historicize experience and identity and beware of the immediacy or "authenticity" of experience, because "it is not individuals who have experience, but subjects who are constituted through experience."[73] As she insists: "Experience is at once always already an interpretation *and* is in need of interpretation. What counts as experience is neither self-evident nor straightforward; it is always contested, always therefore political."[74]

In the realm of feminist politics, I join here Sara Ahmed and her coauthors' call "to think of 'identity' as an effect of the deployment of feminist strategies, tactics and rhetoric, rather than its origin or cause."[75] In this perspective, feminist discourses elaborated and deployed in specific contexts *produce* feminist identities rather than reflect them. These feminist discourses provide interpretations of experiences and identities that lead to inclusions, exclusions, coalitions, divisions, and solidarities. Identities such as Afro-feminist, Muslim-feminist, or white-feminist are not givens but are produced and are to be interpreted. Rather than considering the subject of feminist politics as a pregiven, we must try to understand, in the words of Joan Scott, the "complex and changing discursive processes by which identities are ascribed, resisted, or embraced."[76] By considering identities as always in construction and intimately articulated with experiences always in need of interpretation, we open the analysis of feminist subjectivities and identities to more complexity, and we can make sense of the wide range of differences within minority/racialized and ethnic majority/white feminist groups, and represent the plurality of voices and positions that have been expressed during these debates.[77] In this perspective, debates on Islamic veils should not be understood as only *revealing* a preexisting social location of white privilege on the part of white/ethnic majority feminists in European countries. These debates actually also *produce* the experience and identity of white feminists in both contexts. They shape instances of what I call in chapter 4 *feminist whiteness*. They fuel processes that lead to new feminist identities.

A second characteristic of this alternative genealogy to intersectionality theory is its interest in and account of emotions as an important part of feminist politics and feminist subjectivities. Writings of Black feminists that explore the conflicts between feminists of color and white feminists in the context of the US second-wave movement display and theorize a wide range of affects that appear as symptoms of politicization and as fueling processes of feminist subjectivation. Emotions are symptoms of political and moral wrongs, or of political and moral care and, at the same time, fuel feminists' perception of themselves as part of the political community that feminism creates. The rich emotional vocabulary and poetry used by Cherríe Moraga illustrates the importance of emotions as deeply (feminist) political affects. Writing about the completion of *This Bridge Called My Back*, she stresses the "pain and shock of difference, the joy of commonness, the exhilaration of meeting through incredible odds against it."[78] Talking about racism within the movement, she evokes how the "dread and terror in the room lay like a thick immovable paste above all our shoulders, white and colored alike" and how her feelings were "dark with anger."[79] Moraga also offers a powerful illustration of the politicization of experience and identity when she writes in the next paragraph: "My growing consciousness as a woman of color is surely seeming to transform my experience. How could it be that the more I feel with other women of color, the more I feel myself Chicana, the more susceptible I am to racist attack!" These analyses prompt us to analyze the role that emotions play in sustaining or destroying feminist projects but also in shaping feminist subjectivities.

The articulation between emotions and moral disposition is not specific to feminist politics. Didier Fassin reminds us in his studies on resentment and inequalities that emotions are tightly linked to processes of subjectivation and therefore to politics.[80] Political theorists, from Adam Smith to Sigmund Freud, have recognized the role played by emotions in forging, securing, or destabilizing the political community and the social contract. Sympathy, envy, anger, resentment, love—to name a few—are emotions that constitute the grammar of our relationship to the other members of the political community we belong to, as well as of our relationship to the values that organize the forms of governing this community—equality, freedom, injustice, and so on.[81] Emotional attachments are necessary to sustain political communities. Political passions are not only affective, they are also deeply moral.

These feelings produce political subjects and convey a moral dimension to their relationship to the political community.[82] Public passions therefore convey moral values and moral relations. While many political theorists have investigated the role played by passions in our attachments to a political community and our self-fashioning as good (or bad) liberal or republican subjects,[83] less attention has been devoted by political theorists to understanding the role played by moral emotions in political projects that are not attached to the national political community, such as feminism.[84] What are the moral emotions involved in the *becoming feminist*? What forms of political subjectivation sustain, or erode, this individual and collective project?

Social movement studies have recently given more attention to the role of emotions in social movements, stressing in particular the emotional satisfaction that individuals retain from being part of a collective political identity.[85] However, in this literature emotions are often treated as a means toward collective action,[86] not as symptoms of moral and political dilemmas or as contributing to processes of identification with collective projects and identities that impact moral dispositions and subjectivities. Only a few studies look at how emotions sustain political projects and shape political subjectivities in social movements or "counterpublics."[87] Some social movement studies do look at how emotions denote and produce disidentification among, for example, micro-cohorts of feminist activists, explaining variations in forms of expressive politics over generations—such as when sociologist Jo Reger analyzes "old" feminists' feelings of being displaced in a slut walk.[88] These studies are generally focused on differences in collective identities and how emotions contribute to shape collective feminist identities.[89] They more rarely address the issue of how emotions sustain moral values that shape specific feminist political projects and subjectivities.

An exception is Sarita Srivastava's work on the display of emotions by white feminists and how it can prevent and block antiracist work within women's rights organizations.[90] Indeed, Srivastava notes that exchanges within feminist organizations over racism are rife with "moral undertones, undertones with roots in feminist community, imperial history, and national imaginings." In the context of her fieldwork in Canada, she argues that "in the face of antiracist challenges many white feminists may feel that it is their self-image—as good, implicitly nonracist people—and particularly their shared moral identity as feminists that is under siege. In other words, we can see that the typical pattern of emotional responses to antiracist challenges—anger, fear, and tears—is in part produced by implied challenges to what counts as a good feminist, a good person, a good woman, and a good national citizen."[91] Srivastava's analysis leads us to focus on how emotions sustain moral dispositions as feminists, our ability to see ourselves as "good feminists," and how these moral dispositions are closely articulated with operations of power. What counts as a good woman and a good citizen is intimately intertwined with the historical formation of the liberal modern subject as bourgeois and white, and therefore respectable, allowing white feminists to secure their position as "good" national subjects and "good" feminist subjects through self-righteousness.

In this perspective, feminists' emotions and feminist emotions are understood as laden with moral values, which shape different feminist political projects and feminist political subjectivities. We can explore with such an approach how politics, morals, and emotions are articulated in feminists' discourse and practice, and how feminist discourses police the boundaries of the *good subject* of feminism, regulate feminist subjectivities, and also define how to treat well other participants in this project. We must therefore investigate the politics of emotion that characterize contemporary feminist politics of difference, describing the various attitudes toward different differences, the emotions and moral dispositions they carry with them, and how they produce different feminist subjects. How are feminists' moral dispositions to treat the other well supported by, conveyed through or diverted by specific emotions? What are the types of emotions that have characterized Islamic veiling debates? What are the moral and emotional boundaries that are being drawn or displaced during these debates?

Feminists' Political Subjectivations

To explore these questions, I focus on what I call feminists' political subjectivations. The concept of political subjectivation that I propose captures how feminist subjects are constituted through these intersectional debates that give meaning to and politicize some of their experiences as feminists. It allows us to observe how feminism is mobilized in different contexts through particular emotions and feelings. I argue that feminist discourses elaborated and deployed during these contentious debates over Islamic veiling *produce* and politicize feminist identities and feelings, and that they provide interpretations of experiences and identities that lead to inclusions, exclusions, coalitions, and divisions.

The process of feminist political subjectivation is the process by which feminist political and moral issues become personal ones, through a set of experiences and engagement with a collective subject and a historical and fantasized collective identity.[92] The concept of subjectivation refers to Michel Foucault's understanding of subjectivation as "the forms and modalities of the relation to self by which the individual constitutes and recognizes himself qua subject."[93] Drawing on Foucault's conception of subjectivation, Judith Butler notes the "indistinguishability" between the moral and political dimensions of subjectivation. She observes: "The formation of the subject is the institution of the very reflexivity that indistinguishably assumes the burden of formation. The 'indistinguishability' of this line is precisely the juncture where social norms intersect with ethical demands, and where both are produced in the context of a self-making which is never fully self-inaugurated."[94] In other words, self-formation and ethical deliberation are always bound up with the political context and norms that shape the subject, and moral judgment and social and political critique cannot be dissociated.[95]

However, here my interest is not in the constitution of the subject qua subject, but in the production of a political subjectivity, a political and moral relationship to oneself, which entails a process of political identification with and an attachment to a collective subject.[96] I am interested here in describing the moral dispositions displayed by a variety of feminists toward feminism, that is, toward a political project, and toward other feminists, across relations of power and privilege, difference and identity. To borrow anthropologist Didier Fassin's words, "The sort of subjectivity I try to analyze is not so much psychological as political. I am interested in the formation of subjects engaged in actions they justify on moral grounds rather than in the depths of their unconscious."[97] Hence, my endeavor is not to provide an anthropological account of the ethical practices shaping a feminist ethical self, or a psychoanalytical account of feminist identifications—although these would be fascinating to pursue. In the perspective I adopt, self-formation as a feminist is indistinguishable from processes of ethical deliberation that are historical and contextual. Hence analyzing feminist political subjectivations will require that I engage with the politics of feminist values as well as with ethical questions about how to treat the subject(s) of feminism. Indeed, as I give an account of myself as a feminist, I become engaged in ethical relations with others who also claim to participate in this political project.[98] The concept of feminist political subjectivation thus allows us to understand feminists' moral arguments in their political, social, and historical context with its inherent power asymmetries. Indeed, as Joan Tronto insists, we must understand moral arguments in their political context,[99] and any normative inquiry into feminist ethics must place hierarchies of power at the center of its attention and theoretical care.

However, this process is not only one of ethical deliberation that deploys itself in a specific historical context. It is also a social and psychic process, involving emotions, subjectivity, and affects, since, as Teresa de Lauretis notes, "The constitution of the social subject depends on the nexus language/subjectivity/consciousness— . . . in other words, the personal is political because the political becomes personal by way of its subjective effects through the subject's experience."[100] The importance of emotions in political subjectivation has been underlined by many queer and feminist cultural theorists who are part of the "affective turn" and who explore how affects are enmeshed with ethics and politics, looking at how affects contribute to subjectivation, our sense of belonging, and the formation of historical subjectivities.[101] In particular, Sara Ahmed and José Muñoz have insisted on the role that emotions perform in forging our sense of self and our ability to align with and participate in collective feminist/queer identities.[102] Affects are sometimes presented as first and foremost located in the body and less formed and structured than emotions. I do not share the overemphasis on bodily reactions that seems to subtract affects from critique and from the individual's reflexivity. For this reason, I mostly use the term emotions. However, I do share with these approaches the idea that our relationship to belonging and norms is sustained by emotions and that we may channel and cultivate affective practices that are also ethical practices.[103]

I thus consider processes of political subjectivation as processes that link the moral and the political in individuals' practices, self-understanding, and self-fashioning, processes that do not unfold only through rational behavior but also through emotions, memories, drives, and desires.[104] The concept of feminist political subjectivation thus aims to capture how political positions voiced in the name of feminist values are also intimately articulated with feminist subjectivities that imply affects, memories, and political emotions that often do not lead to political inclusion of a variety of feminist subjects, but rather fuel a drive to reenact injury or its denial. It helps us to describe how, in specific contexts, power relations along racial and religious identities, political structures and organizations within women's movements, individual histories of activism and encounters with feminism, and moral dispositions *as* feminist are connected and produce specific feminist political subjectivations that carry specific ethical or moral dispositions, sustained by a set of emotions. By looking at what feminists care for, when and why they self-identify as feminists, and how specific emotions secure these moral dispositions, we may capture the nature of the promise that feminism holds, as well as what stands in the way of this promise.

Focusing on processes of subjectivation allows us to articulate the political, moral, and emotional dimensions of contemporary feminist politics in a productive and heuristic way. Indeed, by understanding how a variety of feminist political subjectivations are formed in the current context of femonationalism, we can understand how the moral dimension of feminism is appropriated and acted upon by a variety of feminists, and how these appropriations may lead to conflict, separatism, disidentification, or coalition, all processes that shape thepresent and the future of the feminist project.[105] Investigating the various moral and political relationships that a variety of feminists entertain and develop with what they identify as the feminist project and with other feminists, one can attempt to answer the questions put forth by Jonathan Dean and Kristin Aune in their mapping of contemporary European feminism: "How are the boundaries of the feminist subject demarcated and maintained? Which forms of feminist identity and subjectivity are valued and affirmed, and which are erased or cast to the margins?"[106]

Exploring feminist political subjectivations is not only important for social movement scholars trying to make sense of the dynamics of divisions or coalitions among feminist organizations, or for intersectionality scholars who want to show how intersectional social and political processes unfold in the specific context of secularism debates, and how they transform feminist movements, leading to the visibility of new identities. It is also important, I argue, for feminist theory. As Teresa de Lauretis has aptly noted, conflicts over feminism—and I would add, over the good feminist subject—are the very flesh and the history of feminist theory. As she writes, "It would be difficult to explain, otherwise, why thinkers or writers with political and personal histories, projects, needs, and desires as different as those of white women and women of color, of lesbians and heterosexuals, of differently abled women, and of successive generations of women, would all claim feminism as a major—if not the only—ground of difference; why they would address both their critiques or accusations and their demands for recognition to other women, feminist in particular; why the emotional and political stakes in feminist theorizing should be so high, dialogue so charged and confrontation so impassioned."[107]

De Lauretis's point encourages us to understand the complexity of the relationship that feminists entertain with the political project that defines their political and moral identity, and to capture simultaneously both the profound social and political divisions that cut across this political community, and the deep attachments, claims for recognition, and drives toward commonality that feminism awakens. Understood in this perspective, feminism is a project of creating a political community and relationships among feminists. These relationships are both political and moral and are sustained and conveyed through affective politics. In each context, these relationships will take particular forms. For example, Jennifer Nash interprets second-wave black feminism as based on love-politics among women and among black women in particular. Contrastingly, in many contexts, the feminist community created by white feminists is based on caring for distant others so abstract that their concrete needs and interests are misrepresented and the relationship is characterized by asymmetry rather than equality.

I propose therefore to explore emotions as crucial features in the processes of political subjectivation that characterize contemporary feminist politics. This approach directs our attention to the moral and affective nature of the feminist project, allowing us to explore how feminists make promises to each other, create a community, and intend to build relationships based on equality. It allows us to consider the range of moral dispositions that feminists can hold and deploy: the claim to represent others and to improve their condition, the claim to treat others well or to treat them equally, the claim to care for distant others or for concrete and proximate others; and how these moral dispositions are sustained by emotions such as benevolence, self-righteousness, anger, or resentment.

***

In this chapter, I have argued that Islamic veiling debates not only reveal in a singular light the moral nature of feminism, but also enjoin us to take into account the ethical drive that characterizes feminism in our endeavor to elaborate normative proposals when reflecting on feminism's continuing relevance and ability to transform the world. To do so, I have drawn on a genealogy of intersectionality theory that takes into account feminist subjectivities, memories, and emotions, not only identity politics, and therefore that orients our inquiry toward an exploration of the moral dilemmas, political conflicts, and emotional stakes in feminist intersectional politics. In this vein, I propose an approach focused on the processes of political subjectivation that are triggered by debates over veiling and about Islam, race, and gender, which aims at grasping simultaneously the political, emotional, and moral dimensions of feminists' engagement—through separatism, coalition, or exclusion—with their collective political project. I argue that feminist debates and conflicts—sustained by specific emotions—are political, but they are also moral: they help define what is a "good" feminist subject and what is the right type of feminism to adopt. Because feminism is both a political and a moral project, our analysis of feminist divisions must explore both dimensions and their articulation. The moral dimension of these debates is all the more important in that, in fact, it is *connected* with the political and sociological dimensions of these issues. We must thus ask: how does the context of recurring crises over veiling and postcolonial issues shape specific forms of feminist political subjectivations in Europe? The following chapters explore this question by investigating the political subjectivations of white and nonwhite feminists in different contexts.

3
Race, Religion, and Gender

Feminist Intersectional Politics in "Postsecular" Times

Feminism is a project concerned with differences: differences between women and differences between feminists. However, what differences will be the objects of theorizing and political conflicts or alliances depends on the context in which feminist activism and thought are deployed. The salience of differences, their potential to disrupt hegemonic feminist discourses and to shape feminist political subjectivations, therefore varies, and for each historical and social context we must analyze which differences are made to matter for feminist praxis, while others are ignored or sidelined, and with what consequences for the feminist project. The intersection of racialization, migration status, religion, and gender in contemporary Europe has created a specific political configuration for feminist movements, marked by the instrumentalization and co-optation of gender equality in the implementation of anti-immigrant policies,[1] but also marked by a resurgence of older political and moral questions about women's emancipation and the proper feminist subject. While race matters deeply in understanding the dynamics of feminist praxis and coalitions, it is intimately tied up with postcolonialism, immigration, and religion, more precisely Islam. How does this specific configuration, which characterizes many European democracies, shape the feminist politics of intersectionality in these contexts? And what can a careful analysis of this complex dynamics bring to our understanding of intersectionality?

This chapter analyzes the intersectional politics of contemporary feminism in France and Quebec, two contexts that share similarities—notwithstanding differences—and that reveal processes that are also unfolding in other European countries. To do so I explore a set of public debates rearticulating issues of gender equality and secularism—which, following Joan W. Scott's neologism, I will call "sexularism" debates[2]—that occurred in both contexts, tracing the elaboration of specific articulations between racialization, religion, migration/national identity, and gender; and I map how feminists from various strands participated in them. I expose the variety of positions and arguments that diverse women's rights organizations elaborated during these debates, insisting on how the voices and interests located at the intersection of gender and racial/postcolonial/migrant/religious identities have been silenced or misrepresented, while also emphasizing the plurality of voices that emerged despite the dichotomous dominant framings of the debates. While sexularism debates have produced profound divides within the French feminist movement and the sharp decline of one of its main umbrella organizations, in Quebec the main women's rights coalition has moved forward despite important tensions. The fact that in Quebec a feminist coalition was sustainable and that dominantly white feminist grassroots organizations took positions against femonationalism, while this was not the case in France, suggests that we must examine what makes some contexts more conducive to inclusive and critical intersectional feminist politics. I highlight in particular in this chapter how the strength of racialized women's self-organizing, the history of women's organizations (especially the history of their relationships with other radical social movements), and the history of their institutional involvement in addressing racism and racial differences shape the political responses that feminist coalitions can elaborate in troubled times.

Finally, I also interrogate the specificity of the current postsecular context regarding intersectional politics within feminism. As discourses about Islam play an increasingly political role in Europe through political debates on women's rights, we must try to understand the dynamics that they create for intersectional groups and for feminist politics. I argue that the renewed focus on Islam, rather than race or migration, produces a twofold process, in the public sphere in general but in particular for feminist public discourses and praxis. First, the religious dimension of these debates (rather than the focus on immigration that characterized the 1980s and early 1990s) shapes feminist engagements with intersectionality in specific ways because it revives the question of who is a "good" feminist subject and what feminist emancipation and agency should mean. Second, the tight articulation between secularism and national identity in both contexts, which is the product of more than two decades of public debates about religious accommodation and the "integration" of Islam in the national body politic,[3] means that discourses about gender and secularism contribute to defining the boundaries of national identity. Hence, while there is a process of "racing religion"[4] that is surely taking place with regards to Islam in the postcolonial West, we must remain attentive to the specificity that comes with the religious dimension of Muslims' identities as they are socially constructed in the West, which inflects racialization. The fact that those debates and the intersectional politics they trigger concern an identity also perceived as religious means that nationalism is reasserted not through "culture" but through secularism, thereby bolstering a set of moral and political discourses about female emancipation that influence feminists' discourses.

Racialization, Religion, and National Identity: The New Face of Women's Rights

Questions today addressed under the label of intersectionality are not new to feminist theory or feminist praxis.[5] While the concept of intersectionality has contributed in unique ways to make visible structural relations of power, especially within feminist movements, its predecessors—terms such as "triple oppression" or "double jeopardy," also coined by feminists of color—similarly highlighted differences, inequalities, and oppression within women's movements. These terms challenged white privilege, racism, misrepresentation of racialized women's identities and interests,[6] and false universalism within the women's movements, and they also fostered a sense of identity and specific ways to organize and to think feminist praxis among women of color, postcolonial / Third World women, and migrant women.[7] In that perspective, questions now raised thanks to the concept of intersectionality are intrinsic and inherent to feminist theory, and certainly not new or marginal.[8] However, each historical, social, and political context raises new intersectional issues and questions—and old issues in new ways—for feminist movements. Identifying what is new and what is not, and what are the specific configurations that intersectional issues and struggles take at a certain moment in time in a certain context, helps us understand how dynamics of inclusion and exclusion evolve within feminist movements, and how feminist activists frame and respond to these processes. It also matters for the study of social movements, which is only beginning to explore how intersectionality shapes social movement dynamics of identity, separatism, and coalition.[9]

In this vein, I use in this chapter an intersectional approach to analyze how structures of power have shaped the dominant framings of policy debates on race, migration, and religion as well as the positions taken by a diversity of feminist organizations in these public controversies, in two contexts, France and Quebec, since the beginning of the 2000s. Muslim and racialized women have occupied center stage in the debates about secularism and Islam, the accommodation of religious differences linked to Islam, and the "integration" of immigrants and their children into national hegemonic cultural values. Indeed, in the past two decades a distinctive nexus articulating immigration, ethnicity, religion, and class has formed in many European countries. The racialization of Muslim religious identities, which overlaps with the racialization of migrants and their children,[10] has occurred in part through a series of public debates on Muslim and immigrant women: veiling, arranged and forced marriages, and female genital mutilations have been discussed in the European public spheres,[11] with policy or judicial outcomes detrimental to migrant/Muslim women's rights and concrete lives.[12] In these two contexts, dominant framings of the public debates on veiling and religious accommodation have invisibilized and marginalized racialized women, especially Muslim women, as political and feminist subjects, while hypervisibilizing them as objects of public policies—a process typical of the contemporary intersectional politics targeting women of color in Europe.[13] The ways in which gender, race, ethnicity, religion, and nationality intersect varies depending on each national context, but at the European level, these debates on Islamic veils have contributed to a shared perception by many nongovernmental organizations (NGOs) and political actors of the European public sphere that there is an incompatibility between gender and diversity, which demands either the abandonment of diversity or the end of gender equality claims.[14]

Islam in Europe today is a cultural product intimately shaped by postcolonialism, racism, restrictive migratory policies, the "civic" turn in immigrant integration policy,[15] right-wing populist nationalism, and what Fatima El-Tayeb has named the "European narrative of racelessness."[16] It is therefore tightly articulated with processes of racialization and the politics of race in Europe. This is evident in the cross-fertilization of policy debates on immigrant integration, the regulation of Islam, citizenship and racial discrimination, and the multiple slippages in legal discourses from one domain to the next. However, it is also important to underline that religion cannot completely be subsumed under race as an analytical category and as a source of discrimination and social marginalization.

How are we to make sense of the specific religious dimension of these debates in an intersectional framework of analysis? Indeed, the focalization on religious beliefs and behaviors, especially those of Muslim women, can lend itself to a form of culturalism[17] that invisibilizes how race, class and migration status shape the politics of secularism and religion. Hence it is important to specify how the politics of religious difference is both different from and articulated by the politics of race and migration.

Critical scholarship on secularism has pointed to the association of secularism with Western modernity and sexual freedom, and its intimate link with colonial discourses on Muslim men.[18] Hence the configuration of secularism, Islam, and gender politics is a historical formation specific to Western and European contexts that provides legitimate tropes in the public space. In particular, the discourse of secularism provides specific legal tools to regulate behavior deemed improper. With these legal tools—banning forms of Islamic veiling and religious practices—secularism can destabilize human rights discourses and erode antiracist and anti-Islamophobia efforts. In particular, it can divide traditional antiracist movements by operating a distinction between racism based on illegitimate racial categorizations, and secularism, what sociologist Nacira Guénif-Souilamas has termed a "virtuous racism,"[19] which supposedly fosters the integration of religious minorities. The political will to regulate Islam and its perceived "difference" thus leads to new discourses about secularism[20] that allow a continuing marginalization of racialized groups from migrant descent despite their formal belonging to the nation-state.

The historical connection of secularism with nation-building also allows for the expansion of femonationalism by associating gender equality not only with the West and modernity, but also with national identity. Indeed, secularism is historically closely linked with the state and organizes the boundaries of citizenship and inclusion in the national community. It is therefore no surprise that religion, especially the religion of colonial and postcolonial subjects in the case of France, should activate discourses and policies that enact the policing of national identity boundaries,[21] and that headscarf debates perform the exclusion of veiled Muslim women from European national imaginaries.[22] The legislations banning Islamic religious symbols in several European countries have operated a resignification of secularism that excludes European Muslims from citizenship, at the cost of bending and curtailing fundamental rights and the existing legal framework organizing the regulation of religious beliefs and practices.[23] This is especially true in France, admittedly the liberal democracy that has gone the furthest in the attempt to restrict the public expression of Islamic faith, equating state neutrality with the invisibility of religion (especially Islam), and thus organizing its disappearance from public spaces. In that sense, race and Muslimness are categories of difference that are, in contemporary Europe, heavily coconstructed, but which do not totally overlap.

What is more, for a majority of white, nonimmigrant feminists, and also for some racialized feminists in both France and beyond in Europe and in Quebec, religion, contrary to race, raises the issue of faith—that is, a form of submission to a religious authority—and therefore also the issue of women's agency and emancipation in potent ways.[24] Religion, contrary to race, therefore lends itself to moral discourses and boundary work that police the frontiers of good and bad feminist subjects, emancipated agents and oppressed women. This boundary work does not neatly follow the lines of racial categorizations. French Muslim women and girls from migration descent who adhere to secularism and modernity discourses may receive benefits from their conformity to majority norms.[25] More largely, debates over Islamic religious symbols raise the question of the relationship between the state and organized religions, and therefore, in countries such as France and in Quebec with a long history of struggle between the state and the Catholic Church for social hegemony, the question of who should emancipate/protect individuals from religious influence.[26] This history of virtuous feminist struggle against the Catholic Church bolsters feminists' moral claims and righteousness in their opposition to Islamic religious practice.[27]

If there is a denial of racism in many corners of white women's movements in many contexts both in the United States and elsewhere, there is also a historic commitment by most white feminist movements to fight against racism, and there is historical evidence of coalitions to support immigrant women's rights in the 1980s and 1990s in many countries (more on this below). Hence, race does not elicit from white (and racialized) feminists the exact public emotions and political responses as religion does. Of course, reactions to religious *Islamic* practices are heavily shaped by racism and, in Europe at least, by colonial history and discourses. However, I argue that we must also be attentive to these other factors, such as feminists' understanding of emancipation and religious agency, which have contributed to frame specific debates and political responses within feminist organizations on both sides of the Atlantic. In order to grasp *how* racialized Muslim women's voices, identities, and interests were silenced and misrepresented, or on the contrary reclaimed and championed, by a variety of white and nonwhite feminists in these debates, I thus argue that we must take seriously the fact that these debates are shaped by racism and Islamophobia *and* by secularism, understood as a set of political and moral discourses defining oppressed and emancipated female subjects, and tied to exclusionary visions of national identity.

My aim in the next sections is not to expose in detail the various sexularism debates that have occurred since the beginning of the twenty-first century in France and Quebec. Many scholars have told most of these stories, explored the different framings mobilized by various sets of actors, and showed how historical racial and postcolonial formations pervaded the debates (despite the "neutral" focus on religion) and how the boundaries of secularism and of the national community have been contracted through a constant recourse to the value of sex equality, now culturally assigned to the liberal (Christian and white) West and opposed to barbaric orientalized others.[28] For instance, scholars have focused on the legal and political meaning of secularism,[29] and of national models of integration[30] in the two countries, with different interpretations of fundamental rights,[31] and different relationships between national and supranational courts.[32] France and Quebec also differ in the local spread of right-wing populism and its electoral effects on other political parties, and in the relative powerlessness of antidiscrimination agencies—to cite just a few other important elements determining the policy outcomes of these debates. Furthermore, these two national contexts display different "immigrant integration models": that is, distinct politics of race and different regulations to accommodate cultural and religious difference.[33] While Quebec remains in the ambit of Canadian multiculturalism and therefore promotes the visibility of ethnic and immigrant communities through public policy tools, France has sustained a color-blind approach to public policies[34] and a "civic" approach to immigrant integration. Nor do France and Quebec have similar histories of colonization. Quebec was founded on colonial settlement, which seized indigenous lands and oppressed indigenous peoples living where Quebec established its territory.[35] At the same time, its francophone population was also dominated culturally until the 1970s by their Anglophone compatriots, intimidating them into "speaking white," that is, English. Hence, the burst of debates on Islamic religious practices and the development of Islamophobia in the two contexts do not have similar historical roots, even if the French discourse on secularism has found profound echoes in the Quebecois public sphere.[36]

The goal of this chapter is not to survey all the factors that explain how these debates have unfolded differently for feminists in the two contexts. Rather, it is, more modestly, to chart the terrain of intersectionality politics, discursive and political, that women's rights organizations in France and

Quebec have had to navigate, and to the formation of which they have also contributed in important ways. These two countries have feminist traditions that share important commonalities and ties, but very different histories of institutionalization and coalitions among the various strands of the movement. Here I identify actors, arguments, and chronologies that have altered the landscape of women's rights activism since the 2000s, fueling or resisting the rise of femonationalism in both countries. As I explore in more depth the factors that have led to contrasting strategies and alliances of major feminist players in response to these sexularism policy initiatives in both contexts—that is, a profound division within French feminist national coalitions, and a protracted but still workable coalition in Quebec despite important tensions—we gain insights into how feminists have articulated the moral and political issues that legislating veiling practices has triggered for them. This is the background against which the feminist political subjectivations that I explore in the next chapters must be contextualized and understood.

Feminist Tensions in Quebec

I start with the less notorious case of Quebec, which has witnessed, since the mid-2000s, a continuous string of public debates about religious accommodation, secularism, and the place of gender equality among the values that Quebec should promote as a nation, culminating in 2017 with a law (Bill 62) on religious neutrality aimed at preventing forms of face and head covering, mostly for users and agents of public services.[37] To get a sense of how the political terrain has shifted in the past decades, it is useful to remember first that Quebec, while a Canadian province, conceives itself more as a *nation*. This conception is of course contested, inside and outside Quebec, but the Quebecois state has often been ruled by one of Quebec's most important political forces, the Quebecois Party, which openly favors Quebec's sovereignty and independence from Canada. During these periods of nationalist rule, Quebec has adopted laws that favor the French language, and has fought to gain federal political competences, for example on immigration, that no other Canadian province has. What is more, because of its distinctive relation to the rest of Canada, Quebec also opposed early on the development of Canadian multiculturalist policies, proposing its own version of immigrant integration and ethnocultural communities policies under the label *interculturalism*.[38] Hence Quebecois nationalism, in opposition to Canadian federalism and multiculturalism, is an important component of Quebecois political life, and a dynamic that has influenced the way in which secularism and Islam have been debated.

Like many liberal states with an immigrant population, Quebec was faced early on with political debates and legal discussion over the accommodation of religious difference, including the Islamic veil. In 1995, the Commission des droits de la personne et des droits de la jeunesse (Provincial Human Rights Commission) convened to reflect on religious pluralism in Quebec made recommendations on the wearing of Islamic veils in public schools, a clear reference to the debate burgeoning in France.[39] While no case had been publicized or brought to court, the commission examined the issue and stated unambiguously that prohibiting the hijab in public schools would amount to direct discrimination on the basis of religion if the prohibition targeted the hijab only, or to indirect discrimination if the rule was to forbid in neutral terms specific types of garment that would include the hijab. The commission added that such a prohibition would also be contrary to the religious freedom protected in the Canadian Charter of Rights and contrary to Canada's international commitment to the UN International Covenant on Civil and Political Rights. Finally, the commission also pointed out that the Canadian Supreme Court's jurisprudence had developed the *obligation* of reasonable accommodation as an important addition to formal equality—that is, a positive duty to accommodate difference—and that the hijab in public schools met the desired criteria for such a positive accommodation. All in all, this public recommendation did not raise objections, and Quebec seemed firmly anchored on the liberal side of secularism, protecting religious freedom and the right to education. However, this political consensus proved fragile as it was tested by a succession of debates in the following decade.

Sexularism controversies first appeared in 2004 at the margins of the Quebecois public space, in Ontario, when some key players in the Canadian feminist movements engaged in a legal battle against procedures of alternative dispute resolution using religious principles for family issues. Despite an independent review process on religious arbitration that recognized the necessity of accommodating and monitoring religious arbitration practices rather than prohibiting them, Ontario's premier took a position against "sharia courts" in the fall of 2005. The Ontario Arbitration Act of 1991 was revised in February 2006 in order to ban the use of any religious principle when arbitrating family matters, and Ontarian family law was revised to introduce legal safeguards for alternative dispute resolution procedures.[40]

While some feminist voices clearly stated their opposition to this framing of the debate and the resulting policy outcome, they were marginalized in the public sphere.[41] Also to be noted is that among the opposition to religious arbitration were several important organizations of Muslim women that, despite internal dissent over the issue, favored a ban, which seemed, in their view, to better protect devout and nondevout Muslim women.[42]

Echoes of the Ontarian debate filtered to Quebec, in particular with a point of debate introduced at the Quebecois Parliament by MP Fatima Houda-Pépin to forbid the establishment of religious tribunals in Quebec and Canada. The point was debated and adopted symbolically by the Quebecois National Assembly.[43] Many Quebecois women's rights activists and the provincial women's rights federation, the Fédération des femmes du Québec (FFQ), followed the debate in Ontario and identified religious arbitration as a typical excess of Canadian multiculturalist policies that had to be circumvented, and lent their support to the No Religious Arbitration Coalition. However, this was only the prequel to a wider public storm debating reasonable accommodations, which would contribute to redefining Quebec's conception of nationhood and secularism.[44]

Indeed, in February 2007, Quebec's premier, Jean Charest, nominated two important Quebecois public figures, Gérard Bouchard, francophone sociologist, and Charles Taylor, anglophone philosopher, to constitute a consultative commission (the Bouchard-Taylor Commission) that would deliver to the Quebecois government a series of recommendations on accommodation practices related to cultural differences in Quebec. The creation of this commission was meant to assuage anxieties about the supposed proliferation of religious accommodation claims in the province.[45] While sex equality did not figure as an issue in the controversial court cases regarding religious accommodation that originated in Quebec,[46] things changed rapidly as women's rights organizations voiced their concern that sex equality should figure more centrally as a national value to be fostered.[47] This point of view was backed up by Quebec's premier when he stated, as he announced the creation of the Bouchard-Taylor Commission, that the "Québécois Nation has values, solid values, that is: equality between women and men, primacy of the French language and the separation between Church and State."[48] Important provincial women's rights institutions, such as the Conseil du statut de la femme (the provincial women's policy agency), pressed for the inclusion of gender equality issues in the discussion, as did intersectional groups such as No One Is Illegal–Montréal—although in opposition, as they criticized as racist and sexist the dominant feminist framing of the debate pitting women's rights against ethnic and religious communities.[49] The centering of women's rights in the public debate about reasonable accommodation led Quebecois MPs to propose and adopt Bill 63, amending the Quebecois Charter of Rights to include a sex equality clause on June 10, 2008.[50]

This act was more than anything a symbolic gesture, as gender equality was already entrenched in the Quebecois Charter.[51] But it was also the public legitimation of a dominant framing of the debate, one in which women's rights and gender equality should be given a prominent place in the legal order, above the right to religious freedom. The attempt to organize a hierarchy of rights, which is contrary to the nature and aim of the Quebecois Charter, displays the typical feature of sexualism debates: a dichotomous understanding of women's rights as opposed to minority/religious rights, a belief that secularism is inherently propitious to gender equality, and a framing of migrants and Muslims as adhering to backward values incompatible with the democratic nature and values of the national community.

However, enshrining sex equality in the Quebecois Charter of Rights did not put an end to the debate. Quite the contrary, the Bouchard-Taylor report, made public in 2008, was vividly contested from all corners of Quebecois society, including in some feminist ranks. Here again, what started as a question of punctual religious accommodation became, quite consciously—since the mission of the Bouchard-Taylor Commission was framed in these terms—a province-wide debate on national identity, immigrant integration, and the limits of tolerance. The liberal government, trying not to lose too much electoral ground to an emerging right-wing populist party[52] and to the nationalist Quebecois Party, decided to legislate on religious accommodation with the project Bill 94, introduced by Minister of Justice Kathleen Veil, which, among other measures, introduced in ambiguous terms the requirement for public service employees, and potentially for clients, to have their faces uncovered.[53] The occasion to introduce the bill was found with a concrete case, that of Naima Atef Ahmed, who had been expelled from French language classes in Montreal on the grounds of wearing a niqab and who lodged a complaint with the Quebec Human Rights Commission in March 2010.[54] During the lengthy consultation process in the provincial parliament, many feminist organizations were called and voiced different concerns and positions on the bill, as I detail below. The parliamentary debate was finally closed in the fall of 2011 with no vote, since the Liberal Party feared that the Canadian Supreme Court might overrule the bill.

This absence of definite closure to the debate left the door open for the nationalist Quebecois Party to take on the issue for electoral purposes in 2012 and to campaign on a project of a Charte de la laïcité (Secularism Charter). Its victory in the fall 2012 legislative elections led to the opening of parliamentary debate on Bill 60, introduced in 2013 by the nationalist government, proposing the Charte des valeurs (Charter of Quebecois Values), a name deemed more proper for the project at hand of redefining the boundaries of the Quebecois political community around core values, including secularism and gender equality. Hence, the debate on the Charte des valeurs was, as in many European countries, a debate about the boundaries of national identity.[55] Religious difference was heavily racialized, focusing on Muslims and attributed to migrants that had failed to interiorize the values of the province. The Quebecois Party's severe defeat in the general elections of spring 2014 put an end to these legislative attempts. The Liberal Party, back in power, was aware of the complex nature of any claim to redefine the legal grounds of Quebec's secularism in the context of Canadian federalism and the liberal jurisprudence of the Canadian Supreme Court with respect to religious freedom.[56] It therefore proceeded with more caution and at a slower pace. A bill was introduced in June 2015, with debates and public consultations beginning only in the fall of 2016. With the Quebecois Party agitating nationalist issues in the public sphere, and a vast majority of the public opinion in favor of what it perceived as an act to finally regulate and put a limit on reasonable accommodations for religious minorities,[57] the conditions were met for the Quebecois National Assembly to act. Although the debates lasted for more than a year, and although the vote was not an overwhelming one (with sixty-six deputies in favor of the ban and fifty-five against), the law was passed on October 18, 2017. It states that public servants and many employees working in parapublic institutions and publicly funded bodies—such as day care centers—must work with their face visible, and that users of public services (which include public transportation) must also unveil for identification or service provision (an interpretation of the law concerning users of public service is so far wanting). The law preserves the possibility of reasonable accommodation if the accommodation that is requested "respects the right to women and men's equality."[58] In a typical double-standard rationale about minority and majority religion, the law states that Christian religious symbols, such as the cross still hanging in the Quebecois National Assembly "blue room," are not susceptible to being forbidden in the name of state neutrality.

It took longer in Quebec to redefine legally the nature and scope of secularism, and the law finally adopted is less stringent than those in France (and is still on hold as it faces judicial review); however, these public debates and legal regulations have not been without consequences for women's rights organizations. Quite the contrary, they have contributed to the surfacing and development of tensions and of reconfigurations of the movements. In particular, a chasm emerged starting in 2008 between on the one hand the Quebecois women's policy agency, the Conseil du statut de la femme (CSF)—a nominally independent body but a close ally of the Quebecois government (and funded as a governmental agency)—and on the other hand the largest umbrella organization of women's rights centers and organizations in Quebec, the FFQ, as well as organizations self-identified as run by and for women from ethnic minorities, such as the South-Asian Women's Center of Montreal (SAWC).[59] SAWC insisted that women's rights implied their right to wear a headscarf and practice their religion and that diversity should be nurtured in Quebec. At the opposite of the spectrum of positions on the issue of veiling in public institutions, the CSF opted for a framing opposing in radical terms religious accommodation and women's rights, and promoted a muscular version of secularism—as opposed to the "open secularism" encouraged by the Bouchard-Taylor report. While the CSF started with a middle-ground position—interrogating the question of women's rights in a context of diversity of faiths—with a conference organized in 2006, the same year, the nomination of its new head, Christiane Pelchat, a former MP from the Liberal Party, legal scholar, and strong advocate in favor of secularism, led to a hardening of the CSF line.[60] It interpreted the role of religion and of ostentatious religious symbols such as full veils as vehicles for patriarchy and women's oppression in unambiguous ways, arguing that a naked face is, in Quebec, a protection against patriarchal religious traditions and the best way to protect women's rights.[61] The position of the CSF displays all the tropes familiar to sexualism debates. Veiling is understood as a sign of oppression and secularism identified as the natural ally of women's rights under attack by Islamic religious fundamentalism. The CSF calls for the state to protect public order, which means that it

> cannot tolerate that some individuals renounce to their right to human dignity. In our opinion the argument of a willful consent must be rejected for all act that is opposed to human dignity, including those accomplished in the name of a religious belief.[62]

As early as 2007, and clearly borrowing from the new French secularist vocabulary, the CSF demanded that the Quebecois state prohibit the wearing of any *ostentatious* religious symbols[63] by civil servants and representatives of the state. While the CSF declared all religions as women's potential enemy, using examples of far-right Christians and evangelists in Canada along with examples of Muslims in its 2011 opinion on secularism, its lengthy discussion on the history and nature of secularism interestingly ends with a development on *interculturalism*, the Quebecois model of immigrant integration, thereby shifting the grounds of discussion from the relationship between the state and religions to the issue of migrant integration and (excessive) cultural difference.[64] In a typical cross-fertilization of public debates, in 2008 Quebec adopted a declaration that immigrants must sign a statement upon arrival in which they affirm their adhesion to Quebecois values, including a recognition that "political and religious powers are separated in Quebec . . . women and men have the same rights."[65]

In the case of Quebec, numerous references to Quebec's Catholic past and the identification of the struggle for women's rights with the Révolution tranquille (the Quiet Revolution, which led to the secularization of Quebecois society and the rise of Quebec nationalism) are meant to assert that women's rights are strongly tied to what is perceived as a Quebecois model of secularism that has pushed the church out of the public sphere and out of political institutions.[66] This narrative is all the more evocative in that Quebec's identity as a *nation*, not as a province, is based on its long-lasting opposition to anglophone Canada, not only as a territory with a linguistic difference but as a nation with different views on nationhood and immigrant integration. Quebec's rejection of the Canadian Charter of Rights, which enshrined in its section 27 the value of multiculturalism, indicated its opposition to a certain model of race relations and immigrant integration. In this context, Quebecois secularism has been defined during the reasonable accommodation debate as a model opposed to Canadian multiculturalism, one in which multiculturalism's excesses of tolerance are limited by state power through the refusal to accommodate religion's visibility in public spaces and religious practices in public institutions.[67]

While the CSF adhered to a nationalist narrative of secularism as freeing women and implying that Islamic veiling practices should be forbidden in public institutions, the FFQ tried to articulate a position that would not pit women's rights against religious freedom—a position that would not alienate those of its members who strongly adhered to the Quebecois nationalist project, and that would not fuel rampant Islamophobia. As the FFQ's 2007 position paper for the Bouchard-Taylor consultations argued in its introduction:

> The defense of the principle of equality between women and men should not and cannot be used to elaborate a racist discourse against immigrants belonging to specific religious communities (such as Muslim and Jewish communities). In other words, the instrumentalization of feminism cannot cover up racism.[68]

The FFQ's position advocated an inclusive feminism that does not presuppose that religious freedom is the enemy of women's rights.[69] This position was a complex move for the FFQ, given the proximity it had developed during the 1990s to the nationalist Quebecois Party, a party that now claimed a muscular version of secularism and flirted with a populist antimigrant discourse.[70] The FFQ also pointed to the implicit link between racism, migration, and religion, used by the CSF and many Quebecois politicians to argue against multiculturalism. Instead, for example, in a document to its membership in 2009 the FFQ remarked that the CSF's proposal to ban ostentatious religious symbols would disparately impact Muslim women wearing the veil and added: "This question is being asked in a context in which migrant and racialized women and non-veiled Muslim women . . . are already underrepresented in our public administration. Shouldn't we fight for the improvement of their integration and their representation?"[71] In its public statements the FFQ always clearly linked its discourse on secularism with the Quebecois social context marked by racism and systemic discrimination against immigrant women.

As many of the FFQ's publications claim, its implication during the 1990s with the organization of the World March of Women and its establishment of an internal committee representing women from cultural communities in 2003 had contributed to an increased awareness of differences among women and of discrimination against racialized women among the FFQ members.[72] The framing that the FFQ developed was therefore oriented toward the idea of a "feminist secularism" (*laïcité féministe*) that takes into consideration intersectionality. However, the FFQ distinguished between accommodating religious symbols in public service, such as clients wearing a niqab, and the wearing of the niqab by public service employees, which it rejected (a point criticized by organizations such as

SAWC). Not surprisingly, the FFQ position—summarized by "no obligation (to wear the veil) no prohibition"—which aimed at critiquing religious fundamentalism's treatment of women's rights and, at the same time, at supporting women's right to choose their faith and the degree to which they want to practice it, was not easy to reach among the constituency of the organization and proved constantly contested during the following decade.[73] Some members left the FFQ, accusing it of being infiltrated by Islamists, and interpreted the FFQ's position on religious accommodation as a betrayal of the nationalist secular project that the FFQ had supposedly historically endorsed for Quebecois society. They expressed their grievances in vivid terms, lamenting the silencing of their secular voices inside the organization and contesting the accusations of racism that targeted them. A typical narrative of the tensions that characterized the 2013 Estate Generals of the FFQ, published by an ex-member of the FFQ, opposes the historical commitment of the FFQ to defend "*all* women" and a common project for Quebecois society with particular divisive religious claims aiming at leveling differences at the expense of gender and the fight against patriarchy.[74] Interestingly, in this narrative the author regards the term "intersectionality" as akin to the Marxist claim in the 1970s Quebecois feminist movement that class should be taken into account—that is, as a dangerous, divisive difference. Use of the term "racialized" instead of "women from migrant and cultural communities" in the official vocabulary of the organization is interpreted as a form of propaganda to "guilt white women." The obvious moral overtones of this discourse display well-known features of white feminists' resistance to antiracist discourse: claiming the need to universalize the feminist subject and interpreting identity politics by women of color as divisive, and refusing to acknowledge responsibility for white privilege.[75]

Hence, in Quebec, while sexualism debates gave rise to clear tensions among feminists, the umbrella organization representing the leadership of the movement opted for accommodation and articulated an analysis that placed Muslim women at the center of the policy issue—rather than the "protection" of the supposedly Quebecois value of gender equality. The FFQ's reaction to the 2017 ban in public service illustrates its ability to denounce the racism and Islamophobia inherent to the law, and to articulate the fight against racism as a primary feminist concern. The vice president of the FFQ at the time, Marlihan Lopez, reacted to the law in the following terms:

While only a very small number of women wear the niqab or the burqa here in Quebec, this law affects all women. It is a feminist issue because this "religious neutrality" law, which pretends to have as its overt goal ensuring women's security and promoting their liberation, in fact only produces the exclusion of a specific group of women from the public space, and therefore their marginalization. Law 62 victimizes some women and makes them vulnerable to gendered violence.[76]

Hence, in the end, the FFQ managed to articulate a critical position against femonationalism and denounce the instrumentalization of women's rights while also pointing to the harm done to pious Muslim women by the law. This is not to suggest that the feminist movement in Quebec is homogeneous and deprived of tensions. Quite the contrary, racialized women's organizations have their own organizations, and created their own umbrella committee, the "committee of women from diverse origins," in 2002. However, this separate committee was not spurred by debates over veiling or religious accommodation. Rather, it arose from the desire to self-represent as a component of the Quebecois feminist movement, and it has not meant a break in the collaboration with the FFQ. While, as I will detail in chapter 5, many self-identified intersectional and racialized Quebecois feminists were not satisfied with how the FFQ handled the debate, it is nonetheless notable, especially when one compares the situation in France, as I do below, that the FFQ did distance itself from the national narrative of secularism implying the invisibility of (minority) religious symbols, and from the discourse using the fight against sexism to legitimize anti-Muslim and racist policies. What can account for the FFQ's ability to keep a critical distance from femonationalist discourses?

Remaining Critical

How can a "mainstream" and mostly white women's rights coalition such as the FFQ maintain a critical distance from femonationalist discourses in the context of increased Islamophobia in the public sphere? What type of feminist practice and legacy leads a majority of nonracialized feminist organizations to adopt an intersectional perspective and discourse? The literature on feminist movements and intersectional coalitions delineates various factors that foster the adoption of intersectionality, as well as various strategies that minority women's organizations or "mainstream" women's organizations deploy to achieve their political goals, strategies that can foster or impede coalition politics across differences.[77] Among the factors that might foster coalition politics, a central one is the acknowledgment of power relationships among participants in the coalitions. Such acknowledgment may take various institutional forms, such as separate commissions, veto power, commitment to descriptive representation of marginalized groups,[78] and antiracism work inside feminist organizations. While the acknowledgment of power relations leading to the institutionalization of dissent, separatism, or descriptive representation inside a coalition is certainly necessary for it to maintain itself in an inclusive way without suppressing conflicts or excluding differences, one may wonder what factors explain the adoption of these practices in the first place. What makes feminist organizations aware that they should acknowledge power relations along lines of race, religion, or migration status? A first answer that the Quebecois case highlights is the strength of racialized women's self-organizing. The power relations between racialized/immigrant women's organizations and white women's organizations will determine in great part the ability and willingness of feminist coalitions among these actors to adopt inclusive practices. Indeed, the ability of racialized/immigrant feminists to self-organize in Quebec since the 1980s has provided them with an institutional support structure, funding, and a public voice in Quebecois feminism that has put them in the position of deciding their own terms for their collaboration with white feminists. This has not been the case in France, for example, and I develop in more detail the consequences of this ability to self-organize, or not, for racialized feminists' political subjectivations in chapter 5.

I propose to analyze more closely two other and interrelated historical legacies that, I argue, influence the FFQ's ability to remain critical during sexularism debates. The first one is the historical legacy of the FFQ's position in the broader field of radical left protest politics—that is, the history of intermovement relations. A feminist coalition's relation to other segments of the protest arena and formal politics shapes its organizational capacity to include differences.[79] The second historical process that shapes a feminist coalition's ability to adopt intersectionality is its history and memory of organizational relationships across racial differences. How were race and ethnic diversity historically articulated and addressed within white feminist organizations in Quebec such as the FFQ? To answer this question we must retrace the history of the politicization of race within white and racialized feminists' discourses. Of course, this history is also dependent on the strength of racialized/immigrant women's self-organizing in each context, but it should not be reduced to it.

The FFQ is almost fifty years old, with historical roots in a reformist-liberal approach to feminism and, during the last decade has had on average a five-person permanent staff, important funding from the federal and the provincial governments,[80] and numerous individual (an average of three hundred) and organizational members (around two hundred during my fieldwork). FFQ members are, for the most part, grassroots women's rights organizations, and the FFQ does not accept membership from political parties (or their women's groups) but does accept union's women's committees. To understand the FFQ's positions on the Islamic veil it is important to go back to its historical roots as a feminist organization, and to its relationship with other important actors in the field of protest politics.

The FFQ was founded by Thérèse Casgrain in 1966 to push for more women in Quebecois politics: twenty-five years after Quebecois women had been granted the right to vote, their absence in elected bodies called for more action. Initially a reformist, apolitical, and moderate organization with ties to the main Quebecois union, the Confédération des syndicats nationaux, the FFQ has lobbied for the creation of state feminist institutions in Quebec and issued numerous memoirs and reports on women's condition in Quebec over the years. The FFQ evolved in the 1980s and 1990s, becoming more radical and more clearly in favor of Quebec's independence. While during the Quiet Revolution the FFQ did not have ties with the radical Left and was closer to the Liberal Party (despite its formal commitment not to be politically identifiable with a specific party), in the 1980s, a crisis in the leadership and the continuing social mobilization around the constitutional status of Quebec within the Canadian federation altered the FFQ's initial DNA.[81] The ties of some of the members of the FFQ with the nationalist Parti Québécois contributed to changing the position of the FFQ, which, without pledging allegiance to any party, decided to affirm itself, in the name of Quebecois women's interests, in favor of Quebec's sovereignty.

Despite intense political involvement in the debates on Quebec's political future, the economic crisis and the budget cuts initiated by the right-wing government in the first half of the 1990s negatively impacted the FFQ's membership, then at one of the lowest points of its history. To remobilize feminists across the province, then FFQ president Françoise David organized a large Bread and Roses March in 1995, which drew media attention and mobilized feminists around concrete demands directed toward the government, especially alleviation of poverty. This provincial mobilization would morph, five years later, into the World March of Women, coordinated from Quebec with a team originating from the Bread and Roses March.[82] This decade of intense activism drew more members to the FFQ and increased its public profile. In 2009, an anglophone self-identified lesbian and mother, Alexa Conradi, took over the leadership of the FFQ and therefore headed the organization through the turmoil of the charter debate.[83] One of few anglophone leaders of the FFQ and with an immigrant background (from Britain), as well as the first out lesbian to be president, she embodied the politicization and radicalization of the FFQ in the 2000s.[84]

The weakness of the radical Left in the 1970s in Quebec meant that the FFQ was not really challenged by a radical fringe. The more radical Québécois Front de Libération des Femmes, (Women's Liberation Front, FLF, founded in 1969 and close to the Quebec nationalist party) sought alliances with the FFQ.[85] The FLF and the FFQ shared analyses about women's oppression but diverged on the means to be used, without expressing antagonism toward each other. Moreover, the FFQ was founded in the 1960s, before radical-left politics really emerged on the Quebecois political scene. This heritage gave the FFQ anteriority and exteriority vis-à-vis leftist and nationalist political parties. Today, left-wing parties on the Quebecois political stage are headed by former FFQ members (rather than the reverse), and the FFQ therefore appears as an autonomous actor that can ally with the radical Left but has organizational and political autonomy. Hence, the FFQ reflects the history of the Quebecois feminist movement: although often allied with leftist/nationalist movements, it did not depend on or compete with them to exist, and did not have to struggle against them, as was the case for second-wave movements in many other Western countries, France and the United States included. This specificity is important because, as Benita Roth has argued for the United States, the competition of the women's liberation movement with radical-left politics during the second wave encouraged white feminists to frame their claims as universal in order to resist the tendency in radical-left politics to sideline gender issues.[86] Not facing such a strong pressure from radical-left allies, the FFQ did not have to universalize gender equality issues and could remain more attentive to differences between women. However, the ties of the FFQ to the Parti Québécois, which strengthened during the 1990s, have had an impact on some of its members' ability to remain critical toward Quebecois nationalism. With important ties to nationalist leaders and a history of adhesion to Quebecois nationalist discourses, several white feminists from the FFQ decided to leave the organization, in the name of their adhesion to secularism but also because of their refusal to critically reflect on Quebecois nationalist claims.[87]

The second important historical process that has shaped the FFQ's ability to remain critical about femonationalism, and to elaborate a critical feminist discourse on female religious agency, secularism, and nationhood, is its legacy of addressing racial differences and power asymmetries at an institutional level. Indeed, the FFQ was confronted early in its history with the question of the inclusion of what was then conceived as ethnic difference. Its foundational charter from 1966 states that the FFQ's mission is to assemble "without distinctions based on race, ethnic origin, color or belief, women and organizations willing to coordinate their activities in the domain of social action." This commitment reflects the specific Quebecois situation of the 1960s, marked by the emergence of indigenous claims and the historical segregation between anglophones and francophones (considered as "races" or ethnic groups at the time). As early as the mid-1960s, the FFQ defined itself as a "bridge between three solitudes," mainly francophone, anglophone, and Jewish communities, while maintaining its religious neutrality.[88] While many Jewish women in Quebec were arriving as immigrants from Morocco or Hungary, the FFQ was keenly aware of the need to integrate them in the organization. As Amanda Ricci notes about the period from the 1960s to the 1980s, the FFQ was well aware of the importance of being inclusive, while admitting difficulties in implementing this priority, especially with respect to actually recruiting non-Catholics and non-Protestants. The election in 1977 of the first Jewish president of the FFQ, Sheila Finestone, marked an important step in this process.

In 1973, the FFQ held a joint meeting with Canadian Black women's organizations. It reflected on the opportunity of organizing, inside the FFQ, a specific conference on women doubly discriminated against as indigenous, immigrants, or Black. However, here again, there was no concrete outcome of this symbolic statement.[89] Things began to change in the early 1980s, when under the auspices of the Quebecois ministry of immigration and cultural communities, the FFQ organized a conference titled "Immigrant Women, Our Turn to Speak."[90] It led to heightened networking and visibility of migrant women's organizations, which helped them articulate in a more forceful way their critique of the invisibility of their issues and concerns in "mainstream" Quebecois women's rights organizations such as the FFQ. Simultaneously, in the 1980s the FFQ was forced to consider its relationship with the Fédération des Femmes Autochtones du Québec (Federation of Indigenous Women from Québec, FAQ).[91] In 1991, the FAQ decided to leave the FFQ, stating that it did not recognize itself in the cultural Quebecois identity promoted by the FFQ. This breakup encouraged the FFQ to critically reflect on the question of colonial domination and to include in its 1994 political platform the idea that Quebec's sovereignty (openly promoted since the mid-1980s by the FFQ) should have constitutional bases "just and equitable for women, for cultural minorities and for indigenous nations," thereby breaking with traditional sovereigntist discourses.[92] In 2004, a mutual solidarity protocol was signed between the two organizations. This relationship with indigenous women paved the way for critical reflection inside the FFQ about other forms of oppression than gender that the FFQ could not simply dismiss from its analysis.

In line with its work to establish a relationship with indigenous women that was free of domination or racism, and reacting to the pressure exerted by the Coordination of Migrant Women, founded in 1983, the FFQ began to reflect on its own practices with respect to racism and inclusion of immigrant women in the early 1990s. Many activists argue that the first official commitment of the FFQ to represent minority women goes back to the 1992 presidential declaration: "The [feminist] movement will no longer ignore the issue of cultural pluralism. We must achieve a real articulation between the feminist movement and women from ethnocultural communities." However, this commitment was put into practice only in January 2000, when the FFQ created the Comité des femmes des communautés culturelles (Committee of Women from Cultural Communities, CFCC). This committee, which was composed mostly of immigrant and racialized women, had a mandate to

> defend the rights and interests of women from ethnocultural communities as a marginalized group, by fostering the openness of the women's movement to cultural diversity and national and international solidarity and reinforcing the relationship between women from cultural communities and visible minorities and women from the majority.[93]

Following this commitment, in 2004 the FFQ launched a three-year-long process to develop "an inclusive perspective and a shared leadership with cultural communities' organizations ... a strategy to fight racism and ethnic and religious discrimination."[94] The CCFC surveyed minority women's status inside member organizations of the FFQ and the distribution of resources among member organizations to conclude that a rebalancing of resources toward migrant women's organizations was in order, as well as an increase in their descriptive representation inside the FFQ structures.[95] What is more, the fact that the FFQ initiated the World March of Women at the end of the 1990s is also important to explain why the abstract commitment to cultural diversity enshrined in 1992 became a concrete policy in 2000. Indeed, organizing a worldwide event with women from different nationalities and with pressing concerns regarding imperialism or poverty meant acknowledging other types of oppression than gender alone. As an FFQ activist notes:

> This march is an important moment in our reflection process. We have decided to widen our perspective to consider multiple discriminations and also to think in terms of and to apply intersectional analysis. . . . We wanted this fight against discriminations to be totally integrated into the federation's work.[96]

In March 2015, the FFQ held a general assembly to orient its future actions and proposed to its members adopting the fight for the elimination of all forms of oppression (including racism and colonialism) in its charter, as well as intersectionality as an analytical tool shaping the FFQ's position in the public sphere.[97] This adoption was not smooth—far from it— and left marks for many racialized Quebecois feminists, as I examine in chapter 5. However, it does appear to be the result of a decades-long history of partial, and then more sustained, attention to the question of race. The various institutional forms that have been devised by the FFQ to address the question of race also show an increasing politicization of this issue. The institutional vocabulary evolved from the promotion of "plurality" among women in 1992, to the establishment of a special committee of "women from immigrant and cultural communities" in the early 2000s with a mandate to investigate the presence of immigrant women in the organization's membership, to the institutionalization of the descriptive representation of "racialized women" on the board of the organization and the hiring of an officer in charge of "intersectionality." While the FFQ's efforts to institutionalize and politicize race may still appear insufficient or devoid of concrete effects on its mainly white constituency,[98] they denote a capacity to articulate a critical discourse on race that not only provides a social critique of racism in Quebecois society but also reflects on racism *within* the Quebecois feminist movement and aims at revising its practices.[99] This legacy of being accountable on the issue of racial privileges and racism certainly provided the grounds for the organization to elaborate a feminist analysis critical—to some extant—of the rampant femonationalism championed by the Quebecois government. Of course, a gap remains, as in many other organizations, between the rhetorical commitment to intersectionality and actual intersectional practices, a gap that attest to what Sara Ahmed has termed the "nonperformativity" of antiracism.[100] However, critical public discourses against femonationalist projects, and the election at the head of the FFQ in 2018 of a trans* woman, also attest of the capacity of the organization to critically reflect on the privileges of white cis-women in its ranks, and to enlarge its definition of who can embody the good feminist subject. The unfolding of sexularism debates within the French public sphere and within the French women's movements since the beginning of the 2000s provides a strikingly different, and darker, picture.

Feminists' Divides in France

The veil(s) debates in France have been well documented, and the conflicts and crises they precipitated within feminism have also been analyzed, although only punctually.[101] Indeed, while the first law prohibiting veiling in public school shattered the feminist movement to the ground, subsequent laws and debates (in 2010 with the legal ban on face-veiling in public space and in 2016 with the public debate on the burkini) revealed the long-term consequences of these conflicts on women's rights organizations and their relations with each other, which have been less scrutinized. I retrace here the most important fractures that have delineated the grounds upon which women's rights are discussed and implemented in the French public sphere today.

The story of the 2004 law banning Islamic veiling in public school has been told often.[102] Its consequences for the French conception of secularism (and of immigrant integration) have also been analyzed. Among the effects of this piece of legislation and the vast public debate it occasioned, the conflicts it raised among feminists (but also within labor unions, human rights organizations, and the radical Left in general)[103] are noticeable but much less investigated. However, they are crucial to understanding the rise of femonationalism in France: with the 2004 debate, the issue of postcolonialism finally emerged with force within the French feminist movements, and revealed many women's rights activists' adhesion to the French republican universalism and its color-blind, secularist narrative.[104]

While feminists did not initiate the 2004 law, they took part in the public debate and defended opposing views on the legitimacy of a ban on headscarves in public schools. Their contribution to the debate started when, in the spring of 2003, the controversy over headscarves emerged through a passing mention by then minister of the interior, Nicolas Sarkozy—despite a historic low number of girls wearing headscarves in public schools that year—and was rapidly instrumentalized by several political actors, leading to both a parliamentary commission (Commission Debré) and a presidentially mandated commission, appointed by President Jacques Chirac and headed by Bernard Stasi, to provide the government with recommendations on the implementation of secularism in France.[105] Leaders of the wider national umbrella organization for women's rights in France, the Collectif national pour les droits des femmes (CNDF) stated in January 2004[106] that their organization was divided on this issue, and that personaly they opposed both the wearing of the Islamic headscarf and the right-wing government's intention to legislate against the headscarf in public schools. While they acknowledged discriminations against Muslims and migrants in France, they interpreted the choice made by "some young people of Muslim faith, inspired or not by fundamentalist imams, to fight for the right of young girls to wear their headscarves in school, or in public service as employees" as the "wrong struggle," a strategic error in their fight against humiliations.[107] In a typical leftist vein, the heads of the CNDF denounced the focus on religious symbols at a time when socioeconomic questions, poverty, and austerity should have occupied center stage and could have united feminist movements and the Left around a common agenda. Furthermore, in their view:

> Whatever the meaning that a minority of young women give, at a personal level, to the wearing of the veil (and we know this meaning is plural), the wearing of the veil takes on the same meaning in all monotheist religion when it is presented as a compulsory religious requirement. It is not at all a symbol of emancipation.[108]

Interestingly, the acknowledgment of the multiple meanings that a headscarf can be invested with is quickly made irrelevant by the claim that the veil as a religious symbol *cannot* be emancipatory. This authoritative argument simultaneously erases the agency of this "small minority of young women" previously mentioned by the authors.

The CNDF leaders' position, while representative of the positions of many members from the "class struggle" trend inherited from the second wave of the French feminist movement,[109] did not manage to build consensus among women's rights organizations, despite the CNDF's status as the umbrella organization and main network for women's rights in France. Indeed, on one side a novel alignment emerged, grouping together feminists who often had participated in the second-wave movement's "autonomist" trend (meaning autonomous from radical-left organizations or from the Communist Party), such as Anne Zélensky, Anne Vigerie, and Liliane Kandel, and who started to define themselves as secularist feminists (*féministes laïcardes*),[110] feminist members of women's rights organizations close to the Communist Party,[111] and a rising women's rights NGO, Ni putes ni soumises (NPNS), founded by Fadela Amara to represent young girls from the ghetto who wish to be emancipated from religious and ethnic communities.[112] While the vast majority of the individual and institutional members of this formation were not representatives of racialized/immigrant groups, some of them, like Fadela Amara and her organization, specifically defined themselves as such.[113] Prominent figures presented as witnesses of the horrors of religious fundamentalism, like Bangladeshi writer Taslima Nasreen, activist Zazi Sadou (at the time president of Algerian Democratic Women), and Algerian activist Wassyla Tamzali,[114] joined these secularist voices. All these components identified the defense of republicanism and secularism as the most important battle to be fought, and the Islamic headscarf as a dangerous sign of religious proselytism and of the dismantlement of republican values. In an op-ed published in May 2003, Anne Vigerie and Anne Zélensky wrote:

> The question of the veil . . . has been a source of anxiety for feminists for a long time. Young women or girls wear it in the name of the freedom to practice their religion. But the wearing of the veil is not a sign of religious belief. It symbolizes women's place as defined by Islamism. This place is in the shadow, the relegation, the submission to man. That women claim this right does not change anything about the meaning of the veil. It is well known that the oppressed are the most fervent advocates of their own oppression.[115]

They further identified a public space devoid of any religious symbols as the only way to preserve women's rights and the Republic's heritage and denounced a "postcolonial guilt" that encouraged leftist activists to accept encroachment on women's rights in the name of cultural tolerance. NPNS as well presented the veil as a regression in women's rights and a strategy of young girls in urban ghettos to protect themselves from the violence of their male counterparts.[116] After having accused the CNDF of being infiltrated by "Islamists," and in order to voice disapproval of the CNDF's opposition to the law, in NPNS decided to organize a demonstration for women's rights on March 6, 2005, so as not to demonstrate side by side with the CNDF's demonstration on March 8.

On the other side of the feminist spectrum, op-eds were published in May and in December 2003[117] by prominent intellectuals and politicians associated with the Left[118] stressing the context of discrimination and racism against Muslims and the colonialist overtones of the debate. Cautious not to appear as proponents of veiling, they did not insist on religious freedom or women's agency but on the emancipatory nature of public schools and the importance of including Muslim girls:

> How can feminists support a law that excludes these young women from school, often the only place where they can emancipate themselves, to send them back into their families that supposedly oppressed them?[119]

These public appeals coalesced with the creation of a new network, Une école pour tou-te-s, contre les lois d'exclusion,[120] and a new organization, the Collectif féministe pour l'égalité (CFPE), in which prominent radical second-wave feminist Christine Delphy participated. Members represented a heterogeneous mix that never managed to form an effective political coalition.[121] However, with respect to the transformation of the feminist movements, this network marked the emergence of a new discourse and identity, which denounced a misinterpretation of secularism and, more than anything else, the rampant Islamophobia[122] and postcolonial aphasia[123] present in the debate. In feminist terms, they denounced the implicit paternalism that the ban fueled toward Muslim women as well as the idea that the Islamic headscarf could have only one meaning, that of women's oppression. Here again the coalition was a mix of feminists who identified as postcolonial subjects or *indigènes*, such as Houria Bouteldja, who participated in the creation of the

CFPE,[124] and nonracialized feminists coming from human rights organizations or women's rights organizations. Of importance, this coalition for the first time addressed the issue of racism and of the colonial continuum *within* French feminism itself. They presented the necessity of jointly addressing feminism and racism as a precondition for any true feminist project. The divide with the CNDF (as well as with NPNS)[125] crystallized for the celebration of international women's day on March 8, 2004, as the CNDF refused to include the CFPE in its call for demonstrations. This scission would lead, slowly but surely, some years later to parallel demonstrations in Paris on March 8, one organized by the CNDF,[126] and marching toward the Place de la République, and the other organized by the CFPE, Afro-feminists, feminist organizations from the Parisian suburbs, LGBT organizations, and the union of sex workers in Belleville, a neighborhood with an important migrant population.

The debate on Islamic veiling continued beyond the 2004 law, as the conservative right-wing party of Nicolas Sarkozy tried to preserve its electoral gain against a populist far-right National Front in constant progression during the 2000s. Attempts to enlarge the prohibition to other spaces than public schools surfaced first with a discrete jurisprudence by the highest administrative court (the Conseil d'État) in which it refused to grant French citizenship to a woman wearing a niqab in 2008,[127] and later with a public debate and subsequent legislative ban on full veiling in public spaces in 2010.[128] The scope of the prohibition of Islamic veils in public schools broadened with the "Circulaire Chatel," a regulation by the minister of education that forbade mothers wearing a hijab from accompanying pupils during excursions organized by schools, as well as with an ongoing judicial battle over the wearing of Islamic headscarves by an educator in a publicly subsidized private day care center, the crèche Baby-Loup.[129] This constant widening of the scope of prohibition led Socialist president François Hollande to suggest, on March 24, 2013, the possibility of regulating/prohibiting Islamic veiling and religious symbols in private workplaces in France. Feminists were not indifferent to this evolution and expansion of the legislation against Islamic veiling. Indeed, on the one hand, organizations such as NPNS were instrumental in the birth of the 2010 law. They contributed largely to the publicity around the debate on full veiling and made dramatic calls to the legislature to take action.[130] NPNS argued that the French state could not leave women in deprived neighborhoods at the hands of their oppressive husbands and brothers and that republican values had to be extended to these French citizens and these remote territories. NPNS described the banlieues as a war zone for women, using usual feminist tropes about one's right to control her body and sexuality.[131]

While feminist organizations were divided over the 2004 law, a majority was in favor of the 2010 ban on full veiling in public spaces—with the exception of the CFPE and some feminists from the former "class struggle" trend.[132] At the other end of the spectrum, new petitions appeared in 2013 to counter Hollande's proposal to legislate veiling practices in the workplace, especially regarding jobs where one interacts with children. They declared, "We are all veiled women" and argued that

> such a new law would be racist for it would, under the guise of protecting children from some sort of imagined contamination, subject women to domination by proponents of national purification and reduce their conditions to unemployment or invisibility.[133]

While the signatories used "we women" rather than "we feminists," they also used the feminist trope of control over one's body: "The imposition of any dress code whatsoever, whether it involves prohibiting the veil or making wearing it mandatory, is a form of violence and we condemn it as such. Our bodies belong to us and our choice of clothing too." In 2016, feminist figures mobilized again to oppose the multiplication of municipal bans on burkinis.[134] Their open letter clearly articulated the chasm among French feminists, firmly criticizing what they called the "feminist" argument from which women wearing burkinis are alienated:

> We should liberate them from men's oppression by unveiling them. But what do the persons concerned think about this? And where does this idea that a woman must undress to be free come from? This is, alas, an argument used by many "feminists" that has trouble hiding a conception of "emancipation" that is totally dependent on Western ethnocentrism.[135]

While both initiatives gathered support from prestigious feminist scholars in France and abroad, the absence of any major women's rights organization among those who signed the petitions is telling. The CFPE, which introduced the 2013 petition, was the only feminist organization to sign it. This isolation highlights its marginalization within the landscape of women's rights organizations, as well as the weakness of Muslim women's mobilization in such an adversarial context.[136] Conversely, the high number of signatories who belong to academia suggest a growing divide between grassroots women's rights organizations and feminist academics over this issue. This is certainly not to say that feminist academics agree on the subject. Quite the contrary, the controversy over feminist colonial aphasia erupted in academia as well, in particular with the publication in 2012 of a book/pamphlet *Les féministes blanches et l'empire* by Félix Boggio Éwanjé-Épée and Stella Magliani-Belkacem, which traced, albeit sometimes with historical partiality, white French feminists' attitudes toward the veil debates back to colonial times and the complicity of the Third Republic feminists in the colonial campaigns.[137]

Both in France and in Quebec, sexularism debates reconfigured the relationship between secularism, national identity, citizenship, gender equality, and the nexus race/religion/migration/Islam. Because of the heterogeneity of women's rights organizations in both contexts, it is difficult to evaluate if public discourses voiced by prominent feminist organizations or feminist figures reflect the dominant opinions among grassroots feminist activists. In chapters 4 and 5 I document the wide variety of opinions among white and racialized feminists in both contexts. However, without reifying the complexity of the French and Quebecois feminist landscape, the comparative analysis of feminists' public participation in the name of women's rights in both contexts shows that French and Quebecois feminists did not elaborate similar discourses. The desire to protect women's rights and the feminist project led to different articulations of the issues at stake. In both contexts, some white feminists used a feminist discourse about women's emancipation, the memory of women's struggle against the Catholic Church, and a secularist discourse to promote restrictive policies with Islamophobic implications. However, the impact and visibility of this discourse was not comparable in France and Quebec. While a majority of Quebecois feminist organizations—white and nonwhite—maintained a critical distance toward the instrumental use of secularism, nationalism, and gender equality as vectors of anti-immigrant and racist policies, a majority of French feminist organizations adopted a *republican* and *nationalist* discourse in which *laïcité* and universalism were heralded as the best safeguards of women's rights in France. They were unable to develop a critical discourse about the successful political attempts to redefine the boundaries of secularism and nationhood with racist overtones.[138] While attempts to legislate veiling did spur debates and tensions within the Quebecois feminist movements, it

RACE, RELIGION, AND GENDER 75

literally shattered any feeling of unity and of common identity within the French feminist movement.

Perpetuating Ignorance, Participating in Femonationalism

How can we account for the way in which important French feminist organizations have adhered to femonationalism with a discourse that associates Muslim women's religiosity with patriarchy, resorting to state power to regulate the practices and subjectivities of pious Muslim women? Notwithstanding the fact that these feminist organizations have demonstrated historical commitment to antiracism and activism against restrictive immigration policies, how can we make sense of their lack of intersectional critical reflexivity when it comes to assessing the concrete needs of pious Muslim women and girls, and their responsibility as feminists in representing, and caring for, these needs? To explore further this issue, I detail the history of an important feminist organization in the French women's rights landscape, the CNDF, focusing on its ties to radical-left politics and its institutional legacy of addressing racism in its midst, as important factors in explaining its inability to resist femonationalist discourses.

The CNDF is a coalition-type organization with no legal status, no permanent staff, and no budget of its own (because it is not a legal entity). The list of its members varies depending on the actions it launches and is not recorded anywhere (but is in sharp decline, in contrast with the late nineties). CNDF members represent political entities (the Green Party's women's group, unions' women's committees) and women's rights organizations. In contrast to the reformist-turned-radical history of the FFQ, the CNDF has direct roots in the radical/class struggle of the second-wave feminist movement as well as in the broad social movement protest that destabilized the French public sphere and the right-wing government over pension reform in 1995.[139] In the beginning of the 1990s, new, spectacular forms of opposition to abortion rights emerged in France (with pro-life activists chaining themselves to clinics' gates, interrupting medical operations, etc.). This attack on women's rights alerted the already existing coalition for abortion and contraception rights (CADAC),[140] and in 1995, in response to a proposed legal amnesty for persons convicted of this offense,[141] the CADAC called for a broad national demonstration on November 25, 1995. The date was unknowingly scheduled for what would turn out to be the biggest French social movement since 1968. This timing enabled a large feminist mobilization (forty thousand people at the demonstration on November 25), and the CADAC was able to create strong solidarity links with unions and political parties, which led to the creation of a stable, although informal, coalition in January 1996: the CNDF. Very active at the turn of the century, with congresses in 1997 and 2002, and active participation in the debate on the 2006 law against violence against women,[142] the CNDF lost some of its initial steam late in the decade.[143]

From its creation up to 2016, the leadership of the CNDF has not changed: it was co-presided over by two historical figures of the second wave, who self-identify with the "class struggle" trend of the movement, and who were involved in radical-left politics in the 1970s. This leadership testifies to the strong historical links and legacy of the class struggle trend of the feminist second wave that the CNDF harbors within its ranks and in its modus operandi. While radical-autonomous French feminists decided to break with leftist organizations during the 1970s in order to organize on their own and prioritize the struggle against patriarchy,[144] class struggle feminists chose to address the two forms of oppression jointly, a strategy that put them in constant relation to leftist politics, trying to convince leftist organizations and unions to include a gender perspective while attempting to also exist on their own and to forge coalitions with the radical feminists during the 1980s. Leaders from the CNDF were socialized in revolutionary groups (the Cercle Dimitriev and Revolution) and continued to have very strong links throughout the 1990s and 2000s with the Ligue Communiste Revolutionnaire (Communist Revolutionary League), and the Nouveau Parti Anticapitaliste (New Anticapitalist Party). The situation of the CNDF vis-à-vis the French field of radical/leftist protest has had important consequences with respect to its positioning on the Islamic veil issue. While the FFQ in Quebec could provide its own analysis without fear of upsetting political allies, the CNDF, and in particular its leadership, could not ignore the positions taken by other leftist organizations. The fact that the CNDF comprises representatives of political parties and unions, and the fact that these organizations were internally divided over the issue, meant that it was very difficult for the CNDF to reach a common position on the 2004 proposed bill, or to impose its analysis on its political allies.

Another important feature that explains the CNDF's inability to critically reflect on femonationalism and its participation in it relates to the CNDF's historical lack of institutionalization of antiracism. The class struggle trend of the second wave has always had punctual, and sometimes more permanent, relationships with migrant women's movements.[145] While the current organizational landscape does not show many traces of the joint actions between feminists and migrant women that occurred during the 1980s and the first half of the 1990s, those relationships existed, and punctual solidarity and support was the norm. For example, one of the migrant women's organizations created in 1985 (the Nanas Beurs) was founded at a meeting that took place at the Parisian "Maison des femmes," a place run by radical and class struggle feminists.[146] However, the issues faced by migrant women and women of migrant descent were always quite marginal on the agenda of the class struggle second-wave feminist organizations and, subsequently, at the CNDF.

In 1997, the CNDF organized its first national convention on women's rights, with over two thousand women participating in roundtables, workshops, and plenary talks. While supposedly the ambition of the two-day conference was to address all the concerns and needs of women, from work and family to politics, violence, and international solidarity, the CNDF did not plan any specific workshop or roundtable for migrant and racialized women. Racialized women and migrant women were represented in the program only in the context of panels on female genital mutilation and international issues—for example, solidarity with women in Algeria and other African countries. While the proceedings addressed issues relating to work, family, and health, these themes were not analyzed with an intersectional lens. Women from migrant descent claimed, during the convention, the right for some space to discuss their concerns, which was granted in the roundtable dedicated to economic precariousness. Retrospectively the organizers simply stated that migrant women, "who had not participated in the preparatory work for the convention, claimed and obtained a space to meet [*un espace de parole*].... Was it not necessary that it would explode like this? That the unpredictable would happen? Beyond emotions and tensions, these voices [*paroles*] were heard."[147] This explosion, however, did not lead to any new items on the CNDF's future agenda. The needs and priorities of migrant women were always left to a few specific organizations, mobilizing a very limited number of activists, and were not brought from the margins to the center of the CNDF's attention.

Similarly, five years later, the proceedings from the 2002 forum "New Challenges for Feminism" organized by the CNDF[148] also show little inclusion of racialized women's concerns (despite their symbolic presence on the cover of the book). Indeed, the CNDF this time chose three topics to discuss: freedom of choice in a globalized era, women's unity in an age of increased inequalities, and the marketization of bodies. Of the more than three hundred pages of proceedings from the two days of debate, only five are dedicated to racism and discrimination experienced by migrant women in France (designated as such; whether they are indeed migrants or French citizens remains unaddressed).[149] The question of racism *within* the French feminist movement's structures and institutions is not addressed.[150]

Hence, despite relationships between CNDF's members and migrant women's organizations, despite punctual solidarity actions and regular discussions of migrant women's issues, French organizations followed separate roads. While the fight against racism and imperialism might appear in the CNDF's political statements in the public debate, the fight against capitalism is much more prominent, and the CNDF has not launched actions or a working group to address racism specifically. This lapse is in part due to its organizational structure: very limited funding, no permanent staff, and networking activities only. However, the material conditions of the CNDF's political activities is only part of the answer. When confronted with the issue of Islamophobia and the first debate on veils in public schools, the CNDF was caught unprepared, caught in the webs of its own ignorance based on its unspoken privileges as a mainly white women's organization. It had not developed a vocabulary or political grammar to reflect on these issues and used old leftist frames—that other problems such as poverty and unemployment matter more for women, even for those who are Muslim—to address what was in fact a new political configuration. While the "explosion" of migrant women's voices was at least rhetorically welcomed by the CNDF, the punctual presence and voice of veiled women in its organization was met with suspicion and hostility. In the absence of any collective effort to address racism and intersectionality inside the coalition, the presence of veiled women at the CNDF meetings in preparation for the 2004 International Women's Day march, in the midst of the legislative debate over prohibiting the veil in public schools, provoked violent reactions from CNDF members. As one of the veiled participants recalled:

> "Feminists" asked us, those who were wearing the veil, if we were for or against the right to abortion, if we were for or against equality between men and women, our position on homosexuality, and so on. We had to prove we

were feminists, but whatever our response, the piece of cloth on our head disqualified us.[151]

Nor did the CNDF anticipate tensions that occurred during the International Women's Day marches of 2004 and 2005 between some feminist organizations and veiled women marching, and the subsequent alternate feminist march.[152] Nor did it engage in a reflection on the descriptive representation of racialized women in these instances. The CNDF coordination meetings were deemed always "open" to whoever wanted to participate, and the issue of *who* was in fact represented was never addressed. Hence, despite a political commitment to addressing the intersection of class and gender, inherited from the second wave, the intersection of gender and race or migration has remained a low priority, and there has been no particular institutional effort to address racism inside the organization. The CNDF's participation in femonationalist discourses in France, its mild criticism of the 2004 law, and its support for the 2010 ban can thus be understood as the result of its privileged position of ignorance—not that the CNDF has not been active in fighting against racism, but it has been reluctant to perceive the instrumentalization of secularism in fueling Islamophobia. The absence of strong, organized, and recognized racialized women's organizations during this period also meant that counterdiscourses that resist femonationalism were rarely publicly articulated in feminist events and discourses. The two cases scrutinized here, Quebec and France, thus suggest that the strength of minority-feminist organizing is a crucial element in countering femonationalism.

* * *

These tensions and conflicts that arose within feminist movements in the context of policy regulations on Muslim women's religious attire are not unique to France and Quebec. They have also characterized women's movements in other European countries[153] and penetrated the European public sphere in a time of rising populism. While not all women's rights organizations have participated in this exclusionary discourse and process, it has been a major—and often dominant—feature of the new face of women's rights in the European public sphere in "postsecular" times.

Still, we must explore feminist reactions and contributions to the contemporary politics of intersectionality in Europe beyond the simple dichotomy between inclusion and exclusion. Indeed, these debates have also revived, transformed, and challenged women's rights organizations. The period

I scrutinize has been a time of intense activism and debates that, as I showed in this chapter, prompted new forms of alliance and transformed existing coalitions. I have suggested in my analysis of Islamic veiling debates that the postcolonial, secular, nationalist, and racial issues that permeated and shaped the political conflicts they triggered within feminism were articulated with the defense or activation of moral boundaries to define who can be the "good" subject of feminism and about what values feminist emancipation should uphold. These moral concerns were of course intimately articulated with hierarchies of power based on race, immigration, religion, class, and citizenship among feminist activists, but not reducible to them. In the next two chapters, I propose to deepen the analysis of the articulation between hierarchies of power and moral boundaries by examining more closely how the veiling debates reconfigured feminist political subjectivities. Shifting the gaze from organizations and coalitions to feminist activists themselves, I explore *how* exclusion is performed—and contested—and with what feminist values, identities, and emotions it may be articulated.

4
Feminist Whiteness

Reflecting on the formation of political subjects, Judith Butler has insisted that there is no such thing as a pregiven identity, a "pregiven point of departure for politics," and that we must "remember that subjects are constituted through exclusion, that is through the creation of a domain of deauthorized subjects, presubjects, figures of abjection, populations erased from view."[1] It is therefore theoretically and politically necessary to trace the operations that have led to both the construction of the subject as seemingly pregiven, and the erasure of the deauthorized subjects it is based on.[2] In this chapter, I attempt such a task by investigating the political subjectivations of white feminists, and the operations of construction and erasure they rely on. I argue in this chapter that debates on Islamic veiling not only reveal whiteness as the privileged social location occupied by white feminists, but also produce contextualized forms of what I call *feminist whiteness*, the outcome of a process of political subjectivation as a white feminist. Feminist whiteness is a location of privilege to articulate and enforce the moral and political boundaries of the legitimate feminist subject, a location based on ignorance of its own constitution and on the creation of "deauthorized subjects."

Feminists of color, from Audre Lorde to Sara Ahmed, have conceptualized whiteness as an invisible and unmarked category—for those who inhabit it, not for those marked as nonwhite—as a position of privilege and ignorance,[3] as an effect of racialization processes that mark some bodies as others, and as an orientation toward the world that shapes subjectivities.[4] Whiteness as a critical concept must be understood as a process of subjectivation that results from racism and racialization,[5] rather than as a given identity. Whiteness is a material, cultural, and subjective location of privilege; it cannot be reified to a skin color.[6] It changes over time and, as Ruth Frankenberg notes, "It is a complexly constructed product of local, regional, national, and global relations, past and present. . . . It is also a relational category, one that is co-constructed with a range of other racial and cultural categories, with class and with gender."[7] As Ahmed has underscored, whiteness reveals how racial privilege assigns race to others and impacts those bodies recognized as nonwhite.[8] In

Feminist Trouble. Éléonore Lépinard, Oxford University Press (2020). © Oxford University Press.
DOI: 10.1093/oso/9780190077150.001.0001

these ways, the process of whiteness/whitening is premised upon the active effects of racism in marking others as others.

In this chapter I argue that whiteness shapes white feminists' political subjectivation, their relationships to feminism and to other feminists, and, by doing so, deeply affects feminism as a political project. In studying the formation of white feminists' whiteness in this chapter I thus wish to document *how* whiteness informs white feminists' political subjectivation as feminists, and how it changes over time and depending on the context. My interest here is not to give an account of white feminists' *subjectivities*,[9] but rather to investigate how this location, which is both political and subjective, is constructed in the context of white feminists' activism, and how it is premised on a set of discourses and rhetorical devices that universalizes white feminists' experiences while marking other feminist subjects as nonwhite—as well as on a set of memories and legacies, and on political hegemonic discourses. I am interested in particular in how white feminists are constituted as political subjects through their relationships to nonwhite feminists, and to those whom they perceive as "bad" feminist subjects. Indeed, I argue that feminism is made white through a set of discourses that label nonwhite feminists as bad and improper subjects, to be cast away or educated in order to be reclaimed by feminism. By focusing on whiteness, I do not want to suggest that other axes of inequalities and power within feminism and between feminists do not matter. Certainly, class and sexuality have produced important conflicts over who is a good or bad feminist and what feminist emancipation should look like,[10] and they have shaped forms of feminist political subjectivation— in interaction with race. However, I do argue that in order to understand the Islamic veil debates and the ways in which they have shattered, disrupted, and fragmented feminist organizations and the feminist project, we must focus on whiteness, as a location of privilege and ignorance. While there are many different instances of feminist whiteness, not all fueling femonationalism, I argue that some hegemonic forms of feminist whiteness are instrumental in doing so, and they are the focus of this chapter.

Many critical race scholars have noted that whiteness is partly discursively produced, through a specific set of discourses and, mostly, through an absence-presence of race.[11] Hence, tracing the construction of *feminist whiteness* means documenting how feminism is discursively made white, how white feminists' desire to ignore realities of racism preserves their "innocence,"[12] and how they contribute to mark nonwhite feminist subjects as others, racialized and improper subjects to be excluded from the feminist collective project.[13] In this chapter, I first reconstruct whiteness, its contents and markers, through an analysis of how white feminists talk about their activism, their organizational practices with respect to cultural or religious difference, and how they describe migrant women or Muslim women as good or bad feminist subjects. I identify a variety of discourses that contribute to construct and position white feminists *as* white feminists: that is, discourses that denote feminist whiteness as a process of political subjectivation. These discourses vary greatly, and this variation is as important as the common whiteness shared by these interviewees. In fact, in describing feminist commitment and practice, white feminists also share many discursive repertoires with nonwhite feminists. This approach allows for a dynamic exploration of variations and contradictions, and understands whiteness as a historical and contextual social process.[14] I show how in two contexts, France and Quebec, white feminists use different repertoires to address race issues. Some work around or evade race, while others recognize its political salience. These different repertoires therefore point to different ways in which (and extents to which) feminism is made white and the location of white feminist privilege made invisible or acknowledged.

Exploring further how whiteness shapes white feminists' political subjectivations, I then investigate how specific moral dispositions and emotions displayed by white feminists effectively draw boundaries that close the feminist subject and produce "deauthorized" subjects. In her study of white innocence as it is present in the Dutch cultural archive, Gloria Wekker notes that whiteness is saturated by affects and moral dispositions—such as entitlement—and that postcolonial melancholia also feeds anger and violence.[15] Similarly, I document the contours of affective responses to race displayed by white feminists. I argue that women marked as "others" by white feminists—the woman migrant, the veiled woman, the non-white woman—elicit two types of moral, political, and emotional dispositions on the part of white feminists.

A first orientation of white feminists toward "othered" women, and in particular toward migrant woman, is animated by a conception of feminism and feminist practice as a *social* project—that of responding to the need of vulnerable women. In this conception, which characterizes in particular, but not only, white feminists working in service-providing organizations, feminist whiteness translates into specific feminist moral dispositions such as the suspension of judgment, self-improvement, benevolence, and the ignorance of white privilege. It also gives rise to specific emotions such as satisfaction, but also ambivalence. In the second case, which entails an understanding of feminism as a historical *political* collective project of transformation that bonds women together, feminism fuels a different process of political subjectivation as white feminist. Here religious and racial differences are highly politicized and define improper feminist subjects. This process of political subjectivation as white feminist entails moral dispositions such as disapproval, indignation, and self-righteousness, and emotions such as melancholy, fear, and anger.

In the last section in this chapter I argue that debates on Islamic veiling have, in particular, operated a shift in feminist whiteness, from feminist whiteness as *ignorance* to feminist whiteness as an active participation in *national identity*, or what Sarah Farris has called "femonationalism."[16] Characterizing feminist whiteness as a form of ignorance does not mean that it is not actively socially produced. Following feminist epistemologies and epistemologies of ignorance's tenets, what we know and what we ignore are shaped by our social location, and privilege entails the ability to actively ignore relationality with those situated across power lines.[17] I argue that feminist whiteness in the context of femonationalism is not only based on ignorance: the shift I describe emphasizes the more overt and active embrace of republican and nationalist discourses by white feminists in the wake of the laws banning Islamic veiling in France.

Because whiteness is not the product of a preexisting identity, but a political and social construction, the analysis of feminist whiteness I propose is an inductive one; it is reconstructed from the empirical material collected, tracing discourses that retrace processes of political subjectivation.[18] The feminist activists that I interviewed and categorized as white feminists self-identified as members of the ethnic majority group.[19] Or, more precisely, they did not identify racially, thereby adhering to the idea typical of whiteness that they are not marked, even when some might have some parents with a migrant background. They were also officers or volunteers in organizations that did not self-identify as representing a specific ethnic or national group. These organizations—shelters, community centers, and advocacy groups—identified as feminist or women's organizations[20] and, often in Quebec, as multicultural as well.[21] In both France and Quebec race and racism have been publicly problematized in recent history (since the 1980s) in conjunction with issues of immigration and, more recently, religion—meaning in fact Islam, the religion of the formerly colonized, persons who became the immigrant, and then have become, in public debates since the 1990s in France and the 2000s in Quebec, the Muslim man/woman.[22] Hence, my focus here is on how feminist whiteness has been produced in the last decade in relation to women and feminists who are marked as others through the racialization of religion and immigration. Evidently, other historical repertoires, such as colonialism, immigrant integration, secularism, leftist internationalism, republicanism, multiculturalism, and intersectionality, also constitute the discursive field of race and racism in both contexts and contribute to shape different forms of feminist whiteness beyond the focus on Islam.

In France, interviews were realized after the 2010 law prohibiting full veiling in public spaces—less controversial within feminist circles than the 2004 law prohibiting religious symbols in public schools but still a topic that demanded feminists take a position—and while new feminist forces emerged to counter pinkwashing, colonialist discourses and Islamophobia.[23] In Quebec those were also active times. The debate over the Quebecois "charter of values" that unfolded during my fieldwork forced many feminist organizations to take a stand and to articulate their position vis-à-vis Quebecois nationalism and its Islamophobic undertones. A lot has happened since then as well. New feminist organizations have formed and others have disbanded, new feminist voices have emerged and claimed new public identities, while others may have turned away from activism. This means that new white and nonwhite feminist political subjectivities are in the making, subjectivities that this book has not captured.[24] This sample thus does not exhaust the variation of feminist whiteness in both contexts. It is not representative of the diversity of white feminists in France and Quebec. What is more, I selected excerpts that display more obviously feminist whiteness, especially in France, and which may seem to reflect extreme positions, easy to ignore as nonrepresentative of the broader movement (because of their racist overtones or their association of Islam with extremism). However, while they may be overrepresented in the quotations illustrating my argument in this chapter, these discourses are not marginal, especially in France at the time of my fieldwork. The tendency to universalize gender and to associate Islam with women's subordination was well represented in my sample of feminist volunteers, activists, and NGO officers. Hence, while this chapter overrepresents certain forms of feminist whiteness, concentrating on the effects of privilege and ignorance rather than on what Frankenberg has termed "race cognizant" whiteness, this strategy allows for identifying common repertoires and identifying the effects of whiteness on feminist subjectivation, an important step, I argue, in the direction of understanding the current feminist trouble.

Evading Race: French Repertoires of Feminist Whiteness

In her analysis of the social construction of whiteness in the United States, Ruth Frankenberg pays particular attention to white feminists. In her sample of white women interviewed in her research, white feminists are the most "race cognizant"—that is, aware of race pervasiveness in the American society of the 1980s, of its historical significance and links with colonization, and aware that they are themselves white, occupying a position of privilege and power in these relations. Their repertoire contrasts with the dominant repertoire used by most of Frankenberg's interviewees, which evades race, using color-blindness as a way to evade racialization, racism, and power inequalities.[25] Frankenberg presents white feminists' repertoire of race cognizance as a result of the historical events of desegregation and the civil rights movements of the 1960s, as well as a result of the vivid conflicts that occurred within US second-wave feminism, and the product of the challenges and critiques formulated by US Black feminists and other women of color through texts, public interventions, and activism within feminist organizations. While Frankenberg noticed the relative race cognizance of US white feminists she interviewed, other works have also insisted on the pervasiveness of whiteness as a discursive formation that shapes feminism and secures a privileged position for white feminists in feminist movements and theory.[26] Recent scholarship on whiteness in third-wave feminist movements describes a new set of repertoires of whiteness, which express a desire for "diversity" and the rhetorical inclusion of feminists of color's works.[27] However, these repertoires often reproduce whiteness as privilege, instead of displacing its centrality in feminism, for example through an understanding of diversity as a proliferation of differences. What is more, the gap between the avowed desire for inclusion and the lack of concrete engagement to remedy the absence of nonwhite women from feminist organizations displays what Sara Ahmed has termed a "declaration of whiteness that performs a recognition of privilege without actually dislodging it."[28]

Repertoires used by white feminists in France in the 2010s contrast in important ways with the narratives reproduced by Frankenberg, or with third-wave accounts of whiteness. Race cognizance, as described by Frankenberg, is a marginal repertoire within white feminists' discourses, mainly found in Quebec. This marginality denotes that dominant repertoires on race and racism in France and Quebec differ from those in the United States described by Frankenberg, and also that white feminists' relationship to dominant repertoires on race differs in France from the American context. This marginality also suggests that conflicts about racism within feminism have not unfolded in similar ways in France (or in Quebec). There has been an international diffusion of US feminist debates and arguments, as well as a reappropriation of Black US feminist writings by racialized feminist groups, for example in France,[29] and a (contested) importation of the vocabulary of intersectionality.[30] Nevertheless, these processes of diffusion and appropriation have not always impacted white feminists' political subjectivations, and notable differences remain.

While all French women working or volunteering in white/ethnic majority organizations who were interviewed insisted that the 2004 law banning the veil in public schools had raised thorny issues and heated discussions among their members (contrary to the 2010 law banning full veiling in public spaces, which was presented as quite consensus-based), revealing therefore strong disagreements and political conflicts among them, their discourses nevertheless reflect common narratives that position white feminists in a specific location of privilege, within society and, what I will focus on here, within feminism. Two main discursive repertoires allow French white feminists to work around, in potent ways, the reality of the racialization of Muslims and of Islamophobia, and shape their feminist whiteness: universalism, and locating race outside the nation. The repertoires are interconnected, but are unevenly distributed across the sample of feminist officers and volunteers I interviewed, following differences of generation and of politicization because they are products of history, reflecting the evolution of French feminist movements and of their relationship with republican institutions.[31]

A first potent repertoire in the French context is universalism.[32] This ideal irrigates many aspects of white French feminists' relationship to racial or religious difference, which I detail: their understanding of women's rights, their ideas on the proper forms of feminist organizing, and their opinions on antiracism. A first way in which universalism shapes feminist whiteness is by downplaying differences between women based on race or religion in order to insist on the primacy of gender as a site of oppression. This hierarchy of oppressions denotes a lack of intersectional analysis and posits white women as the main subjects of feminism. For instance, Elsa, a young white feminist in her late twenties who volunteers in an organization created in 2009, Feminists Dare,[33] and is part of the executive as well as in charge of communications, sums up the priorities of her association, listing typical "universalist" priorities:

> We launched this campaign with a website that aims to show that feminism is political, that we can change things, that we can change the lives of millions of women. We chose six themes, parenthood . . . , sexism, women's image in the media, equal pay, economic precariousness, women's rights over their bodies . . . , violence, so that includes prostitution obviously, and parity. . . . We don't really address different groups of women, although of course we are aware that there is a great heterogeneity. . . . We would like not to forget women living in the projects; we don't forget that they have daily lives marked by discrimination that are specific to them. But, let's face it . . . we don't come from there. Feminist Dare is not a group of women from the projects. So it's not that easy. We don't want to mess it up. We try to do some meetings, to understand some things.

Elsa uses the descriptor "women from the projects" (*femmes des quartiers*) to convey class and racial difference, thereby performing a social distance that she indeed acknowledges a minute later in her interview when she admits that these women are in fact mostly absent from her organization. However, this absence, even coupled with the admission that racialized women have in fact specific problems and interests, does not lead her to call into question the universalist platform of her organization. Later in her interview, when asked if her organization has reflected upon the question of discrimination in employment against veiled women, she admits that the subject has not been raised. Hence the universalist approach to the feminist project of her organization makes invisible important issues that concern Muslim women—and also invisibilizes how class shapes gender-based inequalities. Social distance and social exclusion are acknowledged, but never interpreted as producing power asymmetries between feminists.

Claudine, a white woman in her early sixties, the daughter of Polish Jewish immigrants, used to be part of a feminist group for rape victims and now heads (as a volunteer) an umbrella organization called Women's Rights Collective, connecting the major French women's rights organizations and women's sections in leftist political parties and labor unions. She acknowledges that the public of her former and current organizations is not really diverse but she does not perceive the lack of any initiative to remedy the whiteness of the organization (in both her former and her current organizations) as an effect of institutional racism, but rather as an effect of geographical segregation: her organization is located within Paris and she argues that this prevents recruiting a more diverse constituency. However, questioned about the past and the relationships during the 1980s between her organization and migrant and racialized women, she states:

> Well, to go back to the issue of race, in quotation marks. . . . I still don't like that term. . . . I know less but I don't think we did not do anything. . . . There was a coordination of Black women in the seventies. There was a feminist collective against racism in 1984 in the Maison des femmes in Paris and everybody was there. One should not say we did not do anything.

Hence, she simultaneously argues that the white feminist "we" acted in solidarity with migrant and racialized women in the past, and that the issue of diversity of the membership is not really relevant in the present.[34] Race is defined in her discourse either as an American import that does not fit the French context, or as a side effect of an "external" event—that is, immigration. It is rarely articulated with colonialism and never acknowledged as a structuring feature of *French* history, or a pervasive ground for exclusion from full citizenship.[35] This logic illustrates in a striking way what Paola Bacchetta has defined as *internal discourses of colonial feminisms*. These discourses universalize "feminist analyses and categories" and display "amnesia about racism and colonialism."[36] The invisibilization of Muslim women through "universalist" feminist claims from the feminist membership enacts a closure of the feminist collective subject around whiteness, which is perceived as legitimate because it is equated with universalism.[37]

Interestingly, this universalist discourse on gender oppression shares many commonalities with the gender universalist ideology upheld by white American feminists in the early 1970s and analyzed by Benita Roth. Roth argues that white American feminists developed this discourse in part as a response to the claims of the New Left that feminists' interests were divisive and narrower than those of the working class or other liberationist movement. She states: "Gender universalism was constructed, then, because it was a strategic answer to concerns that white feminists had about the potentially problematic nature of their new political concerns."[38] I have also described elsewhere how the policing of political boundaries with radical-left organizations in the seventies led some quarters of the French second-wave feminist movement to promote the theoretical and political primacy of gender over other differences.[39] It is therefore remarkable to see how gender universalism is produced and reproduced, in changing historical contexts, and how the relationship of feminist claims to other claims of social justice is an important part of that process. However, this strategic dimension is only one part of the story. Only because white feminists were white and could represent and imagine themselves as unmarked by race could they actually mobilize such a universalist repertoire to counter radical-left antagonist discourses with so much ease and political legitimacy. Hence, white ignorance is also at the heart of these universalist discourses.

A second universalist repertoire that contributes to produce and maintain the social and political distance with racialized women, and to anchor the position of white women as the preferred subject of feminist claims and mobilization, is the delegitimization of racialized women's organizing based on ethnic identity. Here again, universalism is the favored identity of the feminist collective subject. The idea that organizing along ethnic lines goes against the grain of proper feminist politics fuels a move that operates a closure of the feminist subject around whiteness. Julie, a young Jewish woman who is not of immigrant descent and is employed to manage the public relations of the French organization Girls on the Rise, which identifies as representing marginalized women and girls, in particular those from the "projects" (i.e., daughters of immigrants),[40] makes universalism clear in her response:

> This logic [to organize on an ethnic or national origin basis] is not ours. And I think it's not the right way to do it. Today we are the voice of all the women who believe in the feminist conception of equality under the Republic, that's our conception, and who needs help at one point or another, whatever their origin, their color, their sexual orientation. . . . As far as I am concerned [organizing along ethnic identities] does not bother me, but me I like social diversity. . . . I find it enriching and it's a shame to lose that. Now if it happens that there is, first, a community organization because of language, because of community ties, because of a common experience . . . which helps free the discourse [*libérer la parole*]. Then of course it's necessary. But if it's a discourse that says that nobody other than a Congolese woman is better placed to talk to another Congolese woman . . . it bothers me. Here we never assigned people based on their origins.

Julie insisted during her interview that the philosophy of her organization is in fact to bring universal women's rights to *all* women, including Muslim girls and women depicted as particularly vulnerable to patriarchal oppression because of their economic and social marginality, and because of the specificity of religion as a vehicle of women's oppression.

The previous excerpts reveal several processes through which feminist whiteness is produced. The social distance between white women and racialized women is accepted and lamented, but not challenged. Quite the contrary: the focus on "universal" issues that put gender as the main relation of oppression to be fought, and the mild dismissal of racialized women organizing on an ethnic or community basis converge to position white feminists as the proper and preferred subject of feminism. The color-blindness that characterizes these discourses echoes the French legal, social, and political model of color-blindness and the disapproval of ethnic-based organizations reproduces the very tenets of the French immigrant integration model, following which integration is not mediated by ethnic and cultural communities and arguing that instances of recognition of such communities may lead to the demise of the unity of the French republic.[41] In fact, their conception of racism and antiracism is strongly influenced by French republican universalism.[42] These discourses are striking because they display a total lack of race cognizance, that is, an awareness and recognition of race as structuring major inequalities, and of whiteness as providing privileges and a power position within the racial order. Or more precisely, while they denounce racism as a social problem, and while they identify as antiracist, these white feminists never indicate that racism might shape the relationships between white feminists and feminists of color and may place them in a position of power. Doing so, they help sustain a privileged and preferred subject of feminism that is white.

Another way in which race is downplayed is by arguing that class inequalities are more important that inequalities related to race. This repertoire finds its roots in part of the second-wave feminist movement—the class struggle trend—which has had enduring effects on some women's rights organizations. Claudine, who heads the Women's Rights Collective, was politicized in her teens and youth through her participation in leftist revolutionary groups. They sent her to infiltrate feminist organizations in the seventies, and she ended up "staying there" and breaking up with her political group.[43] However, she kept her strong commitment to class issues and anticapitalist struggle. While class is therefore an important structure of power that Claudine's organization always considers when framing its claims and preparing its demonstrations—she proudly notes that female workers were present in the last demonstration she organized, proof that the movement was truly representative of economically disadvantaged women—it is difficult for her to imagine taking into account other structures of inequality.

This omission comforts the invisibility of her whiteness and the privileges attached to it. She develops her thoughts as she concludes:

> Well, okay, but I don't give up on inequalities. That's it.... There needs to be a transmission of what the class struggle trend did—intersectional. I think we are intersectional, but truly, truly, not a veiled woman, a transsexual woman and a sex worker!

Here there is no omission of race but rather a clear priority of "real" struggles to be fought, and others to be marginalized because they are deemed specific and unimportant. In a similar vein, Anick, the founder of a network of support for immigrant and refugee women who was a leftist lesbian white feminist in the 1970s, in the revolutionary group Proletarian Left, decries the fact that for some, race trumps class, and condemns the idea that race may structure political priorities:

> Me, personally, I am against the fact that the social question has been transformed into an ethnic, or even racial, question. And when it comes to the legacy of the colonial system, of course it exists, as much in the former colonies as in the former metropolitan states, but I don't think it is the central glass through which to see history, be it of the former colonies or the former metropolitan states.... It is an oversimplification that leads to the racialization of society, and that's very dangerous.

For white French feminists who came of age in the leftist nebulae of the 1970s and were politicized in revolutionary organizations, the legacy of this political subjectivation has left a profound mark on their vision of feminism. Anick, who volunteers on a daily basis to support undocumented migrant women and was part of support groups for immigrants within the Left as early as the 1970s, knows that racism is pervasive and that it is tightly articulated with economic deprivation. However, she firmly rejects the idea that race could provide a positive basis for identification and politicization. For her, as for Claudine, the politicization of race runs the risk of fragmenting further an already fragmented feminist movement. Anick's refusal of a hierarchy of struggles in fact implicitly maintains the primacy of gender over other struggles, and the position of invisible privilege of the white feminist subject is therefore secured.

A second prevalent repertoire that evades and works around race, meaning that it bypasses the questions of the racialization of religion, the legacy of

French colonialism and institutional racism, is a repertoire that, in the name of international solidarity, locates race outside the national borders. Asked about their positions on the 2004 law banning the veil in public schools, many white feminists mentioned that they had followed the advice of Algerian or Iranian friends and that in fact, by supporting the ban, they had expressed solidarity with Muslim women ... abroad. These discourses allow white feminists to situate themselves not in the configuration of racial relations in the French contemporary context, but in racial configurations of international solidarity. For example, Corinne, , a white feminist in her forties who heads Sisters Unite, a network of women's rights community centers, elaborates:

> At the beginning [of the debate] we didn't know. Each time we take a position on a law ... we try to ask: Can we have a feminist look at it? Should we position ourselves? We listened, we listened a lot ... and thanks to the diversity within our ranks, that's our diversity, thanks to these women coming from different countries, different horizons, different social strata ... we exchanged. We exchanged with Iranians, with Algerians, with women from different countries and continents and we could say: if we retreat on this, if we open the door to this ... we opened the door to a religious sign in the secular space, a sign of domination ... at least we consider it as such. Well, if we do this, everybody will regress and we open a Pandora's box.

Corinne's reflections start with a declaration of ignorance—"at the beginning we didn't know"—which is typical of whiteness as a privilege of ignorance of racialized women's lives, a denial of relationality with nonwhite people and an erasure of their presence as subjects.[44] Corinne positions herself as what Mariana Ortega would call a "lovingly ignorant" white feminist, who "cares" about Muslim women but expect to be educated on the topic, to gain proper knowledge.[45] However, interestingly, while the law directly impacted French Muslim girls in public schools, Corinne seeks proper knowledge from other Muslim women, not French but Iranian—who fled an oppressive regime in the 1980s—and Algerian—who fled terrorism in the 1990s. Indeed, these women who were persecuted for their feminist activities embody proper Muslim emancipated subjects who adhere to recognizable feminist values.[46] In response to further questioning about what will happen to the young French Muslim girls eventually expelled from school as a result of the law, she elaborates further:

That's not true in fact [that they will be expelled]. Our Algerian friends were telling us: don't fall into that trap. It's false. It's not true. And people who truly are into wearing a religious sign, whatever it is in fact, it could be the skullcap for Jews, and so on—well, there are private schools, which are not secular schools, which are religious schools. So they will go there. So one should not say precisely that we will exclude girls, that they won't go to school. It's false. It's false. And in fact, no more than twenty girls were expelled in the whole national territory.... In the end, we can tell ourselves that we saved a lot of girls. And what's more, we sent a strong message to our friends who were arriving here in 1994 [from Algeria], saying: if I don't wear the veil well, my life is in danger.... So we had our friends in front of us telling us no, if you do this ... it's impossible. We will regress everywhere because France, well, we know that France for the rest of the world is the country of human rights.

This long quotation interweaves several narratives that intimately shape French feminist whiteness. Religion is understood as inherently oppressive to women; feminists must "save" the Muslim girls who do not want to wear the headscarf, but are much less concerned with those that wish to do so and will admittedly be excluded from public education and confined to a religious school. The paradox of sending Muslim girls portrayed as oppressed by religion deeper into the arms of their supposed oppressor is not remarked upon by Corinne—nor by many of her white feminist counterparts who opposed the 2004 ban. Corinne identifies with French universalism—as the country of human rights—as an exemplary stance that not only shows solidarity with Muslim women who are victims of state violence in Muslim countries but also pursues the saving of women all over the world. Interestingly, the interviewee's constant denials ("it's false. It's not true") suggest a tension in her narrative, which is resolved thanks to a focus on international solidarity. Such a focus bypasses race as a local/national issue and constructs a diverse collective feminist subject across borders, rather than at home. In a move typical of feminist whiteness and described also by Françoise Vergès about the French second wave, women victims of institutional racism are not seen *here, at home*. White feminists proclaim solidarity with racialized women in other countries, in a place that is always far away from home, while they stay blind to and ignorant of racism at home.[47] Expulsing race from the borders of the nation[48] bolsters their attempt at denying the racist component of the policy they support. Also noteworthy in this quotation, and intimately articulated with whiteness, is the denial of relationality that is expressed by the interviewee with regards to young Muslim girls. The interviewee's moral horizon is suddenly drastically curbed when it comes to relating and empathizing with Muslim schoolgirls. This closure of the moral impulse contributes to producing Muslim schoolgirls as radical others—a point whose ethical consequences I explore further in chapter 6.[49]

In France, white feminists thus work around race in different ways that always deny race its political dimension by universalizing gender oppression, by privileging class over race, or by locating race outside the national borders. Importantly, while the repertoire that insists on class as more important than race may have a generational component[50]—it characterizes white feminists socialized politically in the 1970s—the other repertoires I identified are shared across generations of activists. These various discursive strategies constitute *active resistance to intersectionality*. They contribute to producing and maintaining a white feminist subject whose privileges remain untold and invisible, and who is positioned as the preferred subject of feminism. These discourses that work around race—acknowledging it as a social phenomenon and a basis of inequalities but evading it as a legitimate ground for politicized identities—produce a feminist whiteness that is specific to the French context and shaped by it. As Ruth Frankenberg argued, discourses on race are part of wider historical and cultural repertoires. The discourses of white feminists I interviewed appear singularly compatible with the republican universalism that has been promoted by French institutions since the 1990s through a staunch politics of color-blindness, a rejection of a multicultural approach to immigrant integration,[51] and the championing of republican *laïcité*. They also exemplify the rhetorical device by which race is made irrelevant, as it is associated with an "outside" of the nation. It is presented by some as an American import, or sometimes associated with a past era—that of colonization—but never quite accepted as a present political issue, relevant for feminist action.

Race Cognizance and Multiculturalism: Feminist Whiteness in Quebec

The picture of the Quebecois women's movement, and the discursive modalities through which feminist whiteness is produced, stands in stark contrast with the French case. While Quebecois feminism also witnessed a second wave, which coincided with the Quiet Revolution and the rise of nationalism in Quebec, the weakness of the revolutionary Left in Quebec and the strength of Quebecois nationalism—associated with a social-democrat vision of the Quebecois welfare state—shaped the feminist Quebecois movement. Quebecois feminism is organized around grassroots community centers and shelters, with one umbrella organization, the FFQ, which adhered openly to the nationalist and socially liberal project in the 1990s. Quebecois feminist organizations are, for the vast majority, service oriented; they cater to populations of vulnerable women and, since the 1980s, they have been important actors in immigrant integration policy, providing French classes and designing their services for immigrant populations. They carry out social service missions (migrant integration, mental health referrals, helping women finding work or housing, etc.), work closely with the social services, and, for the most part, receive funding from social service and/or immigration ministries. Many organizations were founded on an ethnic or nationality basis, starting with women immigrants from Italy in the 1970s, then women from North Africa, Latin America, India, and the Philippines in the early 1990s. Grassroots organizations that were not founded by immigrant women define themselves as multicultural in their identity or in their mission statement.[52]

While French feminists' discourses seem to work around and sometimes evade race as power, locating power "outside" the reality of their feminist practice, in Quebec, white feminists display forms of race cognizance. Two main repertoires characterize Quebecois feminist whiteness. The first one interprets race relations within the policy framework of interculturalism. Following the Canadian multiculturalist policy, the Quebecois government has elaborated an intercultural approach to immigrant integration.[53] This repertoire celebrates cultural differences, but reenacts a dichotomy between racialized immigrant women who must learn to integrate, and white Quebecois feminists who provide services and are the holders of Quebecois values. A second repertoire is that of intersectionality. More and more widespread in Quebecois organizations, the term refers to tools or approaches that must be adopted to ensure inclusion. While interculturalism tends to depoliticize race relations, it does legitimize self-organizing by migrant women and their presence, as active members and not just as clients, in feminist grassroots organizations. Intersectionality more clearly acknowledges race as a power relation, but also raises much more criticism and resistance.

Working with a very diverse public, Quebecois feminist organizations have in recent decades developed an intercultural approach and redefined themselves as multicultural. This move toward interculturalism is perceived as the "logical" consequence of the new demography of Montreal and Quebec. Acting as delegates for social services, feminist organizations have been taking part in the Quebecois welfare-state policy of interculturalism since the 1980s. Sandrine, who heads a network on domestic violence in the Montreal region, asserts:

> In Montreal, of course, we are situated in a multicultural milieu . . . so one of our first priorities was the issue of identifying and adapting intervention to the reality of ethnocultural communities. It is a challenge for all our partners in the network, the shelters, the police, the social services, the justice system.

Interculturalism is presented as a tool, an approach, something one needs to be trained about, and an argument to diversify the workforce in women's rights organizations. This discourse operates a twofold move. It positions white Quebecois women as knowledgeable about other cultures and as possessing the ability to communicate with women from other cultures, and, at the same time it also legitimizes the inclusion of racialized and migrant women within women's rights organizations, hence fostering an actual multicultural setting for feminist practice. Ethnic and racial diversity within Quebecois women's organizations' staff does not mean that racism is acknowledged or has disappeared.[54] It indicates that cultural diversity is recognized as socially important, and the object of a specific expertise to be developed by feminist volunteers.

The dominant approach to interculturalism is a professional—rather than political—one. It is a tool, a skill white women develop to enable them to more easily "understand" migrant women, and therefore to perform in a more professional and efficient way their intervention as social workers. As Marion, a young white Quebecois officer in a multicultural women's center, states in her interview, "We always need more training" on the subject of interculturalism. This approach is consistent with the concrete work performed by most women's community centers and shelters as service providers involved in the broader Quebecois politics of immigrant integration. This approach may thus position white women as knowledgeable, legitimate representatives of the Quebecois culture who can educate migrant women in order to smooth their process of integration in Quebec. Diane, a white employee in a multicultural women's community center founded by migrant women in the 1980s in an eastern neighborhood of Montreal, details what an awareness of cultural difference means in her daily work:

> Well, the main approach we have here, I would say, is to see with the woman what she wants, how she wants, what she is thinking. So from there, the intercultural approach is important.... We are going to start by looking... "Tell me, you, what do you want? Why do you think in this way? How was it back home? Well, see, here it works a little bit differently."... So from there, our work is to make them talk, make connections, Then, at some point, to give them references.... So cultural differences are taken into account. Does it sometimes come with frictions? Yes, we're not perfect. Sometimes we say something and we think: ohhhhh, I just made a mistake. But it's part of the work. We make a lot of efforts so that women do not see us like ... "we're the ones who know, and you, you don't know."

Interculturalism's ambivalence appears in the tension between the position of a knower that "gives references" and the ideal of the feminist social worker who does not position herself as above her migrant client. While this move toward a form of equality in the service relationship is consistent with the feminist practice of letting women make their own choices on their own terms, it also tends to erase the power asymmetry that is linked to whiteness in the interaction since the only asymmetry that is acknowledged, in order to be undone, is that of the service relation. In this vein of feminist professionalism, interculturalism appears as a tool that can prevent cultural miscommunication. Racial difference is circumscribed by cultural differences, which may lead to errors, but which will be corrected thanks to experience and training with the proper expert tools.

The cultural diversity highlighted by the interviewees is not limited to their clientele. Importantly, interculturalism legitimates the hiring of migrant women within women's centers. In 2010, a network of women's rights organizations fighting against violence against women decided to research how and if immigrant women who did not speak French or English could have access to their services. In the report, the network underlined that health services, social services, and women's centers should hire women with a migrant background in order to offer services in the language of the clientele. What is more, the interculturalist repertoire also legitimizes the fact that nonwhite women may organize on the basis of similar migrant or ethnic identity. While in France the idea of separate organizations for nonwhite women raised suspicion, in Quebec it was seldom called into question. The Quebecois multicultural policy of migrant integration based on "cultural communities" self-organizing is widely accepted as relevant for feminist intervention in the social domain as well.

Interculturalism acknowledges racial difference, but mainly as cultural difference. The fact that Quebec is historically a white settler colony is not mentioned in these discourses, and while racism is acknowledged as a social reality, feminist intervention is focused on bridging cultural difference and equipping migrant women with the right set of skills to navigate their integration into Quebecois society. Of course, the prevalence of this repertoire is explained both by the official Quebecois politics of migrant integration and by the important part that many women's community centers play in it (to the point where an important part of their funding depends on these activities), and by the concrete social work that feminists who work in community centers and shelters perform daily. Interculturalism is first and foremost part of their identity as good social workers and, as a consequence, as good feminists as well.

Intersectionality is a second repertoire used by Quebecois women's rights organizations. The term "intersectionality" was officially adopted in 2015 by the umbrella organization comprising the majority of Quebecois women's rights centers and organizations, the FFQ, as well as by the network of over twenty feminist centers and shelters, founded in the 1970s–1980s, which fights violence against women throughout Quebec. It has also been unevenly adopted by the women's community centers that form a feminist network of over ninety centers in Quebec. Thus, at the time of fieldwork, the term "intersectionality" was familiar to most white interviewees in Quebec (which was not the case in France). Intersectionality is conceived as a tool for proper feminist work in centers and shelters welcoming immigrant and racialized women, but, and this goes a step further than interculturalism, it is also presented as a tool for self-criticism and reflexivity, associated with ideas of discrimination and power between women based on racialization. Eliane, a white Quebecois feminist in her thirties working in a multiethnic women's center, Northern Montreal, who says that the staff in her organization is familiar with the intersectional approach, explains that the process of adopting an intersectional approach has been like "self-criticism, so that we don't get stuck in our little Quebecois affairs." She explains:

> We all did some work with the network of women's groups in Montreal on the hiring of migrant women and on maintaining them in their jobs. Very few women's groups really did the exercise. But we are so happy we did it, because it changed our evaluation tools. When we form a selection committee for a job opening, the vocabulary we will use... sometimes we're not aware of it but it can be colored with some prejudice.... If we use the term "popular education," well, sometimes for the woman it does not ring a bell. Surely she must have done some in her country, but it was just not named that.... So that's it, opening up... looking beyond, opening up.... I think women's centers still have a long road to travel to be representative of the diversity of the population in Montreal—inclusion, working toward inclusion, opening up to diversity. It has started to change, changing recruitment tools, activities... we really need to change.

Several interviewees, especially the youngest ones, noted that inclusion of women from "cultural communities" should be a priority for the movement, and that meant that they, as Quebecois feminists, had to change their practice and mindset. They did not shy away from the idea that power asymmetries structure relations between women based on racialization, or, as they also refer to it, based on cultural diversity. The question of power relations is more closely articulated with race and intersectionality by some activists, such as Lorie, who works at the umbrella organization for Quebecois women's rights organizations. She reflects on the discussions that arose during the 2015 general assembly of her organization on the question of intersectionality. She recalls that a lot of the debates were focused on the term "intersectionality" itself, as a strategy of avoiding discussing what it is actually about—that is, inequalities between women based on racialization (she described how a similar nominalist strategy had already been deployed about the word "racialized" a couple of years before).

> Then we don't discuss the real issue and about the violence that can be experienced by these women. So certainly some [nonwhite] women have left frustrated... because some discourses were felt as violent... like this feeling that "You constantly ask us to wait because you need to be trained.... This kind of relationship—well, there are some issues we want to deal with now. We want to build solidarity and you kind of reject us." This was a little bit like this, so of course we have to work, to question the way we bring discussion about topics that we know will be disputed—because we knew it

would—so how to do it so that these discussions will not in fact be detrimental to the people who are concerned in the first place, and have the courage to come to those spaces that are not always welcoming and safe spaces ... because sometimes we feel that we did not do it intentionally, but we put some activists on the spot, women who pay the price; so it calls into question our practices.

Lorie's reflection suggests both an awareness of asymmetries of power between feminists linked to racialization, and a desire not to be considered responsible for these inequalities. While she rightly analyzes her organization's general assembly meeting as a space that is not safe for nonwhite women, and while she identifies racialized women as "paying the price" for the lack of attention paid to institutional racism, she simultaneously denies responsibility for what happened by stressing that it was not intentional. Hence, this repertoire of feminist whiteness oscillates between an acknowledgment of racism as a structural system of domination, which also pervades feminist organizations themselves, and a conception of racism as an intentional action, the product of an individual's will to discriminate or treat unequally. However, importantly, this repertoire leads Lorie to acknowledge race and racism since she does insist on the need for institutional self-reflexivity in order to avoid similar tensions in the future.

The intersectionality repertoire therefore identifies racialization and racism as important concerns for feminists and between women. The need to "work," to be trained and aware—particularly present among younger feminists—denotes a conception in which white feminists must work on themselves in order not to unintentionally reproduce discriminatory practices. While often feminist whiteness presents itself as the desire to be educated by feminists of color,[55] here white Quebecois feminists insist that they must educate themselves; the responsibility is therefore theirs. It is specifically this idea of learning and self-transformation conveyed by the repertoire of intersectionality in Quebec that has attracted most resistance on the part of white Quebecois feminists. Lorie acknowledges that for some white women in her organization there is a deep-seated political opposition to the use of intersectionality as a tool for feminist intervention and as a political principle guiding feminist action in Quebec. For some members, the problem is that intersectionality puts an end to the primacy of gender over other grounds of inequality in feminist mobilization. For other members, who left the organization when it failed to support Bill 94 and the Quebecois *laïcité* charter, intersectionality denotes the fact that Quebecois feminist organizations have been infiltrated by conservative Islamic women with a hidden political agenda. However, the most prevalent form of resistance to intersectionality[56] is noticeable in the discourse that insists on a type of "learning fatigue" from white feminists, a reluctance to be self-reflexive under the guise of a work overload, and a demand for "more time" to implement intersectionality in their daily practices. Lorie illustrates this resistance in the following terms:

> There are wide discrepancies in the ways intersectionality has been adopted in the various community centers working on violence against women.... There are indeed tensions. Some centers have adopted it easily; for others there is a blockage, it bothers them.... There is a form of political resistance that comes from individuals and from some centers that is part of a feminist tradition, more second-wave type if you want. But what I heard several times is that it shakes up women who say, "I spent twenty years to construct my feminist analyses with facts, knowledge and all that, and now I have the feeling that with the intersectional approach, or with queer theories, I am asked to learn many more things and I cannot, I cannot. It took me twenty years to get there. I don't have twenty more years to invest."

The idea that with intersectionality one needs to learn a new approach reveals that what is at stake is more than knowledge. It is in fact an identity, based on "twenty years" of investment in learning feminist theory, but also, one might suggest, in *being* a feminist, that is shaken up by the adoption of intersectionality in women's centers. A profound desire not to trouble the established boundaries of feminist whiteness and of the acquired feminist subjectivity is therefore expressed through a resistance to "new" tools and theories. Of course, Lorie's account also implicitly opposes her own attitude of positive adoption of intersectionality with the attitude of the preceding generation of Quebecois white feminists, revealing that a generational gap is at play in the adoption/refusal of intersectionality in Quebec.

These two repertoires are of course not exhaustive. Marginally, white Quebecois interviewees developed, like white French interviewees, analyses that stressed the universality of gender oppression. They also sometimes criticized the ethnic "ghettos" that migrant women's organizations may foster, and argued that the role of grassroots feminist community centers is to bring migrant women to adhere to their feminist charter, as it has been defined by the historically white Quebecois feminist movement. In these instances, Quebecois women are depicted as having defined the content of the Quebecois feminist project, with important ties to the Quebecois project of national sovereignty,[57] and it is a project to which migrant women should adhere and which is not transformed by their inclusion in it.[58] Reciprocally, in France some white interviewees working in organizations providing services to women with a diversity of ethnic origins mentioned the need to culturally adapt their practices and reflect on their routines to improve their inclusivity. Some newly founded French organizations have also adopted the vocabulary of intersectionality.[59] Hence, intersectionality also enters French feminist discourses, and the need to articulate the fight against sexism and racism also exists in some white French feminist organizations.

However, the differences between the two contexts remain more significant than the commonalities. Quebecois repertoires of feminist whiteness contrast with the French repertoires I have examined. They reveal a more widespread form of race cognizance among white feminists, even if processes of evading race are also visible. Tellingly, multicultural and grassroots feminist organizations in Quebec all systematically provide training on intercultural dialogue to their members. This practice was, at the time of the interviews, very marginal in France. Many Quebecois grassroots organizations that define themselves as multicultural do indeed have a diverse staff and board, a fact they proudly stress in interviews, along with the many language skills that their staff displays. While white French feminists are reluctant to use the term "race" and to refer to racialized women with this term, prominent Quebecois feminist organizations used the term "racialized women" (*femmes racisées*) in their documentation and their discourse. The term raised debates and opposition when it was introduced but is nevertheless now part of the common feminist vocabulary. Quebecois white feminists' race cognizance is, of course, shaped by the context of Quebecois multiculturalist politics, by the role women's centers play in immigrant integration policy, and, importantly, by the institutional reflexivity that has been developed since the mid-2000s with respect to racism. Indeed, as I retraced in the previous chapter, the FFQ has promoted a committee for racialized and migrant women and a survey of migrant and racialized women's positions within its members' organizations. These steps have been crucial in politicizing the question of racial inequalities and marginalization within the (white) Quebecois movement, initiating a decentering of the white privileged subject and of gender oppression as the unique ground for feminist action—a decentering that has elicited debates, tensions, and conflicts within the main Quebecois feminist organizations but that has been ultimately accepted.

Feminist Whiteness: Moral Dispositions and Emotions

The various repertoires I have described must be understood as discourses that produce feminist whiteness—that is, a process of political subjectivation as white feminist—in each context. These discursive repertoires are not only words. They are in fact articulated with moral dispositions and layered with emotions. As Ruth Frankenberg and Gloria Wekker notice in their respective studies, whiteness is secured by a set of emotions, such as fear, anger, or indifference. Similarly, feminist whiteness is not only a set of discourses: it also comes to exist through moral feminist dispositions and specific emotions. These emotions and moral dispositions are relational: they define simultaneously the good feminist subject—and the bad ones. For example, anger toward or moral disapproval of Afro-feminists effectively polices the boundaries of the "good" feminist subject, excludes some women from the feminist project, and secures the privileges attached to feminist whiteness.

I identify two types of moral dispositions associated with feminist whiteness. In the first one, the relationship between white feminists and nonwhite women is one of benevolent help and respect, but also ambivalence toward nonwhite women's autonomy. Contrastingly, the second type of moral disposition is marked by a severe criticism and harsh moral judgment from white feminists of the ability of, especially, nonwhite veiled women to embody the feminist subject and to be autonomous. While the repertoires of feminist whiteness differ between France and Quebec, the types of moral disposition displayed by white feminists do not differ depending on the historical and social context—Quebec or France—but rather depend on the status that is conferred to nonwhite women, and especially to veiled women; that is, either that of being an *object* of benevolent feminist attention, or that of being a possible *feminist* subject.

This distinction between women as an object of feminist attention and as a potential feminist subject draws on Linda Zerilli's contrast between feminism understood as a social question and feminism understood as a political question. Indeed, Zerilli follows Hannah Arendt's idea that the political is too often assimilated to the social, that questions of freedom are too often transformed into social questions that should be solved by politico-bureaucratic means, transforming citizens into passive recipients of state care and political life into an "instrumental, means-ends activity."[60] Applied to feminism, this tendency means that the movement's goal is reduced to "the social advancement of the group in whose name members ... claim to speak."[61] It has meant, in the history of feminism, that more often than not feminists have articulated their claims for freedom and participation in politics in the language of social utility.[62] Zerilli underlines that "the displacement of the political by the social is intrinsic to the history of democratic politics" and a strategy used by many disenfranchised groups.[63] Zerilli see this displacement as crippling feminist arguments for freedom and crippling democratic politics in general. She opposes to this feminism confined to the social question a conception of feminism as a political relationship, a form of "political freedom in the sense of world-building . . . [that] must involve, from the start, relations with a plurality of other people in a public space created by action."[64] This conception of feminism as a form of political freedom is deeply indebted to Hannah Arendt's reflections on freedom in democratic politics.[65] Applied to feminism, it draws attention not so much to the collective subject of feminism as predetermined by a shared sociological identity, "women," but, on the contrary, to the collective subject as a political construction, the product of a world-building activity by which feminists enter into relation; but not any type of relation, for these relations must be, Zerilli insists, free relations.

I take up Zerilli's distinction between feminism as a social question and feminism as a political practice of freedom because it captures the fact that both the individual and the collective subjects of feminism can be conceived in opposite ways. When feminism becomes a social question, all women can presumably be enrolled, as beneficiaries, in the project of the social advancement of this category (whether the category is conceived in sociological, biological, or political terms in fact does not matter). Feminism then does not need to reflect on relationships *between* women. Rather, it is preoccupied with women as an object of care and political attention. Contrastingly, Zerilli's insistence that feminism should be understood as a political practice opens up another conception of feminism. Zerilli promotes an understanding of feminism as a practice of freedom, which means that, for her, feminism's political project is about creating free relations *between* women. While I do not want here to elaborate on how Zerilli, following Arendt, defines free relations and their relationship to democratic politics—which is her main concern—I do want to retain the idea that in this political conception of the feminist subject what is at stake is not "women" as a social category to be advanced, but rather the *creation* of a collective subject: the *feminists*.

Hence, feminists themselves, rather than women, are the subject of this political claim, which implies the reciprocal recognition of *other women* as part of the collective feminist subject. These two conceptions of feminism are not mutually exclusive. Feminists may alternatively refer to one or the other depending on the type of political claim they want to make in the public space, the outcome they are looking for, the practical action they are engaged in, and, importantly, whom they are taking and recognizing as legitimate interlocutors. Indeed, as I will show, what matters is *who* is considered a legitimate interlocutor in defining what is feminism and who can embody this political project. I argue that these two different conceptions of feminism elicit two types of moral dispositions that white feminists in France and Quebec display vis-à-vis racialized women. Hence, feminist whiteness is articulated in different ways when the political subjectivation as white feminist occurs through an interaction with racialized women who are the *object* of a feminist intervention, and when they are considered as possible feminist *subjects* and interlocutors.

Racialized Women as Object of Benevolent and Ambivalent Feminist Care

In many interviews, racialized/migrant/veiled women are conceived as the object of benevolent feminist care and attention. When talking about their feminist practice, white feminists insist that migrant women's choices must be respected and that migrant women themselves can make the choices that correspond to their needs. This moral disposition is particularly displayed by white feminists working in organizations that deliver services to women (such as shelters and community centers). Indeed, it corresponds to a feminist intervention credo, shared across the Atlantic, that women are best positioned to know what they need, and that they should define on their own terms what they want. In other words, while feminist officers and workers in shelters and community centers might have their own vision of what is freedom and emancipation, they should not impose their definition on women who come to receive support. Feminist intervention means giving the woman who comes for help the tools to make her decision. More precisely, as Martine, a French officer at Women's Health put it, "We don't give her the tools, she finds them." In fact, in the context of service provision, feminist ideals are pragmatically revised and adapted to correspond to women's needs because it is not expected that these women will become feminist subjects. What is sought is not their emancipation in the feminist terms held by white feminist activists and volunteers, but a "balance" that works for them. Sandrine, a white feminist officer who heads a network against domestic violence in Montreal, explains:

> Feminist intervention is not always the best for all the women from migrant communities. That is, yes, gender equality—it's perfect, it's fine, it's great, and it is what we must continue to claim. But, on the other hand, divorce or separation, for some women, are not the solutions that should be promoted, and if I must choose between proposing this solution and the woman never comes back in our center to get help, and another solution, which is to adapt the intervention to ensure that, step by step, this woman, she receives, she hears the message, and, finally . . . she puts herself in a safer situation, she puts her kids in a safer place, not necessarily by leaving her husband but by taking more space and keeping herself safe . . . everybody wins.

While here this attitude is presented as an adaption of a feminist practice to the reality of what is framed as cultural difference, this moral disposition expresses a feminist tenet that does not apply only to nonwhite women. Claudine, who used to be an officer in a French organization for rape victims, remembers that while pressing charges was her favored solution, she never encouraged victims to do so because she "always refused to dictate" solutions to women and because of the variety of reactions among victims.

Hence, both in Quebec and in France the vast majority of feminists who work in service-oriented organizations will insist that women should be welcomed, listened to, and respected on their own terms. This translates, for example, into a pragmatic (and sometimes principled) inclusion of women wearing religious symbols in all Quebecois women's centers and shelters that I interviewed. While many women's rights community centers have shied away from taking a public stance in the political debates around laws banning the Islamic veil in Quebec, for fear that it would divide their membership and staff, they have adopted a policy of tolerance in their day-to-day practice. Eliane, a young officer in the women's community center Northern Montreal, reflects on the questions of Islamic veiling for her organization in these terms:

We think about it, we reflect, we revise.... We discussed about: Are we open to all women? A veiled woman who enters here, what do we do? A volunteer here at the front desk who wears the veil ... what do we do? All these situations can spur conflicts. Those are topics that, this year, we thought we should not keep that in the team. We must discuss with women who come here. In fact, veiled women—it's absolutely fine, in the sense that a woman who wears the veil is totally welcome here.

For many Quebecois women's center the central issue of inclusivity—that is, the idea that "all" women should be welcome—has overcome uneasiness or anxiety about religious difference and in particular Islamic veiling practices. Hence, what is displayed and valorized is a benevolent care that does not discriminate among women and is faithful to the feminist commitment of helping "women." Yet, importantly, these women are mostly perceived as passive feminist subjects: they are included in the feminist project as recipients of help and empathy, which brings to the white feminist subject who provides help an enhanced form of morality and respectability.[66]

The situation is slightly different in France, where the veil sometimes raises "discomfort," "tension," and ambivalence among white feminist volunteers and employees. While most white interviewees declared that they would never turn away a woman in need of help because she wears an Islamic veil, this attitude was not based on the idea of inclusivity of their organization but rather on a principle of helping women in need. Martine describes what tends to happen when young veiled Muslim women ask for false certificates of virginity in order to satisfy their family's demands before their marital engagement:

For some counselors, these cases are really difficult ones. There is always this tension, and it's even tenser for certificates of virginity. There's a tension because it's difficult to perceive them as alienated.... It's not right either. Some counselors are okay with it; it depends on their individual history if they can help, if they can discuss with the girls, to try to understand why they wear the veil, why they don't, what it means for them. When a girl comes to the center veiled, it's true, it's a real question for us. It questions feminism. This fact that a woman can accept this ideological domination... it questions us.

The moral disposition of benevolent care is here rife with tension and ambivalence. Interestingly, the internal moral debate brought forth by the encounter with religious Muslim women is expressed as relating to her feminist identity and ideals. The question becomes how "our" feminism can make sense of the agency of Muslim women, bringing an intrusive inquiry into the motivations and the moral disposition of Muslim women. This narrative, and the us/them binary that structures it, denotes, once again, that feminist whiteness positions itself as the privileged feminist subject. While the same interviewee presented the need to let women make their own choices as the basis of feminist intervention, when it comes to Muslim women this principle is in fact amended with a higher scrutiny for "proper" motives and moral dispositions. Yet this quotation also suggests a possible decentering of feminist whiteness, which is left unsaid and unresolved, but rather hovering over the interviewee's consciousness: "It questions us."

Hence, when feminist practice is about "helping" "all" women, nonwhite women are easily conceived as passive recipients of help. Feminist whiteness is characterized here by benevolence and ambivalence toward these passive subjects, who are, on the one hand, proper feminist objects of intervention and, on the other hand, at odds with some of the feminist ideals that they hold dear. These moral dispositions are also perceptible in the emotional vocabulary conveyed when discussing these issues, which denotes both contentment with the proper and professional way of practicing feminism, and anxiety over the challenge that Muslim women's agency brings to a feminist intervention that wants to perceive them as alienated.

However, not all women's centers approach nonwhite women as passive recipients. In some centers, in particular those who have signed a common Quebecois feminist charter, the aim of feminist intervention is also to enroll women in the feminist project, understood as a project for the Quebecois society as well.[67] A white officer in such a women's center explains:

> We are feminists. But of course the majority of women who come here, they don't care if we are feminist or not. They really come for a service, an activity. And we don't start to discuss feminism from the moment they adhere to the center. We wait for a woman to come here, to gain her trust, to let her develop a network and feelings of belonging . . . and a few months later, we start discussing topics like women's rights, violence against women . . . so that slowly she becomes conscious of her own condition. . . . All these

topics, we discuss them, but only after we gain women's trust. This is the compromise that we make to keep all these women at the center.

Here a tension is perceptible between the benevolent care for a passive recipient and the active engagement with a woman in order to enroll her in the feminist project, to *make* her a feminist subject. This political subjectivation of migrant women is realized through "feelings of belonging," that is, the enrollment in a collective subject, the closing of the initial social distance. However, even if the feminist intervention is designed to politicize migrant women, rather than include them as passive subjects, their more active inclusion in the Quebecois feminist project does not imply that white feminists should change their own feminist values. Quite the contrary, it is about enrolling nonwhite women in a predefined collective subject. Here benevolence meets a patronizing impulse that mirrors the asymmetry along racial and class lines that characterizes the white volunteer / nonwhite recipient relationship. This is also the case, in a more blatant way, in some French shelters that, like some Quebecois organizations, adhere to a feminist approach that implies not only helping women on their own terms but also providing them with a "feminist analytical framework on gender inequalities" to show them that violence against women is not an individual problem but a collective issue, as Chantal, a white feminist in her late forties who runs a shelter in a Parisian suburb, puts it.

CHANTAL: I was discussing with a young woman who arrived veiled for the admission interview in our living center, but I asked her to take off her veil because here . . . here there is no [veiling]. . . . She explained to me that she chose to wear the veil. She was twelve at the time she chose to wear it. It's a little bit young to make a choice. But it's true it's a woman who has gone to undergrad, she claims her right to wear the veil, she says it's not compulsory to wear it. So . . . she follows her own path. Maybe with discussions that we will have on women's rights she may evolve or not on this issue of wearing her veil.
QUESTION: And she accepted your proposal not to wear the veil while she was at the center?
CHANTAL: Oh yes, of course.
QUESTION: Why did you ask that from her?
CHANTAL: Because, indeed, I think as far as I am concerned it is a sign of women's oppression.

While Chantal insisted that not wearing the veil was not a precondition for being received for an admission interview at the shelter, it appears as a precondition for staying and benefiting from the protection of the shelter and the services it provides. Interestingly, though she does not deny the agency of her interlocutor, Chantal places herself in the position to actually decide what is a proper age for consent and, what is more, what is the meaning of the Islamic veil. In a move typical of whiteness, she creates a social distance with her interlocutor that is only mitigated by a possible class proximity related to academic achievement.[68] She also omits to reflect on the power relation at play during the interview and on the power she exercises over the woman she interviews, although her position of authority surreptitiously shows in her flat avowal of the result of her demand: "of course" the woman took off her veil—what other choice did she have in her situation? Here benevolent care and respect for a woman's choice have been replaced by moral judgment, righteousness, and a unilateral definition of what type of practices feminist emancipation should entail. This difference in moral dispositions is clearly linked to the fact that in this shelter, women who come for help are conceived as subjects of care but also as subjects enrolled in a political project, that of making women into feminists. As the "Muslim veiled woman" changes status in the relationship with the white feminist, from benevolent object of care to potential feminist subject—and therefore imaginably equal in the relationship—she must be made white by removing her veil. In this transaction, and to use Sara Ahmed's terms, feminism *is made white*. Other moral dispositions that lead feminist whiteness to more extreme emotions, such as anger, as well as to forms of melancholy, contribute to this process, and I now turn to explore them.

Racialized Women as Would-Be Feminist Equal: White Feminists' Anger and Melancholy

When racialized, migrant or Muslim women are conceived as possible feminist subjects—that is, when their relationship with white feminists might be defined by reciprocal recognition and equality, rather than by benevolence and asymmetry—moral dispositions and emotions shift. I have described how in Quebec the topic of intersectionality and the inclusion of racialized women into the Quebecois feminist project raised some objections, on the ground that white feminists already had their own feminist analysis and did not want to be challenged and their whiteness to be decentered. However, as I related in chapter 3, these objections have not stalled the efforts of many Quebecois organizations to include politically racialized women. Some isolated white Quebecois feminists have vocally opposed this process and have sometimes left their feminist organization because of this political divergence.[69] However, interviewees working in Montreal's women's rights organizations never adopted this type of position in interviews. The situation was strikingly different in France, where several interviewees displayed harsh moral judgments about veiled Muslim women and lamented the loss of a true feminist subject.[70] Their moral dispositions and their emotions efficiently drew the boundary between a good feminist subject and a bad one.

When feminism is understood as a social question, all women might be enrolled in the feminist project as passive beneficiaries. However, when feminism is understood, and lived, as a political practice defining political relations between women, feminist whiteness takes on a new face. Indeed, when Muslim or racialized women are perceived as possible feminist peers (and all the more so when they make this claim politically), some white feminists may use moral judgment, indignation, and disapproval alongside anger and melancholy to police the boundaries of what they perceive to be the good, and the right, feminist subject. Asked about her analysis of the mobilization of racialized women in an alternate International Women's Day march in Paris, the "March 8 for all," Claudine declares:

> When I think about the "March 8 for all" I think that these groups of migrant girls—I don't like the term "racialized" at all—I think that these groups of migrant girls who go there are completely wrong. It's true it comes from a divergence on the veil issue, certainly, but I don't think that these people will help them—well, if they need help—because I find this is really a kind of "maternalist"[71] attitude.... They don't even know we exist! ... They hold a lot of wrong ideas about us.

Moral judgments about the right type of feminism and the right type of feminist subjectivity surface and draw boundaries between "us" and "them" in an effective way. On the one hand, Claudine places her conception of feminism, and herself, as a reference point (which should not be ignored or misinterpreted by racialized women, as she thinks it is)—a moral and political standard to be adopted if one wishes to be called and recognized as a feminist. On the other hand, she rejects any responsibility for the deep rift that has emerged between her organization, which is supposed to be inclusive and representative of the French women's rights movement, and racialized women demonstrating on their own terms and in opposition to the official International Women's Day march. A comrade of Claudine's, Nelly, a white woman in her seventies who was also a former member of the class struggle trend during the second wave, talks about a prominent white French feminist who denounced the 2004 law in these terms:

NELLY: She allied with the "Indigenous"![72] They are our enemies! . . . And the veil, is it not a symbol of women's oppression? To pretend that there are *islamiste*[73] women who are feminists, it's a fundamental contradiction for us.
QUESTION: Everybody agrees in your organization on this?
NELLY: Yes, yes.
QUESTION: Did it lead to scissions with some feminist groups?
NELLY: Well . . . there is the "March 8 for all." I don't know, well, they are pro-veil and pro-prostitution. . . . That's new. We never had this type of confusion before.
QUESTION: Did you talk with the organizing committee of this alternate march?
NELLY: No, no . . . it's like with fascists, you don't talk with them, it's useless.

Anger as well as political and moral indignation saturates this interview sequence.[74] The Islamic feminist subject is defined, a priori, as an impossible—and a wrong—one, and dialogue, discussion, or any kind of relationship with this feminist subject is presented as impossible and pointless. What is more, the claims made by racialized women as *feminists*—since the "March 8 for all" is a self-defined feminist march—are presented as bringing confusion, troubling the boundaries and the identity of the proper feminist collective subject. A trace of melancholy is also perceptible, and in fact melancholy permeated Nelly's interview. She longed for the unity of the feminist movement that characterized, in her memories, the early 1980s and the creation of the Maison des femmes in Paris. Hence, racialized women's claim to constitute their own collective feminist subject is perceived as troubling both the interviewee and to feminism.

In a similar vein, the following two quotations from interviews illustrate the ways in which white feminists whose political subjectivation was marked by the revolutionary Left in the seventies police the boundaries of the proper white feminist subject and reject any claim from racialized women to be real feminist subjects, accusing them of false consciousness or attributing to them wrong modes of political subjectivation. Anick comments on the short-lived group that self-defined as "indigenous feminist," one of the first feminist collectives in the mid-2000s to articulate a postcolonial feminist position in the French public sphere:

ANICK: Well, they don't bother me. They can continue with their ravings. I'm not gonna forbid them. Their message, it's not . . . it's a nationalist and racialist vision of the world . . . like other women who decide to assemble on some basis, be it . . . religious or geographical, etc. It's not a problem, but it's not a message. It's not new.
QUESTION: They had a critique of the feminist movement that did not include . . .
ANICK: First it's not true, and second it's never justified, it's never proven.

This attitude of moral reprobation and feigned indifference of course contrasts with the benevolent care that characterized relationships with racialized women in the context of service provision by feminist organizations. The harsh delegitimation and disqualification of the indigenous feminist message and its strong critique of white feminism denotes the adoption by Anick of a moral standpoint of authority and self-righteousness. Here again, discussion with self-identified nonwhite feminists is presented as pointless in the name of irreconcilable positions on what *is* (proper) feminism. Presenting the dispute as one between right and wrong political conceptions of feminism obscures and evades discussion about racism and whiteness within the movement. Asked about her thoughts on a newly created group of Afro-feminists in Paris, Claudine seems at pains to understand why a Black French feminist would create her own organization and participate in the "March 8 for all." Feeling that her organization has been accused of not doing anything to include racialized women, she explains:

CLAUDINE: But Annie and Leila, they published a book [on migrant women organizing]. . . ! She can go to libraries and documentation centers also! Who will teach her that? It's us! There is a generation problem as well. Why didn't she go to the network for migrant and refugee women. . . ?
QUESTION: Well, it's a network for migrant women.

CLAUDINE: But at least she will see real work; she won't be able to say that we did not do anything. . . . Why doesn't she go to the organization against female mutilations? There are African women there!
QUESTION: I'm not sure that is what she is looking for.
CLAUDINE: She wants a nonspecialist organization. . . ? What does she want?! . . . I can talk with her, but it's a little bit tricky if she is pro-veil and for the legalization of prostitution. . . . But we can still talk to her, teach her things, because some things that are being said about us are totally false!

Claudine's exasperation during this exchange denotes her feeling that the demands made by French Black feminists are illegitimate. Her responses operate several shifts that are strategies of deflection and blame avoidance. She suggests the problem is one of "generation" rather than racism, and as she tries to prove that there are some organizations that fit nonwhite women's needs, she operates a series of shifts that work around race and racism. She refers to several organizations or networks for migrant women, or organizations with African women that lobby against female genital mutilation, thereby confusing racialization and migration, and dismissing the very identity of the activist who is the object of the discussion as both French and Black. She then shifts grounds, from trying to "fix" Afro-feminists in an already existing "specialized" feminist niche, to declaring that the question is not the inclusiveness of the white feminist movement, but one of political standing on the veil and prostitution. Here political boundary making preserves Claudine's moral high ground and prevents any challenge to her feminist authority. Her irritated exclamation, "What does she want?!"—while an unintended avowal of ignorance on her part—strangely echoes the second-wave feminist motto "What do they [women] want?" an ironical portrayal of men's angry and ignorant reaction to feminist demands. Finally, throughout her response, Claudine continues to situate herself in the position of the knowledgeable educator, correcting mistakes and establishing a truth that absolves her from criticism and racism: "She won't be able to say we didn't do anything." Initiated to inquire about white feminist organizations' inclusiveness, the conversation spurs irritation and anger and ends with the drawing of a political and moral boundary that preserves the privileged position of feminist whiteness. Hence, when the "other" racialized woman is perceived as a potential fellow feminist, as a possible part of a common political collective subject, she is either "returned" to "specific" organizations that supposedly address her "specific" needs or she is excluded on the grounds that her political position cannot be accommodated by a proper feminist collective subject. Never considered an equal or an interlocutor, she is dismissed before any interaction can occur, before any resentment or criticism she may utter can be heard and recognized as legitimate.

Anger and fear are not the only moral emotions that characterize white feminists' discourse on race and racism inside the feminist movement. Another interesting moral emotion that pervades discourses from older white feminists is that of melancholy, a longing for a long-lost unity of the collective feminist "we." One is here reminded of Cristina Beltrán's interrogation on the subject of Latino politics in the United States. Indeed, she asks, "Is Latino politics a project defined by loss?" and "Does the memory of such passionate and participatory politics inspire future political action—or does it render all that follows a disappointment?"[75] Several French interviewees in their sixties expressed deep melancholy, suggesting that true feminism existed in the past, but that now all that was left to do was to mourn a loss never to be replaced, the loss of unity, the loss of collective action and huge demonstrations. Nelly admits she sees "no future" for her umbrella organization that gathers women's rights organizations at the national level. She remembers the 1990s as a time of great activity, and the 1970s as the time of true unity within the movement (despite the numerous conflicts that in fact characterized this period). Similarly, Claudine depicts the feminist movement as experiencing a setback, an in-between-waves moment, that translates into the impossibility of mobilizing a collective presence for street demonstrations. While in fact numerous new feminist organizations have been created in France in the last two decades, while new racialized feminist subjectivities have emerged, Claudine's perception of the movement is one of a lost subject. One could argue that, in fact, at the very moment when racial difference becomes politicized in the French feminist public space, when racism becomes a political issue for new organizations headed by nonwhite feminists, suddenly, for some white feminists, the feminist subject itself is lost and to be mourned. Of course, turning to melancholy, lamenting the loss of the true feminist subject, evades the question of power and privileges within the current feminist collective subject. While the past is presented as a time of true unity and true feminism, present feminist contestations of pervasive white privilege inside the movement are made irrelevant and illegitimate. Feminism is located in the past, and present-day challenge to feminist whiteness ignored.

I thus described two types of moral disposition that are adopted by white feminists I interviewed when encountering nonwhite women. In the first instance, racialized women are the object of benevolent and professional care. There feminist whiteness is characterized by some degree of ambivalence, because racialized/migrant women are granted autonomy in their decisions, while at the same time portrayed as feminist subjects to be educated. The service relation that typically elicits this moral disposition encourages white feminists to be aware of their own prejudices and entails a self-reflection on the ethical dimension of the relationship with racialized/migrant women. Indeed, white feminists working in shelters or community centers often reflect on the power relations that exist in the context of their social work with racialized/migrant women and try to develop tools to mitigate the effects of these power asymmetries on racialized/migrant women who are receiving help. However, these benevolent dispositions depend in large part on the assumption that racialized/migrant women are part of the feminist project as the recipient of help, the object of care, embodying the social subject of feminism, *women*, and the concomitant expectation that they will not be transformed into *feminists*; that is, that the social, political, and moral distance that marks their relationship to white feminists providing service may not be reduced. Feminist intervention is, most of the time, not about creating a political relationship with service recipients.

A second type of moral disposition displayed by white feminists contrasts with this first benevolent and pragmatic attitude. It is elicited when racialized women are perceived as articulating feminist claims and a self-defined feminist identity. Some white French feminists especially display moral dispositions marked by anger, to some extent also fear—of being criticized and called racists[76]—and by self-righteousness. They work to preserve a moral high ground by rejecting claims by racialized women as illegitimate. They portray veiled Muslim women as *impossible* or *improper* feminist subjects, thereby policing the boundaries of what they consider to be the proper feminist subject. Because feminism, as a political project, rather than a social one, is a project of establishing free and equal relations with women, some white French feminists prefer *no* relations at all with racialized feminists. Indeed, any type of relation would entail *answering* legitimate questions about the historical exclusion of racialized women, and would mean transforming the boundaries of the feminist subject, a topic I go back to in chapter 6.

A powerful rationale that pervades the discourses that present veiled Muslim women as improper feminist subjects and that legitimize their exclusion from the feminist project as defined by white feminists is that of secularism (see chapter 3). To conclude this exploration of forms of feminist whiteness, I thus turn to the complex relationship between nationalism, secularism, and whiteness that is reshaping feminist whiteness, in particular in France.

Femonationalism, Secularism, and the Reshaping of Feminist Whiteness

In this last section, I interrogate the emergence and consolidation of a form of hegemonic feminist whiteness that is intertwined with nationalism through a commitment to secularism. Indeed, an important feature of femonationalism, not always remarked upon, especially in France and Quebec, is that it is intimately articulated with secular discourse. Hence, to conclude this chapter I ask: Is femonationalism a new form of feminist whiteness? To what extent is it coextensive with whiteness and secularism?

The answers to these questions are complex: femonationalism is a dynamic process; new policies and laws are regularly put on the agenda of European countries, reflecting the conflation of women's rights with xenophobic nationalism.[77] The adhesion of some white feminists to a femonationalist discourse happens mostly through an identification with secularism as a set of values that inherently protect women against religious oppression. This feminist adhesion to secularism has historical roots both in Quebec and in France, two historically Catholic countries where a majority of feminists fought actively against the Catholic Church until very recently. With the adoption of a secularist femonationalist discourse, feminist whiteness shifts from an active ignorance and avoidance of race to an active adhesion to a national identity that is premised on the exclusion or the reconfiguration of Islam and Muslim citizens themselves.[78] With this shift, some white feminists position themselves as moral entrepreneurs who can decide under what conditions immigrant and Muslim women may be enrolled as good feminist subjects. However, femonationalism is not restricted to white feminists. Quite the contrary, nonwhite feminists can also embrace this discourse and benefit from its public legitimacy.

Repertoires of feminist whiteness vary with time and space. I argue here that sexularism debates that have agitated the feminist public space are not the product of preexisting forms of feminist whiteness within white women's rights organizations, but rather historical moments in which feminist whiteness has been reconfigured. However, this reconfiguration differs in its scope and direction in France and in Quebec. Indeed, in Quebec a minority of white and nonwhite feminists mobilized secularism as a proxy for national Quebecois identity and portrayed Islam as a menace to Quebecois women's rights. They vocally demanded a charter of *laïcité* to curtail the visibility of Islam in Quebecois society, and the entrenchment of gender equality as a value that should precede freedom of religion in the legal order.[79] As I retraced in the previous chapter, a majority of white Quebecois women's rights organizations nevertheless opted for more accommodating stances and affirmed their attachment to secularism, but a secularism that would not produce the exclusion of veiled women from public spaces or the job market. They tended to refuse the fusion between women's rights and a bounded Quebecois identity that would necessitate the cultural assimilation of migrants and the invisibility of their religious practices, and denounced the open racism of the new Bill 62 in 2017.[80] Hence, sexularism debates in Quebec have precipitated the development and adoption of more critical repertoires of feminist whiteness such as intersectionality. They have put to the test the principled, and often only rhetorical, commitment of white feminist organizations to inclusivity that dates back to the 1960s with the foundation of the FFQ,[81] producing a new and deep conflict between white Quebecois feminists.

The situation has been quite different in France. Indeed, in France, sexularism debates emerged in a context in which many major (white) women's rights organizations have identified for several decades with the boundaries of the nation, and with the French Republic and its universalism. As Françoise Vergès notes, after decolonization, French feminists adopted the idea that colonization was over, and that France was now confined to its continental territory. This "mutilated geography," as she calls it, constituted overseas territories that legally remained French as "outside" the borders of the nation, and outside of the political imaginary of French feminists from the continent.[82] It marks, for Vergès, a form of adhesion of white French feminists to nationalism. More recently, in the context of the debate for gender parity in politics that animated the second half of the 1990s, many white French feminists have identified with a republican universalist discourse. A large number of French women's rights organizations became *republicanized* through their adhesion to the parity motto and its discursive strategy, which claimed that women did not represent a "category" or community that should be recognized by the republic, but rather "half of humanity," a component of a universal difference, that could be recognized by the Republic.[83] This adhesion to and identification with a universalist conception of women's rights that prioritizes gender over other axes of difference provided a favorable context for white French feminists' endorsement of *laïcité*, another cornerstone of the French Republic. In this context, feminist whiteness was reconfigured, with a new repertoire affirming that women's rights and the secular Republic are inseparable. Of course, historically, secularism has been beneficial to women's rights in the context of the overwhelming power of the Catholic Church in France until 1905, when the law separating church and state was adopted.[84] However, the secularism promoted in the 2000s by many white feminists differed considerably from the 1905 law and contributed to the fashioning of femonationalism.

Secularism therefore appears as a new repertoire that reshapes French feminist whiteness. This repertoire argues that religion is inherently oppressive to women, and that French *laïcité* is the only efficient protection for women who are vulnerable to religious extremism. This repertoire has roots in French feminism's anticlericalism. Indeed, the fight for the right to abortion during the second wave was framed as a fight against the hold of the state and of the Catholic Church over women's bodies. One cannot underestimate the influence that the Catholic Church had within French society when the second wave emerged at the end of the 1960s.[85] In this context, the association of feminism with secularism became uncontested among feminists from the "long" second wave.[86]

If memories of the second-wave struggle against the Catholic Church were often mentioned by older white feminists, the idea that the Republic and *laïcité* are the natural allies of women's rights was present in many interviews across generations. For many white feminists, religion is understood as inherently oppressive to women, and the veil epitomizes this oppression. Elsa from Feminists Dare!, who is too young to have been part of the feminist fight against far-right Christian extremism in the late 1980s, nevertheless identifies religion with oppression, and republican secularism with emancipation:

> [Religions] have this ambition to intervene in the organization of society. France has this history of *laïcité*, and I think that globally it has protected women. . . . The three monotheist religions have a clear vision of the society

they want and there is no equality between women and men. So my thing is to fight this. For me *laïcité*... is an ideal. It's like equality.... We know we will not reach it, but it can be a direction. And in a way, we are a laboratory in France because, well, there are very few secular countries.

This secularist repertoire reflects the adhesion of many white feminists to the renewed conception of *laïcité* elaborated by French institutions since the mid-1990s. Following Cécile Laborde,[87] one can define this conception of secularism as a republican conception that is perfectionist because it aims, in a typical Enlightenment narrative, at emancipating individuals, and is premised on the idea that the state is better placed than religion to achieve this aim. This republican conception of secularism also aims at fostering the national civic community, and is therefore identified with national identity. In fact, secularism defines a set of civic values and a public culture that draw the boundaries of the national community.[88] Secularism is not a simple law or a set of rights protecting religious freedom; it has become a bond that unites the national community. The following quotation from Julie, the communication officer of Girls on the Rise, epitomizes the articulation between a defiance toward religion and the idea that the Republic must emancipate individuals from this negative and oppressive influence, as well as the idea that this goal amounts to a model, or, as Elsa stated in her interview, "a project for society." Julie comments on the 2010 law banning the full veil in public spaces:

> There is this idea that equality does not depend, in any instance, on religion or sex.... Do we want that everybody is kind of satisfied, or do we clearly and totally take responsibility that we consider that there is a model, that we are universalists, that men and women are equal and that no religious or sectarian form should contravene this, and this is what we want?

Women's rights are conceived as embodied by the universalism that characterizes republicanism, and protected by secularism.[89] Women's rights become equated with the French nation *via* this renewed conception of secularism as a feature of national identity. Many white feminists were aware that their adhesion to secularism might fuel Islamophobia. However, they operated a hierarchy between women's rights, to be defended only thanks to secularism (understood as the banning of religious symbols from public spaces), and the fight against racism. Anick states about the 2010 law preventing full veiling in public spaces:

> I was hesitant in the beginning because it was about no more than a few hundred persons who wear the full veil. I told myself: it's not that important, etc., and it fuels racism against Muslims, and finally I told myself, yes, they are not numerous, but here again one must impose a limit. Otherwise this practice will develop even more.

Hence the French sexularism debates prompted a new repertoire of feminist whiteness, tightly articulated with secularism. While one may have expected a critical stance of white French feminists toward republican discourses and institutions, in the last two decades many women's rights activists have actively identified with republican discourses and values and their implicit nationalism. At the very moment when feminist whiteness based on the active ignorance of race within the movement was challenged by the emergence of new nonwhite feminist subjectivities and new public discourses on race, the French colonial past, and Islamophobia,[90] a new repertoire of feminist whiteness, actively recuperating secularism—understood as distinct from race and racism—was forged. In this context, secularism presents itself as a race-neutral narrative and opens possibilities for articulating new forms of feminist whiteness. Secularism has enabled many white feminists to position themselves as moral entrepreneurs who can decide if and how Muslim women might be good feminist subjects that can be enrolled in the feminist project, or should instead be cast away.

While this repertoire seems to avoid race, placing discussion on the terrain of religious belief, it is nonetheless actively sustaining the privileges attached to feminist whiteness as a hegemonic, racially privileged position. Muslim women become objects of scrutiny; their motivations are examined and deemed compatible, or not, with feminism. Corinne explains her approach with religious Muslim women:

> So it's that idea, that we are trying to give guidelines, because our aim is also to flag some issues for women with respect to these debates, not to stigmatize a community or a religion. It's about saying, "Wait, let's reflect on this. What does it mean? What does it endanger? Does it make us go forward? Does it make us regress backward? In what type of society do we want to live?" And from there we try to give guidelines to women.

Corinne positions herself as knowledgeable and able to provide other women with answers about the type of society in which they should want to live, and how secularism is the right means to achieve this end of "progress" toward more gender equality, associated with republican institutions, rather than regress under the influence of Islam. Chantal explains why she asked a veiled Muslim woman to take off her veil when she came to stay in the shelter:

> Globally, in terms of how you can think about your femininity . . . To hide women . . . the analysis I have, also with researchers who specialize on Islam, [is] there is no obligation. In many countries, Muslim women do not wear the veil. . . . Then it is our job to talk with them about this and about the enlightened choice they will give to their children.

Secularism and the conviction that religion is oppressive to women enables white feminists to bypass any discussion on racism and on the practical exclusionary consequences of their secularist discourses. The good Muslim feminist subject is the one who will adopt secularism and make her religious identity private and invisible for her white non-Muslim counterparts. Secularist discourses elaborated by some white feminists draw a boundary between the good Muslim girl, who will take off her veil and understand the importance of French secularism and republican values, and transmit them to her children, future members of the national body politic, and the one who will not. The latter is considered an irredeemable feminist subject who is not an object of concern for secular feminists. For example, the fact that the 2004 law expelled young Muslim girls from school is often presented as of no concern to secular feminists, the product of a *choice* made by young girl not to adopt secularism, that thus entails their exclusion from school only because they chose so. Elsa presents the situation offered to Muslim girls in those terms:

> The problem is that you encourage the wearing of the veil if you don't put limits. As far as I am concerned the 2004 and 2010 laws protected girls who could resist the family pressure to wear the veil, since they could say, "Either I go to public school and I don't wear the veil, or I go to private school," and the parents had the choice to let her stay in the public school.

Anick reflects on the 2004 law banning religious symbols in public schools in similar terms:

My position on the law changed because when the debate started, I was not in favor of a law. It seems useless. . . . I hesitated . . . the idea that the law would be a problem for these young girls, etc. And then I thought: no. After all, these girls, that's what they want, they are not forced. They should bear the consequences, and in any case it's just in schools, they can put their veils back on their head after. . . . And to see Islamic extremists, when I saw their street demonstration with these bearded guys and these veiled women . . . then no. I was so appalled that I told myself no. We need to stop this religious extremism.

The contrast in Anick's discourse between her benevolent attitude toward "good" migrant women, objects of care by feminists like herself, and bad veiled women who cannot be included in the feminist project is startling. The contradiction between the secularist assumption that religion is oppressive to women and the assertion that veiled girls, after all, choose to veil, is never touched upon. Veiled Muslim girls are suddenly granted agency to *choose* between, on the one hand, adhering to secularism and becoming the object of benevolent care by white feminists, and, on the other hand, making visible their religious identity and being dropped altogether from feminist concern. What is more, secularism makes anger and even disgust expressed with respect to veiled women appear as legitimate feminist reactions and emotions.

Not all white French feminists adhered to this new narrative of secularism and femonationalism. Reciprocally, not all nonwhite feminist rejected this narrative. In fact, prominent nonwhite feminist voices emerged as embodying the liberating forces of secularism for Muslim women themselves. For example, in France, the hearing of Sihem Habchi, then president of the organization Ni putes ni soumises, in front of the Gérin parliamentary commission in 2009 was widely commented on for her vehement defense of secularism and republicanism, as well as for her performance of partly undressing herself to prove her legitimate belonging to the French nation.[91] In France several nonwhite activists for women's rights have adopted comparable public discourses, stressing the necessity to enforce secularism in order to protect women from Islam. Narratives based on testimonies of women in the hand of oppressive Muslim men have also multiplied in bookshops, attesting to the success of the new literary genre of the "Muslim oppressed women" that fuels the rhetoric for muscular secularism in the name of women's rights.[92]

Similar performances of adhesion to the secular femonationalist narrative in Quebec by Muslim feminists include those enacted by Fatima

Houda-Pépin, an MP who vigorously defended the idea of a charter of *laïcité* in Quebec, and Djemila Benhabib, a public intellectual figure whose book *Ma vie à contre-coran: Une femme témoigne sur les islamistes* (My life against the Koran: A woman testifies against Islamists), published in 2009, was very well received in the Quebecois public sphere.[93] In all these cases the adhesion of nonwhite feminists to femonationalism grants them access to public attention as well as social and political capital. It also simultaneously gives credit to the belief that secularist discourses are not about race. The use of femonationalist narratives by nonwhite feminists reveals the only partial overlap between femonationalism and feminist whiteness. However, while these public figures may use femonationalism as a strategy to gain access to the public sphere, they remain very marginal voices among racialized feminists, as I document in the next chapter.

* * *

I explored in this chapter the various repertoires and forms of feminist whiteness in Quebec and France, and the different moral dispositions and emotions that contribute to producing them. I showed how in many different ways and with a variety of discourses in both contexts, feminist whiteness produces white women as the privileged subject of feminism, how repertoires of feminist whiteness work around race and depoliticize race and racism through a culturalist lens, but also how they can sometimes acknowledge power relations along racial lines and attempt to decenter the privileged white feminist subject. While some repertoires of feminist whiteness denote an active discursive resistance to intersectionality, others show how the concept can contribute to transforming feminist whiteness. I have also argued that feminist whiteness and the moral dispositions that sustain it differ depending on the type of relationship white feminists envision between themselves and racialized women. Indeed, when the relationship is one of service provision, when migrant/racialized women are conceived as objects of feminist care, the moral dispositions associated with feminist whiteness are benevolence and ambivalence. On the contrary, in France, when the relationship is politicized—that is, when migrant/racialized women are not perceived as in need of feminist care but as possible feminist subjects—moral dispositions are often self-righteousness, anger, and melancholy. That is, by expressing negative moral judgments, irritation, or exasperation when it comes to issues of racism within the feminist movement, white feminists efficiently police the boundaries of the proper feminist subject.

Secularism has also been enrolled in this policing project, which more often than not demands racialized women silence their claims and their identities to be recognized as equals. Tellingly, young veiled girls have been dropped from the white feminist agenda in the name of protecting women's rights through secularism. Finally, I argue that in France, sexualism debates have indeed changed and refashioned feminist whiteness. While feminist whiteness was based on typical forms of white ignorance and race evasion, since the mid-1990s many white feminists have actively identified with republican values, effectively forging a historically new white feminist subject under the guise of universalism and secularism. But this is only one part of the story: if sexualism debates have efficiently produced new forms of feminist whiteness, they have simultaneously fashioned new processes of feminist political subjectivation for racialized women, which I explore in the next chapter.

5
Resisting Whiteness, Claiming Feminism
Racialized Feminists' Moral Addresses

> It still matters that we feel more properly recognized by some people than we do by others.
> —Judith Butler, *Giving an Account of Oneself*, 33

> You have to accept that we are here, and you have to love us. Otherwise it's not gonna work. You cannot just tolerate us!
> —Mani, South Asian feminist activist, Montreal

When feminist discourses are dissociated from feminist whiteness, what kind of feminist identities, political ideals, and moral dispositions do they regulate? And how do they contribute to a critique of femonationalism? The sexualism debates that have reconfigured white feminists' political subjectivations in many European countries have also impacted and shaped the organizing of racialized feminists and their political subjectivations in those contexts. While I described in the previous chapter the various discursive repertoires and moral dispositions mobilized by white feminists to produce a form of political subjectivation that I have called feminist whiteness, I turn in this chapter to racialized feminists and their modes of political subjectivation in relation to white feminists as they have unfolded in the same period of debates and conflicts among feminists. I argue that racialized feminists' discourses constitute forms of moral address vis-à-vis white feminists, and that racialized feminists elaborate a critical discourse that resists the dominant assumptions that fuel femonationalism, and thereby provides alternative feminist visions, anchored in different moral dispositions and emotions. Of course, racialized feminists' discourses about the sexualism debate and their feminist ideals are not solely directed at white feminists. They are also focused on racialized women, in order to create the constituency they aim to represent. However, I am interested here in analyzing specifically how feminist whiteness is resisted.

My intention in this chapter is not to retrace the history of racialized women's groups and movement in France and Quebec in the past decade, or to explain why they have emerged and perpetuated themselves or didn't survive. While this chapter certainly contributes to documenting racialized women's movements in both contexts—an important task given the fact that very few studies exist and that there is a socially organized lack and loss of memory of those movements—my main aim is different. Indeed, I analyze how sexularism debates have shaped different forms of feminist political subjectivities for racialized feminist groups, and in particular how racialized feminists have forged specific political vocabularies to name and politicize their relationships with white feminists in this heated context. I also argue that these political vocabularies are articulated with a set of emotions and moral dispositions that fashion specific forms of feminist political subjectivation. I propose in this chapter to capture the formation of (collectively produced) moral, political, and ethical dispositions that are intimately linked to and shaped by the context of postcolonialism and postsecularism in France and Quebec. In particular, I ask: How do nonwhite feminists consider their political and moral relationship to the mainly white feminist movement in both contexts? What are the moral dispositions and emotions that the encounters, conflicts, or alliances with white feminists elicit for racialized feminists? How do they resist racism and the exclusions from white feminist spaces it performs?

I argue that by calling themselves feminists, racialized feminists in both contexts enter—among other processes—in relation with white feminists, a relation that they attempt to fashion with their own vocabulary, concepts, and discourses. Since their emergence as organized social movements in different contexts, racialized feminists have produced analyses of their raison d'être and relationships with white feminist organizations. In the United States, Black and Chicana organizations that emerged at the same time as their white counterparts, at the end of the 1960s, produced writings reflecting on their identities, goals, and strategies in order to organize and survive as independent movements.[1] In the contemporary context of sexularism debates and divisions on these issues within feminist movements, racialized feminists have elaborated specific discourses and counterdiscourses to empower themselves and resist the political ideals and identities imposed on them by hegemonic and secular feminist whiteness. Since they occupy a minority position, in the Deleuzian sense—that is, not an identity or a sociological "object," but a position of endogenous conflictuality within a hegemonic normative system[2]—racialized feminists seek to create a new language, a new position, from *within* a dominant discourse.

I insisted in the previous chapter that feminist whiteness is a relational process of political subjectivation. Likewise, racialized feminists' forms of political subjectivation are relational. They are relationally connected to white/mainstream/hegemonic forms of feminist discourse. This relationship is both political and moral. Indeed, I posit that calling oneself an Afrofeminist, a feminist of color, a Muslim feminist, or a South Asian feminist is not only a political choice in a given context. It is also a claim to be recognized as such, by other fellow feminists; it is, to borrow Judith Butler's words, to *give an account of oneself*[3] as a racialized feminist; it is to enter a scene of address and therefore relations with others, relations that delineate a specific moral horizon and specific ethical responsibilities. In particular, I explore in this chapter the political emotions, such as indignation, frustration, pain, unease, anger, or lassitude, that sustain racialized feminists' relationship to white feminists, and the forms of moral address they convey. I argue that racialized feminists' political subjectivities are articulated through both resistance and resentment.

In her analysis of theories and practices of French lesbians of color, Paola Bacchetta contends that resistance can be transgressive, transformative, or oppositional, and that these various forms of resistance allow for the creation of subjectivities and imaginaries thanks to the creation of a collective "we" formed by intersubjective relations.[4] Hence, she insists that queer-of-color subjectivities are coconstituted by various power relations that they resist, leading to the production of new subjectivities and to disidentification processes. I document such forms of resistance through discourses that are opposed to the hegemony of feminist whiteness.

I also document forms of resentment, which I interpret as moral and political addresses that racialized feminists direct to white feminists. There is a philosophical tradition that interprets resentment as a negative political passion. For example, Wendy Brown suggests that resentment fixates wounded identities on their injuries, preventing them from unfolding politically in more positive and productive ways.[5] Resentment tends to orient political action toward the claiming of rights—rights to protection, which reinstate the status of victim. Sara Ahmed insists that feminists of color are assigned the position of a feminist *killjoy* within feminist spaces: as they raise the subject of racism, they are perceived as the problem, because they threaten the preservation of "white fragility" by their very presence.[6] Racialized women's resentment may be described as the product of being a feminist-of-color killjoy, that is, a feminist who "does not make the happiness of others [here white feminists] her cause."[7] However, resentment, like the figure of the killjoy, exceeds negativity. It also bears the mark of a will. Indeed, like the willful subject described by Ahmed,[8] resentment also creates the possibility for a *we*, at the same time as it interrupts the "flow of a conversation."[9] Indeed, following Audre Lorde[10] and bell hooks,[11] Ahmed underlines that bringing up the question of racism within feminism, that is, politicizing race in the context of feminism, means interrupting the flow of the conversation of white feminists. Resentment is therefore a form of willfulness.

In this vein, I argue that resentment is not a way of adopting and safeguarding an identity as a victim, but rather a way to attempt to fashion new relations. It is both a moral disposition and a political action directed at white feminists. Resentment can thus be interpreted as a moral address, as Margaret Walker has argued,[12] directed toward those who have wronged others. Thomas Brudholm has shown that, in the dramatic aftermath of World War II, Jean Améry's writings as a Holocaust survivor had no other aim than to posit resentment as a positive moral demand expressed to his German contemporaries.[13] Harboring resentment may therefore be a political and moral action that is not limited to the foreclosure of political subjectivation on the figure of the victim but rather an action that is principally oriented toward others. While analyses of racialized women's movements often rightly focus on their claim to their own identity and their difference from white feminist movements, I suggest in this chapter that resentment is, among other emotions and moral dispositions, a way to recognize what Hannah Arendt calls "the world between us."

I first explore the contexts of racialized feminists' activism in France and Quebec to underline the difference in their dynamics of self-organization and politicization of their racial identities. I show that they share, across the Atlantic, similar repertoires of collective self-organizing, but also that they approach religious and racial identities in contrasting ways, and that they hold a diversity of positions with respect to sexularism debates, depending in part on the type of organization they are part of, that is, organizations devoted to providing services to women in their communities or consciousness-raising groups. Then I analyze what intersectionality means for racialized feminists, that is, both a lived experience that is conducive to developing a form of feminist subjectivity, and a tool to resist whiteness and claim more and better representation among feminist movements. Finally, exploring further the political subjectivations of racialized feminists, I investigate the range of political and moral emotions that they express with respect to white women. I argue that these feelings nourish both resistance to whiteness and resentment toward white feminists as a form of moral and political appeal to refashion feminist relations.

The Politics of Racialized Feminists "Organizing One's Own"

In most countries where feminism experienced a second wave, during that period racialized women self-organized and produced theoretical reflections on their relationship to the white feminist movement. However, it took quite some time before their dynamics as social movements became the object of scholarship that interrogates and revisits central themes of social movement theories such as identity formation,[14] movement's success,[15] or coalition building.[16] Today there is a developing field of social movement studies that analyzes racialized women's movements and their relationships with white women's movements,[17] and that also investigates the extent to which racialized feminists' claims and identities have been discursively or practically integrated in the political agenda of white/mainstream feminist organizations, through intersectionality discourses and practices.[18] However, these developments are of uneven nature depending on the case under scrutiny. In particular, while there have been several important studies on racialized women's movements in the United States and the United Kingdom,[19] there is a dearth of studies on other European countries and Canada,[20] and the history of Black French women's movements has only recently begun to burgeon.[21] The timing and scope of these processes of self-organizing differ depending on the historical and social context. It is important to understand these differences because they delineate the backdrop against which racialized feminists' political subjectivation unfolds.

In the United States, Black and Chicana feminists organized early on at the end of the sixties and produced an important legacy of writings that formed the foundations of Black feminism and intersectionality as a field of studies, thereby cementing a lasting impact on feminism as a field of protest and as a field of theory.[22] Studies on racialized women's movements in the

United States have brought important insights on the dynamics of formation and dissolution or fading of these organizations. They have in particular underscored that Black and Chicana women's organizations are not the "natural" product of race relations in a given context. As Benita Roth suggests, "Selecting the label 'feminist' was not a simple or automatic act but a political choice among other political choices,"[23] and Black and Chicana women in the United States could have opted at the end of the 1960s to participate in their respective racial groups' social and revolutionary movements rather than create their own organizations. Kimberly Springer also points out the risk of homogenizing these groups, erasing their internal class and sexual diversity. As she outlines in her history of Black women organizing in the United States between 1968 and 1980, the desire to center organizations around Black women's identity, rather than Black women's identit*ies*, created new margins in these movements.[24] Equally important, Chicana and Black feminists in the United States decided to create their own organizations following two impulses of different nature. First, in a crowded social movement field, they felt the need to "organize one's own," an activist ethos that was typical of that time, as Benita Roth has argued. Second, white women's desire to preserve their class and racial privileges made alliances difficult or impossible, despite existing relationships between Black, Chicana, and white women's movements.

France and Quebec provides contrasting pictures to the US history of racialized women's organizing. Racialized feminist's organizations have emerged in France and Quebec at different times and places, and with different political logics and genealogies. In France, despite the existence of racialized feminist activism in overseas territories during the same period and the emergence of migrant women's activism in the 1980s, no such process occurred.[25] Rather, each generation of racialized feminists has strived to achieve visibility, recognition, and influence within the feminist movement. In Quebec, indigenous women's activism and migrant women's activism not only emerged in the 1980s but also were partially institutionalized and funded by the government, thereby impacting the organizational landscape of Quebecois feminist activism.[26]

Differences between France and Quebec, and between these two contexts and the United States, are in great part due to the different histories of the politics of race and immigration that provide the backdrop for racialized feminists to organize. Indeed, Quebec and France offer two contrasting models of citizenship, immigrant integration, and race politics. Quebec, as a Canadian province and despite its official claims to the contrary—including the use of another label, that of *interculturalism*—has, since the 1980s, implemented a close variant of the Canadian policy of multiculturalism, which has become well entrenched legally and institutionally, especially at the federal level but also in the bureaucratic structures of the Quebec state.[27] In Quebec, mobilization around ethnic and immigrant identity is common and encouraged by public authorities as an important dimension of multicultural and immigrant integration politics, and the use of ethnic categories, as well as claims based on ethnic identities, do not raise public debates in Canada.[28] Logically, racialized women's organizations in Quebec take for granted that cultural and ethnic identities are important elements to consider when counseling a woman, thereby following the precepts of multiculturalist policies. Most organizations self-identify on the basis of an ethnic and/or regional origin (South Asian, Philippine), on the basis of a religious identity (i.e., Muslim), or on a shared identity as immigrant women. All these organizations provide services (i.e., counseling, shelter, language classes) to women and are part of Quebecois feminist networks (such as l'R des centres de femmes, a network that asks its members to sign a feminist charter), which enables them to get funding from the Quebecois government as women's rights organizations. However, most of the funding of the self-identified ethnic/religious women's organizations I interviewed came primarily from the then-called Ministry of Cultural Communities and Immigration in Quebec. Finally, these organizations also actively engage in advocacy in the name of their community, lobbying the government on issues of immigration reform, secularism bills, women's rights, and welfare policies.

Conversely, what has been labeled the French "republican model" promotes a contrasting philosophy of integration, which emphasizes a common, national, civic culture instead of pluralism, an abstract concept of citizenship, color-blindness, and civic and cultural assimilation on the part of migrants[29] as well as religious minorities. In this context, ethnic categories are deemed suspicious in public debates and often controversial, which has made mobilization around ethnic identity difficult.[30] Hence, while in Quebec the ministry for immigration and cultural communities funds organizations that organize on an ethnic basis, in France the administrative agencies in charge of immigrant integration have mostly used territorial categories (such as housing projects or banlieues defined by urban planning policies) or economic categories (such as poverty) to define their beneficiaries, rather than ethnic categories. In this context, while in

France, too, racialized women's organizations sometimes receive funding from governmental agencies dedicated to immigrant integration, these agencies encourage organizations to present themselves as defined territorially (an identity bounded by the quartier, i.e., neighborhood) rather than ethnically. Often, women's centers' funding comes from local political and administrative bodies (at the municipal or regional level) in charge of social welfare. What legitimizes their funding is the social work they do—language classes, literacy classes, afterschool programs for children, support for administrative procedures, shelter, counseling—in specific deprived neighborhoods, not their self-organizing within an ethnic community. Hence, in the Parisian region where I conducted interviews, the few racialized women's organizations that provide services in their communities often have names that do not refer to a specific ethnic origin or to racial identity, but rather stress their local roots in the neighborhood, or adopt a mix of both that underlines their immigrant identity (such as "Franco-African women in Paris"). Finally, a handful of organizations that operate as consciousness-raising and activist groups—which do not provide services to women in their communities—put forth feminist of color identities that politicize both their racial and gender (and sometimes sexual) identities, but not specific ties to ethnic communities.

The contexts and timing of the emergence of racialized women's organizations in Quebec and France are therefore quite different. In Quebec, women from immigrant communities were encouraged as early as the beginning of the 1980s to self-organize on an ethnic basis to provide services that would foster immigrant integration (language classes in particular) and simultaneously empower women (screening for domestic violence, temporary free day care for young immigrant mothers, etc.). These women's rights organizations have adopted the vocabulary and political project of multiculturalism, promoting their ethnic and religious difference.[31] However, their involvement in the multiculturalist project is often also a critical one: they tend to question the culturalization of difference at the expense of a class analysis, contest many Quebec policies for immigrant integration as reproducing inequalities and power asymmetries, and often actively lobby against racism (instead of promoting multiculturalism per se).[32] Many immigrant women's organizations based in francophone Quebec are run by anglophone immigrants and have also developed a critical stance toward Quebecois nationalism. Some organizations operated by migrant women and women of migrant descent have also developed ties of solidarity with native women's organizations, as a way to recognize their own participation in the Canadian settlement project and its ongoing colonial legacy for indigenous peoples.[33]

In France, several groups of immigrant women were created at the beginning of the 1970s, but they mostly assembled women from Latin American and North African countries who were in political exile in Paris.[34] Their political activism was geared toward their country of origin or toward international organizations. In 1976, a Black Women's Coordination (Coordination des femmes noires) was created to voice the concerns of racialized and immigrant women; however, it was short-lived and was disbanded in 1980.[35] At the beginning of the 1980s, women of migrant descent started to be politically active, but mostly in organizations devoted to fighting racism or to fostering immigrant solidarity. Only in the mid-1980s did specific migrant women's organizations start to form.[36] The first organizations were generally short-lived, but new organizations quickly formed to replace them. These groups constitute nowadays a much more heterogeneous and less visible activist field than in Quebec, with some organizations based on national origin and politically active with respect to their home country's politics, while others are much more grassroots and cater to a specific neighborhood's diverse population of migrant women and women of migrant descent, and with a few organizations doing critical political lobbying in the name of racialized women and with a postcolonial perspective, which emerged a few years after the turn of the century. This late emergence and singular weakness of an activist field of racialized women within the French feminist field of protest is striking in a country with such a long colonial history and resulting postcolonial migration policies, and which still comprises overseas territories that are legacies from its colonial project. As Françoise Vergès notes, it reflects a French ideology of "decolonization" that has excluded the French overseas territories from French modernity and performs an erasure of colonial history.[37] In this context, the politicization of race and racial identities has been stalled and obscured.

Politicizing Intersectional Identities: Culture, Race, Postcoloniality

This short overview of migrant and racialized women's activism in both contexts indicates that there is a wide variety of organizations in this field, with various forms of politicization of racial and postcolonial identities. How are these different contexts shaping the political subjectivations of racialized feminists? How do legitimate discourses about race and racial identities impact the politics of intersectionality that racialized feminists promote? In each context, different processes of politicization of racial, immigrant, and religious identities provide the backdrop against which the political subjectivation of racialized feminists is set. The politics of intersectionality displayed by racialized feminists is thus variegated. It is shaped by the context in which they organize as feminists, and by the political legitimacy of categories such as culture, race, or religion. It is also shaped by their own trajectory and the generation they belong to. With respect to race, three main types of narratives define intersectional identities. A first one, used by many organizations that deliver services to migrant and racialized women, tends to insist on the *cultural* dimension of racial and migrant differences. Contrastingly, several organizations that provide services to racialized women tend to downplay or suspend the role of race or culture as an important factor in their intervention work. Finally, both in Quebec and in France, some racialized feminists propose an elaborated social critique of racism and postcolonialism that informs their feminist practice. With respect to religion, and more specifically Islam, racialized feminists elaborate also a variety of discourses, marked by ambivalence, tolerance, and rejection. The intersection between religion, race, and gender is thus perceived and politicized differently by racialized feminists, depending on their context and their own trajectory of becoming a feminist. These variations underline how each context—France and Quebec—and its hegemonic politics of race and secularism contribute to shape the political subjectivations of racialized feminists.

Many organizations in Montreal that provide services to racialized/migrant women insist on the specific needs that *cultural* difference generates for the women they seek to help. They underscore that in other organizations that are not run by racialized/migrant women, the women in their community will not find adequate help, because their cultural needs will not be understood or taken into consideration. Nandita, a woman in her fifties from South Asia who works in a center for South Asian women in Montreal, explains her organization's approach:

> We want to make sure her rights are respected, because in some place, in shelters, they try to enforce certain things. They say: you don't have to be in that situation, you can divorce.... But we don't do that. It's her decision. She

has to understand and take it.... What I feel is the social workers who work there, they are not from South Asia. They don't know our culture, they don't know the family values ... so if they don't know, they will make a decision by thinking about their side.... Maybe they don't want to see the culture and the family values. They think the woman is here and she has to adapt to the Quebec society, to live like that. I don't agree with that.

A common discourse among racialized immigrant feminists in Quebec stresses the fact that women from their communities are not adequately served by mainstream feminist shelters because these tend to be insensitive to the cultural dimensions that structure immigrant women's situations of domestic violence. Shelter officers who are not immigrant women themselves are perceived as pushing immigrant women to separate and divorce, while in fact this may not be what these women really want, or it may come at a cost that is not suspected by nonimmigrant women. Naima, an officer in a center for Muslim women in Montreal who is from the Middle East, tells a similar story:

> For newcomers, I find that if the person is from the same culture, it will be easier. They trust you more easily, they are more open. Often they will feel like they don't have to explain themselves ... in some ways, women who are in a relationship, who are married, and they're being abused.... To understand why they're not leaving, in the sense of what are the stakes.... And I don't say this is specific in our culture. This happens in all cultural communities, but the idea of losing faith, of bringing dishonor to the family ... how important it is to keep the family together. All these things. Because I realize how important it is. If I feel like the woman is not ready to take certain steps, I won't force her. I will let her know if I feel she is in a dangerous situation.

What is noticeable is that these discourses share to a large extent the feminist motto that women should make their choice on their own terms and that feminist intervention is about respecting a woman's choice, whatever it is. However, immigrant feminists argue that white feminist organizations tend not to respect this feminist tenet because they are insensitive and unaware of the importance of culture and cultural differences. Hence, self-organization on the basis of shared culture and cultural experience is necessary to provide an adequate feminist response to migrant women's needs.

These discourses echo the narrative of interculturalism and benevolent care expressed by white women working in multicultural organizations. However, while for white feminists interculturalism was a tool that had to be learned, for racialized/immigrant feminists the emphasis on cultural difference is based on lived experience. Of course, the idea that there is a commonality of experience between immigrant women who work or volunteer in immigrant women's organizations and their public, a commonality that guarantees a form of authenticity, is partly fictional.[38] Migration trajectories, class background, and education are often very different between volunteers or managers and beneficiaries.[39] Nonetheless, in Quebec this idea is central to migrant women's self-organizing and their emphasis on cultural difference. Hence culture, rather than race, is politicized and operates as a ground for identification and feminist practice.

In a French context in which race talk is politically risky, some racialized/immigrant women refute the idea that a common racial or cultural identity is necessary to perform a good feminist intervention with racialized/immigrant women. Samira, whose parents are from Algeria and who now manages her own organization in a Parisian suburb, and who argues in her interview for the necessity to self-organize on the basis of a shared immigrant experience and a shared experience of racism, rejects the idea that one must be of a similar cultural background to perform the right intervention:

> I think that when somebody suffers or was victim of violence, etc., it's international. She is here with her suffering.... You just have to be yourself and to be open. Suffering is universal. What's good here is that we have a lot of volunteers from very different cultural origins, different ethnic origins.

Samira's opinion at the same time contests the idea that a shared cultural background enables the right intervention, and, simultaneously, promotes the variety of cultures that are represented through her volunteers, thereby implicitly endorsing the idea that this variety allows the organization to address the cultural and ethnic variety that is found among its beneficiaries. Recognizing that immigration and cultural difference shape women's experiences and their needs, and therefore should be taken into account—in part through the experiences and identities of the volunteers themselves—and believing that a woman's suffering is universal reflect two competing narratives that orient Samira's and other racialized feminist activists' practices. On the one hand, her own experience of racism and exclusion from other types of social services underlines the structural and political nature of racism and justifies self-organization on the basis of immigrant or racialized identity. On the other hand, the feminist ethos of intervention that advocates helping women on their own terms suggests that the identity of the listener does not matter; rather professional and activist experience do. Underlying this discourse is the idea that "suffering is universal," that is, that the women who seek help and support from her organization are victims primarily as *women*. The forms of violence they experience are culturally defined—Samira evokes forced marriage among other cases her organization deals with—but mostly, they fall on the spectrum of violence against women. They are rarely presented as the product of institutional racism or discrimination. In that sense, gender identity comes first in Samira's analysis.

Mariam, a woman from Mali who heads Women Mediators in a northern Parisian suburb, also argues that a common racial or cultural identity is not necessary to perform well in one's job of helping immigrant and racialized women. Mariam gives the example of one of her white French employees who can perform the same job as Mariam does once she establishes trust with the woman with whom she is working, and as long as she abides by the principle of not making decisions in the name of the woman she is helping. Mariam further explains:

> Among our officers now there are a lot of French women. All nationalities . . . French, Greeks . . . some are recognized because they speak several languages. I have Maghrebi women, also South Africans in the team. I don't look at immigration; I look at the person's experience, her ability to listen to people. It's important. At the start, we said we would be immigrant women to help and support immigrant women. That was at the start, but it changed a lot. Even the French, they can intervene with these populations. You just need to listen, to have empathy, to be trained, just to be human, that's all.

As in Samira's discourse, there is both a valorization of ethnic and cultural diversity within the organization, and the clear refusal of the idea that one must share the same culture or immigrant background to provide the right service and support to immigrant women. However, this principled position that rejects the idea of a community-based feminist organization reflects a larger constraint that is specific to the French context. Indeed, asked whether she would prefer to have an organization only for women from Mali, Mariam replies:

MARIAM: No, no, no. If we do that . . . I am against this also. I don't want to be trapped in my culture. And if you do that the state will say: now these associations are based on ethnicity, and well . . .
QUESTION: You might not get funding from institutions then?
MARIAM: No, certainly not.

Hence Mariam's refusal to organize only within her own immigrant and cultural community reflects both the primacy of gender as the basis for her organization's identity, and a political constraint specific to the French context that makes organizing on the basis of racial identity suspicious and unlikely to be funded. In France, a deep tension is perceptible between the claim that a shared cultural or immigrant experience is a necessity and justifies self-organization, and the claim that the cultural or racial identity of the volunteers does not matter in providing immigrant and racialized women with the support they need. This tension means that sometimes, in racialized feminists' discourse, the centrality of race is interrupted, suspended.

In contrast to this repertoire, a handful of organizations in Quebec and France politicize racial identity as an important dimension of their identity. For them, fighting against racial discrimination is as important as empowering women in their community. These groups generally are oriented toward advocacy or consciousness-raising, with no institutional funding and often no office space, and do not provide services to women. These organizations articulate a discourse that politicizes race and colonialism as a social relationship of domination that is as important as gender in understanding racialized/immigrant women's position in society.

Representing a network of racialized and migrant women in Quebec, Karima, an immigrant woman from Algeria in her early fifties and an activist in Montreal, provides a related analysis that centers on colonialism and on the intersectionality that characterizes migrant women's situation in Quebec:

> We consider that our priority is to fight against the neocolonial oppression we are experiencing, because the majority of immigrant and racialized women . . . we come, especially in the past ten years, we come from former colonized countries, [colonized] by the same colonizers, France and Great Britain. And today, when you look closely . . . you realize that there is almost a colonial relationship that is imposed on immigrants.

Immigration and race are politicized within a post and neocolonial framework of analysis. Immigrant women are not presented as defined by their culture and as having specific needs related to their situation as immigrants. Rather, they are presented as oppressed by an interlocking set of cultural and economic relations of domination, which form a system that is defined and denounced as perpetuating under a new guise the former colonial domination. While Quebec was not a colonial power in the usual sense, the comparison with indigenous women allows Karima to draw a parallel between Quebec's settler and colonial policy vis-à-vis indigenous people and the European colonial powers that colonized, among others, her country of birth. Doing so, she draws a historical and political line between colonization and the contemporary politics of immigration in Quebec.

In a similar vein, in France some racialized feminist organizations politicize race and the legacy of colonialism in their discourse and identity as an organization. Maleiha, a woman in her mid-thirties originally from North Africa, who founded a group of lesbians who define themselves as lesbians of color, explains her reasons for creating a group based on a double separation from men and from white women:

> We say "of color," as in the United States. I will answer you like Aimé Césaire when he was asked about Negritude. . . . It's a movement of analysis, of resistance. So I will tell you maybe "of color" is not totally satisfying. But we chose the term because . . . it seemed full of the meaning and analysis of our American predecessors. When you say "of color," there is this recognition of all the work of intersectional analysis. And also, it seemed a broad enough term to encompass all the lesbians who have a history linked to colonization and slavery, to memory, exile, immigration, be they of immigrant origin or migrant themselves, etc. Because if you use "racialized," I don't like that term that much, it reduces women of color to only one oppression, that of racism. "Of color" is more open. It is more political.

For Maleiha, her organization must tackle the various oppressions that lesbians of color experience at once, without introducing a hierarchy between them. The politicization of racial identity is evidenced in the importance of the separation from white women and white lesbians—which was one of the reason to create the organization, after Maleiha experienced unproductive collaborations with white lesbians in a former group. In a similar vein, Sandra, a young woman in her twenties originally from central Africa, who founded an Afro-feminist group in Paris with other women of African descent, explains the reasons for the creation of her association:

> Well, whatever the type of feminism, it always comes from your experience as a woman, and that's the start, starting from your experience as a woman in a given context, and for us, we are Black women who live in a white and patriarchal society.... Clearly we live in a white and heteronormative patriarchy, so it's becoming aware that our position exposes us to several oppressions that are interlocked because of sexism and racism, and that many other oppressions can be added; the idea is not to create a hierarchy between these oppressions; they are an integral part of our trajectory, our experience.

Sandra's and Maleiha's analyses echo the discourses of Black American feminists in the 1970s as analyzed by Kimberly Springer,[40] as well as the analysis of intersectionality proposed by Kimberlé Crenshaw.[41] A specific position at the intersection of several relations of oppression shapes a specific social experience. To politically represent and address this experience correctly, one must not, as is usually the case in social movements, introduce a hierarchy between oppressions but, on the contrary, one must consider simultaneously their effects. This intersectional analysis clearly politicizes race and posits that race is *as important as* gender for political action.

Intersectionality with Religion: Ambivalence, Tensions, and Redefining the Feminist Subject

Given the various ways in which racialized feminists conceptualize racial and immigrant identities, it is not surprising that they also have different discourses regarding Islamic veiling practices and the sexularism debates that have unfolded both in Quebec and in France. For a vast majority of racialized feminists, race and religion do not raise the same issues: religious identities cannot be subsumed under racial categorizations, and intersectional identities that concern Islam differ from those that concern immigrant and racialized women. While race raised the question of culture, racism, and systemic discrimination, religion is mainly understood as a question of choice—from the women who decide to wear the veil—rather than as primarily a practice linked to culture or as a ground for systemic discrimination.

Because of the centrality of the idea of choice and freedom, racialized feminists' discourses on religion differ from those they elaborate on race.

Indeed, religious beliefs raise the question of the relationship between feminism and emancipation. When discussing Islamic veiling, racialized feminists redefine the contours of the good and the bad feminist subjects. While some racialized feminists insist on the notion of choice and therefore the duty to respect religious identities and practices, others condemn the display of religious beliefs, and some express tensions and ambivalence in their discourses between their feminist commitments that condemn what they perceive as oppressive religious practices, and their awareness of Islamophobia. Others wish to recuperate discursively veiled women in the feminist project or propose to place the needs and experiences of these women at the center of their feminist analysis.

In Quebec, the majority of women activists share an accommodating position, be it on the niqab or on the hijab, and reject the government's attempts to regulate these religious practices. Adhering to a multicultural framework that protects religious freedom and legitimizes the expression of cultural difference, they favor solutions that place the decision in the hands of the women who would be targeted by the possible regulations, be it at a collective or individual level. Nandita places the issue of the hijab within the broader framework of multiculturalism and cultural difference:

> When you see a woman's point of view, how she sees that . . . for example, the *hijab*, if she's comfortable with that, what is the problem? All these years it never came out as an issue. Why is it coming now? The whole process of reasonable accommodation—I feel it has to be in two ways. When you respect every culture and all values, there won't be a problem. What I feel is we shouldn't mix the values of the cultures with abuse and control. That's two different things. A woman who is wearing a hijab or who is not wearing a hijab, that has nothing to do with the family and control. That's her own way to define herself. Not all the women wear hijabs. That's her own wish. and I think it should be respected. . . . Before they get in the issue of going into seeing that, they should have consulted these women first, how they feel about that.

Paola, one of the founding members of the same center for South Asian women in Montreal, recalls that her organization took a stand against the project of restriction of reasonable accommodation and against the position of the FFQ, which was to authorize hijabs but to forbid niqabs (in public service, for employees and also possibly for clients). Paola summarizes the position of her organization saying, "Any kind of interference, like telling women what to do, is a problem." Kahina, a young woman in her twenties of Algerian descent who works in a Muslim women's center in Montreal, holds a slightly different position. While Paola and Nandita defend veiled women's right to choose for themselves, whatever the religious garment they decide to wear, in the name of women's agency and the respect for culture and religion that is typical of Canadian multiculturalism, Kahina denounces the bill project for more pragmatic reasons:

> Will interdiction of the niqab in public institutions eradicate niqabs? I don't think so. Did the interdiction of the veil in France eradicate the veil? Did we free these women? I don't think so. For women who are forced, it did not change a thing. And today, in the West, are there really women who are forced to wear the veil? I did not see any.

Kahina also draws a line between the veil and the full-face veil, however, and here again she privileges a pragmatic approach that places women's needs at the center of her analysis

> Personally, it's clear that [with] the niqab, there is a security question, the question of interpersonal relations also. It's clear it has an impact. However, I am against the bill project in Quebec because it would prevent women from consulting social workers or from going to learn French. . . . You will keep them isolated, that's what bothers me.

Despite some uneasiness, most immigrant and racialized women's activists in Quebec are critical of the desire to regulate forms of Islamic veiling and denounce the racist discourse that the sexualism debates have encouraged in the public sphere and popular culture. Their analysis draws both on the Canadian multiculturalist discourse that promotes respect for cultural difference and on a feminist analysis that considers that women are able to choose for themselves. Even those who might disapprove of the practice of veiling assert that these regulations will in fact not benefit the women they are supposed to "protect." Hence, what is being elaborated in these discourse is an alternative definition of the feminist project, one in which the goal of feminism is not to endorse and enforce abstract feminist principles (emancipation, gender equality), but rather, in a more pragmatic fashion, to place racialized women, perceived as already vulnerable to racism, at the center of attention and care. Rather than defining what is the right feminist politics by measuring it up to ideals such as emancipation, racialized feminists suggest that the *concrete* consequences of veiling ban policies should be scrutinized. Feminism therefore becomes a project of caring what will happen to these vulnerable subjects, rather than deciding how they should be emancipated.

In France, racialized feminists hold a wider range of opinions on politics regulating Islamic veiling practices. Several of them express tensions and uneasiness about the issue of the Islamic veil, especially, but not only, those who are Muslim themselves. While they also denounce the practical negative effects that the 2004 and 2010 laws have had, they are also often critical of girls who decide to veil. Mariam, who migrated from Mali and is now in her fifties, explains about the 2004 law forbidding religious symbols in public schools:

> Everybody agreed in our organization. Me I am against this law.... In the public space it depends where you wear it. At our offices, a lot of women come for French classes and they wear a veil, because there are some Turks, Maghrebi women, African women who veil. What bothers me are the young girls who were born in France, are French, our children who veil.... This bothers me, it bothers me a lot, because they are just children.... I am tolerant, I tolerate everybody.... My interns, I have one who is an educator. She is in her third year, she wears a veil. She is from Mali like me. She came with her CV. We were a little bit surprised, but well, I said to myself, a future educator who wears the veil? But I looked at her CV; she started her internship. And she does a very good job. As long as you do your job well and you are not telling the others what they should do ... but here everybody agreed that there was no reason to pass a law. It's like saying to nuns they cannot wear their head covers.

Mariam both mildly disapproves of young women wearing the veil, and denounces a law that was useless and unfair because it targeted only Muslim women. Her decision to hire a veiled woman as an intern is not presented as a political act of resistance, and she does not hide that she was surprised when she received the application. However, she advocates for a neutral and fair approach based on abilities rather than religious identity. Samira, who is originally from Algeria and runs a grassroots organization for migrant/

racialized women in a northern Parisian suburb, is much more critical than Mariam of veil-wearing girls and women:

> Some girls wear it naturally because they grew up in societies where you wear it at the youngest age. These women, I know very well it might be very hard for them to take it off, but it's not compulsory to wear it. But many girls wear it as a provocation. They consider themselves victims and they add something on top. You just have to take it off to find a job. They are a pain, you see. So it's something I really don't understand. I am full of prejudices on this.... The ones I have met, most of them, they don't really know why they wear it. Some could not find jobs before while they were not wearing it... and it's like they tell themselves, well, I will lock myself up with some social recognition. They switch from unemployed to good practicing Muslim.... I met women who are active in organizations and did a conference on Muslim women's volunteering in civil society; there was a lot of veiled women.... I told myself, it's not possible, all these feminists with veils, what is happening?

Samira's own trajectory is important in understanding her position. She is old enough to have witnessed as an adult, from France, the Algerian civil war in the early 1990s, and the terrorism of the Front Islamique du Salut (FIS) in Algeria. In fact, at the time (1992–1993), she even founded an organization to support democratic and feminist activists from Algeria. She associates veiling with "regression" for women's rights, as has been the case in her home country. While she interprets young Muslim women's decision to veil also as the result of a legitimate "anger," especially against colonization— an anger she admits that she shares—she rejects their strategy of resisting through veiling. Not only does she question the motivation—and religious knowledge—of young Muslim women who veil, she also affirms that she cannot ally with veiled women's associations or allow a veiled woman to sit on the board of her own organization because she is convinced that these women are "antidemocratic" and are not truly in favor of women's emancipation. What is more, she interprets white feminists' position against the 2004 ban on the veil in public schools as a mistake due to their privileged location, as women from the bourgeoisie:

> They came here to put us back on the right track, to explain. They were against the ban and we were in favor of the ban.... I told them: "You are in

your nice little bourgeois neighborhoods in Paris and you want to think in our place." I think that law is crucial, because otherwise a majority of young girls will wear the veil. It will be a catastrophe.

For Samira, class differences are as important as race when it comes to understanding the complexity of the politics of veiling and its regulation by authorities. In this case, and because of her own trajectory, she positioned herself within a common class background with the girls who are targeted by the law (rather than a common racial or religious identity). Her common class position authorizes her both to know what's best for veiled girls in public schools and to refute white bourgeois feminists' analysis objecting to the ban in the name of choice.

In both Mariam's and Samira's accounts of their relationship to Islamic veiling practices and veiled women, one recognizes, in a minor mode, a discourse prevalent in the French sexularism debates and following which girls *born* in France should not veil because this practice denotes a refusal to assimilate and to be fully French.[42] However, this does not mean that they are not critical of racism or that they euphemize the importance of colonial legacies and neocolonial policies in France.

Maleiha, who heads an organization of lesbians of color in Paris, illustrates this paradoxical position, that is, one that strongly rejects Islamic veiling and, at the same time, clearly politicizes the veil bans as racist laws.

> The problem I have is that I am totally against the veil. And I say this while I claim my own Muslim spirituality. . . . I have the chance to know Islam and to critique it from within, and from a Muslim point of view I am against the veil. . . . I am upset, upset. It upsets me because once again these girls . . . claim the right to wear the veil or the niqab, and then they fuel policies that are racist, xenophobic, etc. So our thinking is not settled. . . . I don't think that in the name of fighting racism I will support the demand for segregated swimming pools for veiled women. . . . It's complicated, because I fight against a racist government, and against some feminists . . . because it's true some white feminists are Islamophobic. . . . We denounced the 2004 and 2010 laws, which are xenophobic and racist, not republican and secular. That's very clear. But for the reasons I mentioned, I think feminists of color are trapped. . . . It's very unhealthy because they are against the veil but at the same time they feel obligated to support veiled girls. The line is thin. That's why I haven't yet settled my thinking.

Maleiha's complex position is torn between her understanding of veiling as a form of traditional practice that is not religiously founded and is oppressive to women, and her reading of veil bans as fundamentally racist laws. Her commitment to French secularism clashes with her critique of institutional racism. Interestingly, however, she does not position veiled women at the center of her analysis, contrary to Quebecois racialized feminists. While Mariam is mostly benevolently indifferent to young women who veil, despite her admitted lack of understanding of their motivations, Samira presents them at best as driven by false consciousness and at worst as antifeminist enemies, and Maleiha only reluctantly supports them. In all these instances, veiled women are not presented as active agents or possible feminists. Despite the fact that the three interviewees disapprove of the 2004 and 2010 bans, the needs and rights of veiled women are not put at the center of their critical analysis of the law. These discourses testify to the strength of hegemonic discourses in the French public sphere about secularism as necessary to emancipate women, and about the veil as a sign of oppression.

Sandra, who is younger than the three previous interviewees, offers a different discourse that does not oppose feminism to Islamic veiling. She shares the analysis of veil bans as racist policies and criticizes feminists who oppose veiling. However, while other racialized feminists admit their apprehension or refusal to work with veiled Muslim women or Muslim feminists, Sandra, on the contrary, welcomes such an opportunity, drawing a connection and a political alliance between her own fight against racism and the fight against Islamophobia:

> In our group, on the question of the veil, at the last March 8 women's march we clearly positioned ourselves: we are not at all against the veil and if there are possible events or alliances to do with groups of Muslim women, it will be discussed collectively, but we share the same perspective: it will not be a problem. At the moment, there is so much Islamophobia, including in many [feminist] groups, it seems really difficult to work with these groups. . . . As far as we are concerned, we would really like to welcome veiled Black women in our group, clearly, to support them.

The variety of positions that racialized women activists hold is produced both by the different politics of race and secularism that characterize France and Quebec, and by their individual backgrounds as feminist activists. The Canadian multiculturalist discourse provides racialized feminists in Quebec with a legitimate narrative to critique the government's attempts to regulate and/or partially ban veils or niqabs. By contrast, in France racialized feminists sometimes adhere to some of the hegemonic republican and secular rationale that presents veiling as an oppressive practice incompatible with true belonging to the French nation and its modernity.[43] They therefore sit uneasily between their commitment to feminist emancipation and their critique of the veil bans as racist and neocolonial policies. In this perspective, one can argue, following Françoise Vergès's insight that an important dimension of the coloniality of power is its ability to fragment the subalterns,[44] that veil bans—along with the hegemonic discourses they have produced in the French public sphere—fragment the possible solidarity of racialized populations and racialized feminists. Pitting feminism against religion, in a context in which Islam is heavily racialized, produces a fragmentation of racialized feminists over the veil. It may also produce alliances, as Sandra's case shows, but they have remained, so far, marginal.

Differences in activists' trajectories and their belonging to different micro-cohorts[45] also matter to understand these various discourses on Islamic veiling. Activists who are older, especially those with ties to Algeria or Iran, tend to remain very critical of veiling practices. For young activists coming of age as feminists in France in the 1980s or early 1990s, veiling was not really a desirable or possible option. The practice was much less prevalent, and their route toward feminism, given the scarcity of racialized feminists organizations at that time, often was through participation in white feminist groups, as I detail below. In this context of relative absence of Black or Islamic feminism, their "sense of social location"—to borrow Jo Reger's expression[46]—is marked by a dominant white feminist discourse, inherited from the 1970s, that presents religion as incompatible with women's rights. The situation of younger racialized feminists such as Sandra, who came of age as feminists in the 2010s—that is, at a moment in which the ideological discourse of Black feminism and the critique of Islamophobia were much more available in the French public sphere—is that of a different micro-cohort who, "although sharing a set of experiences that largely aligns with the overall ethos of the generation, experience some significant differences in ideology, identity, or goals."[47] In Quebec, activists from Algeria also tend to be more critical of the veil than their South Asian counterparts, suggesting here again that their political subjectivation as feminists did not happen in similar ways. In this case, the politics of language matters. Indeed, South Asian feminists are mostly anglophone and therefore endorse the multiculturalist Canadian discourse, contrary to francophone feminists from the Maghreb (often educated in French schools in their home countries) who identify more easily with Quebec's nationalist discourse and its corollary critique of multiculturalism.

As for white feminists, debates over Islamic veiling have thus produced new forms of political subjectivations among racialized feminists. As those debates have transformed the political vocabulary about race and postcoloniality in both contexts, opening up avenues for new forms of injurious racist and nationalist discourses, they have provided racialized feminists with new issues to address, new realities to contest. They have led, as the case of Sandra shows, to new forms of politicization of the articulation of race and religion and to a displacement of the boundaries of the good and bad feminist subjects. While for some racialized feminists, the Islamic veil remains the marker of an impossible authentic feminist subject, for the vast majority of others, especially in younger generations, the Islamic veil reveals the problematic boundaries of the feminist subject, its foreclosure around whiteness and its ignorance of its own postcolonial legacy. The desire to include veiled women in Sandra's collective thus expresses not only a political will for inclusion, but also a desire for relationality with those supposedly abject feminist subjects, a will and a wish to expand the boundaries of feminism's moral universe and its promise of treating equally its members. Such a moral desire strikes at the heart of the feminist project of emancipation, a project it proposes to dismantle, or at least to critically question. Indeed, Sandra reflects in those terms on the feminist promise of emancipation

> What is emancipation? . . . It goes back to a simple question: well, is a woman free to choose how she dresses, what she wears? . . . There is this paternalist impulse. We want to save them, but to save them from what exactly? That questions us, to save them from what? From big bearded machos? So . . . the problem behind this is, what type of feminism do we want? . . . A paternalist feminism, or maternalism, that is moralizing but is not mindful of the trajectories, the histories of those persons, those women's histories? . . . It puzzles me.

Sandra's puzzlement manifests her radical questioning of feminism's ambition to emancipate female subjects. Her practice of questioning, which leaves the answer open, expresses her ability to remain critical of the feminist project, all the while she defines herself a feminist. This questioning enables a nonclosure of the feminist subject that becomes hospitable to "bad" subjects such as veiled Muslim women and prostitutes. Importantly, this critical return on feminism's ideals is made possible by a distinction Sandra makes between moral *principles*, and a form of moral pragmatism, one attentive to singular stories and histories. This opposition opens up a moral space to think the *who* of the feminist subject in different terms. I return to this issue in the next chapter.

Racialized and immigrant feminists both strongly adhere to feminist principles that are shared by white feminists—such as the idea that women should choose for themselves and that a proper feminist intervention should not impose specific choices on women, even if they are in a vulnerable situation—and, at the same time, they often argue that a common cultural or immigrant background is necessary to rightly perform this feminist intervention with other racialized/immigrant women. This discourse clearly positions them both within the ambit of feminism, a term and an approach they claim for themselves, and in a position to resist and contest the domination of white feminists in this field. However, differences are also perceptible in the ways in which racialized and immigrant feminists politicize their racial and immigrant identities.[48] These differences show that the context of each country's politics of race deeply impacts feminist discourses and identities. What is more, belonging to different micro-cohorts and working in an organization that is more oriented toward service provision or consciousness raising also impact how they conceptualize the intersection of gender and race.[49] However, and despite these variations, racialized feminists also develop similar narratives, accounts of themselves as racialized feminists, narratives in which they resist and challenge feminist whiteness.

Becoming Feminist in a White Space

Racialized feminists in France and Quebec have come to call themselves feminists through various paths depending on their immigrant or native background, their generation, and the context in which they became politically active. However, they all have encountered the whiteness of mainstream and dominant feminist movements. These encounters shape their activism as racialized feminists and the ways in which they politicize their racial or immigrant identities as feminists. What is more, they develop counterdiscourses and practices to contest and resist the whiteness that characterizes dominant feminist discourses—especially those feminist discourses that aim at regulating their identity. They challenge in particular their marginalization in terms of representation, using intersectionality to claim visibility and representation as racialized feminists; they challenge the collusion between feminism and nationalism; and, finally, they resist white feminists' attempts to fetishize their racial difference. All these processes, which constitute, following Paola Bacchetta's insights, circuits of resistance,[50] shape racialized feminists' identities, as well as their active disidentification with white feminists. In that perspective, the political subjectivations of racialized feminists attest to the importance of collective action as an avenue toward challenging subordination.

As Amy Allen notes in her discussion of Judith Butler's account of psychic subjection, an account that insists on the idea that subjection implies the attachment of the subordinated subject to its own subordination: "What is missing is the realization that a possible way out of this attachment to subjection lies in collective social experimentation and political transformation."[51] Racialized feminists' narratives precisely illustrate how giving an account of oneself as a racialized feminist, rather than as a feminist, constitutes a collective political experimentation that challenges feminist whiteness and the subordination it perpetuates.

Racialized/immigrant activists have come to call themselves feminists through different paths. Giving an account of oneself as a feminist is the product of a process of political subjectivation; that is, the elaboration of a specific relationship to oneself, made possible in a given context that provides discourses that sustain, and norms that constrain, this identity. The practice of calling oneself a feminist is, by definition and like other ethical practices, also an exercise in social critique that exposes the limits of norms historically produced. As Judith Butler argues, following Foucault, any practice of subjectivation is a creative practice of self-constitution because "To make oneself in such a way that one exposes those limits is precisely to engage in an aesthetics of the self that maintains a critical relation to existing norms."[52] The process of political subjectivation as a feminist is both the elaboration of a specific relationship to oneself that politicizes one's gender identity, and a relationship to the world that becomes critical of social/gender norms. For racialized/immigrant feminists, this process of subjectivation as a feminist is intimately tied to their racialized identity and their position as a *minority subject within* feminist discourse.

Three different generations of French racialized feminists describe quite a similar story of exclusion and invisibility in white feminist spaces as they came of age as feminists, and their need to organize among racialized women to counter this invisibility. However, each of these women belongs to a different micro-cohort, and therefore the discourses and possibilities to self-organize varied for each of them. Samira, the oldest, is in her late forties. Born in France of Algerian descent, she was socialized and politicized as a feminist through her encounter in the early 1990s with radical feminists who had been part of the Mouvement de libération des femmes (Women's Liberation Movement, MLF) and often of the Communist Revolutionary League as well. While she praises the women she encountered as true radical feminists, she questions their sense of solidarity and their heavily Marxist ideological framework. Hence, despite participating in meetings at the Maison des femmes, the iconic feminist space inherited from the MLF in Paris, she felt a great gap between her own trajectory and the socialization within this group. While Samira recalls she had already read Simone de Beauvoir and Benoîte Groult, and that she found some themes really interesting, she felt unease and a sense of violence during these meetings.

> There was such a gap between my desire to become involved in some feminist activity. . . . If you like, these women from the Maison des femmes, they scared me. They are feminist and reject everything that is feminine. . . . They were so negative about heterosexuality. They were so very politicized. Honestly, I did not know what the Communist Revolutionary League was. When you don't know and you want to discover, you really feel a great violence in words, expressions. It freezes you. I found their opinion like a sword that did not leave any place for exchange. . . . I think they were open to all women, except that all women did not find their place in this organization, did not feel welcome. But well, they are political activists, after all.

Samira's reaction to the politicized and radical feminist discourses directly inherited from the 1970s struggles shows how generation and the "sense of location" matter: the set of experiences that have socialized these activists and Samira are radically different. In this context, she feels alienated; and what is for the MLF activists a common and obvious feminist vocabulary is received by Samira as a form of violence. In the early 1990s, while MLF feminists were still active (mostly in their forties and fifties), there were not many feminist organizations run by younger women who had not been part of the MLF. Samira's choice was therefore limited. However, this feeling of a generational and political gap was reinforced by an experience that framed

Samira's understanding of the limits of feminist solidarity across class and racial boundaries. Indeed, she recalls:

> At the time, I lived in the Parisian suburbs, and I had to commute through all Paris [to come to meetings]. I had more than an hour on public transport, and one night I stayed late, and at half past midnight I did not have any public transport, nothing. And that's when I thought: it's funny because they talk about solidarity, but none of them was concerned that I had to commute back, and that I had no public transport.... And that's when I thought, you political activists, you really are bitches. You talk about international solidarity with women who suffer in the world and you did not even notice that I had a problem.

Samira contrasts MLF feminists' abstract desire to care for remote others, "women in the world," and their inability to care about a concrete other, because they actively ignore the complex class and racial difference that lies between them and shapes their relation. In Samira's story MLF feminists appear unable to take into account this difference in their practice of solidarity. This experience explains why, when Samira encountered a woman from Morocco who had founded an organization for women of immigrant descent, she suddenly felt the desire to get involved.

In the mid-2000s, Maleiha encounters a different situation in the radical lesbian feminist movement in Paris. Maleiha characterizes her position, and that of other lesbians of color, at the time as a "contradictory experience of exclusion and inclusion in the LGBT milieu and the feminist milieu," an experience that encouraged her to develop a strategy of separation from white lesbians. Indeed, in the early 2000s Maleiha had first founded a group with white lesbians and lesbians of color to fight against discrimination. However, this group proved limited in its ability to provide a space in which lesbians of color could recognize themselves without having to decide on a hierarchy between the oppressions they wanted to address.

> First, it was not based on an intersectional approach because there were white members, obviously. And whites who were part of the organization said that they were aware of racism from white women, which they wanted to fight. But where it got complicated is that as soon as we wanted to dig deeper to analyze racism and its consequences ... discriminations, lack of interest for the memory of people of color, etc., well, we could not discuss

in a coherent way with white women. I don't mean it was impossible, but we could not deepen our analysis with people who were not concerned. We were concerned as [women] of color because we suffer these oppressions. They don't. So, I thought, we cannot continue to think about racism together with this logic. We need a more specific group.

Maleiha's experience was shaped by a new context in the French feminist movement. New organizations appeared at the end of the 1990s and a group of lesbians of color, the Groupe du 6 novembre, had already produced its own analyses and translated some work from American Black feminists.[53] Moreover, starting a few years into the twenty-first century, translations in French of seminal works on intersectionality and feminism of color started to appear, as well as the diffusion of French research adopting an intersectional perspective.[54] The context was therefore more favorable to an analysis based on a conception of intersectionality that encouraged a separation from white feminists as an important step. While Maleiha did not denounce feminist whiteness as an active form of racism or complete exclusion in the LGBT milieu, she felt that feminist whiteness meant a form of indifference and distance from white feminist lesbians vis-à-vis issues that were, for her and other lesbians of color, crucial to their understanding of their experience and their identity as feminists and lesbians.

A decade after Maleiha, Sandra encountered yet another context, and she constitutes with other fellow Afro-feminists another micro-cohort of racialized feminists in Paris. Here again, her feminist identity as a racialized feminist who politicizes race and gender is not a given or the natural product of her experience, but the result of a process by which she has come to politicize, as interrelated, experiences of racism and sexism, and through which she has encountered a collective identity and feminist discourses that can sustain this account of herself as an Afro-feminist. In her twenties in the 2010s, Sandra encountered feminist discourses and Black feminism at university during her work toward a master's degree. This encounter with feminism not through activism first but through academic knowledge testifies to the transformation of French academia after the turn of the century and the incorporation of gender studies in academic programs, fueling a new generation of feminist identifications. What is more, that same year the law enabling gay marriage in France was discussed and intensely contested by the Catholic right wing, prompting intense politicization not only of LGBT rights but also of gender politics.[55]

In this context Sandra became aware of many feminist and LGBT organizations. However:

> Rapidly, as I got involved in these spaces, I became aware that there were very few nonwhite or racialized persons, and it's true I found it intriguing. ... And still issues of gender matter for us, issues of sexuality as well, so from then on I started asking myself questions, and rapidly in feminist spaces I realized that when it was time to address issues of racism, the question of race, there was a blockage, as in movements that are really leftist, that give a priority to class struggle that will liberate us all.

Sandra's experience in a way joins that of Samira, as she also encountered a strong leftist ideological framework and discourse that did not leave room to analyze racism, testifying to the ability of this political trend to sustain itself over time in the French political space.[56] What is more, Sandra's account also suggests that Marxist-oriented leftist organizations are particularly inimical political settings for racialized women.[57] In this context, Sandra felt literally voiceless:

> I did not question them because, truth be told, in these spaces I did not talk; that is, I observed a lot. I was starting to get involved and it felt complicated to express myself and take the floor.

Sandra's voicelessness manifests how, in those white spaces, she could not find an adequate expression for her own political subjectivity. The language of feminism as it is elaborated and conveyed in those spaces does not provide her with the possibility of finding her voice through this language, to participate in this community of locutors. Here, we are reminded of Stanley Cavell's and Sandra Laugier's analysis of language and voice: we are in agreement in language, that is, our agreement in language makes a *we* possible and, at the same time, makes my own voice possible.[58] In order for my voice to exist, to be found, it must be recognized and spoken by others, and my words accepted by them.[59] For Sandra to find her voice, as she later describes in her interview, she needed to share a language with others, a collective voice and a collective identity: Afro-feminism.

The unease and ethical violence Sandra felt is similar to that described by Samira, of getting involved but still feeling that one does not fit, that one's voice finds no place in the language that is shared by the feminist community.

A specific incident marked, for Sandra, the necessity to organize collectively as racialized feminists without white feminists:

> Once I had the chance to participate in a consciousness-raising group [*groupe de parole*] on intersectionality in a lesbian and trans bar in Paris where nonwhite, racialized persons had made the choice to organize a group in which white persons could not talk. . . . I was struck by the fact that despite the guidelines that were given, white people expressed themselves with discourse like, "I feel uneasy about this talk about race and racism. I don't understand why you are so . . . with your hair. Why you don't like it when we comment on the fact we like your hair?" . . . I told myself, this is really a serious problem, and I was impressed by racialized persons who took the floor and said they were fed up with explaining again and like, "First, you cannot talk because these are the guidelines, and beyond these, exoticization, you see, does not come from nowhere. Touching our hair, there is a history, and how come you have the guts to say this here when we are trying to do something interesting"—in a space where we deconstruct, a space that presents itself as willing to fight any form of racism, LGBTphobia. . . . That was the most memorable experience for me and I realized that in the end the issue of race, whiteness, was not at all questioned. . . . And that's when I started to have this feminist consciousness, and I wanted to affirm myself as a feminist, and rapidly I discovered blogs by Black women, like *Mrs Roots, miss Dreadfull*.

Sandra admits that it took her some time to call herself a feminist, in part because this form of political subjectivation is not recognized in her cultural community, and for her feminism remained "something white." While she admits she could have used another word than "feminism," she thinks the word should not be left to others and claims it as hers. Her coming of age as a feminist happens in a context in which consciousness-raising groups of feminists of color are a recognized (although still contested by white feminists) form of feminist practice, texts are available through academic training and, more importantly, blogs; and a first feminist documentary film on the experience of Afro-descendant women in France is being shot by an Afro-feminist activist and artist, Amandine Gay, giving visibility to the experience of women like Sandra.[60] In this context, Sandra does not invest primarily in feminist spaces with white feminists, like Maleiha did for several years. She observes the absence of racialized persons in these groups and rapidly decides to organize collectively with other Afro-feminists. Contrary to two decades earlier, this mode of organizing is self-evident; it has become an available repertoire of organization for racialized feminists, in part through the diffusion of texts from American feminists of color, and through the production of blogs and texts from French Afro-feminists.

These three trajectories of becoming a racialized feminist in a white space show how different contexts shape different micro-cohorts of racialized feminists who do not politicize race in the exact same ways. However, they do share the experience of exclusion from white feminist discourses and spaces, an exclusion that is felt as a silencing or a feeling of not being welcomed and recognized, of not "fitting" into the preexisting white feminist discourse.

Claiming Representation and Challenging Whiteness

An important way in which racialized feminists resist feminist whiteness is by claiming self-representation and visibility within the feminist movement. This means both privileging self-organizing to self-represent and using intersectionality discourse to claim adequate visibility and representation within the broader feminist movement. Sandra insists that separation from both men in the African diaspora community and white women was a very important principle in forming her organization, in order to "claim back [their] own voices." Maleiha describes a similar process in which the members of her organization wanted to come together "without self-justification, to decide our actions, our reflections, our analyses, our struggles, with organizational autonomy from a political point of view, and a better consistency with our lives and claims with respect to intersecting oppressions." The need and desire to self-organize seems to operate along the same lines throughout the decades represented by these women. Soraya, a Muslim feminist activist in her thirties who emigrated from the Middle East to Montreal as a child, was part of a committee of racialized women in a mainstream Quebecois feminist organization. She explains why she now desires to create her own group with only racialized feminists after having experienced on several occasions how white feminists she knew personally "forgot" to invite Muslim feminists to events regarding the Charter of Quebecois Values promoted by the government, which is a primary concern for Muslim feminists because of its secular, anti-religious-symbols approach:

We don't pretend to create something that will compete with mainstream organizations, but what has been important in this experience, even if it was painful, is to realize, as many racialized women before us, many Black women that (sigh) there is this idea that if you don't participate in recognized, institutional white spaces, you don't work. But it's not true. . . . In big mainstream organizations your work is short term, in damage control mode, reacting to crisis, as always when it comes to Muslim activists. . . . But instead of working against something, we will start working for something, and that something is us.

Sandra's words, in Paris, echo Soraya's in Montreal. Assessing the changes that the creation of her Afro-feminist organization brought, she insists on the ability to self-represent collectively to articulate her own feminist discourse that she can now voice:

Now we take the floor, we voice, and I think that is the power of this kind of project. . . . Until then you did not talk. . . . The fact of having a collective group, to do things together—in fact, our organization is about giving each other power. I think that is what feminism is about, giving each other power, and when you don't have it anymore, another sister can give it to you, and that's good.

Here again, the voice appears in Sandra's discourse, not so much as a metaphor but as the material embodiment of her political subjectivation as an Afro-feminist, a political subjectivation that is made possible through the constitution of a collective subject. This collective subject enacts a form of care, giving to one another, which is lived as powerful and is a materialization of feminism as a form of life.[61] This will to self-organize and self-represent is also presented as a way to ensure the representation of racialized women's voice within the women's movement, forcing white feminists to acknowledge their presence and their discourse. Liz, who runs an organization of Filipina women in Montreal, explains why she created this organization:

The idea is to have . . . to be visible, for our groups to be visible. For example, the issue of domestic workers, the issue of the minimum wage, was not supported by the main feminist organizations. And then, on the International Women's Day, we were kind of invited. . . . So you sit on the chair and you never hear us. The idea was to be out and to present what our problems are because nobody else will talk about them except us.

Not only did she create her own organization, starting in the 2000s she organized with other racialized women's groups their own demonstration for International Women's Day. Her colleague Mary recalls:

> There was one year that we really became disillusioned with the women's movement in Quebec. We were ignored as immigrant women, ethnic community women . . . and besides, we want to represent ourselves, not a white woman representing us, because you know it's like being a system of patriarchy. It's the authority who has the voice, not us. It will remain like that if we don't bring up our voice.

Mary's explanation of how racialized women's groups came together to organize their own march shows how self-representation also means visibility inside the women's movement, which is understood as a place of power relations that needs to be challenged collectively. Similarly, in France, Maleiha recalls the motivation to create her own group of lesbians of color in Paris:

> The objective was for lesbians of color . . . to reinforce our visibility in terms of analysis, of struggle, in terms of the specificities in the LGBT milieu and in the feminist milieu, to enable a space of expression and autonomous struggle for lesbians of color, to fight against racism and invisibilization.

For racialized/immigrant feminists, the claim to self-represent is intimately linked with a challenge to the whiteness of the movement. Self-organizing is a way to challenge white hegemony in feminist discourses and feminist practices. Paola, who runs a South Asian women's organization in Montreal, explains why she allied with other racialized women's groups in Montreal such as Liz's to organize their own march of racialized and immigrant women on International Women's Day. Interestingly, this march was later on recognized as the official event for International Women's Day by the Quebecois Women's Federation.

> For many years, there was a women's March 8 event [organized by mainstream women's rights organizations] and then that stopped, but the unions, the big unions often had something and would bring their members from

the region and big trucks and balloons. But it was very white; we said, we need to have a women's event that represents, you know, all kind of women, and that's why we chose the name "diverse origins," class, race, age, etc.

For racialized/immigrant feminists, the concept of intersectionality is used to combine the struggle against patriarchy with the struggle against racism and to unveil whiteness and privileges. While for white feminists it was a tool for intercultural feminist intervention and a tool to try to account for differences between women and to attempt inclusion in practice, for racialized feminists it is a claim for the representation of their interests and analyses, a means to challenge whiteness and its privileges. Maleiha explains:

> The LGBT milieu and the feminist milieu in general as well, it's really a milieu which is very white. As long as they haven't elaborated a solid reflection, and acknowledged that they have privileges as whites, they won't understand the intersectional approach and intersectional claim. That's what we bring.

Challenging whiteness in the feminist movement means also redefining some of its principles and priorities, first and foremost refuting the idea that gender oppression can be tackled on its own, independently from other relations of power. Mary, a Filipina activist in Montreal, explains how her organization understands its feminist commitment as articulated with other struggles rather than independent:

> Our goal is to push for workers. That's the majority of our constituents. Class first . . . our members need their class conditions to change, but they are feminists. It's another idea about feminism. Their condition as women . . . we fight to change it. This condition comes from exploitation based on gender, but also exploitation from social condition, race, class. But we also struggle. . . . We want the men from the same social condition to support us, because if we divide we cannot go forward.

In Quebec, the majority of racialized/immigrant women's grassroots organizations stress the fact that they do not exclude men from their struggle and practice. They often accept that men accompany their spouses to their offices for consultation, a practice that is not tolerated by mainstream Quebecois feminist organizations and has raised tensions between racialized feminists and white feminists. Indeed, in Quebec most feminist community centers are part of a network, l'R des femmes, which has a common charter of principles (called a basis of political unity) that all organizations have to adopt. In return, they are granted the status of member and can benefit from government funding. In the charter the presence of men in women's centers is forbidden. Mani, an activist at a South Asian women's center in her late fifties who is Indian-Canadian and grew up in Montreal, recalls the discussion on this issue with white feminist organizations:

> Yes, [the basis of unity] has three things that you need to do: you have to lobby the government, you have to educate your members, and the last thing . . . , I used to know it by heart, I would be like, "Yes, we do all those things!" And they would always say, "Don't let the men in," and I would always, like me and the Italian women and the Greek women, we would all go, "We serve women and their families. We don't see a woman outside her family context because the culture does not allow it." But they [men] are not allowed to vote, they're not allowed to be members and are not allowed to speak at meetings, which is very hard for them. They have to sit at the edge and just shut up, and wait until their wives are finished. They mostly don't come.

Not only does Mani refute the idea that what white Quebecois feminists define as proper feminist intervention is applicable to her organization and her community, she also challenges the idea that white feminists "invented" feminist practice. She explains that her organization had been doing what is prescribed in the basis of political unity long before it was formalized for white feminist organizations in Quebec: "lobby the government, which we did anyways, . . . provide front-line services to women in abusive relationships and help them get out, and educate their members. We were always doing all those things. We could have written that basis of political unity even before they thought of it. We did all those things in the mid-1980s!" This statement challenges the pervasive tale of the white origins of feminism that always presents white organizations as the precursors and pioneers of the movement. Mani also challenges the idea implicitly promoted by the white Quebecois feminist discourse that whiteness is the norm and that white women represent all women, contrary to racialized women who are not perceived as representing all women.[62] In the end, Mani managed to convince her interlocutors to accept her organization in the network so it could access provincial funding. However, she continuously challenged their whiteness. Similarly, when Mani was sent as a representative of her organization to assemblies and boards of the Quebecois federation of women's rights (FFQ), she fought to unveil the fake universalism of white Quebecois feminist claims.

> So a big part of this was me arguing at meetings all the time that groups like ours should be considered mainstream, right? Like if you have a South Asian women's center and it has a feminist mandate and does political lobbying and helps women in sometimes very difficult situations, in their language it's not marginal. . . . Everybody would always say we are an ethno-specific center. It was the same with the network of community centers. That was tricky because they would say you have to be accessible to all women, and they would always say, "You are only for women from South Asia."

During meetings with the FFQ in the 1990s, as she constantly confronted unacknowledged privileges and white women posing as the norm and as owners of Quebecois feminism, Mani invented a term, forged after the term "WASP," to challenge their assumptions frontally:

> When they would say, *notre pays* [our country] or *nous autres pis vous autres* [you people and us people], whenever they were really unaware of that, I would say, "When you say, 'us people,' you mean CFCB?" And they would say, "What is CFCB?" [I'd answer,] "Canadiennes Françaises Catholiques Blanches [White French-Canadian Catholic Women]." They really hated it (*laughs*). They would be really insulted, but I think these women got the point: if you have a label for us, you just gonna have to accept we have a label for you. Why don't we stop using labels at all, but you have to stop first cause you started first!

By self-organizing and by challenging assumptions about feminist principles, racialized feminists unveil whiteness, and resist its various manifestations. However, the ability to challenge whiteness within a mainstream setting varies in Quebec and France. Indeed, in Quebec, racialized/immigrant feminist organizations have been organized on an ethnic/immigrant basis for decades and are recognized as such by the government. They have always engaged critically with the mainstream white organization that associates all women's rights organizations in the province, the FFQ, both by participating on its board, as Mani did for years, and by setting up their own march for International Women's Day, which means having a network for racialized/immigrant women's organizations. This strategy of both inclusion and separation has sometimes proved exhausting and disappointing because the FFQ has not always reacted promptly to racialized feminists' demands. However, it testifies to a possibility for punctual—and sometimes more lasting—alliances. This strategy is in part made possible by the fact that the FFQ itself allows racialized women to caucus during its meeting to elaborate their own propositions. This alliance with mainstream white women's organizations is perceived as demanding by Paola, but also necessary to promote her organization's political agenda:

> When we are trying to confront the government position on honor crime or forced marriage, it's very significant that the FFQ takes a position because they're speaking for all the women of Quebec, so for us I see that as very significant.

Hence, despite disappointments regarding the pace of change in the FFQ, racialized women's organizations manage to have alliances that are seen as productive. In France, by contrast, resisting whiteness and challenging white feminist organizations' agenda means mostly voicing an external critique and organizing among racialized feminists, for example, in the context of the alternate International Women's Day march, which is held in another part of Paris than the "official" march organized by the World March of Women. The organization of separate marches testifies to the very limited possibilities for alliances between white feminist organizations and racialized feminists who voice a critique of whiteness in the feminist movement. This critique is often articulated by advocacy or consciousness-raising groups rather than by organizations that provide services to racialized/migrant women. Indeed, for the latter the situation is different: they are often part of networks or federations (of shelters or community centers) and therefore engaged in practical collaborations with white feminists. For them, confronting white feminists about their privileges seems almost impossible, as Mariam testifies about a recent event at which the head of a white women's organization was rewarded with a medal of honor by the regional council:

We have been around for more than twenty years. We had to get by, volunteering.... When I see this medal of honor thing... it hurts. You work like a dog, you work, you go to demonstrations . . . flyers, you are active. You fight, you get insulted, and they get the medal. The federation gets the medal, and the federation, it's white women. . . . When I started I did not believe it, but it's been twenty years I work in this field. I noticed it's always the domination of white women over Black women. We were colonized in Africa and this colonization continues here, even if it's veiled. . . . Nobody talks about it. The person who talks gets excluded.

Mariam's analysis reflects the pervasiveness of racism within French feminism and the power of whiteness in a context in which it is not legitimate to politicize race. The privileges attached to whiteness are impossible to challenge, and voicing critique means being sidelined, from organizational networks and related funding. While Mani could confront her white feminist peers in the context of collaboration in a coalition, Mariam cannot voice her concerns and critiques to the white feminists she works with and who run bigger and better-funded women's rights organizations in her city and region. Here again, the difference between Quebec and France highlights the ways in which the politics of race in each context shapes racialized feminists' opportunities and constraints in their attempt to challenge and resist whiteness within the feminist movement.

Challenging Nationalism, Resisting Fetishization

In Quebec, challenging the whiteness of the Quebecois women's movement means also challenging its nationalism. Indeed, many grassroots women's rights organizations that have been institutionalized through government-funded networks, as well as the Quebecois umbrella organization (the FFQ), have tended to define themselves through their francophone identity and as partners or allies of the Quebecois nationalist movement. In particular, since the 1990s the FFQ has deepened its links with the Parti Québécois,[63] the Quebecois sovereigntist party, and has advocated for Quebec's sovereignty as a means to realize the feminist society it is fighting for. Racialized Quebecois feminist activists, who are often of migrant background and do not all have French as their mother tongue, have been critical of the nationalism that is implicit in many women's rights organizations' discourses and practices. They have criticized the dominance of French inside women's rights organizations when most immigrant women speak another language as their mother tongue, sometimes English. For years, racialized/migrant women's organizations have asked that all the documents produced by the FFQ be produced in French and in English, without much success. Mary, who volunteers in a Filipina domestic workers organization, recalls how, in the 1990s, her organization fought with the FFQ about language in the context of the organization of a broad movement against women's poverty throughout Quebec:

> We worked so hard, but nothing was being put forward of our issues. We had meetings. . . . The thing was the language barrier, you know. They were so strict in the meetings not to, to do the meeting in French, so how can we, the minority, understand what is being said?

Of course, language is one of the vehicles of Quebecois nationalism. Mani, a colleague of Paola, recalls her meetings at the FFQ board in the 1990s and their position on this issue. She explained to white Quebecois feminists her organization's position in these terms:

> You need to realize that the centers you have built, which are great, cannot serve these women because these women don't speak French! And you guys don't even speak English. How can you help them? It was a huge battle. I got so tired cause I had to say the same thing at the same meetings. . . . The FFQ is a clique kind of organization. It's very political and nationalist, and because we are not at all nationalist in the Quebecois sense—we are federalist—so each time they would say something nationalist, I would say something, I would be a dissenting voice. But I was not speaking for me, I was speaking for my group, I was always representing my group. I would always have to say, "On est pas d'accord. Je veux que ça soit sur le rapport" [We don't agree. I want this noted in the report]. "Oh, okay, right."

Racialized feminists also critique what they perceive as a tendency of French-speaking Quebecois feminists to take on the role of the victim (as francophone Quebecois who have been oppressed by the power of the English-speaking elite in Canada)[64] without scrutinizing the ways in which they might as well contribute to relations of oppression. Soraya comments on this tendency:

It's race, it's the Quebecois people, it's impossible.... There is a discourse of exceptionalism, of total and exclusive appropriation of the label of victim. Nobody else can be a victim because Quebecois, and *Québécoises* in particular, it's impossible for them to share this. The nationalist discourse is really one of "We are the ones who have been oppressed and it's unimaginable that we may be oppressors now."

Soraya analyses the nationalist discourse as a protection that white feminists use against accusations of racism and exclusion. This hegemonic discourse sustains feminist whiteness as a position of invisibilized privilege by making the identity of victim still available to white Quebecois feminists, despite the historical changes that have happened since the 1980s. The inability of white Quebecois feminists to recognize the complexity of the power relations they participate in is supported by their political commitment to Quebecois nationalism. In that sense, Quebecois nationalism works like a powerful legitimizing discourse by which Quebecois feminism is made white. It fuels an epistemology of ignorance that blinds white Quebecois feminists to other forms of oppression, in a way similar to what republican values and secularism have done in France,[65] providing hegemonic discourses that obscure inequalities *inside* the national territory.

Another important way in which racialized/immigrant feminists resist whiteness is by resisting postcolonial fetishization of Black bodies. Indeed, as Franz Fanon captured,[66] race power relations work in part through processes of fetishization of nonwhite bodies, bodies made vulnerable to racist injuries.[67] Both in France and in Quebec racialized feminist activists recall moments in which they have refused this process of fetishization, thereby putting a halt to the ongoing, power-infused postcolonial racialization that is projected onto them by white feminists. Sandra recalls her participation in a demonstration to celebrate the forty-year anniversary of the law decriminalizing abortion in Paris, and the tension she felt with white feminists during the march:

> Exoticization, it also exists in activist spaces, and with our Afro-feminist signs, we encountered attitudes that we felt were totally out of place, discourses, for example people telling us that we were beautiful ... like "Girls, you're beautiful!" So we did not really understand, that's not possible. And this hymn, this song about women that played a lot during the demonstration ... this parallel between the history of slavery, that is about

Black peoples, and the parallel with women, that's a problem, when they say they are the Black continent, we really did not feel at ease.

Sandra presents the creation of her Afro-feminist group as a precise response to this type of event, a way to voice her own claims on her own terms and to resist the postcolonial fetishization that is still going on in feminist activist spaces and which reproduces the colonial gaze onto nonwhite bodies. This racial fetishization operates in a typical postcolonial manner, linking the colonial past to the present, imposing on racialized bodies racialized markers from colonial times.[68] Sandra's critique of the women's hymn[69] recalls the debate in the United States on the comparison between women and Black people during the 1970s (and reactivated in the context of slut walks, and in particular the one in New York City).[70] However, in France, it was only in the 2010s that a similar critique could finally emerge, thanks to the self-organizing of Afro-feminists.

Similarly, in Quebec, Soraya recalls how she managed to resist fetishization during a conference panel she organized on Islamic feminism in Montreal in 2015. After her presentation about women participating in Quebecois mosques, a white feminist asked her about "the difficulties that Muslim women face in mosques." Soraya analyzes the dynamic of the following exchange with this white feminist:

> You know, it's porn, it's porn about Muslim women's oppression. It's voyeurism. I just told her, "It's not original you know, madam, it's not exotic. It's sexism, basic misogyny. I don't need to go further. Apply what you know in your own context and you will find the same thing." And you know for me it was an intense moment because I refused to go into the terrain of "Give us Scheherazade histories of Muslim women oppressions."

In this pivotal moment, Soraya, who was in a position to define the rules of the interaction because she organized the panel and sat on it, had the means to stop the process of fetishization and to reframe the discussion in the terms she chose. As she explains, the problem of participating in white feminist institutions, such as the conference she mentions, is that instead of developing her own reflections, she spends her time doing "popular education" to prove that "yes, you can be feminist and Muslim." On this occasion, she could, however, change the terms of the debate by refusing to engage in a fruitless discussion that fetishizes Muslim women and their oppression.

Racialized feminists in Quebec and France resist whiteness through various strategies and discourses. They contest exclusion by organizing on their own, both to elaborate their own claims—claims that give as much importance to gender oppression as to racial oppression—and to become visible in the eyes of white feminists. By self-organizing, they ensure their representation inside the feminist movement. Challenging the whiteness of other feminist organizations means often calling into question their priorities, making race and racism visible, critiquing the implicit nationalist bias and resisting fetishization. These strategies demonstrate that racialized feminists are not outside of the mainstream white women's movement. Rather they occupy the political position of a minority, a position of insider dissent that relentlessly proposes to reframe what "true" feminism should be. Doing so, they constantly displace the boundaries of the "good" and the "bad" feminist subject, expanding the moral and political horizon of the feminist project as it is defined by many white feminists. In that sense, racialized feminists' strategies aim both at constituting their own constituency and configuring their own collective identity, and at challenging whiteness, which means reformulating feminism in new terms. By doing so, racialized feminists are addressing white feminists in political and moral terms about their definition of feminism and of the collective feminist subject. This address is often rooted in experiences of failed coalition and failed promises of inclusion, and it therefore expresses itself in the form of resentment and of political emotions such as indignation, frustration, or pain.

Resentment and the Failed Promises of Equality

As several previous quotations have made clear, racialized feminists' discourses are often rife with emotions: anger, frustration, tiredness, indignation, uneasiness, and pain. These emotions are rooted in political and ethical grounds. They express the difficulties that arise when one is put in a minority position, forced to articulate her claims with a language that has been forged by others to express another consciousness and another sensitivity, that of a hegemonic and empty universal norm.[71] As Paola Bacchetta suggests, using a Foucauldian lens to analyze the coformation of lesbians of color groups in Paris, these minoritized political subjects are created as an effect of the power exerted over them and, principally, through resistance to this power.[72] This resistance can be oppositional or centered on the creation of a collective identity, but, for Bacchetta, what matters is that subjects are coformed; formed through a variety of processes of circulation of power. These subjects are an effect of power but still remain in the process of being formed and reformed through their resistance. While her approach captures the process of political subjectivation as both an effect of power relations and of the resistance to these relations, it does not, however, consider these relations as also moral relations.

I argue here that the emotions expressed by racialized feminists are certainly an expression of their resistance to power, as Bacchetta suggests, but should *also* be interpreted as moral demands. While certainly the emotions and discourses of racialized feminists denote their resistance to power—as it manifests itself in patriarchy, racism, and heteronormativity—and the simultaneous affirmation of their collective identities through this resistance, these emotions and discourses also manifest, I argue, a certain form of relationality with white feminists that is not reducible to an effect of power. Racialized feminists contest the various forms of political and ethical violence that they are submitted to by the hegemony of feminist whiteness. However, they also make claims that white feminists acknowledge relationality, that is, their participation in the feminist collective subject.

Demands for recognition from oppressed minorities and the resentment—*ressentiment*—that they express are often interpreted, in a Nietzschean fashion, as demands for the recognition of a fixed identity or of an injury, that is, as demands for revenge that in fact may repeat the injury and transform it into a desirable identity, although one that is locked in the past.[73] However, this interpretation may be misreading these manifestations of resentment. Indeed, I argue that expressions of resentment also point to a desire for political action and to establish moral relations on the basis of equality and freedom rather than on the basis of an asymmetrical relation between universal and particular. Resentment and the desire for recognition operate, as Linda Zerilli suggests,[74] following Hannah Arendt, as a way to make the "world between us" appear and exist. Resentment is also an ethical call to action. Calling themselves feminists, racialized feminists create the political space of a possible "we." Mani's powerful words at the inception of this chapter ask for more than tolerance, recognition, or solidarity. They ask for reciprocity and love,[75] a powerful metaphor for a collective political and moral bond: love is unconditional and demands that one place herself in the perspective of the other. Love acknowledges the existence of a reciprocal relation and of the responsibility it equally creates for both parties.

In this respect, resentment here is an ethical disposition that reminds white feminists of their failed promises of inclusion, and opens up a political space for action for racialized feminists.

Racialized feminists' resentment often expresses a demand to white feminists to relinquish power and space. Their demand is not a demand to recognize differences or to promote a pluralism based on a diversity of identities. Rather, they ask, as Soraya puts it, for the right to be at the table and to not be treated like "a little sister" but rather like a feminist peer. This means, among other things, that their concerns should not be considered as particular or accessory, which is often the case. Nadia, a volunteer in an organization that promotes Iranian women's rights in Paris, recalls how the rights of immigrant women are regularly forgotten by white feminist organizations when petitions and demonstrations are organized:

> The minute you are not there, and it's forgotten. I lived it myself [during] the call for the March 8 demonstration. I could not be present at the meeting, and I saw the list of claims, not a line on [immigrant women]. So the next meeting I said it, it was immediately accepted, and they said they were sorry. But it got me thinking.... They should know—our physical presence should not be the reminder.

Hence even on a consensual topic such as migrant women's rights, white feminist organizations need a constant reminder to include these issues on their political platform. Best intentions seem not to be met by a change in practices, which fuels resentment from racialized feminists. This resentment sometimes surfaces as what Sabrina Marchetti has called *postcolonial* resentment,[76] that is, a resentment that links the relationships between white and racialized feminists today with colonial relations in the past. Karima insists that while feminist movements may recognize colonialism as a historical fact, the persistence of colonial relations within Quebecois society remains largely ignored:

> Even if it recognizes that there was colonial domination on countries in the South, the feminist movement has a hard time admitting that this domination continues here through immigration. Why is it so difficult for the feminist movement to recognize this? Because the feminist movement is part of the problem.... Where are immigrant women in the feminist movement here?

Karima's resentment toward Quebecois feminists points to the ways in which white feminists ignore the realities of racism and neocolonialism, circumscribing colonial relations in the past and in another place and hence preserving their innocence here and now. In Quebec, several racialized feminist groups were also particularly disappointed in the outcome of an extended process of consultation organized by the FFQ in 2013 and 2014. The process was supposed to lead to the adoption of intersectionality as a principle for the FFQ and to improve the inclusion not only of racialized feminists but also of trans activists. These aims were formally reached during the Estates General of feminism in Quebec, organized by the FFQ, with the adoption of new principles that included intersectionality. However, the process by which intersectionality was finally adopted, and the resistance with which this claim was met, filled racialized feminists with frustration and anger. Indeed, during the consultation process, a group of white feminists, self-named Les Yvettes, decided to leave the FFQ, arguing that it was infiltrated with Islamic feminists. A year later, when the general assembly had to vote on the propositions formalized during the Estates General, opposition to intersectionality surfaced once again. Some representatives of grassroots feminist community centers, especially from outside Montreal, argued that intersectionality was too complex a principle and impossible for them to implement, at least for now. They asked for more time and contested the idea that intersectionality was necessary for their feminist praxis. In the face of this resistance, Soraya expresses her frustration, disappointment, and tiredness:

> I'm on my way out. We are tired, it's enough (*sigh*). The conclusion is a lot of effort, not a lot of gains. . . . You realize at some point it's really violent, you still go back. People said the Estates General were a great victory, but you realize organizations have not changed their practices. People voted almost unanimously to integrate diverse women, indigenous women, intersectionality, but a year later, last spring, you have people from grassroots centers saying, "We don't want to vote on this." They say, "Women in our center are not ready for this."

Paola expresses a similar dismay at the resistance that emerged against intersectionality during the process. While finally the vote went through despite the opposition, the voicing of resistance against intersectionality, as well as asking racialized women to delay their claims, was interpreted and felt as a form of political violence and a painful moment:

It felt a bit sad. They said, "Look, we are not racist, but you have to understand that not everybody—and we represent women's centers throughout Quebec—not everybody is on the same page. So give us some time so we can go back and work with them and when we're ready . . ." And we asked, "Does that mean we have to face the oppression until they are ready? They're not ready, we are ready, but we have to . . . ?" It's like telling Black people, "Wait for apartheid to end till everybody gets that it's really not correct."

For both Soraya and Paola, this event became a sign of the difficulty that white feminists have in relinquishing power. Soraya analyzes the resistance from grassroots organizations as a lack of political will but also as a way to refuse to relinquish power: "You know, it's like 'We have been the guardians, the pillars of the feminist movement, in Quebec for forty years and we don't want to leave some space for others.'" This event thus made visible a latent conflict over *who* really represents the feminist cause, as well as the common space that feminists are supposed to share equally.

The claim that white feminists must relinquish power is both political and moral. It is a claim for the recognition of equal participation in the feminist project, as well as equal moral worth in this project. Indeed, Soraya's pain and frustration display features like those Noémi Michel has described as the reactions to racialized discursive injuries in postcolonial contexts.[77] Michel reads claims against racial injurious discourses as claims for equality, rather than identity, because racial injuries enact a form of exclusion from full humanity for racialized subjects. While racialized feminists have not been victims of racialized discursive injuries in the context of the FFQ's meetings, they have felt injured by the way in which their own claims have met with new demands to be patient, to wait for equality. Paola's comparison with apartheid and Soraya's feeling that she has been subjected to forms of violence both capture the injurious power and unjust character of the demand for patience, tolerance, and self-restraint that white feminists have placed on racialized feminists. In this context, anger and resentment do not reveal a feeling of exclusion from humanity, but rather an exclusion from the feminist project, from the collective subject that it is supposed to create. Hence, what is being claimed by Soraya when she contests demands placed on her to be patient, is that those demands exclude her from the feminist collective subject and perform, discursively and socially, a form of inequality and a form of ethical violence. These demands to be patient breach the promise of equality intrinsic to the feminist project. Her resentment thus expresses a demand for equality, as equal participation and equal discursive presence in the feminist project, a demand to recognize her equal moral worth as a feminist subject. It thus troubles and displaces the usual boundaries between the particular and the universal, the "good" and the "bad" feminist subjects.

Resentment here performs a refusal to abide by postcolonial structures of power and discourses. Michel argues, following Butler, that it is our fundamental relationality with others, our ontological condition as subjects of language, that makes us *injurable* because we are in need of the recognition of others for our existence.[78] For Michel the postcolonial condition, the historical legacy of colonialism, makes racialized subject specifically vulnerable to racialized discursive injuries. I bring this insight to bear on the analysis of Soraya's discourse to highlight how, in her case, the injury is located at the level of the nonrecognition of her equal moral worth as a *feminist* subject. White feminists' discourses asking for patience are not interpreted by Soraya as performing a racialized injury that denies her belonging to full humanity, but rather as an injury that denies her belonging as a feminist subject to the political community created in the name of feminism. While this injury is of course related to her racialized body, what she resents specifically is the denial of equality performed in the context of a feminist community that is supposed to be a community of equals. This reading of resentment as manifesting a claim to equality, rather than the repetition of an injury, is confirmed by the joy Soraya first felt when the FFQ voted during a special assembly on the issue of the hijab and did adopt a position against the ban in question. She recalls how she felt then:

> The majority went for the position of the executive [of the FFQ], which was no to banning the veil, no to forcing women to wear it. We were so happy, we were filled with joy, it was great, everybody was giving hugs to each other, everybody was happy. I remember my friend, who wears the hijab, and she tells me, "Today"—and I still shiver when I think about it—"today I feel like I could really belong to this society." . . . So there you are.

This event was for Soraya full of promises. Promises of inclusion, belonging, and participation. Promises that her voice would be not only heard but would shape the agenda of the FFQ for the coming years. A promise that she would be considered as belonging, as a feminist subject, as a feminist equal. Her disappointment was all the greater that these promises did not materialize as she had wished. Failed promises have broken the possibility of a common "we" she aspired to. On another occasion, she experienced a lack of solidarity from white feminists that also led her to question the possibility of a common future. When the debate on the Charter of Quebecois Values emerged in 2013, she asked white feminists with whom she had a history of common activism to express their solidarity with an informal network of Muslim women in Quebec, and to publicly take a position against the proposed Charter. However, none of them agreed, and this refusal performed once again a form of injury and denial of equality.

If promises have failed, making a collective "we" difficult to imagine, at least in Quebec promises have been made, and some may be kept. Soraya herself recognizes that the FFQ has shown solidarity and made efforts to include racialized feminists and has paid a price with the departure of some members. Paola also recognizes that the FFQ has supported the International Women's Day march organized by racialized women's groups for several years:

> We often invite the president of FFQ to speak, and the FFQ has been great about that to say, "It's your league, you organize, tell us what you want us to do." . . . So I think maybe things like that have been heard, and the fact that the FFQ president sees us as allies too means there is a recognition that we have a common cause.

Importantly, Paola's remarks show both that on this occasion her position is not that of a minority and that the relationship with mainstream white organizations may be envisioned as one of common cause, a collective "we" in which they are equal interlocutors. Similarly, in France, Maleiha explains that some strategic and punctual alliances with white women's organizations may prove productive. While Maleiha argues that there is a need to decolonize feminist activism, here alliances were possible because her organization decided the terms that would frame their solidarity:

> They talk very clearly about violence against lesbians, and this is thanks to us and other organizations that the fight against lesbophobia is on the agenda . . . but also double violence against immigrant women. . . . It started last year and it was clear. And we are satisfied because we were very clear. We said we agree to come but you need to articulate these issues clearly.

Hence, under specific circumstances, coalitions might succeed. While all racialized/immigrant feminists express in various forms discontent, criticism, and resentment toward white feminists, they also recognize possibilities for alliances, if they are not placed in a minority position but can use their own language and priorities, and see these recognized and adopted by white feminists. Importantly, they demand that their equal moral worth as feminist subjects be recognized. I explore more fully in the next chapter the implications of these politics of coalitions.

* * *

In this chapter I have described and analyzed a variety of processes of political subjectivation by which racialized feminists come to give an account of themselves as racialized feminists. These processes and these accounts vary. In particular, racialized feminists politicize race and religion in different ways, depending on the context and the feminist generation to which they belong. Despite their differences, they all provide trenchant critiques of their encounters with white feminists, and recount their attempts at challenging the whitening of feminism by claiming feminism for themselves, outside of the universalist narrative provided by many white feminists. The discourses through which racialized feminists resist the regulation imposed by feminist whiteness on good and bad feminist subjects are of course eminently political. They denote their resistance to power, and how it contributes to shape their identities and subjectivations as racialized feminists. They also convey moral issues at the heart of the relationship between white and non-white feminists.

Failed promises of solidarity and inclusion leave the possibility of ethical violence looming. Indeed, following Adorno's reflections on violence and the emergence of morality, Judith Butler notes that morality emerges from a divergence between what is posited as a universal interest and what is posited as the interests of particular individuals. This division happens when the universal "fails to agree with or include the individual."[79] In this context, universality "can exercise violence" because it ignores "the social conditions under which a living appropriation might become possible."[80] Transposed to the issue and subject of feminism, Adorno's and Butler's reflections on universality illuminate how the ignorance by white feminists of the social conditions under which the appropriation of feminism by racialized feminists becomes possible performs a form of ethical violence, which is felt as such. The dialectic between the minority position occupied by racialized feminists and the dominant one, parading as universal and occupied by white feminists, is therefore one of structural conflict. Deleuze has described well the position and the dialectic of minority subjects: speaking from within a dominant language that they have not forged themselves, they also try to subvert its meaning in order to account for their position outside of its claimed universality. Deleuze's concept of minority is important because it shows how minority claims seek to deterritorialize the majority's claim to universality, a process clearly at play in racialized feminists' discourses.

However, Deleuze overlooks the question of the attachment of minorities to their identity category and their moral relations to the majority. Deleuze's analysis of the minority position is mainly a political one, looking for strategies of alliances among minorities to rethink emancipation and a revolutionary becoming outside of the narratives of the hegemony of universal subjects. While Deleuze recognizes that minorities are tied to "objective" identities (such as ethnicity or gender), he argues that they must be detached from these identities to become politically relevant, to be articulated with other minorities and to become a "universal minority consciousness."[81] Hence in the dialectic between minorities and universality that must allow for forging a revolutionary political subject, the question of emotional attachments to minority identities,[82] and the moral dimension of the relationship to the majority—marked by resentment in the case of racialized feminists—is left unexplored. Revisiting Deleuze's metaphor of the minority position as similar to that of a minor/minoritized language or dialect forged from within the majoritarian language, one can perceive how a minority position carries more than just resistance to power, and how minority subjectivity is not engulfed in or produced only through power. Indeed, language is not just a set of hegemonic rules to be subverted from within by its minoritized iterations, as Deleuze suggests. Language is also spoken; it is what enables my voice and my being a subject. As Sandra Laugier beautifully remarks in her analysis of Wittgenstein's and Stanley Cavell's approach to language as *spoken*: "The voice is both a subjective and a general expression: it is what makes it possible for my individual voice to become shared. In voice, there is the idea of a claim. The singular claims a shared, common validity."[83] Language, as the voice, is therefore this locus of my subjectivity and, at the same time, the place and the form in which I seek commonality, the possibility of being recognized by others.[84]

In this perspective, the minority position is not only one of subversion or deterritorialization of the majority, it is also a position that seeks common validity. The resentment and emotional grievance that racialized/immigrant feminists justly feel fuel in that respect a call to responsibility that they address to white feminists, a moral call. Hence, while for Deleuze the minority is first and foremost a political position, one that articulates a tension and a conflict from within the hegemonic norm, racialized feminists also affirm their full participation in the feminist project not only at the political level but also in moral terms, through an address to white feminists.

Here Drucilla Cornell's words about the recognition of differences between women come to mind: "This call to responsibility inheres in the aspiration to the ethical relationship and is, as a result, a crucial aspect of what I call ethical feminism. It can call us to both acts of identification and disidentification. But it demands of us that we deconstruct the claim that there is an identity that we share as women and that the differences between us are secondary."[85] As racialized/immigrant feminists invent various new languages from within the hegemonic feminist norm to describe and politicize their own experience and thereby resist whiteness, this invention brings with it conflicts but also implies a possibility and a promise, the promise that this language, as a voice, both singular and claiming common validity, might open up a common space for collective political action, a space defined by feminist moral relations of equality.

6
Toward a Feminist Ethic of Responsibility

> "Solidarity" as an ideal of a political altruism is rooted in some degree of identification, which it will also transcend. But its invocation is immensely delicate.
> —Denise Riley, *The Words of Selves*, 9

> Solidarity does not assume that our struggles are the same struggles, or that our pain is the same pain, or that our hope is for the same future. Solidarity involves commitment, and work, as well as the recognition that even if we do not have the same feelings, or the same lives, or the same bodies, we do live on common ground.
> —Sara Ahmed, *The Cultural Politics Of Emotions*, 189

Already two and a half decades ago, Judith Butler reflected on the modern feminist project in the following terms:

> Through what exclusions has the feminist subject been constructed, and how do those excluded domains return to haunt the "integrity" and "unity" of the feminist "we"? And how is it that the very category, the subject, the "we," that is supposed to be presumed for the purpose of solidarity, produces the very factionalization it is supposed to quell? Do women want to become subjects on the model which requires and produces an anterior rejoin of abjection, or must feminism become a process which is self-critical about the processes that produce and destabilize identity categories?[1]

Butler's considerations find a profound echo in the current politics of feminism in a majority of Western countries. As I have documented in previous chapters, far from having rejected or critically reflected upon the false universalism and unity of the "we women," numerous contemporary feminist organizations in Europe and beyond have been enrolled in an exclusionary project contributing in many respects to the "rise of femonationalism";[2] that is, the enrollment of feminist values in nationalist far-right political projects. However, as Butler predicted, these excluded domains return to haunt, challenge, and disrupt this exclusionary discourse, also in the name of women's rights, simultaneously shattering liberal categories of emancipation and agency.

In the previous chapters I have documented and analyzed these two processes—the exclusion and the haunting. I have first shown how feminist whiteness, in its many forms and incarnations, polices the boundaries of the feminist collective subject, performing the symbolic and practical exclusion of "bad" subjects and/or positing that nonwhite feminists' political subjectivities must be regulated and put in line with feminist ideals historically and socially defined as white (and secular). This process can be critically read as the product of power relations within feminism based on race and religion. These discourses delineate the boundaries of feminist whiteness and secure for many white feminists their already privileged position within the movement. Moreover, and as Butler's citation suggests, this process of political subjectivation is also profoundly intertwined with emotions and moral dispositions. Attachment to identity categories, to the unified "we," is also the product of a psychic and emotional impulse. I have also shown how race especially comes back to haunt this feminist project, as Butler predicted. I have considered how racialized feminists reclaim the feminist subject on their own terms, contesting the boundaries drawn by white feminists, while, at the same time, seeking recognition of their belonging to the feminist project, first among themselves, but also in relation to white feminists. In that sense, racialized feminists' discourse must also be heard as a moral address directed at white feminists.

The exploration of the political subjectivations of white and racialized feminists in the context of sexualism debates has therefore exposed the dyadic nature of feminism, as both a political and a moral project. Conflicts about what gender equality means, or what freedom means, and the impossibility of ever agreeing on this topic are, I maintain with Linda Zerilli and others, inherent to the feminist project. That those values are debated and contested is the very mark that feminism is a political project. As Zerilli notes: "There can no more be *the* final or conclusive argument for the equality of the sexes than there can be *the* final and conclusive argument for the beautiful. Every political or aesthetic argument must be articulated in relation to a set of particulars."[3] In this perspective, feminism is thus a political activity that is defined neither by a shared identity nor by an agreement on political values such as gender equality or autonomy, but rather by its aim to create a political community. Hence, to critically think about the feminist project and its future, we should not be concerned with defining gender equality or female autonomy in a way that would assuage the conflicts within feminism sparked by sexularism debates, but rather reflect on the conditions that enable this political community to be sustained and define its nature (as a community of equals, for example).[4] Instead of inquiring about the limits or the impossibility of a subject, a "we women," that would found or embody feminism, we should then interrogate what political community feminism pretends to create, and on what moral bonds this community might be based, questions I explore in this chapter.

Indeed, feminism, I argue, is also a moral project. Debates over Islamic veiling reveal conflicts about what gender equality and female autonomy mean for feminists, but they also reveal that some subjects may be considered proper feminists subjects while others are considered improper subjects, outside the scope of the feminist project of emancipation. In that perspective, the future of the feminist project does not only depend on an ability to be critical about the "we" that it invokes in its claims, a subject that has fueled much of feminist theory's inquiries.[5] It also lies in our ability to critically reflect on the moral boundaries and moral relations that the feminist project creates. The moral relationships that characterize the political subjectivations of white and racialized feminists—from benevolence or indignation to resentment—indicate that moral relations between feminists are at the heart of feminism. Hence, I am concerned with the moral dimension of the feminist project, the bonds that enable feminism to be embodied in a political community.

In that sense, I argue that we need to be self-critical not only about the boundaries of the "we" that we intend to claim when we make claims as feminists, as Butler suggests, but that we also need to be self-critical about the relationships we forge or imagine between those who might claim that "we" with us, in the very process of claiming it. Indeed, disagreeing on political outcomes should not lead to ignoring power asymmetries between feminists, and should not reinforce moral boundaries and exclusion. On the contrary, feminism should be an exercise in critique of moral boundaries. I argue that we must therefore concern ourselves with the moral dimension of the feminist project, the bonds that enable feminism to be embodied in a community, and that ensure that its claims will be picked up by others. This is not a turn to morality as opposed to politics. Rather it is an attempt to elucidate what moral relations can create a political community of equals. How can feminism define a community that is not marked by hierarchies between "good" and "bad" feminist subjects? How can our feminist imagination define bonds *between* its members that do not reproduce exclusions, abjections, and privilege?

In this chapter, I argue that such a conception of feminism as a moral and political project, which creates bonds between those who declare themselves feminists, can reorient our critical inquiry. Grappling with sexularism debates, our attention has been fixated on the subject of feminism, debating who can be part of this project—with religious Muslim women being evaluated as proper or improper subjects of feminist consideration—and the type of agency these subjects should display to be included in a political project of emancipation. Rather, I suggest concentrating our attention not on the subject of feminism but on the relationships that feminists create among themselves, the nature of the bonds that a feminist project requires. Hence, what we must explore are the moral bonds we create when we invoke feminism. Can we imagine feminist moral bounds that sustain a community of equals?

While Butler is right to promote a nonfoundationalist account of feminism, one in which this political project does not rely on the belief of a "we" grounded in a common identity, this does not mean that feminism should not aim at creating a *community*, in the sense of creating and sustaining moral and political bonds between its participants. What I have described in the preceding chapters, thanks to the concept of political subjectivation, is not only a problematic passionate attachment to the category or identity of "women," but also a passionate desire to name oneself a feminist and to be recognized by other feminists as a feminist. The passionate attachment to feminist ideals such as gender equality and autonomy is matched in intensity only by the affective and moral bonds created *between* feminists. Whether this community is based on an identity category or is self-critical about this identity, feminism as a political activity generates emotional attachment, not only to the identity category or to its destabilization (I can be as emotionally invested in the maintaining of the category "women" as I can be affectively engaged in its dislocation) but to the other participants in that project.

This chapter is an exercise in political imagination. As Amy Allen has emphasized, any critical analysis rests in fact on an anticipated future for the feminist project.[6] This utopian dimension must be specified; otherwise it will necessarily create new exclusionary domains, as has been the case in the past—for example, with feminism's uncritical adhesion to liberal values and its attachment to modernity.[7] I therefore here explore in normative terms the moral bonds that feminists may create among feminists, and that may avoid reproducing hierarchies, privileges, and exclusions.

The figure of the coalition is a good place to start such an inquiry. Coalitions have been repeatedly presented as a *solution* to the *problem* of differences and of power relations among women. Most of the literature has focused on the organizational modalities of coalitions, exploring what makes feminist coalitions succeed or fail as political endeavors. I argue that while indeed we learn important pragmatic feminist politics from these studies, coalitions are not only attempts at broader political inclusion or political alliances between minorities that may ally on tactical issues. They also constitute moral endeavors that necessitate forging specific moral bonds and developing a form of feminist ethics. I then explore different theoretical propositions of such a feminist ethics. In particular, I discuss how the concept of enlarged mentality, or enlarged thought, first elaborated by Hannah Arendt in her theory of judgment, has been used by feminist theorists such as Linda Zerilli and Iris Young to capture the type of moral disposition that could define a feminist ethics. In the last section, I propose to build on and nuance these insights into the ethical dispositions that can create a feminist political community. I argue that what I call a *feminist ethic of responsibility* may provide normative yardsticks that take into account the affects and moral dispositions that characterize feminists' political subjectivations, and redirect them toward the aim of disestablishing the moral hierarchies and political exclusions within feminism. I show how such an ethics can address the pitfalls described at length in this book and by others, and help us conceive feminism as a political community of equals, while leaving open political disagreements about the values at the heart of this project, such as autonomy and equality.

Coalition as a Political and Moral Promise

Many feminist scholars have presented coalitions as the solution to the problem of the exclusionary domains created by the "we women," a "we" too often appropriated by white and privileged feminists. Coalitions are said to offer a solution by acknowledging differences, especially differences in privilege and power, while at the same time creating a temporary united "we."

I first review theoretical arguments in favor of this mode of feminist organizing, and I specify, using my fieldwork in France and Quebec, under which conditions coalitions are said to have reached their objective or to have been experienced as successful. These experiences of "successful" coalitions give us insights about their nature—as strategic, political alliances—but also about the ethical dispositions they require from their participants, a dimension rarely explored in the literature. Indeed, as the quotation from Sara Ahmed that opens this chapter suggests, solidarity, expressed through coalition building, requires that we recognize that "we live on common ground." However, this requirement and its ethical implications are rarely fully articulated within coalition politics or in feminist theory.

Talking about Black feminist politics in the United States, Bernice Johnson Reagon famously opposed "home" and coalition: "You don't go into coalition because you like it. The only reason you would consider trying to team up with somebody who could possibly kill you, is because that's the only way you can figure you can stay alive."[8] To the safety and recognition of home, Reagon contrasted coalition politics as *hard work*, a place that is not safe but is a necessity. She emphasized that feminist work for the twenty-first century must be about coalescing, which entails a risk, and therefore carefulness because "you can't know everything when you start to coalesce with these people who sorta look like you in just one aspect but really they belong to another group."[9] Hence, belonging is about home and people who look just like me in every aspect, while coalition is about not belonging, not looking alike, not recognizing myself in the others, and, however, *working* with them. Because coalition work is based on the premise that the participants do not share a similar identity, or a similar pain as Ahmed remarks, it supposedly quenches the question of differences and recognition. It proposes a self-critical understanding of the feminist "we" that has been upheld as the practical solution to the "problem" of the "we women" by many theorists from various theoretical traditions.[10] Central among the reasons that explain the theoretical success of coalition as a viable figure for feminist politics is thus the idea that coalition is centered around work, action, or communication rather than identity.

This antiessentialist predicate supposedly offers a guarantee that calls for commonality and identity will not be used to mask power disparities nor to protect the privileged subjects of feminism at the expense of those who are multiply marginalized. Coalitions are supposed to avoid what María Lugones calls a logic of purity, a logic based on the "fundamental assumption that there is unity underlying multiplicity."[11] This assumption is misleading for feminist practice or for any emancipatory politics because it rests on a longing for unity, community, and shared subjectivity as a premise and precondition for political action, whereas such a premise is always flawed and exclusionary, enacting a closure of the political subject, and whereas this premise ignores, or travesties, the fact that identity building is the product of political work.[12] In fact, coalition may be the model to follow even for groups that present themselves as identity-based. Indeed, and as chapter 5 illustrated, identity-based feminist groups are not the product of an immediate, prepolitical identity. They also are the product of collective processes of political subjectivation that necessitate work to create a common identity, a feeling of security and a vocabulary to politicize the intersectional nature of their identity.[13]

Hence, coalition may be a model for feminist practice not only to bridge across difference but for any type of feminist collective action. Coalition is thus favored by feminist theorists of recognition who value communicative ethics as a way to foster understanding across differences,[14] as well as intersectional theorists who wish to ensure minoritized women's inclusion in the feminist project as well as their self-organizing.[15] Coalition can offer a figure of inclusive feminism, by multiplying the available and accepted feminist figures, like in the intersectional version of the Rosie the Riveter poster, an image with three racialized women posing as Rosie, used by racialized feminist groups in Paris (and in the United States) in 2015,[16] or in material metaphors such as the quilt seamed by different women groups in over fifty countries for the World March of Women organized by Quebecois feminists in 2005. In both these visual and material metaphors the feminist subject is multiplied, embodied by a multiplicity of figures rather than by a univocal one.

Beyond the theoretical assumption that coalition is an adequate form for feminist practice, scholars of social movements have also documented under which conditions coalitions succeed, meaning that they manage to forge a short-term alliance on specific issues. Empirical studies show that for a coalition to sustain itself, despite difference in identities and power, there needs to be a recognition of the power differential[17] and a specific representation for the disadvantaged group so that their viewpoint is not suppressed through the coalition building.[18] The institutionalization of what Laurel Weldon calls "norms of inclusivity," to secure the self-organizing of minorities within the coalition and their descriptive representation, provides the necessary safeguards to ensure minorities' interests are taken into account and for the coalition to thus be sustainable.

However, both the theoretical account of coalition and empirical studies of successful coalitions tend to sideline important dimensions of coalition work. Here I explore further these affective and moral dimensions of coalition, both between racialized and nonracialized feminists and between differently racialized or marginalized feminist groups, in France and Quebec, to delineate when and why feminists experience a coalition as successful or as a failure, and what these moral and political evaluations tell us about the potential and the limits of coalition as a figure of inclusive feminism. I argue that while, as has been noted by other scholars, acknowledging power within a coalition is a prerequisite posited by racialized feminists for a coalition to be possible, coalition work—with other racialized feminists or with white feminists—also entails cultivating specific moral dispositions. I first document empirically this claim, and then elaborate theoretically its implications.

Discourses about coalitions across racial and religious divides vary depending on standpoint. While coalition is a leitmotiv of the narratives from racialized feminists in France and Quebec, showing the necessity of including their views if one is to reflect on this feminist practice, it is much less so for a majority of white feminists I interviewed, especially in France. In some cases, the failure of coalition, even for symbolic short-term events, such as the International Women's Day demonstration on March 8, is accounted for by white French feminists by underlining irreducible differences over feminist values and ideals (for example, on the Islamic veil or on sex work)—rather than power, privilege, and racism. In Quebec, the provincial umbrella organization for women's rights, the FFQ, mainly run by white women, has engaged reflexively on this issue since the beginning of this century, mainly through the institutionalization of a specific representation of racialized women inside the organization—an initiative welcomed by racialized feminists, but one that did not appease their concern about the organization's lack of diversity and continued implicit support for Quebecois nationalism. As Mani, an activist and volunteer in a South Asian women's center in Montreal underlines, descriptive representation does not mean inclusion, and the concerns of her organization remain marginalized in the coalition's agenda despite her continued presence there:

> Of course, we were invited to go to the exceptional General Assembly again this September and I looked at their program and I said there is no way I have three days to listen to them all doing all that stuff again, and arguing

about nationalism probably.... So I don't know, I don't have the patience for it anymore.

Contrary to the relative lack of discourse about coalition from nonracialized feminists, racialized feminists in France and Quebec expose their disillusions, but also the conditions that have been conducive to successful coalitions with white women.[19] In line with the literature on feminist coalition, interviewees in Quebec and France underscore that a lack of acknowledgment of the power differential is an impediment to forging effective coalitions. Soraya, a Muslim feminist activist in her early forties who has been a member of the provincial federation for many years and cofounded a Muslim feminist group in Montreal, critically reflects on her experience of organizing with white Quebecois feminists and being included in the events they organize:

> In fact, a real integration of intersectional practice would lead, I think, in this context, to take into account the vulnerabilities of different groups, but their attitude is to say, "It's a level playing field, you just have to make your mark, it's the same rules for everybody, and they apply to everyone fairly."... The same women who said fifty years ago to men that they should favor women's participation, and they cannot see the link.

Lack of awareness of power differentials, the very absence of a level playing field, makes coalition work impossible in this case. Acknowledging racism *inside* the movement and material power differentials is thus a precondition for a feasible coalition. However, examples of successful coalition—where power asymmetries are recognized—show that racialized feminists define this work as temporary, strategic, and on their own terms. Maleiha, who facilitates a group of lesbians of color in Paris, insists on both the temporal limit and the protection of her group's autonomy in coalition work:

> We have reflected on practices of strategic and short-term alliances. That is, we are a radical group, but we find it necessary and useful to have actions with others, we are not closed.... Why short term? Because we protect our autonomy, an autonomous organization, to produce our own reflections and analyses. This idea of temporariness enables us to circumscribe our alliances, so that we are not in the long term, so we're safe. We won't be assimilated, and our conditions will be very clear. With white lesbians, first we ally only with those we know well, and this affective side, this friendship

is very important because, in fact, political lesbians that fight racism, there's not a lot of them around.

As this long quotation makes clear, while the scope and dynamics of the coalition must ensure racialized feminists that their participation will be defined on their own terms, as already exemplified in chapter 5, coalition work is also rife with emotions and affects. Successful coalitions are based on trust, built over time, as well as on friendship and emotional bonds. Indeed, Maleiha emphasizes the need for trust and affective relations even to sustain strategic and temporary coalitions with carefully picked allies. While the literature often opposes identity groups, characterized by emotional safety and shared identity, and coalition work, this distinction seems, on some level, to be inadequate. It is clear that identity groups, such as the one founded by Maleiha, provide her with a collective sense of belonging and with political autonomy, as she often emphasizes in her interview. But this belonging does not suppress the need for affective and trustful relations in the coalition work she engages in as well. Coalition work does not render the affective and emotional dimensions of feminist political subjectivation irrelevant, as Soraya's and Maleiha's words suggest.

Reciprocally, failed coalitions display not only a lack of awareness of inequalities and racism within feminist movements, but also moral dispositions that prevent working together. The political recognition of power asymmetries—or its refusal—is intimately intertwined with moral and affective dispositions. This interweaving can be identified in the following example. When she mentions the organization of an event on Islamic feminism where no Muslim feminist was in fact invited, Soraya contrasts the theoretical commitment of white feminists toward diversity and intersectionality with the practical lack of financial solidarity:

> I can't believe there is no money to have [a Muslim feminist] come from Morocco. It's impossible for me to imagine that there is no possibility of financing her. . . . But if I say this, it is presented as completely wacky on my part, emotional, as if I was asking for preferential treatment. But in theory if you ask them if it's important to take into consideration race, sexual orientation, they will say yes.

Soraya's critique goes beyond the lack of acknowledgment of economic asymmetries. Her demand to recognize power differentials, including financial ones, is met with a moral gaze that delegitimizes this demand and categorizes the one who utters it as "unfit" for proper feminist practice. What is more, and as Soraya develops her reflection, the ability to embody the "good" feminist subject is always disputed by white feminists, especially when it comes to acknowledging Muslim feminists as feminists:

> There is often this, "Well, it would be nice to see you at a demonstration for abortion rights." They put conditions on acceptance, on integration, criteria we are supposed to meet.... The answer is "prove yourself and you will be accepted."

Hence the moral gaze of feminist whiteness that ascribes to racialized feminists a position of "bad" feminist subject, or of a subject who still needs to be regulated, to prove itself, makes coalition work with white feminists very problematic for racialized feminists. The emotional and moral implications of such coalition work also appear clearly in this quote. Beyond the recognition of power asymmetries, racialized feminists recognize coalition with white feminist organizations as also morally meaningful when, contrary to the example given by Soraya, a common belonging to the feminist project is fully acknowledged. Paola, who heads a South Asian women's center in Montreal, reflects on the relationship of her organization with the mainstream umbrella feminist organization, the FFQ—after the latter proposed that racialized feminist organizations grouped under the banner of "women from diverse origins" would from now on organize the March 8 demonstration—in these terms: "The fact that the president [of the organization] sees us as allies too means there is a recognition that we have a *common cause*" (my emphasis). Importantly, the acknowledgment that feminists share a common cause, and live on common ground, implies a recognition not only of equal moral worth but also of relationality—which I will develop further.

The interweaving of political and moral disposition as a precondition for coalition is not limited to coalitions of racialized feminists with white feminists. Indeed, racialized feminists' organizations also need to build coalitions among women of color, or with other oppressed categories.[20] Paola, for example, explains the logic guiding the relationship that her organization tries to build with indigenous women's groups in Quebec. While she states that they do not have a formal working relationship, she explains that they asked the head of the federation of indigenous women in Quebec to come give a talk so that the members of her organization would inform themselves about indigenous women's multiple discrimination and history of colonial oppression in Quebec.

The will to self-educate might therefore be one way to express solidarity. Another is apologizing to groups that one has sidelined in political work. Soraya relates an event that happened during the Estates General of feminism in Quebec, a wide gathering of all feminist organizations, organized by the FFQ but rallying beyond its usual membership. A long discussion occurred to decide if trans* and intersex women should be named as intersectional categories or subsumed under a "sexual diversity" label within the charter that was being drafted. Soraya's group opted for the latter, a political and moral fault as she explains:

> For her [a trans* activist] and another intersex activist it was really important to name them, because they have never been named, and, see, this was a big blunder on the part of racialized women, because we did not vote with them. It was a tragic moment. We thought we were doing the right thing by skipping the list [of sexual minorities]. . . . We really had a hard time. We apologized, but these women will not come back.

Here again, the issue is not only about the *right* political position to take in order to acknowledge the identities and the needs of multiply marginalized groups within the feminist coalition. It is also an issue of acknowledging relationality and a common moral ground between feminists. The fact that Soraya describes this event as *tragic* underlines both the passion with which she invests it as she recalls it, and the unspoken idea that exclusion is unavoidable, a fate that one tries to escape but that repeats itself, despite the best intentions. However, the fact that her group apologized suggests that, to use Hannah Arendt's metaphor, even if promises of solidarity have not been kept, new promises may be made again, and coalition rebuilt. Hence, here again, political stakes, moral dispositions and emotions are intimately interwoven in Soraya's understanding of what has been missed. The failure she expresses is both political and moral. Her moral dismay echoes, and illuminates, Linda Zerilli's analysis, relating the story of a feminist collective in Milan, when she remarks that such collective is based on "a *promise* to make good a claim to community and acknowledge a debt."[21]

Reflecting on these examples, we see that coalition is not only strategic allying or the multiplication of figures that may embody or represent the feminist subject. Coalitions are rife with emotional stakes and moral relations. Failed coalitions between racialized and nonracialized feminists reflect not only a cognitive and political failure on the part of some feminists—that of not acknowledging asymmetries in power along racial lines—they also result from a lack of moral reciprocity, the absence of an acknowledgment of common ground. Conversely, successful coalition work rests not only on institutionalizing norms of inclusivity but also on trust, emotional bonds, and the moral acknowledgment of relationality and, therefore, responsibility, between feminists—I will develop this point further in the following sections.

Hence, coalitions are not only strategic alliances, necessitating that the right norms of inclusivity be institutionalized in order to be successful. Coalitions are also moral endeavors, putting to the test the moral relations that unite—or separate—their participants. The examples of coalitions between minority groups illustrate as well this moral and emotional nature of coalition. Indeed, as the last example, Soraya's tragic mistake, showed, communication between oppressed minorities is neither transparent nor obvious. As minorities, trans* feminists and racialized feminists shared a common critique of the dominant feminist discourse imposed by white cis-feminists; however, this shared critique did not automatically translate into adequate practices of solidarity. There might always be an intersecting power relation, or a logic of resistance, that one might omit.[22] But, maybe more importantly, Soraya stressed the need to apologize, asking for forgiveness, thereby revealing the deeply moral nature of the bond she aimed to preserve. The vision of coalition as mostly strategic, resting upon communicative ethics or on institutionalized norms of inclusivity, thus falls short of capturing what is at stake in coalition work.

These examples of coalitions between racialized feminists and white feminists, as well as among differently marginalized feminists, indicate that coalition is also a promise, a promise one must want to make and that one must try to keep. I want to argue that for this reason, coalition should not be presented as the *solution* to the *problem* of differences among women. The foreshadowing of coalition as the future of feminism is not satisfactory, despite its endearing visual representation of feminism as a collective reuniting different identities in a common project. While coalition politics have proven to be, under the right circumstances, potent ways to organize across racial divides and across sexual orientation or class, I argue that coalitions are the *product* of already existing inclusive political practices, and of specific ethical dispositions, rather than a mode of coalescing that could create new political and moral understandings. Indeed, in many contexts, coalition efforts fail, or, as the case of France suggests, a coalition is not even envisioned as a possible form for a common feminist subject. In a context in which representations of "good" and "bad" feminist subjects are radically entrenched and opposed, via processes of political subjectivation that reproduce feminist whiteness, coalition is *not* thinkable, nor desirable, and cannot therefore provide a productive site to imagine a common feminist future. While we know from political science that successful coalitions are built on specific practices of inclusion and representation of minoritized groups within the coalition, what is left untold by this account is that, before any inclusionary practice may be put in place, feminists have to *desire* coalition in the first place.

The question then becomes, What are the moral dispositions that must be nurtured, learned, and practiced so that coalition becomes desirable? So that promises might be made? In this perspective coalition is the *result* of a successful moral and political endeavor. It is a promise that has been made. But what are the feminist moral dispositions that can sustain a desire for feminism as a coalition, a recognition that feminists share common ground? This question directs us toward an investigation of the ethic of feminism. I now review different theoretical proposals that have attempted to delineate the ethical relations that should sustain the feminist project. A first proposal, elaborated by Brenda Lyshaug, is the development of "enlarged sympathy." I argue that this proposal, centered on self-investigation and imaginary projections onto other women's experiences, is flawed for several reasons. I then turn to proposals by Iris Young and Linda Zerilli that both use Hannah Arendt's concept of "enlarged mentality" as a principle that could, with some alterations, be fit for the purpose of sustaining a feminist collective project. I argue that while those proposals point to important issues, they fall short of offering the fully-fledged feminist ethic of responsibility that postsecular times and intersectional feminism demand.

A Self-Involved Ethics: Enlarged Sympathy

The insight that coalition cannot only be envisioned as strategic, but needs to be based on ethical self-practice, has been developed by Brenda Lyshaug in her account of the ethic of coalition building.[23] I first review here her proposal in favor of the cultivation of "enlarged sympathy" as a way to foster coalition, and the feminist project more broadly. While I share Lyshaug's argument that feminism is a moral project and therefore implies specific ethical dispositions, I argue that "enlarged sympathy" is not the right candidate because it remains focused on the feminist subject, on feminism as grounded in a (wounded) identity.

Lyshaug critiques the strategic orientation of coalition building as feminist practice, as well as the idea that what coalition building needs is more communicative action across differences. Indeed, Lyshaug argues that the question of coalition is not one of cognitive redress—that is, the need for more knowledge or for more equal and symmetrical communicative action of the type promoted by Seyla Benhabib in her account of the "enlarged mentality,"[24] as a way to reverse perspectives and enable deliberation across asymmetries of power. For Lyshaug, the problem is not one of cognitive failure, but one of *identification* and, therefore, emotions. To ensure inclusion despite differences, Lyshaug contends that ethical self-practices promoting tolerance of ambiguity and receptivity to what may seem threatening must be nurtured among feminists.[25] She finds that what she calls "enlarged sympathy"—a disposition toward others that can sustain attentiveness and a sense of accountability and connection with others despite the fact that we do not identify with them—is an important complement to strategic accounts of coalition.[26] For Lyshaug, reflecting on accounts of failed sisterhood alliances during the US second wave, the main issue is that of identifying, ensuring a connection, without ever falling into the trap of imagining that one's feelings and experiences are similar to others', or that one can fully understand and experience the feelings of others. This concern rises from accounts of appropriation of racialized women's experience by white feminists, made possible not only by a cognitive failure—the lack of knowledge about racialized women's concrete experiences—but also by a misplaced form of identification, for example, when white women believe they can understand and share racialized women's suffering. Lyshaug's aim is to make coalition possible without suppressing or denying differences; to promote sympathy and identification, which implies emotional relations, without pretending to abolish the distance that remains between one's experience and others'.

This orientation shares some of the concerns raised by María Lugones that identities are not transparent but multiple, and thus that some degree of opacity always persists in any form of communication.[27] Lyshaug's concept of enlarged sympathy, borrowed from Sandra Bartky and George Kateb, is supposed to achieve this trick of promoting feelings of sympathy, finding connections with others, recognizing some of their experiences as shared with mine, while at the same time recognizing that they are different and therefore avoiding the illusion of transparent sisterhood. Lyshaug's enlarged sympathy is therefore, first and foremost, an "introspective achievement."[28] If Lyshaug calls this disposition an ethical one, it revolves mostly around the cultivation of specific feeling—openness to threat and ambivalence—and a focus on one's identity, in order to learn to perceive it as multiple and changing rather than fixed. Indeed, only if identity is envisioned in this way can the "introjection of differences into the self,"[29] which is necessary to find overlap with and sympathy toward others' experiences, be realized. Lyshaug elaborates this proposal in the context of thinking about what could sustain inclusive coalitions that respect differences. However, if we agree that even feminist identity groups are, by nature, coalitional, because they also entail work across differences to build a common identity,[30] this proposal can in fact be understood more broadly as that of a feminist ethics that can sustain any feminist project that acknowledges differences.

While I agree with Lyshaug that a successful coalition, or an inclusive feminist project, needs more than an effort to ensure cognitive rectification, I remain unconvinced by her proposal to nurture "enlarged sympathy" as the solution to working across differences, especially in postsecular times. Indeed, while Lyshaug tries to find an ethical disposition, or rather emotional attitudes, that could ensure sympathy without suppressing differences, the challenge today for coalition building is rather to find common ground. Differences are not suppressed; they are rather often posited as irreconcilable. Lyshaug wants to emphasize attentiveness to difference, so that empathy and sisterhood do not, deceptively, mean feeling like the other. She aims at ensuring sisterhood while recognizing that differences in positions and identities—and one would add, more importantly, in power—matter and shape experience. In the context of sexualism debates, what prevents coalition building is rather the absence of acknowledgment that feminists might share common grounds. The discourses that police the borders of good and bad feminist subjects exclude from the feminist imagination specific figures with whom they do not particularly want to empathize. The exclusion of those abject subjects from the feminist imagination is often a premise of white feminists' political subjectivation, making it difficult to imagine that sympathy may be nurtured to promote identification with them. Hence, while Lyshaug's argument presupposes that one may desire to identify with other members of one's group (i.e., women), across some internal differences within this group, I question this very assumption, both as a credible account of feminist practice, and as a normative goal to pursue. As I underlined, there may not be any *desire* for coalition in the first place because separation from abject figures, rather than coalition with them, sustains some processes of political subjectivation as feminist. In these conditions Lyshaug's focus on emotions and "imaginative impersonation"—to imaginatively enter into sympathy with others—may prove misguided because it cannot account for, nor instill, the desire to identify with subjects that have been, precisely, defined as outside the perimeter of the good feminist subject.

Lyshaug uses the example of literature as a way to cultivate enlarged sympathy with people and groups that have different experiences of oppression. But if one thinks of the vast literature that summons the image of "the oppressed Muslim woman,"[31] the ambivalent uses of this fictional vehicle to access experiences of oppression appear clearly. Indeed, this literature, based on the sharing of "authentic" narratives of oppression, reproduces stereotypes about Muslim women's specific plight as victims of their religion and their culture and presents their agency in reified ways. Doing so, they present feminist ideals of emancipation as incompatible with cultural diversity and especially Islam.[32] Rather than trouble the boundaries of "good" and "bad" feminist subjects, such a reading of the experience of oppression of "othered" women may indeed nurture enlarged sympathy, but only toward those Muslim women who fit the identity of absolute victim of patriarchy. Here enlarged sympathy might in fact reinforce the boundary between the good and the bad feminist subjects, instilling the conviction that Muslim women may either be absolute victims of their religion or adhere to Western feminist ideals and, if possible, reject their religious identities. More broadly, the strategy of enlarged sympathy poses the question of whose experience I shall try to enter into sympathy with. Are all experiences and all identities comparable and to be included in the feminist project? Are only experiences of oppression worth identifying with?

The ethical disposition proposed by Lyshaug is plagued with another problem, as it tends to suggest that, in fine, the feminist project revolves around an identity, that of women—and one might add, oppressed women. While it acknowledges that women may be oppressed in very different ways, the ethical disposition of enlarged sympathy is supposed to make possible connections between these experiences of oppression, without denying their different nature, degree, or content, as a precondition for feminist coalition. The focus on oppression as a prime locus of feminist identity thus implicitly rests on a common identity; an imaginary sharing of experience that strives for commonality, defined as a partial overlap, fostered by enlarged sympathy, between a variety of experiences of oppression. This idea that the feminist project is in fact about sisterhood, forging a common identity and sharing a partial overlap in experiences of oppression—even while recognizing that there may be wide differences between these experiences—constitutes the feminist project mainly as an identity project. A last assumption central to this proposal seems misplaced. Indeed, Lyshaug presents these ethical dispositions as first and foremost an introspective achievement, that is, focused on a relationship of the self to the self. There are many good reasons to think that a feminist ethics based on such a form of solipsism cannot provide a fertile ground for a collective project in the postsecular context.

Zerilli's Enlarged Mentality: Judgment and Feminist Ethics

Insights from the theoretical perspective elaborated by Linda Zerilli on feminism as a political project can help us explore why an ethics based on self-investigation is misdirected. Indeed, Zerilli has provided a trenchant critique of the focus of feminist theory on the "subject" of feminism rather than on action.[33] Promoting a conception of feminism that envisions it as a practice of freedom, rather than as an identity, Zerilli has argued convincingly that the wish to ground feminism in a common subject, "women," comes with a cost of which we should be wary. This cost is, simply put, that of losing the potential of feminism as a project of world-building. Indeed, freedom, as Zerilli understands it following Hannah Arendt, is an I-can, rather than an I-am. The focus on identity and on the subject of feminism, a focus that implies that emancipation rests ultimately in a form of self-transformation of subjectivity (from oppressed victim to emancipated subject), is misleading because, for Zerilli, it ignores the fact that freedom is a relational creation, not the possession or property of the subject: "No subjective relation of the self to itself, freedom requires a certain kind of relation to others in the space defined by plurality that Arendt calls the 'common world.'"[34] Read in this light, Lyshaug's proposal to direct ethical inquiry toward the self—to improve one's ability for imaginative impersonation—is misguided because it suggests that what needs to be salvaged and championed is some form of common identity, and that feminist practice is mostly a practice of the self, centered on the transformation of subjectivity.

Zerilli's call for a shift away from the "subject" question in feminism—and from the feminist subject—to embrace a conception of feminism as a practice of freedom is powerful. It implies that what feminism needs is not an identity but the capacity *to make and hold promises*. Indeed, following Arendt's argument presented in *The Human Condition*, Zerilli affirms that to address plurality, irreversibility, and the uncertainty of the world, what we have are promises and forgiveness. What makes possible and helps sustain a political we, a political action carried out as a collective entity, is the recognition of what Arendt calls our common world, or "the world between us."[35] Failing to honor this promise of political recognition of what unites and separates us, which is not a promise or illusion that we share a common identity, is what dooms the feminist project. In this perspective, it is not a common identity that grounds feminism as a political project, but the "world-building practice of publicly articulating matters of common concern."[36]

Zerilli's account of feminism directs our attention away from identity to the question of "free relations" among feminist subjects. It defines feminism as a project of articulating claims in the public space, claims that will materialize a collective political subject. The capacity to articulate those claims, so that they can be picked up by others, depends on the ability to exercise imagination and judgment. Here Zerilli draws on Arendt's concept of enlarged mentality that presupposes that one thinks and sees from the standpoint of others, thus viewing the world from different perspectives and, as a result, being able to make judgments.[37] Hence, the ethical disposition that corresponds to Zerilli's account of feminism is an enlarged mentality, understood as the ability that will ensure that my claims can materialize a political community. Indeed, if I do not engage in the exercise of enlarged mentality, in judging from the standpoint of others, then chances are that my claims will not be picked up by others. What is more, envisioning feminism as the political process by which political claims may be picked up by others means that those I might enroll, or exclude, can always "speak back to me."[38] Hence, the enlarged mentality also presupposes that I consider other feminists as my interlocutors, and that I cannot in advance decide who will or will not be part of that political project.

In this account of the feminist project, enlarged mentality is thus a feminist ethics in the service of building a political community. In Lyshaug's account, enlarged sympathy is a feminist ethics in the service of changing my own subjectivity, my relationship to myself, as a way to understand others, without identifying with them. Zerilli's proposal, on the contrary, is about forging a collective subject in the public space. Her account of enlarged mentality revolves around Arendt's conception of judgment. Rather than identification, or self-investigation, what she proposes is to develop an ability to *judge* differences between women. Indeed, Zerilli's theoretical proposal is a response to the debate about "differences" between women and the threat those differences supposedly represent for the feminist project. Using Arendt's vocabulary, Zerilli operates a shift from differences—understood as social differences—to plurality, which is both an ontological and a political concept. Indeed, for Arendt there is no such thing as two objects occupying the same position (ontological premise) and, for Zerilli, our points of view on the world will shape the political claims we make in the public space. With this shift, Zerilli denounces the idea that feminism is a project rooted in a common identity, which intersectional differences may put in peril. She argues on the contrary that plurality is the condition of any political community and that, at the same time, "plurality is a political relation that is irreducible to empirical differences."[39] Empirical, identity-based or social differences are *objects*, while the relations we establish between these differences, through judging, form the political relations that are the basis of a political community. Zerilli argues that the enlarged mentality enables us to learn how to acknowledge and judge such differences among women.[40]

Judging politically is not deliberating in search of a rational argument that everyone will agree upon. For Zerilli, it is rather, as in aesthetic judgment, an act based in a subjective validity that implies quarreling with others. Judging is a rhetorical ability used to persuade others, a creative act that "projects words into a new context."[41] It is not the logic we use that will convince others and enable us to judge differences among us, but, rather, our ability to see from different perspectives. Seeing the world from different perspectives, we can imagine relations between objects, we can judge differences. Hence, recognizing or celebrating empirical differences is not what a feminist project requires. What feminism requires is the continuous building of a public space defined by equality. This space is constructed by the repeated acts of judging our political differences, or quarreling, because only through this activity can I discover with whom I am in community.[42] In this ongoing process of judging and quarreling, I recognize and I sustain the plurality that characterizes my community. The space in which I perform this judgment is marked by equality: I recognize others as interlocutors. This recognition means that I cannot speak for others, and that I can always be spoken back to. There is, therefore, in Zerilli's account a fundamental reciprocity in the political relationship that the act of judging establishes.

Zerilli's account of feminism as an I-can, sustained by a community defined as a public space of equal participants, is invigorating. It proposes a radical alternative to the conception of feminism as a political project based on a shared identity, often reified to a politics of representation of othered women, being spoken for instead of spoken to. Zerilli's approach echoes the discourses of racialized feminists in Quebec and France when they claim the recognition by white feminists that they share common ground. Being recognized as an interlocutor is a condition for feminist coalition politics. However, her account of enlarged mentality as a feminist ethics that can sustain this feminist project needs to be complemented. Indeed, while Zerilli argues that enlarged mentality enables me to judge politically, and that empirical differences do not matter, her insistence on discarding issues linked to identity or social differences—which, along with Arendt, she expels from the domain of the political—might prove problematic. Racialized feminists claim that common ground should be recognized, and they *also* demand that asymmetries of power, entrenched in social differences, be recognized as well. Zerilli seems to believe that a space of equals can be created by sheer political will, abstracting social differences from relationships. But this declaration of will might also obscure concrete asymmetries of power and how they shape the political space, delimiting the boundaries of the community I pretend to make appear. How can I make sure that judging differences will not mean reenacting exclusions or erecting boundaries between those I recognize as similar to me and those that I deem different from me? If I am indeed asking with whom I am in community, if I am tracing the boundaries of a community of equals to whom I speak, am I not also excluding some participants from my community because the claims I make they cannot take up, or because, while they speak back to me, I am deaf to their voices?

Zerilli seems to presuppose that social differences will not matter in determining who is part of my feminist political community, because what matters are the claims I make. If I develop an enlarged mentality, I will be able to make those claims in ways that make them resonate for others. This belief contrasts starkly with the description I have given of how white feminists' claims may be emotionally attached to the preservation of white privilege, and therefore impossible to be picked up by racialized feminists. If a claim to gender equality is intimately linked to a claim that religious belief or Islamic veiling practices are inherently oppressive to women and irreconcilable with gender equality, then it will not be picked up by religious women, who will be excluded from the political community these claims are supposed to create. While white feminists might develop an enlarged mentality when it comes to taking the standpoint of Muslim women as victims of their community's patriarchy, they might be incapable of using an enlarged mentality to see the world from the points of view of Muslim feminists. As I have stated already, asymmetries of power structure feminists' moral dispositions: whiteness consolidates the moral boundaries erected between "good" and "bad" feminist subjects, and claims by white feminists that they embody the "good" feminist subject will be impossible to pick up for those very subjects they define as "bad." I remain unconvinced that the capacity for enlarged mentality, as defined by Zerilli, will translate into the necessary self-critique of experiences and claims that privileged feminists must engage in.

What is more, Zerilli's defiance vis-à-vis social identity is problematic for racialized feminists, or any other minoritized group mobilizing for a voice in the public space and for emancipation. Indeed, as Bruno Perreau underlines, reflecting on queer politics in Europe, "Minorities do not have the luxury of disavowing, once and for all, their sense of belonging."[43] The symmetry that Zerilli suggests exists between all the participants that build, through their claims, a political community thus ignores that we are not positioned similarly toward our social identities, and evades the question of power asymmetries within the political community that is being formed. This inattentiveness toward our different social ascriptions and belonging make Zerilli's conception of enlarged mentality insufficient for the project of forging and sustaining equal moral bonds within feminism. There is no guarantee that the enlarged mentality proposed by Zerilli will destabilize the boundary between "good" and "bad" feminist subjects and provide a feminist community that is more inclusive. While her approach rejects founding the feminist project on a common identity, it does not question the concrete conditions under which an enlarged mentality can avoid reproducing similar exclusions. How can an enlarged mentality be developed in the context of asymmetries of power? What does it mean to see the world from the others' point of view when points of view are shaped by different and intersecting power relations? This question is all the more crucial to ask when it comes to the ability of those in positions of privilege to develop an enlarged mentality.

Young's Enlarged Thought: Asymmetries and Inclusion

Iris Young addresses this issue in her reflection on enlarged thought. Indeed, she notes that there is no such thing as taking the standpoint of someone else in a context in which social asymmetries characterize my relationship with that person. What is missing in the account that Zerilli provides of the enlarged mentality is specifically the questioning of the relation that exists between the participants. While she defines this relationship as one of political equality, she glosses over the concrete inequalities that will also certainly define it. More careful to take into account the impact that social asymmetries might have on moral and political relations, Young states that an encounter carries me beyond my own standpoint but "does not carry me into the standpoint of the other person."[44] For Young, we cannot pretend to reverse position or to grasp the other's position because such a claim "neglects to conceptualize the relation between us."[45] While Zerilli suggests a form of symmetry in the moral and political relation forged through enlarged mentality—speaking to and being spoken to, in a context in which both interlocutors are considered equals—Young insists that there are no symmetrical positions in the world. She insists that "this idea of a symmetry in our relation obscures the difference and particularity of the other position," and risks misrepresenting its claims. Second, she continues, "It is ontologically impossible for people in one social position to adopt the perspective of those in the social positions with which they are related in social structures and interaction."[46] Hence, while Zerilli suggested that we make judgment by being outside of ourselves, seeing the world from others' points of view, Young is more careful in her assessment of the conditions under which enlarged thought can flourish, and indicates that for our moral claims to be valid we must not only take into account one another's interests and claims, but also consider "the collective social processes and relationships that lie between us."[47]

Young's reflection on moral relations in the context of social asymmetries complicates Zerilli's account of enlarged mentality. Young's examples and her analysis suggest that her prime concern in critiquing the idea of symmetrical moral respect is her concern for asymmetries of power. She writes: "When privileged people put themselves in the position of those who are less privileged, the assumptions derived from their privilege often allow them unknowingly to misrepresent the other's situation."[48] To address this situation of social asymmetry, Young argues that in interactive communication with less privileged individuals, privileged ones might refrain from identification, preserve a form of distance, and adopt an attitude of moral humility. Wary of identification with individuals situated in different social positions, Young argues that communication is not about identification but rather a creative act through which, by listening and remaining open to difference, I might transcend my own experience and point of view. For Young, such an ideal and practice of communication as asymmetrical reciprocity will make it possible to build relations of solidarity or similarity. It will foster possibilities of agreement by recognizing the plurality of experiences without presupposing that we must share similar experiences or positions to understand each other.

Hence, Young's response to the acknowledgment of power asymmetries structuring social relations is to promote a form of enlarged thought that is based on "respectful distancing"[49] and moral humility, as well as "wonder" and "gift giving." Indeed, Young argues that communication is always a gift; it is an opening up to the other person, and all the more so when social asymmetries structure relationships. Gift giving is a way to recognize the creative dimension of communication, to enact the sense of wonder—pleasurable surprise in the face of difference—that Young is calling for to define communicative ethics. She complements this proposal in her book *Inclusion and Democracy*, where she argues that real democratic inclusion demands that social differentiation be acknowledged within theorization of communicative ethics and democratic deliberation. She underlines that despite formal presence, "internal exclusion" can affect minorities marked by social differences when they are formally participants in the debate, but in fact are not heard and feel excluded.[50] She therefore proposes several types of communicative practices, such as greetings, that might counteract this informal exclusion. Hence, Young's proposal for ensuring moral respect in the process of communication is both based on the nurturing of moral dispositions, such as wonder and humility, and on practical forms of address intended to reflect and nurture these moral dispositions, such as greetings or what she calls the "affirmative use of rhetoric," which recognizes that emotions participate in communication and orient one toward her audience.[51]

Several of Young's insights about communicative ethics can be recaptured to define a feminist ethics. Her vision of enlarged thought—which acknowledges the asymmetries of positions—and the various modalities of communicating that she suggests can enhance it are, I think, more adequate than the enlarged mentality proposed by Zerilli, which tends to obscure power relations between feminists. Young elaborates her perspective on enlarged thought in the context of reflecting on inclusive democratic deliberation. Deliberation within feminist movements could certainly benefit from Young's insights. Indeed, Young's proposal to define communicative ethics in a way that will not exclude the groups whose identities and interests have been historically represented as marginal, and who have been formally or informally excluded from deliberation, echoes important issues within contemporary feminist movements. Her insights on inclusive political communication are certainly useful to promote feminist coalition building across divides of race, class, or sexuality.

However, Young's aim is to ensure democratic inclusion in order to reach fairer decisions. Hers is an issue of justice in societies marked by plurality, and she acknowledges that the style of communicative ethics she advocates will not make agreement easier to reach because it will multiply standpoints and enliven discussions.[52] While feminism is also marked by plurality, and while many feminist organizations must reach decisions while ensuring the inclusion of the viewpoints of their internal minorities, the questions that have been raised in the context of sexularism debates are not mainly about reaching fair decisions. They rather point to the moral hierarchies and exclusions that are perpetuated in the name of feminism's values, and to the challenge of sustaining a political community of equals in the name of feminism. Young's proposals may seem unable to address these issues. In particular, while she acknowledges asymmetries of power, the enlarged thought and wonder for which she advocates may seem inadequate to disestablish whiteness and its corrosive effects.

There is a tension perceptible in Young's *Inclusion and Democracy* between taking into account asymmetries of power and providing a theory of moral respect that, in fact, places all agents in equal moral positions. A tension thus emerges between recognizing how social injustices and inequalities shape our moral world, and recognizing that they position us in different moral positions. The communicative tactics that Young artfully describes to ensure ethical communication across differences and asymmetries, such as gift giving or storytelling, do take into account the asymmetrical positioning of the participants. Indeed, Young's aim is to provide narrative spaces for the voiceless, and to dissociate the powerful from the belief that her experience can be made universal or that she embodies a "view from nowhere," situated above the particular experiences of concrete others. Hence Young's proposals demonstrate that she is keenly aware of how our positions of belonging to minority or majority groups—to groups historically discriminated against or groups that have been considered to embody the universal standpoint—situate us on different moral grounds, or at least in different locations from where to engage in democratic deliberation.

However, she does not suggest that these positions may assign us different *moral responsibilities*. While she pays attention to the relation that defines asymmetrical positions, emphasizing that because of that very relation I cannot pretend to "put myself in the shoes" of someone else, she does not infer that this asymmetrical relation may place different moral responsibilities on its participants. For example, discussing asymmetrical reciprocity between white and Black American feminists in the context of the Anita Hill Supreme Court hearings in 1991, Young advises that white feminists should have approached the issue with caution and moral humility. She advocates a form of respectful distance, rather than moral responsibility, on the part of those who are privileged because of their lack of appreciation of the complexity of intersectional marginalization. Young considers differences in standpoints important because they produce a more democratic and inclusive discussion, because "having to be accountable to people from diverse social positions with different needs, interests, and experience helps transform discourse from self-regard to appeals to justice."[53] However, she disregards here the fact that these differences are the product of relations, placing some in positions of power *over* others. Those different needs and interests are relational and therefore antagonistic: the needs of the privileged are based on the denial of the needs of those who are oppressed by those very same privileges.

Both Zerilli and Young focus their ethical inquiry into enlarged thought on communication across difference. Zerilli addresses the issue from the perspective of political equality, insisting that, when making claims in the public space that can be picked up by others and act as bonds for a political community, I must accept being spoken back to and, importantly, that my claims convey this promise of hearing when spoken back to. Young argues, from the perspective of communicative ethics, that equal moral respect entails in fact moral wonder, moral humility, and a form of "gift" by opening up a conversation in which I am not sure the other will reciprocate.[54] Here too, then, I will be spoken back to in terms I have not chosen and cannot anticipate.

But is a posture of wonder and gift enough to ensure moral bonds in a common political project? Can my agreement to be spoken back to prove sufficient in a context of deep asymmetries of power? How should the fact of being spoken back to actually affect me? Does my responsibility lie only in listening, or should I be responsible to act upon what has been said to me?

Feminist whiteness, understood as a position of privilege that sustains moral boundaries and exclusions from the feminist project, poses these questions with an acute intensity. Zerilli's and Young's proposals to develop enlarged mentality/thought remain unsatisfactory for reflecting on the types of moral bonds that can build and maintain a political community across differences, and, in particular, a community in which whiteness, as a site of privilege and moral superiority, is disestablished. Whiteness is no mere difference of perception or of position in the world. A property procuring rights and configuring expectations of entitlement, it structures privileges and dispossessions, supremacy and subjection.[55] I explore now what a consideration of feminist whiteness as a form of political and moral wrong can bring to reflection on the features of a *feminist ethic of responsibility*.

Whiteness and the Denial of Relationality

I argue that asymmetries of power within feminism call not only for equal moral respect, or asymmetrical reciprocity, but also for a feminist ethic of responsibility, and that such an ethics may provide an important normative principle to foster moral bonds invigorating a critical feminist community. My argument here is twofold. I first argue that a feminist ethic of responsibility must acknowledge relationality between feminists. Such an acknowledgment provides an important lever to disestablish whiteness and the moral hierarchies it sustains. Second, in the next section I argue that a feminist ethic of responsibility must be understood not as a virtue or disposition one must nurture, a self-involved reflection, but rather as an activity, an instance of moral pragmatism.

First, let's remember again the of racialized feminists in France and Quebec presented in the previous chapter. Their words aim to make white feminists both acknowledge common ground and recognize power inequalities and their privileges. However, they find in many cases resistance to their demands. In particular, what I have described as feminist whiteness—a propensity to universalize one's experience and position of privilege and to draw moral boundaries between deserving and undeserving feminist subjects—presents a site of resistance to the claims made by racialized feminists. This resistance is all the more pervasive because emotions and moral dispositions, such as anger, self-righteousness, and benevolence, sustain many feminists' attachment to feminist whiteness. Hence, despite voicing their discontent, grievances, and resentment, despite formulating their moral address toward white feminists, racialized feminists rarely experience being spoken back to on equal terms or having their discourse picked up by others. This does not mean their moral address always fails and their discourses always remain unheard. As the various examples of coalition I have given in this chapter and the preceding one show, white feminists sometimes act upon—respond to—the discourses that are being spoken back to them by racialized feminists. However, I am interested here in challenging and dislocating the resistance entrenched in feminist whiteness, and in arguing for the necessity to acknowledge common ground as a prerequisite for a critical feminist project.

I analyze here feminist whiteness as driving a denial of the relationality that links white and nonwhite feminists, a denial of common ground. Feminist whiteness secures moral hierarchies between good and bad feminist subjects, as well as the privileged embodiment of feminism by white feminist subjects. In doing so, feminist whiteness also operates a denial of relationality between feminist subjects across racial or religious divides. Not only do some white feminists question the very possibility that pious Muslim women can be feminists, they also reject vehemently any possible ties, any common ground with them. This denial of relationality is not specific to feminist whiteness. Indeed, it is in fact an important feature of racial privilege. Reflecting on how racial privilege is based on an epistemology of ignorance, Sarah Lucia Hoagland argues that "epistemological and ethical practices of ignorance are strategic and involve a denial of relationality."[56] Hence racial privilege is based upon, and secured, by practices of ignorance about the life and material conditions of those who are oppressed by racial subjection. In order to sustain this ignorance and the privileges it secures, whites have an interest in denying that their existence is interdependent with that of those who are oppressed by racism. While our subjectivities are relationally formed, whiteness performs an erasure of that relationality when it comes to acknowledging interdependence with people of color. As Hoagland surmises: "Whiteness doesn't exist independently from engagements with people of color, even, or especially, if those engagements are white practices of erasure."[57]

I have described the practices of erasure and marginalization of racialized feminists that characterize the discourses of some white feminists, and their role in securing feminist whiteness. Understanding these practices as performing acts of denial of relationality helps us to characterize their profoundly moral implications. Different issues are at stake in these accounts of whiteness that deny relationality with racialized feminists. One is ethical violence; the other is a moral posture that identifies feminism with whiteness and prevents the advent of an ethic of responsibility. One of the discursive repertoires sustaining feminist whiteness that I have described in chapter 4 uses the supposed universality of gender oppression to minimize the pervasiveness of racial oppression, or to justify ignoring it for the sake of political efficiency. This appropriation of universality can be defined, following Judith Butler's reading of Adorno, as a form of ethical violence. Drawing on Adorno, who "uses the term *violence* in relation to ethics in the context of claims about universality,"[58] she affirms that if an ethos based on universality "ignores the existing social conditions which are also the conditions under which any ethics might be appropriated, that ethos becomes violent."[59] In other words, violence resides in discursive operations that render it impossible for some groups to appropriate universality. While Butler is more concerned about individual ethical formation, her reflection illuminates some of the ethical stakes of feminist whiteness. By associating whiteness and gender universality, feminist whiteness performs a form of ethical violence. Furthermore, beyond the question of the appropriation of universality, there is, more broadly, ethical violence in the nonrecognition of race as a system of racial subjection and in the nonrecognition of white privilege.

However, as I described earlier, feminist whiteness is not always predicated upon the appropriation of universalism, or on the denial of racism as a structure of power. More often, feminist whiteness hinges on the drawing of moral boundaries that expel "bad subjects" from the feminist community. While some white feminists may define themselves as antiracist activists and act upon that political claim, they may simultaneously perform exclusions, denying other feminists—or other women—the possibility of claiming themselves feminists, portraying them as improper feminist subjects in need of regulation. Analyzing this moral impulse as a denial of relationality with racialized feminists can help us trace its moral implications and delineate an alternative moral account, based on a feminist ethic of responsibility. Indeed, to borrow the words of psychologist Pascale Molinier, "Any of us can, if she wants to, understand,"[60] meaning, here, be attentive to the language of the other: I can choose to know or not to know. I can decide to focus my sustained attention on what will become of the young girls wearing a veil who are expelled from public school, or not to do so. Of course, as Molinier underlines with others ethicists of care, "*Our* responsibility is always limited or restricted by its context; but no position of exteriority is legitimate, we cannot leave the world."[61]

Relationality and Responsibility

Relational accounts of morality, such as those developed by Veena Das[62] or Joan Tronto,[63] ground the moral character of our actions in the social and relational nature of our lives and humanity. All these approaches, whether they define themselves as theories of care or ethics of the ordinary, place (inter)dependency and vulnerability at the heart of human life, and therefore at the center of moral relations.[64] Both Das and Tronto draw on an intellectual tradition, represented by Ludwig Wittgenstein and Stanley Cavell, that conceives morality as grounded in our concrete existence, our form of life. This tradition recognizes that our humanity and subjectivity exist only through the form of life to which they belong. Our voices, as subjects, exist because of language, which is "an inherited form of life."[65] Hence, as Sandra Laugier affirms, "The voice is both a subjective and a general expression: it is what makes it possible for my individual voice to become shared."[66] Here the interdependency between the individual and the context, a form of life, appears clearly. My very sense of being a subject depends on a language, a form of life, which is by definition collective. Theories of care and relational accounts of morality are thus attentive to ordinary life, to what makes possible the perpetuation of a life form, to concrete others and to their needs, always specific, and to the moral emotions and feelings they elicit in us. Far from grand theories of justice, an ethics of care concentrates on the moral implications of recognizing that we share a life form, that we share common ground.

In these relational and contextual accounts of morality,[67] how I relate to otherness is central in defining the moral nature of my actions and feelings. Joan Tronto, for example, starts her reflection in *Moral Boundaries* by stressing that the question of "what our relationship with other people who are close and distant should be" and "the need to be attentive to viewing others' circumstances in a whole context"[68] are the crucial questions for moral inquiry. Such a statement is not a repetition of otherness as difference. Rather, to reflect on our moral relations with others is to reflect on the form of life we share with them. This appears clearly in Veena Das's account of morality, which also places concrete others at the heart of moral inquiry.

Rejecting accounts of morality that place its locus inside the subject, Das explains: "If the ethical subject here is the set of relations rather than an individual who is the locus of decision, then a moral life is crafted as much out of the affective force of an attunement to this other who is not wholly other.... The paths to a moral life do not lie here in either rule following or in taking recourse to technologies of self-making but rather in the attentiveness through which one ties one's own fate to that of the other."[69] For Das, our moral response to others—for example, to their pain—which we identify not primarily thanks to cognitive reasoning but rather through the feelings it elicits, this response that I observe in myself, "reveals what stakes I have in our lives together."[70] Moral feelings are therefore crucial because they remind me that I share common ground with others and that this common ground obliges me: I have stakes in this common life. Refusing to acknowledge this common ground, denying relationality, is therefore a form of moral wrong. It is a moral wrong in the broad or general sense that doing so is to refuse responsibility for my relationships with others, and to strip them of their voice. Das expresses this idea when she states: "Not trusting the words of the other is in effect a lack of trust in the other and in our mutual capacity to have a future together."[71]

Sandra Laugier suggests, in the same vein, that, since we share language as a life form, when I refuse to accept the words of others, I am also depriving them of their voice. She asks: "If my society is my expression it should also allow me to find my voice. But is this really the case? If others stifle my voice, speak for me, I will always seem to consent. One does not have a voice, *one's own voice*. It must be found so as to speak in the name of others and to let others speak in one's name. For if others do not accept my words, I lose more than language: I lose my voice."[72] We hear echoes of Linda Zerilli's analysis of the role of feminist claims in constituting a political community. Relying on Wittgenstein and the idea that we must always project words into new contexts, Zerilli also emphasizes that feminists make claims that must be picked up by others in order to constitute a community. For these claims to be picked up by others, she proposes that feminists nurture enlarged mentality so as to be able to see the world from others' points of view. However, in her view, if my claims are not picked up by others, it is because I did not articulate them in a way that responds to their situation or that meets their judgment of the world. Laugier's account differs here because she stresses that claims might not be picked up not only because our judgments of objects differ but also because my claim, as the expression of my voice, is not recognized, because my words are not accepted. And this, she insists, constitutes a moral wrong, because I, or you, will be deprived of my/your voice. Hence, denying common ground, denying relationality, constitutes a moral harm.

Having said so, the question remains of how we should acknowledge relationality and common ground in the context of feminism. With whom am I in community in such a way that that person can lay claims on me and that I must acknowledge common ground with her? Because they focus on how we relate to others, and on how this relationality should shape our moral lives, relational accounts of morality seem to be a well-suited entry point into the question of how to delineate a feminist ethic of responsibility. Recognizing that we share common ground means that we let this common ground lay a claim on us, that of recognizing "what stakes I have in our lives together," to use again Das's words. Relationality implies here a reciprocal responsibility (which does not mean that it is symmetrical), of one toward another because we share common ground. If feminism is our common ground, because we have come to give an account of ourselves as feminists, therefore laying a claim on other feminists and accepting that they can lay claims on us, what type of responsibility does this political project, and the political community it proposes to constitute, imply?

In exploring this question, Joan Tronto's ethic of care provides important insights. Indeed, it understands morality and moral responsibility as shaped by and embedded in a social and political context. It does not shy away from acknowledging power and, rather, proposes to conceptualize how the political context and the power asymmetries it produces must be incorporated into how we think about moral responsibility.[73] This premise has two implications. For one, care is not only about our relationships with those we care for in an intimate and personal way. Care, as an "ethical practice of making complex moral judgment"[74] that implies attentiveness, responsibility, competence, and responsiveness, can—and Tronto claims, should—also be understood as a political idea. She argues that "the practice of care describes the qualities necessary for democratic citizens to live together well in a pluralistic society, and that only in a just, pluralistic, democratic society can care flourish."[75] This approach makes her ethic of care particularly suited for reflecting on a feminist ethic of responsibility.

The second implication of Tronto's premise that the moral and the political cannot be separated is a proposal to acknowledge power asymmetries in terms of differential responsibilities. Similarly to Iris Young's cautious reminder that we cannot put ourselves in the shoes of others, only meet them halfway, Tronto insists that we cannot project our morality onto others without any consideration for the context in which they are situated. Hence, while her ethic of care recognizes, and is predicated upon, the fact that humans share an ontological position of interdependency—a premise shared also, for example, by Butler's ethical proposal based on the precariousness of life—Tronto's approach to the ethic of care is not confined to this ontological claim but articulates it with the political and social differences produced by the social world, differences that bring us closer together or further away, differences that give us power over others or place us in positions of vulnerability to others' power.

This approach thus complexifies our understanding of the moral claims that an ethic of care lays on us, depending on the context in which we respond to the moral questions that our political relationship with others asks of us. In this vein, Tronto states: "To make simple applications of moral precepts to another's situation as if none of the constraints of power within which people's lives should affect our moral judgments, results in moral thought that is ultimately unresponsive to the genuine lives and moral concerns of 'others.'"[76] Power asymmetries therefore demand different types of responsiveness and attentiveness to others. While Tronto shares with Young the idea that we must be attentive to power asymmetries and, therefore, that we cannot assume that others will share our moral judgments, Tronto is not interested in remedying this social distance, and this power imbalance, thanks to enlarged thought or wonder. Rather than exploring how we must nurture certain moral and affective qualities in order to empathize with or understand others, she insists that what these asymmetries imply is rather a critical reflection toward our own position and what specific responsibility it entails. Indeed, she underscores that social privilege translates as "privileged irresponsibility";[77] that is, that those who are privileged usually don't have to care: denial of relationality is also a denial of responsibility. On the contrary, she argues that privileges should entail *more* responsibility to care, a state of moral engagement rather than a condition of detachment or of denial of relationality and responsibility.

How and when should we be responsible to care? How and when do our relationships entail the responsibility for caring for others, or for working to redress injustices that affect them? Both Iris Young and Joan Tronto propose some reflections on this issue. Considering both that relationality entails responsibility, and that care—as a complex form of moral judgment—must be placed in its political and social context, means that, to borrow Tronto's expression, moral responsibility is *relational*.[78] It will vary depending on the relations at stake. The relational conception of responsibility that Tronto advocates for shares important premises with Iris Young's social connection model of responsibility, which argues that all agents who participate in one way or another in structural processes leading to injustice have a responsibility to work to remedy it.[79] Indeed, both conceptions of responsibility rest on the idea that what connects us, the relationships we nurture with others—partial or extensive and through different mediums, such as kinship, practices, environment, institutions, projects—defines the type of responsibility that we will have to consider and the nature of the demands to which we must respond.[80]

However, how can we find out what type of relation implies what type of responsibility? In order to do so, both theorists explore different venues. Young insists on analyzing and taking into account the position of the moral agent, in terms of power, resources, and capacities to contribute to social change and to redress injustice.[81] For a feminist ethic of responsibility this is obviously a very important principle. Positions of power, within the movement and within organizations, imply access to resources, and therefore a privileged position to address situations of injustice within the movement. They should therefore also lead to a greater responsibility to do so. An example might be, in Quebec, the way that the province-wide federation for women's rights (the FFQ) took responsibility for carrying out a survey of racialized women's positions (their share and their status as officers or volunteers and the according salaries) within feminist organizations in the province. On the basis of this survey the federation suggested giving priority to racialized women in hiring processes in feminist organizations.

Joan Tronto provides another perspective on how to decide what type of relationship leads to what type of responsibility, which can complement Young's proposal and help delineate a feminist ethic of responsibility. She proposes to "measure" responsibility by evaluating the harm done by *irresponsibility*. Indeed, she notes: "From a relational approach, it is not simply the agent's voluntarism, or the strength of the causal chain, but the consequence of acting irresponsibly that determines the degree of harm that comes from irresponsibility. Some elements become more important in assessing the harm of irresponsibility. For example, the imbalances of power in relationships."[82] Assessing the nature of a relationship, and its concomitant responsibility, through the notion of the harm done by irresponsibility in the context of such a relationship draws attention to the fact that it is the *quality* of the relationship that produces a moral obligation, not the formalistic nature of this relationship. Tronto here takes an example from Marilyn Friedman: kinship in itself may not entail responsibility; the quality of the relationship with a family member will determine the type of responsibility brought about by kinship. Of course, power impacts the quality of the relationship, in particular because it means that some actions might have different consequences for both parties to the relationship. The Islamic veil is a good example. Feminist discourses in favor of veiling bans claim to represent the interests of all women, thereby creating a moral relationship between them. Nevertheless, when non-Muslim women favor a ban on Muslim headscarves, they will not bear the direct consequences of their action, while Muslim women will. Hence, the harm that irresponsibility brings with our actions is an important guide, in that it is also an indication of the quality of the relationship. In particular, for Tronto, it indicates the power imbalances that structure this relation. Power brings privilege and the possibility of irresponsibility.

A Feminist Ethic of Responsibility: Caring for Feminist Subjects

Now, thinking about the quality of the relationship and the harm done by irresponsibility, and bringing this discussion back to the question of a feminist ethic of responsibility, I argue that we need to complement the accounts proposed by Iris Young and Joan Tronto if we want to characterize what in the nature of the feminist project creates a relationship, the nature of this relationship, and the responsibilities it entails. Critics of the relational account of responsibility argue that we do not choose the relationships we are drawn into, or at least most of them, especially those that connect us to distant others, such as markets, institutions, or national communities.[83] This critique does not hold for the responsibilities that arise from our commitment to feminism. We choose to give an account of ourselves as feminists—and indeed many people choose *not* to do so. There is here a commitment not only to a political ideal, but also to the political community that may embody this ideal.[84] By claiming to speak in the name of women, we might imagine that we are *representing* all women, and that the political relationship that defines our feminist commitment is one of political representation. Thus, the claim to speak "in the name of women" does carry some political and moral responsibility. Indeed, imagining oneself as representing other women is, to a certain extent, to make a promise to care about other women. The promise to care can manifest itself in weak ways, such as feeling affected by other women's plight, reacting to their pain, or voicing concern about them. It can take a deeper form if I see myself as *representing* the interests of other women; I need then to take an interest in their lives, and I make a promise that I will represent them—their identities and their interests. Hence, understood as a classic relationship of political representation, feminism already carries moral responsibilities to care about other women.

However, this conception of feminism—as producing relationships of political representation that would entail specific types of responsibilities, similar to those of a spokesperson or a political representative—is, I think, inadequate, both to describe the reality of the political community created by the feminist project, and to reflect on the type of moral relationships feminism gives rise to. While this conception may capture some types of feminist activism, especially in its encounter with institutions, bureaucracies, and international organizations, it does not apprehend the experiences of the grassroots feminist activists I encountered, nor the subjectivities and moral relations described in many well-known feminist narratives retracing solidarity and conflicts among feminists.[85] I have argued that to give an account of oneself as a feminist is the result of a process of political subjectivation, which entails deep moral and political connections, both to the subject herself—identifying as a feminist, adhering to a set of beliefs and transforming one's subjectivity according to them—and to the collective subject, the political community, created by feminism. The emotional attachment to feminism as a collective political project that I have described thoroughly in the preceding chapters suggests a specific *quality* of the relationship that feminists may entertain with feminism as a collective project, and with the political community that may embody it in the context in which they are situated. This quality is not adequately expressed by the understanding of this relationship as one of political representation. In claiming to speak in the name of women, or in adhering to feminism as a political community, I make a promise, a promise not only to care about other women, but also to care about other feminists, *to care about the political community that defines itself through this project*.

Relational accounts of morality distinguish relationships, and the moral obligations they give rise to, depending on their nature. Not all relations will imply moral obligations. Soran Reader cites various grounds for relationships that give rise to moral obligations: presence (if some stranger collapses in front of me, I shall help), biology (as creating kinship), history (intertwining of lives over time), practices, environment, institutions, play, and conversation all provide grounds of different nature for different moral obligations.[86] Reader also cites "shared projects" among the relationships creating some type of moral obligation. Feminism can be understood as a shared project, giving rise to moral obligations for its participants. How does a political community such as feminism qualify in specific ways the relationships among its members, and what are the responsibilities it may give rise to? While history and historical legacies, such as those of colonialism or historical feminist struggles, certainly qualify the relationships that feminists may sustain among themselves, the promise that binds them, the promise to care about feminism as a collective project, also gives to these relationships a specific quality. Hence if, following Tronto, we must define the quality of the relationship that defines moral obligation, I argue that, with respect to feminists, it is the *promise, a promise to care for other feminists as equals* and for the collective project of feminism, that binds this political community together and that obligates feminists toward one another. Any discussion among feminists inevitably revolves around not only the right strategies to achieve specific goals, or the rights goods or ends to fight for (sexual safety or sexual freedom, equality or autonomy, etc.), but also the future of the feminist project. Feminists voice a care for the future of their project, which denotes or expresses the quality of feminism as a political community. This community is an exercise in political imagination. It can stretch to the size of the globe, but it is also always embodied in the very concrete relationships that feminists sustain among themselves in a specific context. Most importantly, this community *matters* for feminists, and connects them.

Caring for the feminist project is also expressed in the dismay, trouble, bitterness, or sorrow expressed by those feminists who feel that feminism is in peril, or that their political community, and the project it embodied, has disappeared. Hence the emotional attachment to feminism that I have described in the preceding chapters suggest that giving an account of oneself as a feminist is to claim to be part of a political community, to acknowledge that feminism matters to one's life, and, subsequently, to make a promise that one will care about this community. Of course, as I have shown, who is supposed to be included in this community in practice, who can legitimately embody the feminist subject, is a site of conflicts and competing moral evaluations. Nevertheless, aside from these conflicts—to which I will return promptly—there is a common drive, what de Lauretis called "the ethical drive in feminism,"[87] to be recognized by others as a feminist and to recognize them as such. From this drive a relationship is constituted, which entails responsibilities: first and foremost the responsibility to care, not only for *women*, but also, and more importantly, for other *feminists*. I cannot decide in advance who will be part of this community, and I am morally obliged toward those whose claims relate them to me through feminism.

Is this care the one described by care theorists? I would like to defend the idea that the care that we can place at the center of a feminist ethic of responsibility has a strong family resemblance with the care that is traditionally the object of care theorists' reflections. Tronto defines the values of caring as attentiveness, responsibility, nurturance, compassion, and meeting others' needs.[88] In the context of feminism as the relationship that binds together a political community, attentiveness and responsibility certainly should be part of a feminist ethics. Nurturance and compassion may invoke sorority-like images that have been, for good reasons, criticized as the wrong metaphors to define relationships among feminists, metaphots which have erased power asymmetries within feminist communities. For Tronto, because an ethic of care should be attentive to particularity, it does not posit a "false sense of community or of identity among people within a community,"[89] so that nurturing and compassion do not imply an emphasis on commonality over differences. However, attentiveness to particularity is difficult to enact in the context of relations defined by a common political project such as feminism, because these relations are, more often than not, relations with distant others, and the particularity of their situation will not always be properly grasped. What is more, defining a feminist ethic of responsibility as centered on compassion may miss the very political nature of the feminist project. Linda Zerilli has proposed a useful distinction—drawn from Hannah Arendt's critique of the displacement of the political by the social—between feminism as a project of taking care of a social question (i.e., meeting women's needs) and feminism articulated as a political community, which is the product of a world-building activity. While compassion may certainly be, in certain contexts, a moral force engaged in the building of a political community, I argue that it may not be the case for a feminist ethics. Feminism as a political project should not be defined around meeting *needs*, but rather should be defined from the perspective of the community it aims to create, the transformation it may bring to our lives.

How could this be translated in moral terms? I draw here a connection between Joan Tronto and Veena Das that can help specify the contours of a feminist ethic of responsibility. Indeed, Tronto comments that "caring requires that one starts from the standpoint of the one needing care or attention. It requires that we meet the other morally, adopt that person's, or group's, perspective and look at the world in those terms."[90] The question of adopting a person's or group's perspective, or meeting it halfway, has been discussed when I elaborated on the notion of "enlarged mentality." It is often presented as an exercise of imagination, a demand to change one's subjectivity. This subjective account is challenged by an analysis made by Soraya. She remarks about the FFQ, of which she is a member:

> I am at pains to see more diversity than in this organization, but it does not mean that it translates into [changes in how the organization addresses racial issues] . . . The members have not integrated, in their institutions, in their . . . practices. There is great resistance and a big emotional charge linked to this idea that we are trying to make them feel guilty, that they have no lesson to learn from anybody. . . . They refuse the political consciousness that the movement is proposing to them, especially when it comes to Muslim women who continue to feel attachment to their culture of origin, their religion, their headscarf, etc.

Here we find several elements already discussed in previous chapters: the interweaving of political, moral, and emotional issues when it comes to defining the parameters of who should be included in the feminist project, and the perpetuation of white ignorance thanks to a posture of moral superiority, articulated with a rejection of responsibility through a rejection of guilt. Notable in this quotation is the nature of Soraya's demand to white feminists who resist their own organization's attempts to elaborate an inclusive discourse. She is critical about white feminists' refusal to include, or to adopt, a certain *political consciousness*. She is not looking for compassion or for her needs to be understood. Rather, it is the very political nature of her claims, as claims that could foster and found a political community inclusive of Muslim women, that she wants to be heard and adopted by white feminists. In that sense, she is asking for what Veena Das describes as the ethical activity of "creating a space of possibility for the other."[91] I interpret Soraya's words as a call to include in the life of the feminist political community "some aspects of the life of the other."[92] What is more, this space of possibility for the other is one in which that other is considered an equal, a space that creates equal relationships, as Soraya's rejection of the idea, latter in her interview, that she could join the "common table" as a "little sister" clearly states.

Creating this "space of possibility" should therefore be an important element of a feminist ethic of responsibility, one of the ethical activities through which caring for feminism as a political project and a political community is enacted, a way to make the promise that Hannah Arendt deems necessary for a political community to be constituted.

Caring for Women / Caring for Feminist Subjects: A Feminist Politics of Emotions

Thinking about a feminist ethic of responsibility as a moral obligation to create this space of possibility for the other in the political community created by feminism enables us to draw a distinction between a feminist ethic as *caring* for other women, and as *caring* for potential feminist subjects. This distinction encourages us, I contend, to critically examine common feminist politics of emotions, and to nurture specific emotions and moral dispositions. When discussing feminist whiteness in chapter 4, I contrasted the attitudes of some white feminist volunteers in women's rights organizations toward racialized women when the latter are considered as benevolent objects of care, and when they are considered as potential feminist subjects. The distinction I want to draw now, from an ethical point of view, between caring for other *women* and caring for other *feminists* as members of a political community elaborates on the distinction between these two different moral dispositions. Indeed, I argue that *caring* for other women, a moral disposition that is prevalent in the relationship that many (white) feminist volunteers and activists create with women who benefit from the services of their organization, may prove misguided. Indeed, more often than not, that caring does not take into account that the women that feminists intend to care about are *distant others* who look like them, to borrow Joan Tronto's words: the distance and the power asymmetries that structure the relationship with them tend to be ignored in the very name of the care that feminists want to express. Hence, distant "othered" women are made to embody specific qualities, often revolving around their need for help and vulnerability, that reproduce power asymmetries, as well as the injunction for the powerless to address the powerful in the terms set by the latter.

Caring for other women who are in fact more often than not distant others is a perilous exercise in some contexts: for example, when feminists do not know enough about the context of these distant others' lives and moral concerns, or when they may have difficulty in discerning the terms in which the powerless express their claims, because the powerless might not have a recognized voice or access to public discourse.[93] What is more, the emotions that sustain the moral disposition to care for distant other women may prove misguided for critical and reflexive feminist politics. Postcolonial feminist theorists have largely documented and criticized the posture of benevolence and the emotions that sustain it as deeply embedded in postcolonial representations of the "Other."[94] Indeed, distant others are imagined, rather than encountered, and emotions such as compassion and benevolence, not rooted in actual relations, may evaporate if and when distant others reveal themselves to be different from the "good" subject that was imagined.

The ability to properly care for other women, as a specific feminist moral responsibility, will therefore depend both on distance and on the capacity of feminists to reflect upon power asymmetries. This is evident when comparing the discourses of feminists who work in grassroots organizations that provide services to women and feminists who do mostly lobbying work and are more remote from the field. Indeed, feminists who, through their volunteering or work, actually encounter racialized and othered women display a texture of attentiveness to the context of the women they encounter that leads them to moral reasonings that are much more complex. They evaluate their own political beliefs in the light of the concrete situations of, for example, young girls asking for a certificate of virginity in order to satisfy their family's inquiries or to be able to marry when in fact they are not virgins. In these instances of concrete encounters, feminists can care more appropriately in feminist terms because the distance has been reduced and a singular voice has been heard. What is more, the professional ethos of feminist volunteers and workers is also often characterized by a commitment to respect a woman's choice. This ethical attitude can avoid, to a certain extent, reproducing power asymmetries.

However, to adequately care in these feminist interventions, one would also need to critically and systematically engage with whiteness in order to contribute to disestablish hierarchies. These moral dispositions that do enact a certain form of care within a relationship of service to women contrast with the discourses of feminist activists who have much fewer opportunities to encounter distant others. In the context of this type of lobbying, claims to care for other women may display the pitfalls I have described—that is, relying on certain accounts that better fit their moral views, such as that of "oppressed Muslim women," instead of relying on more complex accounts of distant others' forms of life to elaborate their judgments. Feminists may then end up "caring" for other women by ignoring their moral perspectives altogether.

Another point that makes caring for other *women* an inadequate principle for a feminist ethic of responsibility is that it does reiterate a foundationalist perspective about feminism, reinscribing the subject of feminism in a shared identity, *women*. Defining a feminist ethic of responsibility as caring for women thus fails to take into account the call to remain critical about identity categories and their exclusionary effects.

For all these reasons, I argue in favor of shifting our moral focus *away* from caring for other women as the basis for a feminist ethic of responsibility. However, by critiquing the moral disposition of caring for women as central to a feminist ethics and to feminists' political subjectivations, I do not want to suggest that feminists should be disengaged from other women. Especially with respect to privileged feminists, this would amount to a form of moral irresponsibility. However, I want to emphasize that in the case of feminism, caring must be specified and nuanced. It cannot be about meeting what are perceived to be the *needs* of other women, and it must be able to acknowledge that often women are distant others. The very category that is the object of care, women—perceived as distant others who look like us—must also always be critically appraised. Hence, I would rather scale down, in the case of a feminist ethics, the substantial content of care toward other women, defining it as a form of attention, interest, and responsibility toward other women (but not exclusively women), rather than as an ability to adopt other women's perspectives and to meet their needs.

More importantly, I argue that the subject of attention for a feminist ethic of responsibility should not be first and foremost women, but rather other feminist subjects: those who give an account of themselves as such and claim their rights to participate equally in this political community, and those who we imagine could do so as well, those who are put in relation with us through feminism. Articulating the political and the ethical in the framework of feminism, I argue that *creating a space of possibility for the other, within the political community created by feminism*, is the appropriate way to care about other feminists, and a defining principle for a feminist ethic of responsibility that takes into account power asymmetries. Indeed, creating a space of possibility does not imply that I can see the world from the other's perspective. Rather, it is about finding room within one's own moral and political space to accommodate the other's perspectives and discourses, all the more so if the other is less privileged. Such a form of care, geared toward other feminists rather than other women, opens up a space for political action, without the need to found the feminist project on an identity category. I thus argue that we must distinguish between the responsibility that feminists must assume when they claim to politically represent women's needs and interests (a duty for attentiveness and interest, and a responsibility to take into account power asymmetries and the limits of one's ability to meet distant others' needs), and the feminist ethic of responsibility that must preside over their relationships with other feminist subjects, and which aims at creating a space of possibility for these others within the feminist political community. I also argue that a political and moral focus on the first type of responsibility should be replaced by a focus on the second type of moral responsibility I have defined.

That the ethic of feminism is primarily oriented toward other feminists, understood as those women who are, in a certain context, at a certain time, put in relation with feminism and feminist claims, is beautifully illustrated by the name of a coalition in Turkey between LGBT feminists and religious Muslim women that formed in 2010 and is recounted by Eirini Avramopoulou. Indeed, this context-based coalition, which stretched way beyond the usual feminist politics to encompass pious Muslim women who did not define themselves as feminists, but considered themselves to be victims of state patriarchy, and radical feminist and LGBT groups, called itself We Care about One Another. Most of the coalition's effort was then geared toward finding, in a pragmatic fashion, the right way to care for one another across the divide of political positions and religious identifications.[95]

I also illustrate the idea that a feminist ethic of responsibility is oriented toward caring for other feminist subjects/subjects put in relation with/by feminism with the question of abandonment. Reflecting upon the type of moral harm that results from irresponsibility, Tronto cites abandonment as maybe the worst possible moral harm, because it terminates the relationship without any possibility for the other party to negotiate its terms. The harm of abandonment is also an indication of the power imbalance in the relationship because abandonment is often decided upon by the most powerful in the relationship. I identify a moral regret resulting from having performed such a harm of abandonment in the following quote, again from Soraya. Reflecting on the stance taken by the umbrella organization for women's rights in the province, the FFQ—an organization she is a member of—opposing use of the niqab (full veil) in public offices or public services, but supporting the freedom to wear the headscarf, she states:

> You know, for many Muslim women, we feel that in the end we allied with a position, we sacrificed the girls wearing the niqab. We willingly sacrificed them for the greater cause, the greater good, but in the end, it's a lot of effort for not much.

Here the idea that some women have been sacrificed in the name of a greater cause—feminism—suggests that, in fact, in the name of feminism the harm of abandonment has been perpetrated. Women wearing the niqab have been abandoned, excluded from the feminist promise insofar as they have been considered as impossible feminist subjects, incapable of embodying the feminist community, of being part of that political project. This exclusion is abandonment because Soraya feels that, as feminists, they should have *cared* for niqab-wearing women. This care, the moral relation that is expressed through this feeling of moral wrong, is not linked to a specific, concrete social relationship with these women. They are "distant others," to use Tronto's vocabulary, and Soraya does not illustrate her feeling of moral wrong with specific cases of women she knows. However, she feels she should have cared more, because her promise to care for feminism as a political project should have made her care for those women, I argue, as possible feminist subjects, as women put in relation with her through feminist claims about Islamic veiling. By feeling a sense of moral failure, she manifests that there is indeed a relationship that binds her to these women, and that relationship is, I argue, feminism.

Just as I argued that Islamic veiling debates have reconfigured the moral and political features of feminist whiteness, these debates have put Muslim women in relation with feminists because claims have been made about them in the name of feminism. Being enrolled as subjects of feminist discourses, Muslim women become part of the moral horizon of feminism, and feminists thus carry a moral responsibility toward them. The abandonment of specific groups of Muslim women in both contexts (women wearing the niqab in Quebec, women wearing the full veil but also the Islamic headscarf in France) is therefore not only a political wrong—testifying to the lack of intersectional analysis of some feminists, their active ignorance of racism and Islamophobia and of their material consequences for Muslim women—but also a moral wrong. Indeed, both from the perspective of the consequences of this irresponsibility (the impossibility for these women to go to public school or become civil servants or just find a job) and from the point of view of the relationships that the feminist project is based upon, the support for veiling bans has enacted a form of abandonment.

Our moral responsibility increases with the specificity or the proximity of our relationships. The *quality* of the relationship matters to explore what type of moral obligations it may give rise to. I argue that in the case of feminism, these moral responsibilities exist because we share a common political project, not because we share a common identity. In this perspective, we may not so much have to care *specifically* about women as women but to care about women, or any other subjects, as possible or actual feminist subjects, subjects put in relation with us through feminism. Not only should we desire a responsibility toward other women and other subjects of feminist attention for the sake of our political goal (to be an inclusive feminist movement, to be true to the political ambitions that animate this political community that claims to represent women), but we should also acknowledge that claiming to be a feminist, claiming to be part of this project, endows us with a specific moral responsibility, an attentiveness toward the other subjects who are part of this project or enrolled in it by feminist discourses.

This moral responsibility is not equally distributed among feminists. The preceding explorations into theories of moral responsibility and care have provided ample moral justifications of why asymmetries of power in relationships matter for moral responsibilities. A feminist ethic of responsibility must therefore consider the sets of harms that are produced by power asymmetries within relationships of responsibility. It must be not only attentive to, but also critical of, epistemologies of ignorance that characterize whiteness, and assess the consequences of feminist claims with respect to these power asymmetries. Are my feminist claims reinforcing and exploiting asymmetries? Or are they contributing to discursively undermining these asymmetries? One of the most important consequences of this approach is also that the powerless, or the one who is vulnerable, should not have to appeal to the powerful in the terms that they have had the power to set and impose. This assumption should certainly be part of a feminist ethic of responsibility and amounts to acknowledging responsibility in structures of power and agreeing on the importance of these structures within the feminist political community.

The project of caring for other subjects will, I argue, be based on other types of emotion than benevolence and compassion. Indeed, in the affective politics of caring for distant others, compassion is central. In a context of abstract relations, I will be moved to act, to claim a relation with a distant other, because I witness his or her suffering, a suffering with which I may identify.[96] Caring for feminist subjects will entail other types of emotions, better captured by the affective politics of love. Let's recall the words of Mani, a South-Asian feminist activist from Montreal. Addressing white Quebecois feminists, she exclaimed: "You have to accept that we are here, and you have to love us. Otherwise it's not gonna work. You cannot just tolerate us!" Her injunction to go beyond tolerance, benevolence, and compassion recalls Jennifer Nash's analysis of second-wave Black feminism's "radical ethic of care."[97] Indeed, she argues that love for other Black women, as erotic, sexual, and nonsexual, was a powerful dimension of Black feminist politics, necessary to create and imagine a public sphere in which Black feminism could appear, as an affective community that provides a space to redress harms. In a similar vein, Mani's call for love is a call to challenge the usual affective politics that structure white feminists' relations to racialized feminists, a radical call to envision new forms of political and moral relations. Redirecting powerful emotional drives that are usually put in the service of claims to abstract relations with distant others might therefore be a crucial step in forging a feminist ethic of responsibility based on concrete relations with other feminists.

I have so far drawn the contours of a feminist ethic of responsibility that arises from our commitment to the feminist project as a project to create and sustain a political community. The drive that manifests itself in this ethic of responsibility is one of caring for this political community. Moral qualities that make this caring possible are attentiveness, responsibility (understood as a responsibility to act that varies depending on power asymmetries), and the practice of creating a space of possibility for others in this community. However, beyond the moral qualities that such an ethic presupposes, how can this ethic manifest itself? How do these concepts take life in the context of feminist activism? Inspired by the ethic of care, the feminist ethic of responsibility that I propose is a pragmatist ethic. I argue that we must focus on the consequences of our actions to reevaluate the moral quality of our intentions. Because a feminist ethic of responsibility is attentive to the political context in which it is enunciated, it must take into account the consequences of the judgments and actions that I propose to make. Acknowledging the pragmatist nature of this ethic helps us see how what have been perceived as feminist dilemmas may in fact be approached through an analysis of the consequences of the actions and policies that are proposed, thereby breaking with feminist moral evaluations centered around values such as freedom or autonomy.

Pragmatism and Feminist Responsibility

Applying a feminist ethic of responsibility to navigate issues such as debates on Islamic veiling (but sex work is another domain to which we could apply such an ethic) means being guided by the responsibility to care for the feminist political community and creating a space of possibilities for others, including those so far considered by some as "bad" feminist subjects. Such an ethic is fundamentally grounded in a particular context, addressing particular problems, and it cannot rely only on abstract principles and values to guide actions. Indeed, more often than not, relying on abstract principles in a decision will in fact privilege those who are already privileged.[98] Embedded in relations of responsibilities, a feminist ethic of responsibility is therefore contextual. I cannot rely on abstract values such as autonomy, freedom, or emancipation to guide my actions and shape my relationships of responsibility. Instead, to enact a feminist ethic of responsibility, I must take into consideration the consequences of my actions, because I cannot separate the moral impulse I wish to act upon from its concrete consequences. My decisions on how to respond to claims made by others upon me as a feminist will have to take into account the context in which these claims are made, and in particular the positions of power or disempowerment from where they are enunciated.

In the context of Islamic veiling debates, the question of the position of disempowerment at the intersection of race, religion, and gender would therefore pragmatically shape my response. While, as I documented in previous chapters, some French feminists, white and nonwhite, took a stand based on abstract principles—gender equality, secularism, female emancipation—that promoted the strict regulation or ban of forms of Islamic veiling, the context-based analysis of many feminist organizations in Quebec put at the center of the analysis, and of the decision, the impact that these policies would have on pious Muslim women. From that standpoint, a feminist ethic of responsibility demanded that restrictive policies be opposed, even while some Quebecois feminists may have found that veiling was a patriarchal practice. Typically, here, we can see how—without entering the moral and political arguments that have characterized sexularism debates of whether religious practices such as (full) veiling are incompatible with agency or gender equality—an approach inspired by theories of care will first point to the need to address this issue from the point of view of the consequences that Muslim women, made vulnerable by potential bans on their practices, will bear. Placing the concrete needs and interests of those who are multiply marginalized at the center of the decision therefore responds to an imperative both to contextualize a moral judgment and to act upon asymmetries of power. Such a principle can therefore prove particularly helpful in debating intersectional issues.[99]

Taking into account the needs and interests of others—in particular those who are disempowered in the context in which I am making a judgment—implies, I claim, that I engage in moral practices that are embedded in pragmatism. This is not pragmatism understood as a moral order defined by necessity instead of values, but pragmatism in its philosophical sense, as the art of evaluating morally the consequences of our actions. Because it makes the consequences of our actions as a central guide to define what is ethical and what is not, pragmatism proposes a conception of responsibility that is both political and moral,[100] and is therefore suitable for a feminist ethic. In order to delineate types of ethical practices that can adequately enact forms of care for distant others—women or feminists or both—I take inspiration here from pragmatist environmental philosopher Emilie Hache.[101] Indeed, in her exploration of the moral responsibilities that fall on us as we are relationally connected to the environment, and of how we can adequately respond to the calls that our environment is making, she suggests two types of moral practices that, I argue, can also orient a feminist ethic of responsibility. The first one consists in putting our ends (and values) in relation. The second enjoins us to rely on concrete experience to elaborate our moral responses.

A first important moral practice that will help me to sustain a feminist ethic of care for others is, following Hache's insight, that of relating the moral values that animate our commitment to feminism with other values. This means putting feminist values—such as autonomy or equality—in relation with other moral values that might be important for others in a given context. Putting in relation these moral ends is a way to try to care for them, rather than introducing a hierarchy of values and moral ends or instrumentalizing one value to promote another one. In the context of sexularism debates, such an ethical practice of putting moral ends in relation would, for example, draw attention to the fact that we should promote *both* gender equality *and* antiracism, avoiding the instrumentalization of gender equality in favor of nationalism and Islamophobia. It would also mean combining the goal of caring for disempowered pious Muslim women and girls *and* the goal of protecting secularism or gender equality, rather than opposing them. Lastly, it could mean putting the goal of respecting secularism in perspective with veiled Muslim girls' right to education or pious Muslim women's right to work, including in public services.

Such an exercise of putting our ends in relation to one another exposes us to a risk, that of discovering that our values, what we value, may not be equally valued by others.[102] However, the fear that our values will be marginalized by others' values (such as gender equality being marginalized by religious freedom or by the right to education) should not lead us to refuse this risk and impose our ends as superior to others' ends. While I value my attachment to feminism, I cannot impose on others that they be attached in similar ways and with the same intensity to this political community. Hence, a pragmatist feminist ethic here requires that I put my commitment in perspective with that of others. I cannot ask others to share my values in the same ways as a prerequisite to enter the conversation, or their values might never be considered in my exercise of moral judgment. On the contrary, I must put my ends in perspective with those of others so that they may feel part of my project as well, so that I may interest them in sharing my values. Such an ethic would, for example, discourage Quebecois feminists from asking for gender equality to be enshrined as a more important right than the right to religious freedom in the Quebecois Charter of Rights and Freedoms.[103]

Creating a space of possibility for others in the feminist project, especially those others who have been often presented as "bad" feminist subjects, thus entails that I put my claims in relation with theirs. Such an exercise of putting my ends in relations with other ends—and other people—will certainly encourage me to make compromises. Here Hache understands making compromises not as sacrificing one's moral values,[104] but rather as the result of treating well the others who are part of my project, who are involved in the problem I seek to address. Acknowledging relationality means that I will have to accept being morally engaged with others, and this cannot happen on my moral grounds only; I must leave room for the moral ends of others. To care well about others, to create a space for them, I will have to make compromises. Otherwise I will have imposed on them my moral ends and values as a prerequisite for our being in relation.

A second ethical practice identified by Emilie Hache, and which can apply to a feminist ethic of responsibility, is that of relying on others' experiences to elaborate our moral response. While Iris Young and to a certain extent Linda Zerilli consider the capacity for enlarged thought as crucial for communicative ethics or feminist practice, this capacity relies mostly on moral imagination or wonder—or, for Zerilli, on the ability to make judgment, because I can thus take the point of view of others. Hence, both emphasize a supposed ability to imagine, envision, or adopt others' viewpoints. Such a call to adopt others' standpoints is always fraught with risks and limits. Young identifies these in the asymmetry that characterizes social relationships and thus insists that we can only meet others' viewpoints "halfway." Here, Hache's proposal is to focus on *experiences* rather than viewpoints. What we should strive for is not to try to put ourselves in the shoes of others, trying to imagine or feel what others feel, but rather to make space for their experience—which remains, singularly, theirs and only theirs—in my moral and political space. Rather than projecting myself onto others to try to share their viewpoint, I must open up my moral space and judgment to the narratives of their experiences. This act implies a form of copresence, a sharing of moral space, and therefore an acknowledgment of common ground. Such an ethical practice radically shifts the grounds of our moral inquiry. Indeed, for example, as a white secular feminist, or as a liberal or critical feminist theorist, instead of reflecting upon how pious Muslim women may be attached to their religious beliefs, and trying to reconstruct their moral perspective from this attachment that I do not share, I should rather include in my moral space and moral inquiry their concrete experiences, such as the experience of being expelled from school, or being discriminated against on the job market, or harboring resentment and feeling betrayed by fellow citizens. When I make these experiences available and present in my moral space, I agree to share the space that harbors my moral universe, my form of life, with the narratives and experiences of others. The sharing of this space will make me morally responsive—to the pain and suffering of others or to their joy—and therefore in a better position to respond adequately to the moral claims that have been addressed to me.

I add to these two ethical practices described by Hache, putting ends in relation and taking into account experiences, a third ethical practice that

I believe should be central to a feminist ethic. This practice is that of *translating*. Indeed, while feminist philosophers have insisted on our need to see the world from others' points of view, such an endeavor is based on the premise that my moral imagination or my ability for judgment—carried on through conversation and argument with others—will lead me to understand their moral viewpoint. For Iris Young, communicative ethics—if it takes into account the various practices she recommends, such as greetings and the affirmative use of rhetoric—should lead me to understand and morally respect the point of view of others, leading to deeper forms of agreements.[105] For Linda Zerilli, arguing about my political claims with others, using persuasion to make them see the world from my viewpoint, and being persuaded by some others in similar ways will provide me with an ability to judge, to adopt different viewpoints on an object or on the world. I argue that the risk of both ethical practices proposed is that of promoting only a limited and partial understanding of others' viewpoints and morality. Young's communicative ethics might be appropriate to foster an inclusive democracy with a deeper form of deliberation, as she suggests, but will not be sufficient to enroll new and old subjects in a political community that wishes to transform the world. I need more than exposure to others' narratives to engage with them in a project of creating or sustaining a political community. As I stated earlier, I need to *care* for them as well. In the case of Zerilli's argument, the risk of founding a political community on unending discussion and persuasive arguments is that debates may never end, and I might never be convinced by others' viewpoints. I may be insensible to their persuasive rhetoric because I do not wish to put my ends in relation with them. While Zerilli argues that an argument has force because it makes us "see" things differently,[106] I may resist and stay blind. I may feel that compromising, for example, about what I believe "gender equality" should mean would endanger my claims, my convictions, and my very identity as a feminist. As I have documented, some white feminists are not persuaded by the arguments put forth by racialized or Muslim feminists, because those arguments seem to contradict radically what they have learned to believe is *right* for feminism, and therefore call into question their whole narrative of themselves as feminists committed to care for women.

For these reasons, I argue that we must also learn to *translate* others' claims into claims that are recognizable for us and that will enroll us in others' projects. I borrow here the term "translation" from Bruno Latour, who uses it to describe the process that creates communities (of humans and nonhumans): by translating the claims of a group or community, I try to *enroll* others in my group.[107] Hence, translating is a way to put in relation different actors, and will always imply also some transformation of my claim. I give here an example from Quebec that illustrates how claims can be translated. The commitment of the Quebecois federation of women (FFQ) to adopt a more intersectional perspective in its political agenda led its executive officers in the early 2010s to push for prioritizing claims in favor of migrant women in the FFQ's program. However, the FFQ also wanted its base, which is not composed of a majority of migrant women, to support the inclusion of the question of the official recognition of foreign diplomas (an important policy for migrant women trying to access the Quebecois job market) as a top priority. In order to do so, the FFQ practiced a form of *translation*. It put this claim in relation to other, more traditional, Quebecois feminist claims about access to financial autonomy and work outside of the home. Translating is important because it extends common ground between feminists and enrolls other feminists in my project. Finding connections in claims, translating them so that they echo previous struggles and speak to the moral and political universe of a diverse community of feminism can foster inclusion and create more space of possibilities for others.[108] It can help us redirect and transform emotions usually put in the service of claiming to speak for distant others—such as compassion and benevolence—into a more radical and critical affective politics, based on care.

***

In this chapter I have argued that debates and conflicts about forms of Islamic veiling require that we rethink the question of the moral ground of the feminist subject, and I have sought to reconceptualize political and moral relations among feminists so as to acknowledge relational responsibilities between feminists as well as power differentials in order to delineate the moral relations that can sustain a collective project. While coalition is often presented as the right way to embody feminism so as to preserve the possibility of a collective project while acknowledging structural differences between women, I have argued that coalition cannot "solve" the question of differences and power asymmetries within feminism, because feminists need to desire coalition in the first place—that is, they must feel morally obliged to enter into coalition with other feminists' subjects and emotionally invested in doing so. I have argued that discourses that sustain feminist whiteness and depict certain racialized women or racialized feminists as "bad" feminist subjects prevent such a moral responsibility from materializing in the political subjectivities of many white feminists. Hence, to disestablish feminist whiteness and to provide ways to think, reformulate, and imagine feminism as an inclusive political community, I have proposed to explore the moral relations that feminism must create between the participants in its community, and the types of responsibilities these imply.

Feminists' political subjectivations, the fact of giving an account of oneself as a feminist, cannot be reduced to a set of sociological identities or to social positions. While acknowledging structural inequalities based on race or religion, and ensuring the full participation of racialized women in feminist organizations should be a central goal of the movement, this goal cannot suffice. Racialized feminists' discourses, in particular those about coalitions with white feminists, express moral demands that go beyond their formal inclusion or the representation of their interests. They ask for the acknowledgment by white feminists that they share common moral ground. Doing so, they posit that they are in relation with white feminists, and that these relations imply specific moral responsibilities. Relying on this insight, I have identified the moral impulse, the ethical drive within feminism, as one of being recognized by other feminists as sharing common ground. Such a drive means recognizing relationality and the moral responsibilities it creates for feminists. Those responsibilities vary depending on the position of privilege or disempowerment feminists occupy. Drawing on the ethic of care and on philosophical pragmatism, I have formulated a feminist ethic of responsibility that, I argue, is at the heart of the feminist project. This ethic is based on the recognition of power asymmetries and on the responsibility to *care* for other feminist subjects, defined as those subjects who make claims in the name of feminism, but also those who are put in relation with feminism through their claims—such as a claim to wear an Islamic veil in school or public spaces. Rather than a project to represent other women, feminism is therefore a project to care for those who could be part of this political community, who are put in relation with it through their claims or the claims that are made about them in the name of feminism.

The different ethical practices I have proposed as central to characterizing a feminist ethic of responsibility—putting ends in relation, taking into account experience, and translating—all aim at creating a space of possibility for others in the moral and political project that defines itself as feminism. They foster what Cristina Beltrán call an "ethos of non-closure" for this political subject.[109] These practices are meant to enact the broader moral endeavor of a feminist ethic of responsibility; that is, the moral obligation to recognize relationality with those subjects who make claims that put them in relation with feminism—self-identified feminist or potential feminist subjects—and to create a space of possibility for them in this political community. Importantly, I cannot choose or know in advance who will be part of my community. Claims to appropriate feminism, or to embody it in the "right" way, cannot sustain feminism as a political community and must therefore always be critically assessed. What is more, this community is of course defined by equality: I must recognize that those that may be enrolled in my claims can speak back to me. They are therefore equal interlocutors in this project, and feminism as a political community defines a space of moral and political equality.[110]

I argue that such an approach shifts the focus away from the *who* question, or the *subject* question in feminism: who can claim to be a feminist—and a "good" feminist subject—and whether there is a subject (women?) for feminism. Moral inquiries and regulatory discourses about "good" and "bad" subjects become irrelevant because we acknowledge that the political community we seek to create will not be morally "pure" but rather based on compromises and, first and foremost, on our moral responsibility to *care* for these subjects that are put in relation with us through feminism. Focusing on ethical practices, and rooting them in what I have identified as an ethical drive within feminism that might be shared across power asymmetries, is a way to recognize that disputes over values—autonomy, gender equality, and so on—may not be solved, but that the exclusions that they perform, as they marginalize the identities and interests of some feminist subjects, must be combated. I contend that to struggle against the formation of these excluded domains, we should identify and denounce power asymmetries and racism and we should claim equal participation and representation of multiply marginalized groups. These are crucial tasks and political imperatives. But we must also harness the power of the ethical drive of feminism in order to disestablish whiteness and the resistances and hierarchies it creates. By reformulating feminism as an ethical project that obliges us toward other feminist subjects, I hope we can achieve such a transformation. To do so we must consider feminism also as an ethical commitment, one that means treating other feminists well and treating them equally. Of course, treating the other equally is never a given. There is no measure by which I can be certain that I have achieved equality when it comes to relations between feminists. While I can evaluate statuses and responsibilities within feminist organizations and aim for just representation of racialized and underrepresented women, treating the other equally requires first acknowledging them as interlocutors.

7

Conclusion

Revisiting the "We" of Feminism

> The "we" of feminism is not its foundation; it is an effect of the impressions made by others who take the risk of inhabiting its name. Of course, this "hopeful" narrative has another edge: the "we" of feminism is shaped by some bodies, more than others.
> —Sara Ahmed, *The Cultural Politics of Emotions*, 189

Throughout this book, I have defined feminism as a political and moral project, and I have explored its troubles and its reconfigurations in postsecular times. My aim has not been to settle feminist disputes over values such as gender equality, autonomy, or secularism—now debatably heralded as a feminist value as well.[1] Rather, I have sought to understand feminism's trouble through an exploration of feminists' variegated attachments to the feminist project, and of how these reproduce hierarchies of race and exclusions as well as provide terms for resistance to these exclusions. Indeed, my argument has been that if we are to understand how the recuperation of feminist values for nationalist and xenophobic agendas was made possible, and understand the intractable disputes over the subjects who may or may not be included, as equals, in the feminist project, we must comprehend how attachments to feminism are shaped by race, whiteness, class, sexuality and history, and we must consider their deeply moral nature.

The debates over Islamic veiling practices that have unfolded in the last two decades in liberal democracies, especially in Europe, have captured the imagination of the public with ready-made oppositions between secularism and religious freedom, national identity and religious faith, gender equality and Islamic practices. Ideas about gender equality and emancipation have figured prominently in these discussions, providing a convenient vehicle for modernity—as is often the case—as well as a convenient veil over postcolonial relations, racism, and Islamophobia. Logically, feminists have figured prominently in these debates, on various sides. Their disputes have reconfigured feminist movements in many contexts, creating new alliances and breaking up old ones.

At the same time, feminist discourses about gender equality have been enrolled in nationalist projects that have gained tremendous support in particular in Europe, in the context of the antimigrant politics that has consolidated since the "refugee crisis." In that sense, in many national contexts, feminists' inability to agree upon veiling policies has certainly played an important political role in the current recuperation of feminist discourses for xenophobic purposes. However, the active adhesion of a small or large fraction of feminist activists to secularist discourses and veiling bans—which is not to be understated—does not explain the rise of femonationalism,[2] that is, the appropriation of feminist values to pursue a nationalist and populist politics. Indeed, a vast majority of those very same feminists would openly oppose such a politics, and in fact, many feminists have actively resisted femonationalism and anti-immigrant politics. Rather, I argue that it is the *inability to resist* such a femonationalist discourse, and the *ignorance* of its roots and connections within the feminist movements themselves, that has paved the way to femonationalism, like the perfect epitome of the *return of the repressed*. In other words, the rise of femonationalism calls attention to the roads not taken, the alliances not forged in time, the foreclosure of critique, and the ignorance linked to privilege within feminism.

From that perspective, the sexularism debates provide an ideal vantage point from which to analyze the present—and future—of feminism as a political project. What is more, these debates also had profound echoes in feminist theory. Indeed, by placing religious Muslim women at the center of attention and discourses, a subject depicted as not liberal enough, the debates have encountered a stream of critical reflections, analyses, and anxieties about the feminist subject, understood as the subject to be emancipated by feminism. Indeed, multiculturalist feminist theory has grappled with the conundrum of reconciling the liberal premises of gender equality with minority rights,[3] while critical feminist theory has chastised the political ambitions of feminism to emancipate subjects whose form of life does not follow the political and moral grammar of liberalism.[4] These debates have revolved around the meaning of female agency and its role and centrality for feminist politics.[5] They have therefore provided a critical return on feminism's liberal and modern premises, revealing the extent of the exclusions these perform, but they have also opened up a political and normative abyss—to be explored or to recoil from. It is no surprise, then, that sexularism debates have captured not only the public imagination in many European countries but also feminists' imagination.

In this book, I have proposed to shift attention from female agency and emancipation—a subject at the heart of both the public debate on Islamic veiling and of numerous feminist theorizations—to feminists and the project they inhabit, to use Sara Ahmed's metaphor in the epigraph of this concluding chapter. Instead of scrutinizing the ability of pious women to display agency even in religiously orthodox settings or the potential of religiosity as a medium of emancipation—a site of important empirical and theoretical developments[6]—I have proposed to explore feminists' political subjectivations in the contemporary postsecular moment. The concept of political subjectivation I have forged aims at describing the process by which becoming a feminist implies not only adhering to a set of norms and political visions, but also tracing boundaries between "good" and "bad" feminist subjects, and entering into relations with these subjects accordingly. It thus captures the articulation between politics and morals that, I argue, is at the heart of the feminist project. This change in focus, from the *subject of feminists' attention*—the nonliberal subject to be recuperated, or not, for the feminist project—to *the subjects of feminism*, responded first to a desire to understand the tremendous emotional charge that these debates triggered for feminists on different sides and what these emotions revealed about the nature of the feminist project. Indeed, while analyzing feminist discourses in the context of sexularism debates, I have argued relentlessly in this book that we must consider feminism not only as a political project of collective emancipation and subjective transformation, but also as a moral project. By creating and imagining political relationships, feminism also produces moral relations between its participants, envisioned as distant others to be saved or as possibly emancipated equals.

Second, this shift in focus responded to the ambition to explore Islamic veil debates as the return of the repressed in feminism, as the excluded domains coming back to haunt this project in various guises depending on the context. I have documented how whiteness and its privileges remain actively concealed, through universalist discourses in particular, and how whiteness shapes feminist politics vis-à-vis Islamic veil regulations. Finally, the focus on feminists' political subjectivations aimed not only at operating a critical return on the repressed, but also, by outlining the moral dimension of the feminist project, at reflecting on how the ethical drive within this political project may be put in the service of an anticipatory-utopian moment,[7] reclaiming feminism's imaginative and transformative powers. As I analyzed feminists' discourses, I traced their moral dispositions—the contours of the ethical drive that characterizes this political project—and I reflected critically on the moral harms that feminists may perpetrate, as well as on the asymmetries of power and privilege that shape their relations and the ways in which subjects may inhabit feminism. I also argued that we may harness the potential of this ethical drive in the service of expanding the moral boundaries of the feminist project, in particular to disestablish feminist whiteness.

Feminist Whiteness and Femonationalism

My approach thus shifts our focus and our understanding of Islamic veil debates and femonationalism. While many artful commentaries and analyses of these debates have stressed how they have reconfigured secularism, gender, and sexual emancipation in racialized terms,[8] I have focused on the ways in which they trigger feminists' moral discourses about "good" and "bad" feminist subjects, and how these discourses are shaped by race and postcolonialism, as well as religion and secularism. Seen in this light, Islamic veil debates display well-known features of "difference" debates within feminism. They reproduce what intersectional analyses of feminist movements have critiqued for decades—that is, the centrality of race and racism as mechanisms of privilege and exclusion within feminist movements, as well as the resulting invisibilization of multiple marginalized subjects and subjectivities from the feminist project.[9]

I also argue that these debates reveal new features as well. Indeed, because they revolve around issues such as female autonomy and emancipation, they elicit moral discourses that reveal the moral horizon and boundaries that feminism produces. By defining "good" and "bad" feminist subjects—subjects of equal respect and objects of benevolent care; subjects to be regulated, and abject subjects to be condemned—these discourses delimit who is to be part of the feminist project and benefit from its claims, and who is to be excluded. Doing so, they produce and reproduce power relations, hierarchies, and asymmetries in the very name of feminism, based on race, postcolonial relations, and Islamophobia.

My focus on the moral dimension of feminism, and how it connects with politics, has thus led me to complement intersectional approaches of feminist movements with an attention to whiteness and how it shapes the political subjectivation of white feminists. Indeed, in order to account for white feminists' emotional reactions and their desire to regulate Muslim women's subjectivities in the name of feminism, I have relied mainly on the concept of *feminist whiteness*. This concept designates how feminism is made white through the discourses of white feminists. These discourses vary depending on the context, and they also convey different moral relations. I have in particular distinguished between, on the one hand, feminist whiteness as it is expressed in a benevolent relation of care for racialized women—understood as objects of care, beneficiaries of feminist claims made in their names—and on the other hand, feminist whiteness that enforces the exclusion of those racialized subjects who claim their part as equals in the feminist project. Hence, feminist whiteness is shaped by the social context in which it is performed. It fashions feminism when it is conceived as a social project, one of taking care of vulnerable women and representing their needs, and it also fashions feminism understood as a political project creating political relationships among equals.

I argue that the approach focusing on feminist whiteness I have proposed in this book sheds new light on femonationalism and its political success. Femonationalism can be analyzed as resulting from a convergence of material interests in neoliberal times,[10] but it should also be understood as elicited by feminist whiteness; that is, as fueled by the political subjectivation of white feminists as *white* feminists. White ignorance[11] and white innocence[12] explain why many white feminists did not consider the implications that their claims in favor of veiling bans would have for Muslim women, and how they could be instrumentalized for right-wing and xenophobic political agendas. Indeed, I have argued that feminist whiteness is often predicated upon a denial of relationality with racialized subjects, a denial that fuels the possibility of moral and political irresponsibility. Hence, the political and moral relations with racialized feminists that have been refused, denied, or marginalized by white feminists have transformed into political claims that consolidate and rigidify the boundaries of the national community on the basis of race, class, migration status, and religion.

However, feminist whiteness may be displaced and debunked, for example through the discourse of intersectionality—when it is indeed adopted as an important principle of feminist intervention, as is the case to some extent in

Quebec. Then issues of racism and white privilege become part of a more critical feminist practice. What is more, the feminist ethic of intervention in grassroots organizations, when it is critical of the power relations between the one providing service and counseling and the one receiving them, and considers that women should be listened to on their own terms, also provides a potential lever to critique white privilege by encouraging relationality and decentering feminist whiteness and its supposed epistemological superiority. Finally, the most important site of resistance to feminist whiteness is feminist activism and discourses by racialized feminists. Indeed, racialized feminists provide a trenchant analysis and critique of feminist whiteness within feminist organizations and feminist movements at large. Their discourses also reveal the deeply moral nature of feminism. Racialized feminists' just resentment claims moral redress from white feminists. It demands that they be considered equal participants in the feminist project, and asks as a prerequisite that power relations and white privilege be acknowledged by white feminists. Racialized feminists' moral address and their experiences of failed solidarity or of the promise of inclusion direct us to inquire more deeply into the moral bonds that the feminist promise holds. I explored those bonds, and the nature of the feminist project, in chapter 6, arguing that we must develop and deepen what I called a feminist ethic of responsibility if we want to live up to the promise of caring for other feminist subjects that feminism entails and upon which it is based.

Feminist Trouble / Feminist Futures: Revisiting the "We" of Feminism

The question of foundations—of who is the "we" feminists claim to be, to represent, and to make claims about—has been a central one for feminist theory.[13] At the heart of antifoundationalist accounts of feminism is the premise that for feminism to be a transformative project, it cannot rest upon essentialist categorizations, especially when those have historically performed exclusions based on race, sexuality, or coloniality. While this claim has accomplished a critical return on the feminist project, contesting its boundaries and its normative horizon, it has not led to new ways to imagine what is the nature of the community that feminism claims to create. This anti-identitarian account of feminism has thus elicited what Judith Butler presents as a practice of critique, one that establishes a critical relation to norms "in the sense that it will not comply with a given category, but rather constitute an interrogatory relation to the field of categorization itself, referring at least implicitly to the limits of the epistemological horizon within which practices are formed."[14] For antifoundationalist feminists such as Teresa de Lauretis, Judith Butler, and Linda Zerilli, the lack of foundation of the "we" is what constitutes feminism as a critical project, although for different reasons. For de Lauretis, feminist theory and practice is based on a paradox, that of being at once limited by its social circumstances and identities, and "excessive to them."[15] For Butler, what constitutes feminism is precisely its critical relation to norms, a relation that is vital for any critical political project.[16] For Zerilli, feminism is a project of freedom, creating free relations, rather than a project based on a shared identity, and the question of the "we" is, in fact, irrelevant for this political project.[17]

However, can this critical relation to the normativity embedded in the "we" that feminism pretends to incarnate constitute the basis of an anticipatory-utopian moment for feminism? Or can feminism dispense with its utopian dimension? While I agree with the antifoundationalist perspective on the feminist subject wholeheartedly, I ask: can and should another "we" than "we women" emerge from this operation of critique? For some feminist theorists like Judith Butler, there is no other moment than the moment of critique. There is no outside of norms, and new normative projects must elicit new critical ethics. The "we women" must be understood as undecidable, open to reinterpretations, as "permanent openness and resignifiability."[18] The practice of critique for feminism would then make visible the fact that there can be no anticipatory-utopian moment, only possibilities of mobilization produced by "existing configurations of discourse and power."[19]

What type of political subject can then emerge from this critical practice? Two paths seem to have been opened by the antifoundationalist account of feminism. One is Judith Butler's reflection on coalition based on vulnerability and on a shared precarious life. Indeed, in her recent work Butler has argued that our vulnerability in the face of death and mourning and our social living condition of precariousness are shared conditions of existence—rather than ontological claims—that may lay the antifoundationalist basis for collective action. The precariousness of life, the fact that living makes us dependent on others, is a shared human condition, but also a condition that is unequally distributed among us, with some of us being more exposed to vulnerability than others—a situation denied by those who are shielded from vulnerability by their privileges. Vulnerability is therefore a political relation and can thus lead to political action, in the form of coalitions, presented by Butler as copresence in the public space in the name of a "we" the people, a "we" that exists as copresence and shared vulnerability rather than as an identity.[20]

Can such an account of the "we" delineate the contour of a feminist "we"? I argue that Butler's proposal remains incomplete, in particular because it does not allow us to distinguish between those who are close and those who are distant from us, and this distinction is central for ethical and political purposes. Although we are differently exposed to vulnerability, Butler does not reflect more precisely on how those differences might forge specific political relations, across and within those differences, and therefore constitute different collective subjects. More importantly, while Butler affirms that there is no normative horizon or foundation beyond critique, except a form of collective copresence in the public space to claim forms of protection from institutionalized vulnerability, the very act of claiming rights presupposes an outside of the "we," an authority that one seeks to challenge and replace. There is, therefore, underlying critique, a desire—a utopia maybe—that the world could be different, that an authority could be replaced. Hence, some kind of anticipatory-utopian moment, unexamined in Butler's claim, may be in fact shaping her critique. I agree here with Amy Allen's important reminder that critical feminist theory needs to be both explanatory and anticipatory to be truly a critical project with political potential.[21] This anticipatory moment must be articulated if we want to be able to expose its possible exclusions and limits. What is more, my fieldwork and numerous critical accounts of feminists' relationship to feminism indicate that commitment to this "we," even if an undecided "we" that is exposed to resignifications, exceeds a pure moment of critique and negativity. Hence, this path toward a potential antifoundationalist political "we" remains only partially explored.

A second path that follows from antifoundationalist accounts of feminism is evidently queer theory on politics and identity, or rather on disidentification.[22] While here I will not do a close reading of the various approaches that queer theory has developed to think through the question of collective action without foundations, I want to underline two related concepts that open up a queer feminist theorization of politics. I purposely combine here the terms "queer" and "feminist" as one because, when it comes to antifoundationalist theorizing about politics, the two approaches have more similarities than differences and share the same genealogy.[23] Both José Esteban Muñoz and Bruno Perreau argue in similar ways that a queer conception of a political community implies a retrospective glance, a critical return on a political *experience*. Muñoz underlines the distinctive quality of queerness as an illumination, an ideality, a capacity for imagination especially, but not only, visible in queer aesthetics.[24] Hence, for Muñoz, queer politics cannot be encapsulated in the negativity of critique. We must recapture its ideality as a concrete utopia, one of actualizing potentialities. In particular, Muñoz insists on the desire evidenced in queer aesthetic, a desire for a future and a desire for queer relationality, a sharing of experiences and desires. Analyzing an instance of actualized queer potentiality, in the resistance to antiqueer politics in France, Perreau[25] also defines a queer political community beyond negativity, as a critical return on an experienced event. He argues that a queer politics not only challenges the norms established by the majority, the idea that communities need fixed boundaries, but that it also claims one's belonging to a political community, a return on a shared experience.

I join these queer insights in arguing that we need critical imagination and potentiality—a more adequate reformulation of the anticipatory-utopian moment—for feminism as much as for queer politics, and that indeed, these projects are in many ways one and the same. I have proposed in this book an antifoundationalist account of the "we" of feminism that is not only critical of identities, but also, I argue, full of potentiality. Indeed, I have defined feminism as a political and moral project of caring for feminist subjects, understood as subjects who give an account of themselves as feminists, but also as those subjects who are put in relation with feminism through their claims or the claims made about them. The potentiality of these relations is what brings them into the scope of feminism and into the web of political and moral relations it creates. I contend that such an account of feminism can provide critical imagination, beyond the negativity of critique, because it centers on the ethical drive of feminism, on relationality and its inherent affectivity, dimensions that are crucial for utopianism.

One may then ask: if subjects who do not claim to be feminist but are put in relation with feminism are considered to be part of that political community, is that community indeed defined by feminism as a set of shared values and a transformative commitment? What does this claim imply for the political boundaries of feminism? Indeed, a risk lies precisely at this juncture. The critical imagination I propose for the feminist project implies that we extend our care, our relations, to subjects who lay beyond what have been identified as feminism's shared values and "good" subjects. To take again the example given by Eirini Avramopoulou of a feminist coalition in Turkey, feminism meant here allying with religious Muslim women who do not define themselves as feminist, and "taking care" of each other.[26] However, is this in any way new for feminism? Historically feminism has always enrolled in its project subjects who do not define themselves as feminists—"women"— and has claimed to speak for them and in their names. What is more, there is, in fact, no agreement on shared values among those who identify as feminists: gender equality, autonomy, and emancipation are values feminists are fighting for and fighting over at the same time.

However, the risks of the critical imagination that I propose are, I argue, morally and politically worthier of taking. Indeed, the risks that feminists take when they claim to represent "women" and women's interests are often no risk at all: speaking for and in place of distant others who cannot speak for themselves because they are not listened to may just be an iteration of privilege. What is more, the deep essentialist narrative that these claims fuel enacts closures all too well known. In its place, the risk I propose is a risk inherent to any moral relation because, as Emilie Hache surmises, to treat the other well is never a given.[27] It is a complex moral practice, especially, I would add, when we recognize that it is also a political act. Treating others equally is a deeply political action, as Jacques Rancière has carefully documented, but it is also the sign of a desire to treat them well, to be preoccupied by others and by my relation to them.[28] Hence, we may take the risk that what we have come to know and experience as feminism may be transformed, becoming in part unrecognizable to us. However, doing so, we might in fact recognize new subjects as part of this project and recognize them as equals—a risk worth taking.

Emancipation without Agency

I conclude this book with a last venture into one of feminist theory's preferred and perilous topics, that of agency. In opening this book, I underlined that sexularism debates captured feminists' political imagination in great part because they centered on the nature of agency and autonomy: could pious Muslim women be redeemed as agentic subjects? How could agency be redefined to account for practices of compliance—with conservative gender norms and what were perceived as patriarchal injunctions—rather than resistance? The debate over agency and how best to conceptualize it has provided us with some of the most insightful, innovative and complex reflections in contemporary feminist theory. This centrality to feminist thought is of course intimately linked with the centrality of emancipation in the feminist utopian project.[29] I argue, maybe provocatively, that, for the sake of feminism's emancipatory promise, we do not have to and should not settle the question of agency. My aim in this book has been to decenter our inquiry from the subjectivities and life forms of "distant" others—not-liberal-enough and pious subjects—and to turn away from questions asking whether these subjects can be recuperated for the feminist project, or whether the project's limits have been exposed, making it irrelevant for postsecular times. I have argued that we should rather focus our attention on the political subjectivities of feminists and what we can learn about the feminist project as the project of creating political and moral relations. Now, last, I argue that this decentering also opens up new ways of thinking about the connection between agency and emancipation.

Many feminist theorists have argued that only by transforming our conception of autonomy and freedom can we reconcile the feminist project with political subjectivities that fall outside the scope of liberalism.[30] I have argued, on the contrary, that we need not enter the debate over the definition of what counts as autonomous behavior, freedom, or emancipation in order to decide how we should address questions such as those about forms of Islamic veiling. Indeed, I have argued that the feminist ethic of responsibility that I propose can provide moral and political clues to help us more appropriately address the issues at stake for feminism in these debates because it can erode, or displace, the conflict over who embodies the "good" feminist subject, by shifting our moral inquiry away from the properties of "bad" or illiberal feminist subjects and toward the nature of our relationship with the "others" who are put in relation with us through feminist claims. Rather than asking, Can pious Muslim women—or any other type of eccentric feminist subject—display autonomous behavior? Can they be recaptured as potential emancipated feminist subjects? I propose to ask, How should my relationship to these eccentric feminist subjects be defined? What is its nature? Is it marked by power asymmetries? Do these asymmetries endow me with heightened moral responsibility to care for them as potential feminist subjects?

Now I return to the agency debate to also argue that, while the approach I propose sidesteps the question of agency, it does not leave us in a political vacuum from which emancipation has disappeared. Rather, I offer that we can productively think of emancipation *without* agency. Both Saba Mahmood and Amy Allen have argued for the need to suspend normative (liberal) feminist assumptions in the face of the consequences that these assumptions can have, and have had, for the illiberal or not-so-liberal (female) subjects regulated by postcolonial, neoliberal, and secular discourses.[31] Saba Mahmood's critical appraisal of feminism's normative liberal embrace of freedom leads her to ask the question of feminist responsibility—but not to provide us with a satisfying answer, other than sustaining the critique. She writes: "Do my political visions ever run up against the responsibility that I incur for the destruction of life forms so that 'unenlightened women may be taught to live more freely?'"[32] This critique is a challenge to the feminist project as a normative project of emancipation. It is also a challenge to the liberal understanding of autonomy, and an affirmation that there is a paradox of subjectivation, one in which I may desire to inhabit norms that oppress me or constrain me. As Alison Weir notes, this is only a paradox from the point of view of the liberal understanding of autonomy.[33] From a more socially and historically astute and conceptually rich understanding of subject formation, such as the one developed by Foucault and which precisely inspires Mahmood's reflections, it is no paradox at all but the very condition of subjectivation. However, a nonliberal understanding of autonomy, such as the conception offered by Mahmood of subjectivation as the practices of *inhabiting* social norms, does not provide a sound basis from which to think about the emancipatory potentiality of feminism. Indeed, Mahmood's response to this critique and this challenge is placed on more personal terrain, that of the ethics of the anthropologist herself. As she attempts to give a more complex and comprehensive account of these forms of life, her proposal is to adhere to "a political imperative, born out of the realization that we can no longer presume that secular reason and morality exhaust the forms of valuable human flourishings. . . . A particular openness to exploring nonliberal traditions is intrinsic to a politically responsible scholarly practice . . . and a willingness to reevaluate one's own views in light of the Other's."[34] Interestingly, I find here echoes between what Mahmood describes as the "politically responsible scholarly practice"[35] and the feminist ethic of responsibility I have defined, in that both seek to create a space of possibility for the Other. However, Mahmood does not apply her insights to feminism as a political and moral practice, and her profound reflections on the nature and limits of liberal and critical accounts of agency seem to offer no potentiality for feminism as a critical *and* utopian project, but rather to enjoin us to abandon not only feminism's liberal premises but also its ambition to emancipate subjects.

Reflecting on Mahmood's proposal, Amy Allen also endorses an approach that favors a continuing critical engagement with the identity categories that are mobilized by feminism, and a stance of humility toward the liberal norms that animate the feminist project. She remarks: "The endpoint of this line of questioning is the adoption of a stance of humility toward one's own normative and political commitments, a stance that recognizes its own limits and contingencies and that is willing to have those commitments de-stabilized in the encounter with other forms of life."[36] She therefore proposes to break with the normative certainties inherent to most of modern critical theory about the importance of freedom, autonomy, and reflexive rationality, as well as with the idea of a specific place for the Western Enlightenment within modernity, an idea defended by some prominent critical theorists such as Jürgen Habermas. Allen provides a full and complex picture of the challenges that arise for feminist theory if it is to adopt a critical stance toward its normative ideals because it recognizes that they are also the product of relations of power, of a history not only of enlightenment but also of colonization and racism. Her answer to this challenge first suspends the relation of necessity between feminism and any particular understanding of freedom as autonomy,[37] and, second, offers a negativistic conception of power, inspired by Foucault, that understands emancipation as "the transformation of a state of domination into a mobile, reversible field of power relations."[38] Indeed, this negativistic conception of emancipation does not need to imagine a "power-free utopia" and therefore is based on a more complex understanding of power and of how it shapes agency in ambivalent ways. This proposal, by loosening the normative requirements that define what is emancipation, should open up feminism to subjectivities that are not regulated by liberal norms. Hence, Allen resolves the conundrum of agency and emancipation by proposing a figure of emancipation—a more versatile field of power relations—that can accommodate "thin" conceptions of agentic behavior. For Allen, this conception preserves the possibility of both moments—critique and anticipatory-utopian—because the conception of emancipation is rooted in a more realistic understanding of power and therefore of agency.

While it is important to base our normative endeavors on more realistic representations of power and agency, Foucault's negativistic conception may fall short of satisfying a political project such as feminism that has always defined itself as *transformative* and *collective*. This negativistic conception gives us more appropriate lenses to make sense of how power shapes agency, and of what may fall under a broader scope of emancipatory practices. It gives us a concept that is more adjusted to identify emancipatory possibilities in the complex interweaving of subjectivation and social forces. While I think we must retain such a negativistic conception of emancipation in a critical feminist approach, I argue that it must also be complemented, because this conception is too focused on the individual as the locus of agency or power (and as the subject of power) to make sense of the role of *relations* in emancipation, and therefore it is too limited to capture emancipation as a collective project.

Among the reconceptualizations of autonomy outside of the premises of liberalism and individualism, relational accounts of autonomy have opened a theoretical space to think about autonomy as the product of social, emotional, and moral relations, rather than an attribute of the sovereign individual.[39] Alison Weir has developed this insight in her reflection on the articulation between identities and freedom, arguing that if we take seriously the idea that we are socially constituted, we cannot provide a definite answer to the question of whether we act as autonomous *individuals*.[40] However, this realization must not lead to feminist despair. Indeed, relationships provide us with a sense of identity, home, connections, freedom, and, importantly, possibilities for change. Some relations will foster my capacity for autonomy, and, reciprocally, freedom is also expressed in my ability to sustain the relations I choose to forge, in my ability to choose whom and what I choose to love. Among those relationships are, following Weir, relationships of solidarity and identification that feminists may choose to develop. While Weir's vision of solidarity and shared values among feminists is, I believe, too optimistic, she does provide an important insight when she underlines, using María Lugones's idea of feminist coalitions as a form of "traveling" toward the Other,[41] the transformative nature of solidarity relationships forged among feminists.

However, I have argued that such a transformation is not the product of a subjective imaginative capacity, that of "meeting" the "other" or putting myself in her shoes—even if halfway—as suggested, for example, by Iris Young. I also affirm that it cannot emerge from an "impulse" for solidarity between feminists, as suggested by Weir. Indeed, Weir suggests that identification with shared feminist values, and identification as/with women and as/with feminists, can provide a positive basis for feminist solidarity, forged in resistance and dissent. Contrastingly, I have documented in this book that agreements and identifications with feminist values do not lead to solidarity—as debates on Islamic headscarves have largely demonstrated—and I have also showed that identification with/as women or feminists is the result of a complex process of political subjectivation, which more often than not encloses the feminist subject along racial and religious lines. Hence, Weir's proposal of a transnational feminist subject bonded by solidarity and identification, although both processes are understood as reflective, ethical, and political processes, remains insufficient to bring about the transformations of feminist solidarity she calls for.

The feminist ethic of responsibility I have proposed shares the premise that our freedom as political and ethical subjects is embedded in the relationships we may be able to forge and sustain, the collective feminist subject we may create. Moreover, I argue that this ethic can sustain a transformative collective project because it requires a political recognition of power asymmetries between feminists, and because it involves ethical practices of care that erode boundaries between "good" and "bad" feminist subjects, thereby contributing to disestablishing social hierarchies such as whiteness—but also, importantly, hierarchies based on good and bad sexualities or hierarchies based on ablebodiedness.[42] Caring for those subjects deemed improper and bad is not only an ethical practice that opens spaces of possibilities for the other: it is also both a political promise of equality— treating the other equally is one of the ways in which I treat her well—and a transformative practice challenging the very social hierarchies that sustain forms of oppression. It is in this sense that a feminist ethic of responsibility constitutes a project of emancipation, an emancipation without the prerequisite of agency.

***

A way to disrupt femonationalism, which is proliferating in Europe in particular, is to pay attention to those excluded subjects who are spoken for instead of spoken to, and to the boundaries of the moral world we create by making claims as feminists. National borders, citizenship regulations, religious and racial identities cannot serve as the limits of our communities. Nor can transnational feminist discourses that focus on distant others who are time and again spoken for. What is more, femonationalism, homonationalism, and other attempts to hollow out emancipatory projects to recuperate them in neoliberal agendas (think, for example, of *business feminism*) not only pose a threat to these emancipatory projects, as the conflicts and divisions I described clearly show, they pose more broadly threats to democracy, by emptying political projects that help us imagine the world we have in common of their very ethical drive. What femonationalism does to feminism is not only align it with xenophobic and racist political agendas, but also empty feminism of its potential to create a political community of equals, to engender moral relations.

By contrast, by concentrating our attention on the concrete consequences of our actions and discourses, instead of on the values we say we uphold, we may make space for others in our feminist discourses and communities. Holding to feminism as a treasure in peril to be lost triggers defensive reactions, an abstract adhesion to a set of ideas and an imagined community that in fact forecloses the feminist subject. Instead we must conceive feminism, as Linda Zerilli proposed,[43] as a world-building activity, a work that creates *feminist relations*. Acknowledging that I am in relation with other feminist subjects, and subjects who are spoken for by feminism, rather than believing that I *represent* them or their interests, implies scrutinizing the type of relations that connect us: What are the hierarchies that structure those relations? How can they be undone? This is not an abstract proposal or a naïve project of promoting moral feelings such as love and care among feminists. In fact, promoting love and care as grounds for political relations can be a radical and revolutionary project.[44] It is a concrete project that we can apply in our contexts of work and mobilization. Who is concretely part of my project? What power does she have to voice her concern and be listened to? How are whiteness, racism, classism, ableism, and heteronormativity shaping the relations I create through feminism? What are the consequences of our actions on other subjects we enroll in our political project of community? Can we make a promise to treat the other well, and make amends when we did not?

I am indebted to theories of care that have helped me articulate a utopian vision of feminism rooted in the ethical drive of feminism. This drive is not limited to feminism, and the hierarchies that need to be disestablished, within feminism and beyond, are not limited to race and religion. Some of the insights we may gain from this investigation into feminist ethics and politics may be used to understand coalition politics that go beyond feminism. I do think that feminist theories and feminist ethics of care provide a specific normative vision of politics and democracy. This critical and normative potentiality must be harnessed to oppose the recuperation of feminism by nationalist and xenophobic discourses, and, more broadly by neoliberal political agendas. Rethinking the articulation between moral relations and the political community that feminists create is, I hope to have shown, at the heart of this project of *femoresistance*.

Appendix on Methodology

The empirical fieldwork upon which this book is based comprises interviews with members (volunteers and officers) of fifty feminist organizations in France and Quebec.

These two cases were selected with an eye to comparing the dynamics of their feminist movements and organizations, but also because they provided fertile grounds for this inquiry. Indeed, in both contexts heated debates about Islamic veiling occupied the public sphere; however, feminist organizations responded very differently, in each context and between each context, offering a wide variety of examples to draw from for my analysis. I also had a deep knowledge of both countries, having been educated in one and having begun my postgraduate academic career in the other. Through feminist activism and relations, I had easy points of entries for fieldwork and knew very well the debates raging in feminist circles in both contexts. Finally, Quebec offered a reversed mirror to European developments. While I could observe how French prohibitive policies against Islamic forms of veiling were spreading in several European countries, the dynamics of the policy and public debate in Quebec was very different, due to its political and legal system, and to the position occupied by major feminist organizations that I detail in chapter 3. I found both cases worth researching in and of themselves, to highlight the dynamics between organizations, and worth comparing one to the other to underscore how dominant repertoires about race and religion profoundly shaped feminists' perspectives on these issues.

To trace and analyze the various debates about the accommodation or prohibition of Muslim religious practices in France and Quebec, and the various feminist interventions and positions they gave rise to, I used parliamentary debates in both contexts, media coverage, feminist petitions, interviews, and archives from feminist organizations over the period 2004–2016. I also used public testimonies that narrate in affective and political language the issues at stake for racialized and/or self-defined religious feminists as well as for white and/or secular feminists.

In France, I analyzed the impact of veiling prohibition debates on feminist organizations, with a particular focus on the 2004 ban on veiling in public schools and the 2010 ban on full veiling in public spaces. I asked interviewees how they had positioned themselves and their organizations during these events and how they had navigated the moral terms of these issues, such as freedom, autonomy, and gender equality. In Quebec, I analyzed the impact of the ongoing debate on secularism, starting with the bill project on religious accommodation in public service (in fact targeting forms of veiling for public servants and clients), then reframed as the project of the charter for *laïcité* that captured the Quebecois political imagination beginning at the end of the 2000s, and the well publicized 2007 Bouchard-Taylor Commission on reasonable accommodation, until 2015.

Interviews in my sample were distributed in the following fashion:

	France	Quebec	Total
Feminist organizations that represent racialized women	7	13	20
Feminist organizations that do not represent racialized women	12	18	30
Total	19	31	50

The status of the organizations varies across the sample. While I wanted to restrict the fieldwork to registered feminist NGOs, I decided to include more informal groups in order to ensure the representation of racialized feminist activism. Indeed, in particular in France, several groups of racialized feminists were not registered as NGOs; however, they did hold regular meetings, organize activities, and develop a public discourse of feminist advocacy and they had an updated website. I purposefully did not interview academics, public intellectuals, or femocrats. I also did not interview women identifying as feminist but working in other types of organizations such as unions and antiracist or ethnic-based organizations.

Some organizations did not use the word "feminist" in their name or in some public settings. For example, some racialized feminist organizations that cater to a specific community did not want to identify in all contexts as feminist, in order not to fuel negative reactions in their own community. However, respondents from these organizations identified as feminists among themselves: they see themselves as members in this political project of transformation, and seek to be recognized as such by other feminists.

I designed the sample of these activists and their organizations so as to address the topic at the heart of this book—that is, the conflicts over religious and racial identities within feminist movements. Hence, I chose to compare organizations and groups run by women from racialized minorities and directing their efforts toward specific groups of women defined by their racialized, religious, or migrant identity, with "mainstream" organizations, run by white women, that do not claim a specific ethnic or religious identity but define their identity only around gender. Because issues of postcoloniality, race, and legal status are closely articulated with debates over veiling and the mobilization they reconfigure among racialized women, my fieldwork was not limited to Muslim women organizations but rather encompassed all feminist organizations that defined themselves thanks to a religious, racial, or national identity.

To select organizations, in Quebec I consulted listings of women's organizations compiled by official agencies (such as the Quebec's Conseil du Statut de la femme) and picked organizations representing a variety of racialized and self-identified ethnic backgrounds, with a balance between advocacy-type organizations and service providers in my sample, all located in Montreal. Marie Laperrière, then a master's degree student, provided help with doing some of the interviews in Quebec. In France, no exhaustive listing exists, but I relied on prior knowledge of the landscape of the women's movements, as well as snowballing technique, in order to identify service-oriented organizations that claim an ethnic/immigrant identity. Given the existing networks among service provider organizations and advocacy organizations (on issues such as violence against women, for example), after the first round of interviews, I was able to identify almost all organizations that were relevant for this research and located in Paris, and I was able to interview the majority of them. I do not provide a list of the organizations that were interviewed in order to preserve the anonymity of the interviewees. Interviews lasted between 55 and 115 minutes. I coded them on Atlas-ti software to ensure a systematic content analysis.

A lot has been written in anthropology, sociology, and gender studies on "encounters in the field," positionality, standpoint, and subjectivity in qualitative research. However, more often than not this important question is reified to issues of privileged access to informants or personal narratives that revolve around the author's subjectivity and the transformation she might have experienced through various encounters. In a more Bourdieusian vein, issues of positionality in research morph into finding ways to objectify one's social position relatively to that of the informants and interviewees. While I find it important to reflect on positionality, on how one's position grants access to some knowledge and may prevent one from accessing other information and knowledge, and while I also find it important to be able in one way or another to objectify one's own position, in order to be aware of what discourses one may be given access to and its inherent limits, I find these methodological reflections often reifying, acting as defensive strategies transforming our research into a dead matter rather than a living one, a way of using methodology that Pascale Molinier has well described for researchers in biomedicine but that can apply, as she underlines, to all scholars.[1] More rarely indeed do we truly reflect on the ethical and moral implications of qualitative methods. While there is a push in globalized academia to formalize ethical procedures and accreditations for research, this is obviously not the type of ethics I have in mind. Ethics certificates urge the scholar to formalize and limit the *relation* that will be created with interviewees by the research project in order to minimize risk; they do not encourage us to think about what is unpredictable in the relation that we create in the field: the encounter, the moral texture that can condense during an interview, the feeling of responsibility that comes with interviewees' sharing of knowledge with us.

As I mention in the first chapter of this book, my positionality as a white feminist academic from the global North matters for how I accessed the field and the data I could collect. My feminist previous "credentials" and my knowledge of many organizations helped me to access fieldwork with white/mainstream organizations in particular. My positionality was also marked by extraterritoriality: I did part of the fieldwork in Quebec while I was working there but I was not an active member of the Quebecois feminist movement. In France, while some rare interviewees knew me from previous encounters during my PhD years, they also knew I was now abroad and not an active member of the movement either. Hence, I believe that I was both distant and close—since I was clearly self-identifying as feminist. I had not written on the topic before and my own positions on Islamic veiling and its legal regulation was not predictable by the interviewee before the interview. Of course, as a white academic I certainly did not have access to a range of analyses and opinions, especially in interviews with racialized feminists. Sometimes they surfaced, late in the interview, when some form of trust may have consolidated as I shared concern about racism and marginalization in the movement with the interviewee. Then I felt something very similar to what Pascale Molinier describes in her fieldwork with caregivers in a retirement home:[2] we agreed on the *importance* of racism within feminism (which is something different from its *prevalence*). And I could feel it and understand it more fully: not racism itself but its *importance*, something these interviewees experience all the time, but that I cannot understand without *relating* with my interviewees. I was not interested in evaluating the veracity of claims of instances of racism—my methodological and ethical compass was not pointing to the truthfulness or falseness of the data collected—rather, in these moments, my compass was activated because they made me feel that my project was meaningful also for others.

Sometimes organizations had their own way of neutralizing the potential power relations at stake in the interview situation. In Montréal, a feminist organization for South Asian women had a policy for interviews, asking the interviewer to commit to sharing results and to financially contribute to the organization. I found this type of formalization of the process of sharing information and experience very useful in this specific context. The organization had a collective understanding of how power structures demands for information—pointing out that the same workers and volunteers were, again, asked to give some of their time to educate often privileged academics or students—and it had found a way to alleviate some of this imbalance.

The rest of the story is not entirely mine to tell. I can recount only my part in a set of *relations* that were established during fieldwork. These relations are not reducible to my positionality: my position moved and was in flux during interviews depending on what the interviewee shared with me. I was moved and displaced by interviews. Sometimes I disagreed with the feminists I interviewed, and I did mention my concerns at the end of the interview. This led to heated discussions that were often productive as moral and emotional stakes surfaced just right then. Sometimes, and more often, I listened or encouraged my interlocutor by clearly stating that I agreed with her analyses. In these situations, trust was built, and more analyses were shared and discussed. Investigating such heated and politicized issues, I never believed that an artificial neutrality on my part would allow me to collect better or more interesting data and insights. Certainly, a pretense of neutrality on my part would rather have denied any possibility of establishing a relation with interviewees, of sharing analyses and experiences as feminists. While I did not declare my own inclinations and analyses at the beginning of the interviews, I did engage in discussions when the interviewee opened the door for it, which was in fact always the case. There is a fine line between intruding and caring for what is being said in interviews. Listening to the language that is being used by a person is an art, valued as such in psychiatry, psychology, psychoanalysis, and in some feminist methodology,[3] and it is curious and unfortunate that it is not always valued and taught—to the extent that it can be taught—in sociology. This book is concerned with delineating the moral boundaries and texture of feminist relations; it is therefore not surprising that I argue that these moral relations were also an important dimension of the interviews. I cannot affirm that I listened well, I can only say that often I left interviews with a mixed feeling of joy and sadness: joy for what had been shared and the knowledge I had gained from the encounter, giving me the feeling that I could now understand better the world I shared with the interviewee, and sadness for the story of exclusion, of moral wrong that I had witnessed.

Of course, my perceptions of what happened during interviews, of the moral responsibility that I may have felt and that may have been shared, is limited and subjective. I do not shy away from the nature of the material I collected, because it is this very nature, full of emotions, judgments, ambivalences, that is the flesh of this book. It is rather in the acknowledgment of the subjective nature of this material, and by making space for the various and contradicting viewpoints I encountered, that I hope to provide new knowledge and intelligibility to the question of feminists' attachments to their political project and community. I did my best to make space for the viewpoints and experiences of the feminists I interviewed, and in particular for racialized feminists, by quoting at length their analyses and by putting their *concerns* at the heart of my inquiry and of my narrative. I believe that their language, the choice of their words, conveys the moral texture of the relation that was established during interviews. Of course, inquiring about feminist relations, about how a political project of equality can exist and sustain itself with attention pointed to differential powers and hierarchies within this community, begs the difficult question of how to give voice to others while not speaking in their names.

Knowing the limits of my standpoint, and being a firm believer in standpoint epistemology that stresses that producing knowledge is a collective endeavor with a political purpose of disestablishing hierarchies and is also a moral quest, I can only encourage further research that will multiply and share standpoints and analyses, so as to draw a fuller picture of our individual and collective attachment to feminism.

Notes

Chapter 1

1. Ahmed, "Phenomenology of Whiteness"; Hughey, "The (Dis)Similarities of White Racial Identities."
2. Stoler, "Colonial Aphasia."
3. The publication by prominent feminist philosopher Susan Moller Okin of her essay "Is Multiculturalism Bad for Women?" in 1998 epitomizes this trend.
4. Scott, *Sex and Secularism*.
5. For some comparative analyses of feminists' involvement in these policy debates, see Phillips and Saharso, "Guest Editorial"; Kılıç, Saharso, and Sauer, "Introduction"; Rosenberger and Sauer, *Politics, Religion and Gender*; Lozano, Veinguer, and García-González, "Intersectionality and the Discourses"; Lépinard, "In the Name of Equality?" On France, see Scott, *The Politics of the Veil*; Dot-Pouillard, "Les recompositions politiques du mouvement féministe français au regard du hijab."
6. For analyses of the political and policy dynamics of these debates see Rosenberger and Sauer, *Politics, Religion and Gender*; Joppke, "State Neutrality"; Korteweg and Yurdakul, *The Headscarf Debates*; Bowen, *Why the French Don't Like Headscarves*; Bassel, *Refugee Women*; Barras, *Refashioning Secularisms in France and Turkey*; Selby, "Un/veiling Women's Bodies"; and Fournier, "Headscarf and Burqa Controversies at the Crossroad of Politics, Society and Law." On Nordic countries, see Siim, "How Institutional Context Shapes Headscarf Debates across Scandinavia."
7. Puar, *Terrorist Assemblages*.
8. Farris, "Femonationalism"; Farris, *In the Name of Women's Rights*.
9. Farris, "Femonationalism," 185. Feminist movements have developed variegated relationships to nationalism depending on the historical context, so in a sense the alliance between feminism and nationalism is not totally new; however, its reliance upon a racist, anti-Islamic, and anti-immigrant discourse is specific to the contemporary period. On other times and places, see Jayawardena, *Feminism and Nationalism in the Third World*; Ferree, *Varieties of Feminism*. On Quebec, see Lamoureux, *L'amère patrie*.
10. On Canada, see, for example, Lépinard, "In the Name of Equality?"
11. Scott, *Sex and Secularism*.
12. Several authors use the term "sexual nationalism" to describe how issues of gender equality and LGBT rights have been instrumentalized in an Islamophobic agenda in different contexts. On France, see Fassin, "Sexual Democracy and the New Racialization of Europe." On the Netherlands, see Mepschen, Duyvendak, and Tonkens, "Sexual Politics." On Germany, see Ewing, *Stolen Honor*. On Quebec, see Bilge, "Mapping Quebecois Sexual Nationalism." Sara R. Farris uses the term

"femonationalism" to depict a similar process; however, she favors a political economy approach to the phenomenon. See Farris, *In the Name of Women's Rights*.

13. Debates over Islam and gender in postcolonial Europe have, on the one hand, given a new topicality to the postcolonial feminist theory canon, e.g., Spivak, "Can the Subaltern Speak?"; Mohanty, "Under Western Eyes." On the other hand, they have encouraged feminist scholars to update this theoretical framework and apply it to the contemporary European context, which articulates Islam with race, intersectionality, and postcolonialism. See, for example, El-Tayeb, *European Others*; Bentouhami-Molino, *Race, Cultures, Identités*; Crenshaw, "Postscript."
14. Bassel and Emejulu, *Minority Women and Austerity*.
15. Wekker, *White Innocence*.
16. Farris, *In the Name of Women's Rights*; Arruzza, Bhattacharya, and Fraser, *Feminism for the 99%*.
17. Most of the time, analyses of "feminist discourses" in these debates rely on media statements issued by self-proclaimed feminist figures (whose feminist identity is often contested by other feminist activists). The extent to which these positions represent fractions of the feminist movement is impossible to evaluate. For example, Farris relies on analysis of contested public figures in France, Italy, and the Netherlands in *In the Name of Women's Rights*. This methodology is adequate to understand how feminism is being used and talked about in nationalist and right-wing discourse, but cannot grasp how feminists talk about these issues and how the movement has been transformed or not in the process.
18. See, for example, Dot-Pouillard, "Les recompositions politiques du mouvement féministe français au regard du hijab." For a review on France, Belgium, Greece, and Turkey, see Bouyahia and Sanna, *La polysémie du voile*. On Canada/Quebec, see Lépinard, "In the Name of Equality?"; Baines, "Must Feminists Identify as Secular Citizens?"; Bakht, "Religious Arbitration in Canada." On the importance of concretely documenting the operations that perform "constitutive exclusions," for example, from the feminist subject, and their contestations, see Kramer, *Constitutive Exclusion*, 11.
19. The open letter was published in an online media platform and signed by fewer than a hundred persons, mostly feminist and human rights activists; Les invités de Mediapart, "Lettre ouverte," https://blogs.mediapart.fr/edition/les-invites-de-mediapart/article/260816/lettre-ouverte-aux-maires-l-origine-des-arretes-anti-burkini, accessed May 29, 2018.
20. See Mahmood, *Politics of Piety*; Phillips, *Multiculturalism without Culture*; Phillips, "Feminism and Liberalism Revisited"; Lépinard, "Autonomy and the Crisis of the Feminist Subject." In the French context, where the dominant imaginary is also a *republican* one, Cécile Laborde in *Critical Republicanism*, explores the various understandings of this republican tradition and how they have weighed on the French headscarf debates.
21. Other oppositions to restrictive measures on Islamic veiling in the name of feminism have also been publicly voiced by members and participants in Les Mots Sont Importants. The organization launched a call "Oui à la laïcité, non aux lois

d'exceptions" in May 2003, http://lmsi.net/Liste-des-signataires-contre-l, accessed May 29, 2018. See also the op-ed by Balibar et al., "Oui au foulard à l'école laïque"; Les invités de Mediapart, "Lettre ouverte."
22. Mahmood, *Politics of Piety*; Allen, "Emancipation without Utopia."
23. Braidotti, "In Spite of the Times," 2.
24. Weir, *Identities and Freedom*, 2.
25. For example, Mahmood, "Feminist Theory, Embodiment, and the Docile Agent"; Bracke, "Conjugating the Modern/Religious"; Rinaldo, "Pious and Critical"; Avishai, "'Doing Religion' in a Secular World."
26. Friedman, *Autonomy, Gender, Politics*.
27. Deveaux, *Gender and Justice in Multicultural Liberal States*; Phillips, *Multiculturalism without Culture*.
28. I analyze the consequences of these various conceptions of female autonomy on the feminist project in Lépinard, "Autonomy and the Crisis of the Feminist Subject."
29. See. for example. Narayan, "Essence of Culture"; Bracke, "Conjugating the Modern/Religious"; Singh, "Religious Agency and the Limits of Intersectionality."
30. Mahmood, *Politics of Piety*, 5.
31. Mahmood, *Politics of Piety*, 32.
32. Mahmood, *Politics of Piety*, 34.
33. Mahmood, *Politics of Piety*, 36. Sindre Bangstad provides a powerful critique of Mahmood's simultaneous condemnation of liberal feminism and obliviousness regarding the religious political ideology of her ethnographic subjects; see Bangstad, "Saba Mahmood and Anthropological Feminism."
34. Lépinard, "Autonomy and the Crisis of the Feminist Subject." It has also contributed to framing Muslim women first and foremost in terms of religious identity, foregrounding a form of culturalism (and cultural relativism). See Bangstad, "Saba Mahmood and Anthropological Feminism."
35. Allen, "Feminism, Modernity and Critical Theory."
36. Mohanty, *Feminism without Borders*; Fraser, "Mapping the Feminist Imagination."
37. Mahmood, *Politics of Piety*, 39.
38. On the importance of differentiating between various forms of differences, see Yuval-Davis, *Gender and Nation*. It is interesting to note that conservative religious agency such as the one displayed by French Catholic women during the twentieth century or Protestant American women in the South did not bring a similar political challenge to Western feminism. These illiberal subjects were glossed over as buried in false consciousness, and thus did not fuel theoretical reflections on women's differences. Their whiteness presupposed and secured their accepted—but politically not acceptable—autonomy, foreclosing most inquiries into their agency and their relationship to feminism. For exceptions, see Blee, *Women of the Klan*; Della Sudda, "Par-delà le bien et le mal."
39. See chapter 10 in Braidotti, *Nomadic Theory*.
40. Tronto, *Moral Boundaries*; Rushing, "Butler's Ethical Appeal"; Jenkins, "Sensate Democracy and Grievable Life"; Schippers, "Violence, Affect and Ethics"; Lloyd, "The Ethics and Politics of Vulnerable Bodies." The turn to ethics in feminist

theory has been particularly applied to Judith Butler's work, considering that *Precarious Life* (2004) marks a shift to ethics with references to Levinas becoming central to her theorizing. However, as multiple contributions in Lloyd, *Butler and Ethics* make clear, there is not so much a shift as an ongoing articulation of politics and ethics in Butler's reflections. It is precisely this articulation, rather than opposing the two perspectives as divergent, that, I argue, we must try to think through in the context of feminism and feminist theory. My own attempt is developed in chapter 6.

41. Among many other accounts, see Davis, *Women, Race, & Class*; hooks, *Feminist Theory*; Anzaldúa and Moraga, *This Bridge Called My Back*.
42. Eloit, "Lesbian Trouble."
43. Vance, *Pleasure and Danger*.
44. McRobbie, *The Aftermath of Feminism*.
45. de Lauretis, "Upping the Anti," 266.
46. Butler, "Contingent Foundations," 1995, 48.
47. There is a consensus on an ethical turn in political philosophy at the turn of the twenty-first century, and in feminist theory it has been particularly commented about the work of Judith Butler and her supposed own ethical turn. This debate on Butler's work is rich and, despite claims of the contrary, helps us map the connections between ethics and politics; see Lloyd, *Butler and Ethics*.
48. Relational conception of ethics can refer to the work of Emmanuel Levinas, whose influences on Judith Butler's ethical turn is well known. Relational conceptions of ethics also permeate various authors who developed an ethic of care, such as Carol Gilligan, Iris Murdoch, or Joan Tronto.
49. Fassin, "Troubled Waters."
50. Tronto, *Moral Boundaries*, 3.
51. Tronto, *Moral Boundaries*, 14.
52. de Lauretis, "Upping the Anti," 257.
53. Allen, *The Politics of Our Selves*.
54. Young, *Inclusion and Democracy*, 10.
55. As well as from the general public: see Hesford, *Feeling Women's Liberation*.
56. Fassin, "On Resentment and Ressentiment," 249.
57. See *Intersectionality in Feminist and Queer Movements: Confronting Privileges*, edited by Elizabeth Evans and Éléonore Lépinard, Routledge, 2019.
58. Reger, *Everywhere and Nowhere*.
59. McBride and Mazur, "Women's Movements, Feminism, and Feminist Movements."
60. See the methodological appendix in this book for more details. Feminist activism takes place in a variety of organizational settings, networks, and structures, so that it is sometimes referred to as a "field of action" or a "space" of activism for women's cause; see Ray, *Fields of Protest*; Bereni, *La bataille de la parité*. These concepts aim at capturing the heterogeneity of this field of activism and the various arenas (state institutions, academia, nongovernmental organizations) in which it is deployed. However, my aim here is different. I wish to identify those who actively identify with feminism as a social practice of advocacy and contestation, who participate in

organizations that aim, admittedly in the long run, to achieve some kind of social transformation.
61. Taylor and Whittier, "Collective Identity in Social Movement Communities"; Whittier, *Feminist Generations*; Whittier, "Political Generations."
62. Collins, *Black Feminist Thought*; Harding, "Rethinking Standpoint Epistemology."
63. Das, "What Does Ordinary Ethics Look Like?"
64. Tronto, *Moral Boundaries*, 18.
65. I am especially indebted to Pascale Molinier's artful articulation of some dilemmas faced by feminists as they try to live up to their feminist ethics; see Molinier, "Des féministes et de leurs femmes de ménage."
66. Paperman and Molinier, "Présentation," 29.
67. Yuval-Davis, "Intersectionality and Feminist Politics"; Hancock, "Multiplication."
68. Mills, "White Ignorance."
69. Deleuze, "Philosophie et minorité," 154–55.
70. E.g., Dewey, *The Public and Its Problems*. I draw on Emilie Hache's reading of this philosophical tradition; see Hache, *Ce à quoi nous tenons*.
71. Arendt, *The Human Condition*.
72. From "The Future of Feminist Theory: Dreams for New Knowledge," cited in Pollock, "Is Feminism a Trauma, a Bad Memory, or a Virtual Future?," 30.

Chapter 2

1. Rosenberger and Sauer, *Politics, Religion and Gender*; Korteweg and Yurdakul, *The Headscarf Debates*.
2. Farris, *In the Name of Women's Rights*.
3. A call to shape up intersectional and anticapitalist feminism is also resounding, emboldened by the Million Women's March in the United States, and #MeToo public debates and online mobilizations. See, for example, Arruzza, Bhattacharya, and Fraser, *Feminism for the 99 percent*.
4. Beckwith, "Women's Movements at Century's End"; Reger, *Everywhere and Nowhere*; Walby, *The Future of Feminism*; Evans, *The Politics of Third Wave Feminisms*.
5. hooks, *Feminist Theory*, chap. 2.
6. Ahmed, *Living a Feminist Life*, 3.
7. Introduction to Butler, *Gender Trouble*; Anzaldúa and Moraga, *This Bridge Called My Back*; de Lauretis, "Upping the Anti"; de Lauretis, "Eccentric Subjects"; Spelman, *Inessential Woman*; Butler and Scott, *Feminists Theorize the Political*; Benhabib et al., *Feminist Contentions*; Mohanty, *Feminism without Borders*.
8. However, this very approach has been submitted to intersectional critique. See Bilge, "Plaidoyer pour une intersectionalité critique non blanchie."
9. Zerilli, *Feminism and the Abyss of Freedom*, xi.
10. For genealogies of the field of intersectionality studies and of the concept, see Cho, Crenshaw, and McCall, "Toward a Field of Intersectionality Studies"; Hancock, *Intersectionality*. The 1990s debates on "democracy and difference," to use the title of

a landmark volume in political theory, Benhabib, *Democracy and Difference*, stressed the inherent limits of identity politics. Postcolonial feminism as early as the 1980s and interventions in the "feminism versus multiculturalism" debate during the 1990s and 2000s also reenacted important theoretical antagonisms about differences and feminism. See Cott, *The Grounding of Modern Feminism*. For a critical reflection on the importance of ethnic and national categories and identity politics for women see also Yuval-Davis, *Gender and Nation*.

11. See Butler, "Contingent Foundations," 1994.
12. Zerilli, *Feminism and the Abyss of Freedom*.
13. See Butler and Scott, *Feminists Theorize the Political*, in particular, the following chapters: Riley, "A Short History of Some Preoccupations"; Butler, Scott, and McClure, "The Issue of Foundations." This debate, however, is not the first attempt to deconstruct the category "women," a task that as preoccupied many feminist theorists before; see Hemmings, "Telling Feminists Stories."
14. Butler and Scott, *Feminists Theorize the Political*. The attempt by US-based feminists to deconstruct the category of women and then of sex and sexuality through queer theory has fueled the negative reception of poststructuralist feminist theory and queer theory in the French context. Indeed, many French feminists not only viewed *Gender Trouble* as an American import competing with their own theoretical tradition, but also as a theoretical move that would fragment the feminist subject. On the import and journey of American-based feminist and queer theories in France see Möser, *Féminismes en traductions*. See also Perreau, *Queer Theory*.
15. Mohanty, "Under Western Eyes."
16. Okin, "Is Multiculturalism Bad for Women?" See also Okin, "Feminism and Multiculturalism." And for a critical take on the debate, see the contributors to Cohen, Howard, and Nussbaum, *Is Multiculturalism Bad for Women?*, especially the chapter by Cohen et al., "My Culture Made Me Do It."
17. See Narayan, "Essence of Culture"; Hirschmann, *The Subject of Liberty*; Friedman, *Autonomy, Gender, Politics*; Deveaux, *Gender and Justice in Multicultural Liberal States*.
18. Davis, "Intersectionality as Buzzword," 70. See also Phoenix and Pattynama, "Intersectionality." Many critics, however, remain skeptical of the promise of the concept to carry on this theoretical and political task and to overcome divisions. See Carbin and Edenheim, "The Intersectional Turn in Feminist Theory."
19. Dean and Aune, "Feminism Resurgent?," 382–83.
20. A parallel and overlapping debate on differences and power within minority politics has unfolded in queer theory; for a critical analysis of its theoretical "echoes," see Perreau, *Queer Theory*.
21. Various authors have argued at different moments in time that those theoretical debates hold a potential of negativity for feminist theory because of their focus on identity politics; see Moore, *A Passion for Difference*; Fraser, "Multiculturalism and Gender Equity"; Zerilli, *Feminism and the Abyss of Freedom*; Tomlinson, "To Tell the Truth and Not Get Trapped"; Puar, *Terrorist Assemblages*. For a critique addressed

from within black feminist theory, see Nash, "Re-thinking Intersectionality"; Nash, "Practicing Love."
22. Zerilli, *Feminism and the Abyss of Freedom*.
23. Arendt, *The Human Condition*.
24. Zerilli, *Feminism and the Abyss of Freedom*, 25–29.
25. Butler, *Precarious Life*; Butler, *Frames of War*.
26. Jenkins, "Sensate Democracy and Grievable Life."
27. Tronto, "Partiality Based on Relational Responsibilities"; Plumwood, *Feminism and the Mastery of Nature*.
28. I detail this issue and the question of "enlarged mentality" in chapter 6.
29. Crenshaw, "Mapping the Margins." For an artful definition of the contemporary political and theoretical project carried on by intersectionality, see Hancock, *Intersectionality*.
30. Crenshaw, "Mapping the Margins."
31. In fact, Crenshaw used three variations for intersectionality, the last one being representational intersectionality, which directs attention to how popular culture represents women of color. However, while the distinction between structural and political intersectionality is analytically important, the third term is more marginal for theorizations of intersectionality in social movements.
32. Crenshaw, "Demarginalizing the Intersection of Race and Sex," 140.
33. Crenshaw, "Mapping the Margins."
34. Nelson, *Women of Color and the Reproductive Rights Movement*, 62.
35. Springer, *Living for the Revolution*; Nelson, *Women of Color and the Reproductive Rights Movement*.
36. Roth, *Separate Roads to Feminism*.
37. Strolovitch, *Affirmative Advocacy*.
38. Frankenberg, "Growing Up White."
39. Zajicek, "Race Discourses and Antiracist Practices in a Local Women's Movement"; Smith, "Crossing the Great Divides."
40. Townsend-Bell, "What Is Relevance?"; Townsend-Bell, "Intersectional Advances?"
41. Predelli and Halsaa, *Majority-Minority Relations in Contemporary Women's Movements*.
42. Ouali, "Les rapports de domination au sein du mouvement des femmes à Bruxelles."
43. Guénif-Souilamas, *La république mise à nu par son immigration*; Lépinard, "Doing Intersectionality."
44. Bassel and Emejulu, *Minority Women and Austerity*.
45. Townsend-Bell, "What Is Relevance?"; Predelli and Halsaa, *Majority-Minority Relations in Contemporary Women's Movements*.
46. Bilge, "Plaidoyer pour une intersectionalité critique non blanchie"; Cole, "Coalitions as a Model for Intersectionality."
47. For a review, see, Polletta and Jasper, "Collective Identity and Social Movements." See also the introduction in Armstrong, *Forging Gay Identities*. On women's movements see Taylor and Whittier, "Collective Identity in Social Movement Communities." Reger, "Organizational Dynamics and Multiple Feminist Identities."

48. As compared to the American LGBT movement from the 1970s to the 1990s, for example. Indeed, Elizabeth Armstrong notes that the question of diversity within the LGBT movement spurred conflicts between lesbians and gays, between Afro-American gays and white gays, and between lesbians of color and the rest of the movement; however, she emphasizes that—contrary, one may say, to the feminist movement in the United States—this diversity was also praised and not seen as threatening to the movement's unity. This valorization of a diverse movement was due, Armstrong contends, to the focus of the movement on individual emancipation (and commodification of individual sexual pleasure). See Armstrong, *Forging Gay Identities*.

49. See Chandra Talpade Mohanty's criticism of this tendency toward unity in chapter 4 of Mohanty, *Feminism without Borders*.

50. See, for example, such an approach in Bassel and Emejulu, *Minority Women and Austerity*.

51. El-Tayeb, *European Others*, xx.

52. On the historical continuity of these debates with French colonialism, see Stoler, "Colonial Aphasia"; Vergès, *Le ventre des femmes*; Bouyahia and Ramdani, "D'un voile à l'autre." On Switzerland, see Michel, "Sheepology." On the Netherlands see Wekker, *White Innocence*.

53. Applying an intersectional approach methodologically has meant collecting feminist discourses from white and nonwhite feminists, thereby placing racial inequalities and privileges at the center of the research design and analysis. Second, with respect to the analysis of Islamic veiling debates and their consequences for feminist coalitions, an intersectional perspective has meant analyzing how feminist organizations' discourses about Islamic veiling center on or ignore the experiences and interests of Muslim women, and documenting how these discourses set the stage for possible coalitions across racial divides and inequalities or, on the contrary, how they perform and reproduce the invisibilization of racialized women's identities and discourses (see chapter 3).

54. Collins, *Black Feminist Thought*; Bassel and Emejulu, *Minority Women and Austerity*. The question of visibility (and inclusion) is one of the two features that Ange-Marie Hancock identifies to define the intellectual and political project carried out through the concept of intersectionality. See Hancock, *Intersectionality*.

55. On love politics in black feminism see Nash, "Practicing Love." On the complex relation between identities and coalitions in feminism see Cole and Luna, "Making Coalitions Work."

56. Ahmed, *Cultural Politics of Emotion*, 178.

57. On the lability and ambivalence of the category of hospitality in feminist thought, because being a host means, in French, at the same time hosting and being hosted, see Gardey, "From Hospitality to Coalition."

58. I do not adhere to the idea that our era is, in actuality, more postsecular than previous historical periods of modernity. However, the term "postsecular" draws attention to the conundrum that the realization of the limits of the modernity narrative has

brought for feminist theory. On the "postsecular" see Habermas, Blair, and Debray, "Secularism's Crisis of Faith."
59. Lesselier, "Pour une histoire des mouvements de femmes de l'immigration en France."
60. Guénif-Souilamas, *La république mise à nu par son immigration*.
61. The wish to politicize a postcolonial feminist identity sometimes leads to an ahistorical understanding of experience. See Bruno Perreau's critique in *Queer Theory*, 126, of the book by Boggio Éwanjé-Épée and Magliani-Belkacem, *Les féministes blanches et l'empire*. See also Jennifer Nash's carefully articulated critique of the tendency to reify the intersectional categories in intersectionality approaches; Nash, "Re-thinking Intersectionality."
62. See, for example, in the French case, the positions described in Bassel, *Refugee Women*; Selby, "French Secularism as a 'Guarantor' of Women's Rights?"; Fernando, "Exceptional Citizens." See also, on Belgium, Fadil, "Not-/Unveiling as an Ethical Practice." Similar variations can be observed in the Canadian context with respect to the Sharia tribunal debate; see Lépinard, "In the Name of Equality?"
63. Bassel, *Refugee Women*.
64. Bassel and Emejulu, *Minority Women and Austerity*.
65. Ahmed, *Living a Feminist Life*, 1.
66. It is beyond the scope of this chapter to trace the contours of this theoretical body of work and its relationship with the more canonical writings in intersectionality theory. However, it is important to note that there is a discussion about whether this alternative genealogy should be labeled intersectionality as well, and about its parameters. Ange-Marie Hancock identifies this body of work, from multicultural feminist theorists prior to Crenshaw and Collins, as pertaining to intersectionality, although they did not use the term itself. She labels them "intersectionality-minded" theories, and places them in the broader arc and genealogy of the concept. See Hancock, *Intersectionality*. Contrastingly, Jennifer Nash labels several black feminist theorists as postintersectional and opposes their conceptualization to the one proposed mainly by Crenshaw; see Nash, "Practicing Love." While there is certainly analytical purchase in insisting on the differences between these two bodies of theories, these genealogical distinctions are less useful for the purpose of providing a comprehensive account of how intersecting power relations shape feminists' political subjectivations, in particular outside of the US context. What seems important to retain from this critical elaboration is, first, that there is an alternative genealogy to identity-focused intersectionality theory that should be unearthed, and second, the need to be wary of identity-based analysis, because, as Leah Bassel underscores, the identity approach repeats "the closure of subjectivity in ascribed identities or pre-given scripts of collective political projects." Bassel, *Refugee Women*, 6.
67. As whiteness studies have shown, the question of the articulation between experience and consciousness/subjectivity for the privileged is also a complex one. See Cervulle, "La conscience dominante. rapports sociaux de race et subjectivation." Barbara Ellen Smith also notes, about racial divides in feminist organizations, "Whatever the relative potency of these various forms and mechanisms of oppression in unifying the

oppressed, they do not necessarily generate a proportionate unity and group consciousness among the privileged." Smith, "Crossing the Great Divides."
68. For a critical reflection on feminist identities and identifications see Weir, *Identities and Freedom*, chap. 3. Aimee Carrillo Rowe's analysis of alliances among racialized and white feminists in academia also draws on the idea of a politics of location and stresses how it informs a politics of relations rather than identity; Rowe, *Power Lines*.
69. Mohanty, *Feminism without Borders*, 106. See also Yuval-Davis, *The Politics of Belonging*.
70. Mohanty, *Feminism without Borders*, 118.
71. Mohanty, *Feminism without Borders*, 109.
72. Mohanty and Martin, "What's Home Got to Do with It," 86.
73. Scott, "Experience," 25–26. Authenticity is also performed in movements, and always subject to contestation; see Luna, "Who Speaks for Whom?"
74. Scott, "Experience," 37.
75. Ahmed et al., "Introduction," 17.
76. Scott, "Experience," 33.
77. There is sometimes a tendency to consider (and oppose) "minority" and "majority" women as monolithic blocs, glossing over their internal dissensions, which are described but not analyzed as conceptually or sociologically meaningful; e.g., Predelli and Halsaa, *Majority-Minority Relations in Contemporary Women's Movements*.
78. Moraga's preface to Anzaldúa and Moraga, *This Bridge Called My Back*, xiv.
79. Anzaldúa and Moraga, *This Bridge Called My Back*, xv. White feminists have also testified to the multilayered emotions that take hold of them when they begin to take racism seriously and confront their privileged position and whiteness; Pratt, "Identity"; Mohanty and Martin, "What's Home Got to Do with It"; Hull, Bell-Scott, and Smith, *But Some of Us Are Brave*; Frye, *The Politics of Reality*.
80. Fassin, "On Resentment and Ressentiment."
81. See Nussbaum, *Political Emotions*. Since Montesquieu and the Scottish enlightenment, we associate specific emotions—or to use Montesquieu's term, *passions*—with specific political regimes. For Montesquieu, fear characterizes despotism, honor is the main passion that organizes monarchies, and virtue is the passion of republics; see Montesquieu, *Esprit des lois*. Alexis de Tocqueville similarly noted that democracy fostered a specific set of emotions among citizens, the most important being the love of equality; Tocqueville, *De la démocratie en Amérique*, vol. 2.
82. As Anne Simonin brilliantly showed in the case of France, the Republic's public law that defines citizens' rights and their belonging to the nation is based on deeply meta-legal moral notions of solidarity, fraternity, and moral worth. In Simonin, *Le déshonneur dans la république*.
83. See Nussbaum, *Political Emotions*.
84. An exception is Cristina Beltrán's analysis of *latinidad* as a political identity that is "not only strategic but also emotive and experiential." Beltrán, *The Trouble with Unity*, 7.
85. Polletta and Jasper, "Collective Identity and Social Movements," 290.
86. See, for example, Hercus, "Identity, Emotion, and Feminist Collective Action."

87. For an exception, see Muñoz, *Disidentifications*.
88. Reger, "Micro-Cohorts"; Reger, "The Story of a Slut Walk."
89. See Reger, "Organizational 'Emotion Work' through Consciousness-Raising."
90. Srivastava, "Tears, Fears and Careers." About white women's discursive strategy to avoid confronting racial issues in women's organizations see also Zajicek, "Race Discourses and Antiracist Practices in a Local Women's Movement." Davis, "Avoiding the 'R-Word.'"
91. Srivastava, "'You're Calling Me a Racist?,'" 30.
92. Subjectivation here is not to be understood as a translation from the French *assujetissement* used by Foucault and Althusser. Rather, it is a process of identification with a collective political identity that entails specific emotions, norms, and values and a specific relationship to oneself in order to call oneself a feminist.
93. Foucault, *The Use of Pleasure*, 6.
94. Butler, *Giving an Account of Oneself*, 8; Butler, "What Is Critique?"
95. Butler, *Giving an Account of Oneself*; Butler, "What Is Critique?" I use here interchangeably the terms "moral" and "ethical." However, my use of "ethical" departs from how the term has been used in the literature that sparked the ethical turn in feminist theory, and which implies a focus on individuals' inner selves and ethical practices, and an endeavor to describe psychic mechanisms with the help of psychoanalytical theory; see Butler, *The Psychic Life of Power*.
96. The concept of political subjectivation may be another vocabulary to capture the processes that underpin what Chandra Talpade Mohanty defines as the "politics of location" of feminists, that is, the set of "historical, geographical, cultural, psychic, and imaginative boundaries that provide the grounds for political definition and self-definition" and "necessarily implies self- as well as collective definition, since meanings of the self are inextricably bound up with our understanding of collectives as social agents." See Mohanty, *Feminism without Borders*, 106.
97. Fassin, "On Resentment and Ressentiment," 250.
98. Sara Ahmed depicts this relation as "picking each-other up"; see Ahmed, *Living a Feminist Life*, 1–2.
99. Tronto, *Moral Boundaries*, 5.
100. De Lauretis, "Eccentric Subjects," 115.
101. Ngai, *Ugly Feelings*; Ahmed, *The Promise of Happiness*; Berlant, *Cruel Optimism*.
102. Muñoz, *Disidentifications*; Ahmed, *Cultural Politics of Emotion*; Nash, "Practicing Love."
103. Rushing, "Butler's Ethical Appeal."
104. Mahmood, *Politics of Piety*. And more precisely on the psychic dimension see Butler, *The Psychic Life of Power*. On the articulation between politics and emotions and the political nature of emotions see Ahmed, *Cultural Politics of Emotion*.
105. The approach I propose shares a premise with Paola Bacchetta's analysis of resistance among French lesbians of color, that is, the articulation between political activism and subjectivities, when she argues that the decolonial resistance of the Groupe du 6 Novembre, a lesbian of color organization based in Paris, allows for the

simultaneous creation of subjectivities, imaginaries, and alternative practices. See Bacchetta, "Co-formations."
106. Dean and Aune, "Feminism Resurgent?," 383.
107. de Lauretis, "Upping the Anti," 257.

Chapter 3

1. On France, see Scott, *The Politics of the Veil*. On France, Italy and the Netherlands see Farris, *In the Name of Women's Rights*. Farris argues that the phenomenon is a *convergence* rather than an instrumentalization. She also discusses the concept "sexualization of racism," which has a long tradition of scholarship that predates the convergence between populism and women's rights. On northern Europe see Meret and Siim, "Gender, Populism and Politics of Belonging."
2. Scott, "Sexularism."
3. Lépinard, "From Immigrants to Muslims"; Hajjat, *Les frontières de l'identité nationale*.
4. El-Tayeb, *European Others*, 2011, 81; Galonnier, "The Racialization of Muslims in France and the United States."
5. Cho, Crenshaw, and McCall, "Toward a Field of Intersectionality Studies." I follow these authors and their reminder that intersectionality is not a grand theory, nor a static analysis of identity categories. It is a concept, a theoretical tool aiming at social transformation, used to capture dynamic processes and power relations. I also follow Ange-Marie Hancock's proposal that for this concept to produce the political effects it was crafted for, we need to be attentive to the way we use it; that is, we should aim to make visible categories and groups who are marginalized, especially because of racism, and to reshape "the ontological relationships between categories of difference." Hancock, *Intersectionality*, 20.
6. Crenshaw, "Mapping the Margins"; Collins, *Black Feminist Thought*; Nelson, *Women of Color and the Reproductive Rights Movement*; Springer, *Living for the Revolution*. On France, England, and Scotland see Emejulu and Bassel, "Minority Women, Austerity and Activism"; Bassel and Emejulu, *Minority Women and Austerity*.
7. Anderson-Bricker, "Triple Jeopardy"; Collins, *Black Feminist Thought*; Roth, *Separate Roads to Feminism*; Chun, Lipsitz, and Shin, "Intersectionality as a Social Movement Strategy"; Tungohan, "Intersectionality and Social Justice"; Bacchetta, "Co-formations."
8. The discrepancy between the historical archives and studies on the US context and the French one is wide on this subject. The question was raised in writings about the US second wave that have become canonical in the English-speaking world; see, for example, Lorde, *Sister Outsider*. Historians have also shown that women of color have organized, written texts, and been part of the movement through multiracial coalitions since its inception, and in its many occurrences; see Roth, *Separate Roads to Feminism*; Springer, *Living for the Revolution*; Baxandall, "Re-visioning the Women's Liberation Movement's Narrative"; Carroll, "Unlikely Allies"; Cobble, *The Other Women's Movement*; Townsend-Bell, "Writing the Way to Feminism." In

French and on France, there is much less historical work available so far: Bacchetta, "Co-formations"; Moujoud, "Femmes sans-papiers et exilées dans les mobilisations féministes"; Paris, "Un féminisme anti-colonial."

9. This statement of course does not apply to the literature specifically on racialized women's movement cited above, which has precisely investigated the dynamics of intersectionality on racialized women's organizing. On how intersectionality reconfigures a nonracialized women's movement, see Strolovitch, *Affirmative Advocacy*; Predelli and Halsaa, *Majority-Minority Relations in Contemporary Women's Movements*; Agustín, *Gender Equality, Intersectionality, and Diversity in Europe*; Laperrière and Lépinard, "Intersectionality as a Tool for Social Movements."
10. Mohammed and Hajjat, *Islamophobie*.
11. Rosenberger and Sauer, *Politics, Religion and Gender*; Siim and Mokre, *Negotiating Gender and Diversity*.
12. Brems, *The Experiences of Face Veil Wearers in Europe and the Law*; Elver, *The Headscarf Controversy*.
13. Bassel and Emejulu, *Minority Women and Austerity*.
14. Siim and Mokre, *Negotiating Gender and Diversity*.
15. Joppke, "Beyond National Models."
16. El-Tayeb, *European Others*, 2011. See also Guénif-Souilamas, "The Other French Exception"; Nordmann, *Le foulard islamique en questions*; Delphy et al., "Sexisme et racisme"; Delphy et al., "Sexisme, racisme et postcolonialisme"; Barras and Guillaume, "The Safety of Authenticity"; Keaton, *Muslim Girls and the Other France*; Scott, *The Politics of the Veil*. On the denial of race in the French public imaginary, see Keaton, Sharpley-Whiting, and Stovall, *Black France / France Noire*.
17. Bangstad, "Saba Mahmood and Anthropological Feminism."
18. Ewing, *Stolen Honor*; Scott, *Sex and Secularism*.
19. Guénif-Souilamas, "The Other French Exception."
20. It is important to underscore that in France the laws enacting prohibition of veiling practices are not so much the result of the legal organization of secularism as they are an opportunity to radically alter this framework and to create a new legal understanding of secularism; see Vauchez and Valentin, *L'affaire Baby Loup ou la nouvelle laïcité*; Lépinard, "Writing the Law."
21. Asad, *Formations of the Secular*; Fernando, *The Republic Unsettled*; Stoler, "Colonial Aphasia."
22. Andreassen and Lettinga, "Veiled Debates."
23. For critical legal analyses of these regulations see McGoldrick, *Human Rights and Religion*; De Galembert, "La fabrique du droit"; Lépinard, "Writing the Law"; Bowen, "How the French State Justifies Controlling Muslim Bodies"; Corral, "Some Constitutional Thoughts"; Rorive, "Religious Symbols in the Public Space"; Malik, "Complex Equality"; Vakulenko, *Islamic Veiling in Legal Discourse*; Hennette-Vauchez, "Derrière la burqa."
24. On the historical convergence between promoters of secularism and feminists who equate religion and women's submission in France, see Rochefort, "Foulard, genre et

laïcité en 1989." On the contemporary situation, see Chetcuti-Osorovitz, "Féminismes contemporains et controverse du pacte laïque en France."
25. Guénif-Souilamas, "The Other French Exception."
26. Cécile Laborde retraces the republican historical roots and philosophical tenets that irrigate the discourse of veil ban promoters as well as feminists in the French context; see Laborde, *Critical Republicanism*.
27. In France, for example, Camille Masclet's research on feminists who were active in the second-wave movement in Lyon and Grenoble shows that their adhesion to prohibitive laws against Islamic veiling are rooted in their previous political involvement against the Catholic Church in the seventies and eighties; see Masclet, "Sociologie des féministes des années 1970."
28. For a general perspective, see Abu-Lughod, "Do Muslim Women Really Need Saving?" For Quebec and Canada, see Razack, *Casting Out*; Bassel, *Refugee Women*; Lépinard, "In the Name of Equality?"; Bakht, "In Your Face"; Bakht, "Were Muslim Barbarians Really Knocking on the Gates of Ontario"; Baines, "Must Feminists Support Entrenchment of Sex Equality?"; Selby, "Un/veiling Women's Bodies." For France, see Tevanian, *Le voile médiatique*; Scott, *The Politics of the Veil*; Kian, "Le voile islamique"; Guénif-Souilamas, "The Other French Exception"; Fernando, *The Republic Unsettled*. On Europe, see Rosenberger and Sauer, *Politics, Religion and Gender*; Korteweg and Yurdakul, *The Headscarf Debates*; Kılıç, Saharso, and Sauer, "Introduction"; Ferrari and Pastorelli, *The Burqa Affair across Europe*; Brems, *The Experiences of Face Veil Wearers in Europe and the Law*.
29. Hennette-Vauchez, "Derrière la burqa"; Bowen, "How the French State Justifies Controlling Muslim Bodies"; Siim, "How Institutional Context Shapes Headscarf Debates across Scandinavia"; Koussens, "Sous l'affaire de la burqa"; Baubérot, *Une laïcité interculturelle*. For a comparison, see Lépinard, "Writing the Law"; Amiraux and Gaudreault-Desbiens, "Libertés fondamentales et visibilité des signes religieux en France et au Québec."
30. Lettinga and Saharso, "The Political Debates on the Veil in France and the Netherlands."
31. Rorive, "Religious Symbols in the Public Space"; Vauchez and Valentin, *L'affaire Baby Loup ou la nouvelle laïcité*; Baines, "Must Feminists Identify as Secular Citizens?"; Fornerod, "The Burqa Affair in France."
32. De Galembert, "La fabrique du droit"; Ringelheim, "The Roma Minority and the Utility of Human Rights."
33. On the articulation between race and citizenship in France, see Chapman and Frader, *Race in France*; Mazouz, *La République et ses autres*; Larcher, *L'autre citoyen*; Thomas, "Keeping Identity at a Distance." On French secularism and its links with citizenship and republicanism, see Fernando, *The Republic Unsettled*. For a comparison of religious accommodation in both contexts see Wayland, "Religious Expression in Public Schools"; Lépinard, "Writing the Law." I have explored the impact of the different models of immigrant integration and secularism on feminist organizations in both countries in Lépinard, "Doing Intersectionality." See also Laperrière and Lépinard, "Intersectionality as a Tool for Social Movements."

34. Simon, "The Choice of Ignorance."
35. As a settler nation, Canada/Quebec of course enforced colonial law on indigenous men and women; see Stark, "Criminal Empire."
36. Baubérot, *Une laïcité interculturelle*.
37. "Loi favorisant le respect de la neutralité religieuse de l'État et visant notamment à encadrer les demandes d'accommodements pour un motif religieux dans certains organismes" (An act to foster respect for state religious neutrality and promoting and regulating religious accommodations requests in certain bodies) adopted on October 18, 2017. Despite its intent to clarify what is allowed and what is prohibited, and to propose clear limits to religious accommodation, the law was criticized as soon as it was adopted for its need of interpretation. Contradictory statements from various Quebecois government members on when and where the law would apply added to the confusion. Finally, the law will be subjected to judicial review following the complaint lodged by Muslim citizens. Dominique Scali, "La loi 62 sera contestée en Cour supérieure," Journaldemontreal.com, November 7, 2017, http://www.journaldemontreal.com/2017/11/07/la-loi-62-sera-contestee-en-cour-superieure-1, accessed November 8, 2017. Unsurprisingly, the law is currently under judicial review, and therefore on hold: https://www.ledevoir.com/politique/quebec/514479/la-cour-superieure-suspend-l-article-10-de-la-loi-sur-la-neutralite-religieuse, accessed May 28, 2018.
38. Kymlicka, *Finding Our Way*; Banting and Soroka, "Minority Nationalism and Immigrant Integration in Canada."
39. Commission des droits de la personne et des droits la jeunesse, "Le pluralisme religieux au Québec, un défi d'éthique sociale."
40. Bill 27, The Family Statute Law Amendment Act passed on February 14, 2006.
41. Bakht, "Religious Arbitration in Canada"; Bassel, "Intersectional Politics at the Boundaries of the Nation State"; Korteweg, "The Sharia Debate in Ontario"; Razack, "The 'Sharia Law Debate' in Ontario"; Korteweg and Selby, *Debating Sharia*.
42. Lépinard, "In the Name of Equality?"
43. Assemblée nationale du Québec, "S'opposer à l'implantation de tribunaux dits islamiques au Québec et au Canada."
44. See Laxer, Carson, and Korteweg, "Articulating Minority Nationhood"; Eid et al., *Appartenances religieuses, appartenance citoyenne*.
45. The story of the "crisis" of religious accommodation in Quebec is told in Baubérot, *Une laïcité interculturelle*.
46. Two cases were judged by the Quebec appellate court and then reversed by the Canadian Supreme Court, one involving the right of orthodox Jews to build succahs on their balconies (*Syndicat Northcrest v. Anselem*, 2004 SCC47), and one involving the wearing of a ceremonial Sikh dagger on public school premises (*Multani v. Commission Scolaire Margueritte-Bourgeoys*, 2006 SCC 6). See Bosset, "Les fondements juridiques et l'évolution de l'obligation d'accommodement raisonnable." See also Koussens, "Neutrality of the State and Regulation of Religious Symbols in Schools in Québec and France."
47. Baines, "Must Feminists Support Entrenchment of Sex Equality?"

48. Déclaration du Premier Ministre, February 8, 2007.
49. No One Is Illegal–Montréal, "Statement on the Racist Quebec Debate about 'Reasonable Accommodation.'" See also the critique of Quebecois sexual nationalism made by Sirma Bilge, in "Mapping Quebecois Sexual Nationalism" and in "Alors que nous, Québécois, nos femmes sont égales à nous et nous les aimons ainsi."
50. "An Act to amend the Charter of human rights and freedoms," S.Q. 2008, c. 15.
51. For the details of this history and a legal analysis of its consequences, see Baines, "Must Feminists Support Entrenchment of Sex Equality?"
52. The Action Démocratique du Québec funded by ex-nationalist and *péquiste* Mario Dumont.
53. Projet de loi no 94, "Loi établissant les balises encadrant les demandes d'accommodement dans l'Administration gouvernementale et dans certains établissements," Chap. II, sec. 5, 2010.
54. Selby, "Un/veiling Women's Bodies."
55. Dalpé and Koussens, "Les discours sur la laïcité pendant le débat sur la 'Charte des valeurs de la laïcité.'"
56. Lépinard, "Writing the Law."
57. An October 2017 public opinion survey indicated that 76 percent of Quebecois were in favor of a law. Agence QMI, "Une majorité de Canadiens voudraient de la loi 62," Journaldemontreal.com, October 27, 2017, http://www.journaldemontreal.com/2017/10/27/une-majorite-de-canadiens-voudraient-de-la-loi-62, accessed November 8, 2017.
58. Projet de loi no 62, Chap. 19, p. 10, 2017.
59. SAWC sent a memo to the Bouchard-Taylor Commission and was interviewed during the consultation process. See Bouchard and Taylor, "Building the Future."
60. Lefebvre and Beaman, "Protecting Gender Relations."
61. Conseil du statut de la femme, *Avis*. This framing dominated the majority of the contributions made by politicians and collective actors during the legislative debates on the Charte des valeurs. See Beaman and Smith, "Dans leur propre intérêt."
62. Conseil du statut de la femme, *Affirmer la laïcité*, 100. Translation to English is mine for all quotes from documents originally in French.
63. While the French 2004 law designated the forbidden signs as *ostensibles* (conspicuous), meaning clearly visible, in the debate the term was largely and rapidly replaced by the phonetically similar word *ostentatoires* (ostentatious), which suggests in French an excess of visibility for the wrong reasons. The term *ostentatoire* was used in France in 1994 in a ministerial decree trying to prohibit headscarves in public schools. It is therefore interesting that the CSF chose to use a term that was not legally approved in France.
64. Conseil du statut de la femme, *Affirmer la laïcité*.
65. Ministère de l'immigration et des communautés culturelles, *Pour enrichir le Québec*, 12.
66. The CSF presents women's "march" toward equality as intimately linked to Quebec's secularization in Conseil du statut de la femme, *Affirmer La Laïcité*, 100–103. On the way in which secularism is used as a proxy for national identity in Quebec, see

Koussens, "Une mise en scène nationaliste de la laïcité." On how the memory of the Catholic past bears upon current debates about Islam in Quebec, see Rousseau, "Le travail obscur de la mémoire identitaire."
67. Of course, the limits placed on religious visibility are in fact placed on minority religions (mostly Islamic, Sikh, and Jewish religious practices) rather than on the majority religion, as the debate on the presence of the Catholic cross on the wall of the Quebecois parliament attests. Koussens, "Symboles et rituels catholiques."
68. Fédération des femmes du Québec, "Mémoire présenté par la Fédération des femmes du Québec à la Commission de consultation sur les pratiques d'accommodements reliées aux différences culturelle," 3.
69. Fédération des femmes du Québec, 5.
70. On the relationship between the FFQ and the nationalist Quebecois Party, especially under the tenure of Françoise David, see Trudel, "L'engagement des femmes en politique au Québec."
71. Fédération des femmes du Québec, *Débat sur la laïcité et le port de signes religieux ostentatoires dans la fonction et les services publics québécois. Proposal from the Board for the Special General Assembly of May 9th 2009.*
72. Giraud and Dufour, *Dix ans de solidarité planétaire.*
73. See the FFQ leaflet, Fédération des femmes du Québec, "La laïcité."
74. See the testimony of Gagnon, "Ma rupture avec la Fédération des femmes du Québec."
75. Frye, *The Politics of Reality*; Srivastava, " 'You're Calling Me a Racist?' "
76. "CONTRE LA LOI 62: Contingent féministe de la FFQ à la grande manifestation contre la haine et le racisme le 12 novembre," Fédération des femmes du Québec, October 30, 2017, http://www.ffq.qc.ca/2017/10/contre-la-loi-62-contingent-feministe-de-la/, accessed November 8, 2017.
77. An answer often provided by activists themselves about the failure to build a coalition across differences linked to race, ethnicity, or religion is that they don't agree *politically*. This is the case when French feminists from the CNDF explain the impossibility of allying with those who oppose the ban on veiling in the name of opposed conceptions of feminism. However, to take this explanation at face value is to obscure the social processes that have led to these opposing political positions and to endorse the idea that political dissent prevents coalition, while one could argue that coalition or solidarity presupposes dissent and difference.
78. Laurel S. Weldon, for example, shows that norms of inclusivity in the successful transnational coalition against violence against women she studied included a commitment to descriptive representation and separate organizations for disadvantaged groups. Weldon, "Inclusion, Solidarity, and Social Movements." Isabelle Giraud also shows that the representation of young women in the World March of Women was ensured, in line with Weldon's analysis, by separate organizing and formal descriptive representation. Giraud, "Intégrer la diversité des oppressions dans la Marche mondiale des femmes." Elizabeth Cole also addresses a similar issue when she argues from empirical evidence that power differentials need to be addressed directly for a coalition to sustain collaborative work. See Cole, "Coalitions as a Model for Intersectionality."

79. For a similar argument that stresses the importance of intermovement relations, see Ferree and Roth, "Gender, Class, and the Interaction between Social Movements."
80. In 2003 the FFQ budget was around one million Canadian dollars; see Trudel, "L'engagement des femmes en politique au Québec."
81. Trudel, "L'engagement des femmes en politique au Québec."
82. Giraud and Dufour, *Dix ans de solidarité planétaire*.
83. http://www.ffq.qc.ca/a-propos/qu%E2%80%99est-ce-que-la-ffq/les-presidentes-de-la-ffq/
84. The leadership since the mid-1990s has reflected this change in its political ties: Françoise David left the FFQ to create a radical left-wing political party, Québec Solidaire. The FFQ therefore has strong links (in terms of ideological affinity and membership) with this radical-left party.
85. Trudel, "L'engagement des femmes en politique au Québec," 118.
86. I have argued that a similar dynamics characterized the French second-wave movement; see Lépinard, "The Contentious Subject of Feminism."
87. Nationalist Quebecois feminists consider that the historical oppression of francophones by anglophones makes them victims, and tend to refuse that identity to nonwhite feminists; see Pagé, " 'Est-ce qu'on peut être racisées nous aussi?' "
88. Ricci, "Un féminisme inclusif?"
89. Ricci, "Un féminisme inclusif?," 109.
90. In June 1982; for a detailed analysis, see Ricci, "Un Féminisme Inclusif?"
91. On Mohawk women's activism in Quebec, see Ricci, "Contesting the Nation(s)."
92. "Le referendum s'en vient." Cited in Trudel, "L'engagement des femmes en politique au Québec," 372.
93. Fédération des femmes du Québec, "Débat sur la laïcité," 7.
94. Fédération des femmes du Québec, "Débat sur la laïcité," 5. This process included education and training for unions and women's organizations to promote migrant women's contribution to Quebecois society.
95. For several years, the FFQ hired a former representative of the Association des aides familiales du Québec (Quebec Caregivers Association), a Quebecois Black woman, as an officer in charge of intersectionality. Trainings were proposed to member organizations on intersectionality with role-play sessions in order to address unconscious racism.
96. Interview with the officer in charge of intersectionality at the FFQ, June 2012. Translation is mine for all interviews originally conducted in French and quoted in this book.
97. See Fédération des femmes du Québec, "Résister construire transformer. Congrès d'orientation, 27 Au 29 Mars 2015."
98. See in chapter 4 the critique proposed by racialized Quebecois feminists.
99. On this issue, see Hamrouni and Maillé, *Le sujet du féminisme est-il blanc?*
100. Ahmed, "The Nonperformativity of Antiracism." For empirical evidence of this phenomenon in white feminist organizations regarding the adoption of intersectionality, see Reger, *Everywhere and Nowhere*; Evans, "Intersectionality as Feminist Praxis"; Schuster, "Intersectional Expectations."

101. Many academic and nonacademic feminists commented, while taking a position on the issue, upon the consequences of the 2004 debate on the movement, as is evident, for example, on the website *Les mots sont importants*, which has more than eighty pages of comments on the veil debate; see "Le voile et ce qu'il dévoile." See also Guénif-Souilamas and Macé, *Les féministes et le garçon arabe*; Guénif-Souilamas, "The Other French Exception"; and the conclusion in Ali, *Féminismes islamiques*. Fewer sociological studies provide a social movement analysis of what happened. See, for example, Dot-Pouillard, "Les recompositions politiques du mouvement féministe français au regard du hijab." But Dot-Pouillard's analysis is focused on 2004–2006 and uses only texts produced by feminists during the debate. See also Garcia, "Des féminismes aux prises avec l'"intersectionnalité""; Asal, "Au nom de l'égalité!" Jennifer Selby in *Questioning French Secularism* devotes one chapter to a feminist organization in a Parisian suburb and its relationship to secularism. See also Selby, "French Secularism as a 'Guarantor' of Women's Rights?"
102. Among the numerous accounts of these events, see the thorough analyses of Lorcerie, *La politisation du voile*; Lorcerie, "La 'loi sur le voile'"; Scott, *The Politics of the Veil*; Bowen, *Why the French Don't Like Headscarves*.
103. On the extreme-left relationship with secularism see Pereira, *Les grammaires de la contestation*.
104. Dot-Pouillard, "Les recompositions politiques du mouvement féministe français au regard du hijab." See also Lépinard, "Doing Intersectionality."
105. Lorcerie, "La 'loi Sur Le Voile.'"
106. The op-ed was signed by three prominent members, and not by the CNDF as an organization, because it remained divided over the issue—which is also why it did not manage to take a position earlier; see "En France, des femmes et des hommes dénoncent 'toutes les violences' envers les femmes," Sisyphe.org, December 2003, https://sisyphe.org/spip.php?breve64, accessed November 8, 2017. A similar tiptoeing position characterized another feminist network, Ruptures, at the time; see "Sur le foulard / 6 octobre," Collectif & réseau féministe "Ruptures," November 9, 2011, http://www.reseau-feministe-ruptures.org/spip.php?article225, accessed November 8, 2017.
107. Rojtman, Surduts, and Trat, "On ne peut taire les critiques à l'égard du voile au nom de la solidarité avec les jeunes des quartiers populaires."
108. Rojtman, Surduts, and Trat, "On ne peut taire les critiques à l'égard du voile au nom de la solidarité avec les jeunes des quartiers populaires."
109. Usually three trends are identified within the second-wave French feminist movement: the "class struggle" trend, emanating from extreme-left Trotskyist or Lambertist organizations such as the political group Révolution and the Ligue Communiste Révolutionnaire; the "autonomous" trend, ideologically close to the class struggle trend but in favor of a feminist movement independent from political organizations and critiquing their sexism; and finally the "difference" trend, animated by figures close to Lacanian psychoanalytic theory, such as Antoinette Fouque, Luce Irigaray, and Hélène Cixous. See Picq, *Libération des femmes*; Stetson and McBride, *Women's Rights in France*; Delphy, "The Invention of French Feminism."

110. Organizations such as the Cercle d'études de réformes féministes, the Ligue des droits des femmes, and the Coordination féministe laïque exemplify this trend, as does the journal *Pro-choix* and its editors at the time, Fiammetta Venner and Caroline Fourest. Many members of the Collectif contre le viol also adopted a secularist position. The Coordination féministe laïque was also very active, in France, in the movement against sharia arbitral courts in Ontario.
111. Such as the NGO Femmes solidaires; see, for example, its press release of October 12, 2003.
112. It is important to note that when it was created, NPNS did not identify as a feminist organization, and later on defined its feminism as *opposed* to the mainstream movement described as intellectualizing and removed from the reality of life in urban ghettos. See Garcia, "Des féminismes aux prises avec l'"intersectionnalité.'" However, it was clearly identified as a feminist organization by the media, and fueled this identification with its vocal participation in the March 8 demonstration.
113. Including NGOs such as Mouvement des Maghrébins laïques de France and D'ailleurs ou d'ici mais ensemble.
114. See her op-ed in *Libération*, Tamzali, "Féministes, je vous écris d'Alger," reprinted in the *Pro-choix* issue of spring 2004. On Muslim women critiquin secular discourses in the Western public sphere as a new form of orientalism, see Mahmood, "Feminism, Democracy, and Empire."
115. Vigerie and Zelensky, "'Laïcardes,' puisque féministes."
116. Amara and Zappi, *Ni putes ni soumises*.
117. Boumediene-Thiery et al., "Un voile sur la discrimination." Here again, prominent feminist figures, including Françoise Gaspard and Christine Delphy, signed the op-ed. See also Tevanian, "Une loi antilaïque, antiféministe et antisociale," 8.
118. Balibar et al., "Oui au foulard à l'école laïque."
119. Boumediene-Thiery et al., "Un voile sur la discrimination."
120. In January 2004 the collective issued a press release, Collectif Une école pour tou-te-s, "Communiqué du collectif Une école pour tou-te-s." http://lmsi.net/Communique-du-Collectif-Une-ecole.
121. See Françoise Lorcerie's analysis in Lorcerie, *La politisation du voile*. Among the signatories of a first petition against the law, one finds Muslim organizations such as the Collectif des Musulmans de France, Jeunes Musulmans de France, Conseil des imams de France, Etudiants musulmans de France, personalities and NGOs representing the "ghettos" and migrant integration issues such as Divercité (an NGO from Lyon led by Saïda Kada), Dounia Bouzar, MIB (Mouvement de l'immigration et des banlieues), human rights and antiracist NGOs such as the Human Rights League and the MRAP (Mouvement contre le racisme et pour l'amitié entre les peoples), labor unions like SUD (Solidaires Unitaires Démocratiques), and political parties (the Greens and the Communist Revolutionary League).
122. Tevanian, *Le voile médiatique*; Bouteldja, "De la cérémonie du dévoilement à Alger (1958) à Ni putes ni soumises." See also the video documentary by Host, *Un racisme à peine voilé*.

123. I borrow the term from Stoler, "Colonial Aphasia." The degree to which the prism of the colonial continuum is mobilized depends on the organization, as does the degree to which a "white feminism" is accused of complicity with neocolonial policies targeting young racialized men. See Garcia, "Des féminismes aux prises avec l'"intersectionnalité.'"
124. Houria Bouteldja also founded the Mouvement des indigènes de la République, later transformed into a Parti des indigènes de la République, and led the Indigenous Feminists, a collective that existed in the first years of the movement (2005–2008) and issued a press release in January 2007. See Garcia, "Des féminismes aux prises avec l'"intersectionnalité'"; Grewal, "'Va t'faire intégrer.'"
125. See, for example, Houria Bouteldja's criticism of NPNS as promoting forms of colonial politics in "De la cérémonie du dévoilement à Alger (1958) à Ni putes ni soumises."
126. Or alternatively by the World March of Women French section
127. Koussens, "Sous l'affaire de la burqa"; Hennette-Vauchez, "Derrière la burqa."
128. Selby, "Un/veiling Women's Bodies"; Tissot, "Excluding Muslim Women"; Lépinard, "Writing the Law."
129. See Vauchez and Valentin, L'affaire Baby Loup ou la nouvelle laïcité.
130. In 2009, NPNS president Sihem Habchi was interviewed by the Commission Gérin on the burqa with a performance that impressed the commission (see Tissot, "Excluding Muslim Women"), and in January 2010, NPNS demonstrated wearing burqas in front of the headquarters of the Socialist Party, denouncing its unwillingness to legislate on the matter. See Equy, "Ni putes ni soumises manifeste en burqa devant le siège du PS."
131. See Selby, "Un/veiling Women's Bodies"; Beaman, "Overdressed and Underexposed or Underdressed and Overexposed?"
132. See Trat, "Non à une loi contre le voile intégral."
133. "Pétition: Nous sommes toutes des femmes voilées." The online petition was signed by 3,195 individuals.
134. Les invités de Mediapart, "Lettre ouverte." Veiled women also voiced their concerns after the minister in charge of women's rights made derogatory comments about Islam and veiling in a media interview in April 2016. Les invités de Mediapart, "Pour en finir avec le contrôle politique du corps des femmes." This statement constitutes one of the first public statements made by veiled women in their own names that invokes feminist values to criticize the femonationalist discourse of public authorities.
135. Les invités de Mediapart, "Lettre ouverte."
136. Kassir and Reitz, "Protesting Headscarf Ban."
137. Feminist union activist Josette Trat responded to what she considered false and phantom accusations, in Trat, "Les féministes blanches et l'empire ou le récit d'un complot féministe fantasmé." For a criticism of the underlying essentialism that characterizes the arguments set forth in the book, see Perreau, Queer Theory.
138. Lépinard, "Doing Intersectionality." Because the majority of French feminist organizations are run by white women, this means that a majority of white feminists

had trouble elaborating a critical discourse on the way secularism was being transformed in the name of women's rights. However, as I document in chapter 5, opinions among racialized feminists were not uniform, with some in favor of the bans and others strongly opposed.

139. This social protest remains the longest (almost a month) and biggest (two million participants are estimated to have attended the December 12 demonstration) workers' strike in recent French history.
140. Created in 1993, it broadly mobilized political parties and unions to lobby the government to create a new offense, *délit d'entrave à l'avortement* (crime of interference with abortion procedures)
141. Each new president of the Republic can provide amnesty for certain types of offenses. In 1995, newly elected president Jacques Chirac proposed to amnesty persons convicted of having interfered with abortion procedures.
142. But, in contrast, less active in the debate over gender parity in politics that took place at the same time (1998–2000)
143. The CNDF deplores the lack of involvement of participants, and its difficulties in recruiting new members as a side effect of the ebb in protest and social movement politics that characterizes the current austerity period.
144. In a similar way as radical feminists in the United States described by Roth, *Separate Roads to Feminism*. See Picq, *Libération des femmes*. In previous work on the French feminist movements I showed that inherited conceptions of gender oppression that left little place for intersectionality were tied to the structural place of the feminist movements of the second wave vis-à-vis the extreme Left and to the internal division (between radicals and "class struggle" trends of the movement). See Lépinard, "The Contentious Subject of Feminism."
145. Lesselier, "Pour une histoire des mouvements de femmes de l'immigration en France."
146. Oral communication in Benani, "Faire et écrire l'histoire."
147. Collectif national pour les droits des femmes, *En avant toutes!*
148. Collectif national pour les droits des femmes, *De nouveaux défis pour le féminisme, forum du Collectif national pour les droits des femmes*.
149. To be noted, among these five pages dedicated to "Racism, xenophobia and discrimination against migrant women," two are dedicated to Tunisian women discriminated against in Tunisia. As often in CNDF events, issues related to women in formerly colonized countries are bundled up with issues related to migrant/racialized women in France and articulated with concerns about American imperialism, the global rise of neoliberalism and neoconservatism, the alliance of religions at the global level against women, the Algerian civil war, radical political Islam and terrorism, etc. This tendency is also visible in Trat, "Les féministes blanches et l'empire ou le récit d'un complot féministe fantasmé." See chapter 4 for details on how this international solidarity invisibilizes racial discrimination in France. For similar reflections about the French feminist movement in the 1970s and 1980s, see Vergès, *Le ventre des femmes*.
150. Collectif national pour les droits des femmes, *De nouveaux défis pour le féminisme, forum du Collectif national pour les droits des femmes*.

151. Paye, "Stop!"
152. During the 2004 march itself tensions were palpable between the official organizations, which were in favor of the law banning religious symbols in public schools, and veiled women who came to march; see the narrative given by one participant in Java, "La marche de toutes les femmes ?" A year later, similar events of violence against veiled women participating in the World March of Women in Marseilles were related; see Collectif des féministes pour l'égalité, "Pour les droits des femmes, contre les exclusions, pour un monde plus solidaire."
153. Lettinga and Saharso, "The Political Debates on the Veil in France and the Netherlands"; Selby, "Hijab Debates in Europe."

Chapter 4

1. Butler, "Contingent Foundations," 1995, 47.
2. See also Kramer, *Constitutive Exclusion*.
3. White ignorance has been conceptualized in different ways. Some authors insist on its epistemological dimension, as the systematic production of false perceptions and distorted knowledge about racism that sustain the dominant group's interests through cognitive dysfunctions. See Mills, *The Racial Contract*; Mills, "White Ignorance." Other scholars insist on white ignorance as the product of a cultural work of self-representation by white people that systematically denies memories, histories, and realities linked to imperialism and domination of nonwhites. See Wekker, *White Innocence*, and Yancy, *Look, a White!*. My approach is situated in this second category of work, which investigates self-representation and the desire *not to know* that characterizes whiteness.
4. Ahmed, "Phenomenology of Whiteness"; Lorde, *Sister Outsider*. In Sara Ahmed's phenomenological account, whiteness is an ability to inhabit a world historically made white, an orientation toward this world that makes it reachable and livable as one's own.
5. Frankenberg, *White Women, Race Matters*; Frankenberg, "Growing Up White"; McWhorter, "Where Do White People Come From?"
6. Frye, *The Politics of Reality*.
7. Frankenberg, "Growing Up White"; Frankenberg, *White Women, Race Matters*, 236. On the European context see Griffin and Braidotti, "Whiteness and European Situatedness."
8. Ahmed, "Declarations of Whiteness."
9. I am not therefore investigating the issue of white *subjectivity* and how it is shaped by power and domination, an issue that has preoccupied the field of critical whiteness studies. For a discussion of this issue, see McWhorter, "Where Do White People Come From?"; Cervulle, "La conscience dominante."
10. On the conflict over sexuality in the French second wave feminist movement see Eloit, "Lesbian Trouble."
11. Rowe, "Locating Feminism's Subject"; Mane, "Transmuting Grammars of Whiteness."

12. See Gloria Wekker's powerful analysis of white innocence as a dominant cultural feature of white Dutch self-representation, in Wekker, *White Innocence*.
13. In the next chapter, I explore the consequences of feminist whiteness for nonwhite feminists and how they respond to it and challenge it.
14. For a similar approach see Frankenberg, *White Women, Race Matters*; Mueller, "Producing Colorblindness."
15. Wekker, *White Innocence*, 16–19.
16. Farris, *In the Name of Women's Rights*.
17. See the various contributions to Sullivan and Tuana, *Race and Epistemologies of Ignorance*.
18. I chose the concept of whiteness over other available terms used by other scholars of feminist movements, such as "minority"/"majority" women (used in Predelli and Halsaa, *Majority-Minority Relations in Contemporary Women's Movements*), "dominant" / "(multiply) marginalized" women, and "mainstream"/"minority" feminists. Ethnic minority and ethnic majority organizations (or members) can be accurate descriptors of the various feminist organizations that take part in the feminist landscape of each country. However, in Quebec, for example, many organizations define themselves as multicultural and ethnically diverse. Sometimes they were founded by immigrant women and are now run by feminist officers from a diversity of ethnic backgrounds; sometimes they were founded by white Quebecois women and their staff remains mainly white. Hence the dichotomy minority/majority does not cover the complexity of cases, in particular in Quebec. What is more, even as the term "majority" carries a political meaning, it does not convey the idea of a privileged position, ignored as such by the one that occupies it, as whiteness does. Marginalized/dominant carries an interesting focus on the positions that organizations occupy within the feminist movement, but is not easily operationalized in the field and tends to reproduce the idea that Afro or Muslim feminism is marginal to feminism, therefore reinforcing the binary it is supposed to deconstruct. Finally, mainstream/minority also does not apply well to the complex field of feminist organizations and tends to legitimize some organizations (and to overstate their status and influence) while delegitimizing others.
19. In a previous piece using the same empirical data, I focused on organizations, rather than individuals, and categorized them into single-axis organizations (identifying as women's rights organizations in a universal way and, implicitly, representing mostly women from the majority ethnic group) and dual-axis organizations (self-identifying as defending women from a specific ethnic or national group); Lépinard, "Doing Intersectionality." However, this categorization could not capture how whiteness shapes feminist consciousness and activism.
20. There was, for some organizations run by and for racialized women, and often for shelters, a gap between members' self-identification as feminists and the organizations' identification as a women's organization for the wider public.
21. See table of interviews in the appendix for more details on methodology and interviews sample.

22. I retrace this shift in France from immigration to religion in Lépinard, "Migrating Concepts."
23. For example, in 2011 an event on feminism and Islamophobia led to the creation of a (short-lived) "front du 20 mars" in Paris, a network that gathered several organizations. http://frontdu20mars.github.io/qui-sommes-nous/ (accessed August 19, 2017).
24. For example, while other scholars have noted the centrality of intersectionality and diversity for the younger generation of feminists in the United States and the United Kingdom, at the time of my fieldwork this was not the case in France—although this movement might have developed since then. Talk about intersectionality is, however, rarely met by practices to implement it. On the United States see Reger, *Everywhere and Nowhere*. On the United Kingdom see Evans, *The Politics of Third Wave Feminisms*; Evans, "Intersectionality as Feminist Praxis." And on New Zealand see Schuster, "Intersectional Expectations." To be noted, these studies review mostly *white* feminist activism in both contexts.
25. Frankenberg, *White Women, Race Matters*, chap. 6.
26. Rowe, "Locating Feminism's Subject"; Ortega, "Being Lovingly, Knowingly Ignorant."
27. Reger, *Everywhere and Nowhere*; Mane, "Transmuting Grammars of Whiteness"; Evans, "Intersectionality as Feminist Praxis"; Schuster, "Intersectional Expectations."
28. Ahmed, "Declarations of Whiteness."
29. See chapter 4 of this book and Bacchetta, "Décoloniser le féminisme"; Bacchetta, "Co-formations."
30. For an overview of debates on the diffusion of intersectionality through Europe and France in particular, see Fassa, Lépinard, and Roca i Escoda, *L'intersectionnalité*.
31. I explored feminists' relationships to the French republican ideology in the context of the campaign for political parity in Lépinard, *L'égalité introuvable*; Lépinard, "For Women Only?"
32. A wide literature in history and sociology has explored the features of French universalism, e.g., Perreau and Scott, *Les défis de la République*. On universalism and race in France, see Larcher, *L'autre citoyen*.
33. Names of organizations have been anonymized.
34. However, one should note that here again in the acknowledgment of the existence of immigrant and racialized women's movements in the 1970s there is also a move toward race evasion. Indeed, French women from the overseas departments and territories are never mentioned. While in the 1970s they were victims of massive illegal sterilization, a scandal widely mediatized then, this historical episode, a clear instance of French institutional racism and colonialism that reveals race as a French political reality (and not an American import or a side effect of immigration), is never mentioned or acknowledged by white French feminists. See Vergès, *Le ventre des femmes*; Paris, "Un féminisme anti-colonial."
35. Vergès, *Le ventre des femmes*; Guénif-Souilamas, *La république mise à nu par son immigration*; Saada, "The Empire of Law"; Shepard, *The Invention of Decolonization*.
36. Bacchetta, "Décoloniser le féminisme." Translation from cited works in French are mine.

37. Such a universalization of the white feminist subject has been documented in many other contexts, first and foremost by feminists of color; see, for example, Anzaldúa and Moraga, *This Bridge Called My Back*; Crenshaw, "Demarginalizing the Intersection of Race and Sex"; Hurtado, *The Color of Privilege*; Rowe, "Locating Feminism's Subject."
38. Roth, *Separate Roads to Feminism*, 188.
39. Lépinard, "The Contentious Subject of Feminism."
40. This organization was founded by the daughter of Maghrebi immigrants with the aim to create a popular movement whose mission is to represent the women "forgotten" by bourgeois feminism. It was rapidly promoted by the media as an organization representative of racialized women living in deprived neighborhoods. However, and interestingly, it reframed its identity as representing all women marginalized in society (including, for example, women living in rural areas with little access to public services) and in 2015 elected a white woman as president. Its regional groups are also often headed by white women or men.
41. On French color-blindness, see Sabbagh and Peer, "French Color Blindness in Perspective"; Simon, "The Choice of Ignorance." On the historical formation of the French republican model of integration, see Favell, *Philosophies of Integration*. On the fear of disunity and the need for the invisibility of difference, see Lépinard, "Migrating Concepts"; Lépinard, "Writing the Law."
42. Analyzing the emergence of French antiracism in the 1930s with the birth of the first French organization devoted to antiracism and anti-Semitism, Emmanuel Debono shows that its universalist approach was adopted in order to downplay the actual focus of activists on the protection of Jews from violence and from anti-Semitic propaganda; see Debono, *Aux origines de l'antiracisme*. The color-blind and universalist approach to racism continued after World War II, see Bleich, *Race Politics in Britain and France*. See also Larcher, "Troubles dans la 'race.'"
43. This structural conflict within French feminism, produced by the strength of French far-left organizations during the 1970s, fueled the "universalization" of gender oppression and is not unrelated to the tendency of many white feminists to embrace the claim for political parity and the universalist repertoire on gender in general. On the long-lasting impact of the second wave's debates over the category "women" on the historical trajectory of French feminism, see Lépinard, "The Contentious Subject of Feminism."
44. Hoagland, "Denying Relationality," 99.
45. Ortega, "Being Lovingly, Knowingly Ignorant."
46. Camille Masclet's research on French feminist activists from the second-wave also suggests that they were deeply influenced in their political analysis of the Islamic veil debates in the 2000s by their relationship with Iranian and Algerian feminists in exile in France in the 1980s and 1990s; see Masclet, "Sociologie des féministes des années 1970."
47. Vergès, *Le ventre des femmes*.
48. On this rhetorical device, see Michel, "Sheepology."
49. On the denial of relationality, see Hoagland, "Denying Relationality."
50. Whittier, *Feminist Generations*; Whittier, "Political Generations."

51. Mueller, "Producing Colorblindness." See also the long-standing discussions on the elimination of the word "race" from the French constitution: Balibar, "Le mot race n'est pas 'de trop.'"
52. On the structure of the Quebecois women's movement and its approach to the inclusion of racialized and immigrant women, see Laperrière and Lépinard, "Intersectionality as a Tool for Social Movements."
53. Taylor, "Interculturalism or Multiculturalism?"; Banting and Soroka, "Minority Nationalism and Immigrant Integration in Canada."
54. See Srivastava's study on anglophone Canadian organizations' antiracist programs; Srivastava, "Tears, Fears and Careers."
55. Hurtado, *The Color of Privilege*; Ortega, "Being Lovingly, Knowingly Ignorant."
56. This discourse resisting intersectionality was expressed during the general assembly in 2015, but also on other occasions of feminist gatherings in Montreal (fieldwork notes, observation August 2015, Montreal). Geneviève Pagé rightly links these resistances to the attachment of older white feminists to the figure of the oppressed that was central to the Quebecois sovereignty project, a project that portrayed francophones as oppressed by anglophones and therefore as the oppressed "race"; see Pagé, "'Est-ce qu'on peut être racisées nous aussi?'"
57. Lamoureux, *L'amère patrie*; Pagé, "'Est-ce qu'on peut être racisées nous aussi?'"
58. See Laperrière and Lépinard, "Intersectionality as a Tool for Social Movements."
59. For example, more in line with other accounts of third-wave feminism, in 2015 the organization Feminist Dare adopted intersectionality as one of its core values and stressed the need to work with antiracist collectives. This rhetorical commitment was nevertheless not perceived as sufficient by one of its sister organizations based in a major French city, which broke with Feminist Dare at the same moment on the grounds that its position against the Muslim veil amounted to Islamophobia and racism.
60. Zerilli, *Feminism and the Abyss of Freedom*, 3.
61. Zerilli, *Feminism and the Abyss of Freedom*, 2.
62. For a historical analysis of American and French feminism along these lines, see Riley, *"Am I That Name?"*; Scott, *Only Paradoxes to Offer*.
63. Zerilli, *Feminism and the Abyss of Freedom*, 7.
64. Zerilli, *Feminism and the Abyss of Freedom*, 16.
65. Especially in the chapter "Freedom" in Arendt, *The Human Condition*.
66. This echoes Sarita Srivastava's remarks on the articulation between whiteness and respectability in feminist organizations; see Srivastava, "'You're Calling Me a Racist?'"
67. See Laperrière and Lépinard, "Intersectionality as a Tool for Social Movements."
68. On how school shapes class expectations and relations in France, see Laacher, *L'institution scolaire et ses miracles*.
69. A prominent collective voice opposed to the FFQ's accommodating position in sexularism debate is "Pour les droits des femmes du Québec," http://www.pdfquebec.org/, accessed November 13, 2017.
70. These interviews are not representative of course of the variety of positions adopted by white French feminists (see for a counterexample the queer feminist approach

developed by the Front du 20 mars, http://frontdu20mars.github.io/, accessed January 5, 2018). The interviews I use in this section are, however, representative of how feminism is made white, which is why I focus here on their moral dispositions.
71. Claudine is using the word "maternalist" here as the feminized version of paternalist.
72. Nelly refers to the Party of the Indigenous of the Republic, a leftist organization that fights the persistence of colonial relations and racism in French society.
73. In French, the neologism *islamiste* qualifies individuals who adhere to a political form of Islam linked to jihadism and terrorism. Here, Nelly's confusion between *islamiste* and Islamic (*islamique*) reveals a confusion between Islam and jihadism.
74. Anger and indignation are common feminist emotions that sustain feminist collective identity in the face of antifeminist sentiments. See Hercus, "Identity, Emotion, and Feminist Collective Action." However, here these emotions are directed not at a broader public that is not welcoming to feminist ideas, but at nonwhite fellow feminists.
75. Beltrán, *The Trouble with Unity*, 75.
76. An attitude that is not limited to French white feminists. See Srivastava, "Tears, Fears and Careers."
77. Farris, *In the Name of Women's Rights*; Bilge, "Mapping Quebecois Sexual Nationalism"; Hadj Abdou, "Gender Nationalism."
78. On the ways French institutions reconfigure Islam, see Fernando, *The Republic Unsettled*.
79. Baines, "Must Feminists Support Entrenchment of Sex Equality?" Another way in which Quebecois white feminists identify with Quebecois nationalism has been to insist, for example, that exchanges within umbrella organizations and women's rights forums and congresses occur only in French, while numerous racialized women's organizations in the Montreal region work in English. This political demand has effectively undermined the possibilities of including racialized women in the Quebecois women's movement's largest networks.
80. An important exception to this statement was the governmental body for women's rights, which on the contrary elaborated a discourse with heavy femonationalist overtones; Conseil du statut de la femme, *Affirmer la laïcité*.
81. Ricci, "Un féminisme inclusif?"
82. Vergès, *Le ventre des femmes*.
83. See Lépinard, "The Contentious Subject of Feminism," and Lépinard, *L'égalité introuvable*.
84. Rochefort, *Le pouvoir du genre*.
85. Della Sudda, "Par-delà le bien et le mal."
86. Between 1987 and 1995 many women's rights organizations mobilized to pass a new law criminalizing the actions taken by far-right Catholic groups to prevent women from accessing medical facilities to have an abortion, and in 1988, a far-right Christian committed arson against a Parisian theater showing Martin Scorsese's *The Last Temptation of Christ*.
87. See Laborde, "On Republican Toleration"; Laborde, *Critical Republicanism*.
88. This is what Laborde identifies as *laïcité C* in Laborde, "On Republican Toleration."

89. Selby, "French Secularism as a 'Guarantor' of Women's Rights?"
90. On this turning point, see Fassin and Fassin, *De la question sociale à la question raciale?*
91. See Tissot, "Excluding Muslim Women"; Selby, "Un/veiling Women's Bodies."
92. A similar cultural trope is analyzed for the United States in Ahmad, "Not Yet beyond the Veil."
93. See Amélie Barras's analysis of Benhabib's narratives in Barras, "Travelogue of Secularism." These cases, both in France and in Quebec, are exceptional but not isolated ones. Barras notes in Quebec at least four other public figures with similar discourses: Yolande Geadah, Leila Lesbet, Rakia Fourati, and Blandine Soulmana. In France, one can cite another prominent figure of the Ni putes ni soumises organization, Fadela Amara, as well as Gaye Petek, the head of an organization of Turkish women. Of course, Ayaan Hirsi Ali's case and her writings also come to mind.

Chapter 5

1. Anzaldúa and Moraga, *This Bridge Called My Back*; Lorde, *Sister Outsider*; Nelson, *Women of Color and the Reproductive Rights Movement*; Roth, *Separate Roads to Feminism*; Springer, *Living for the Revolution*; Beltrán, *The Trouble with Unity*.
2. Deleuze, "Philosophie et minorité," 154–55; Deleuze and Guattari, *Mille plateaux*, 133–34.
3. Butler, *Giving an Account of Oneself*.
4. Bacchetta, "Co-formations," 2.
5. Brown, *States of Injury*.
6. Ahmed, "Feminist Killjoys"; Ahmed, *Living a Feminist Life*, 177–79.
7. Ahmed, *Living a Feminist Life*, 74–75.
8. Ahmed, *Willful Subjects*.
9. Ahmed, *Living a Feminist Life*, 83.
10. Lorde, *Sister Outsider*.
11. hooks, *Feminist Theory*.
12. Walker, *Moral Repair*.
13. Brudholm, "Revisiting Resentments"; Brudholm, *Resentment's Virtue*.
14. Roth, *Separate Roads to Feminism*.
15. Springer, *Living for the Revolution*.
16. Nelson, *Women of Color and the Reproductive Rights. Movement*; Cole, "Coalitions as a Model for Intersectionality."
17. Predelli and Halsaa, *Majority-Minority Relations in Contemporary Women's Movements*; Townsend-Bell, "What Is Relevance?"
18. Strolovitch, *Affirmative Advocacy*; Laperrière and Lépinard, "Intersectionality as a Tool for Social Movements"; Evans, "Intersectionality as Feminist Praxis"; Lépinard, "Doing Intersectionality"; Emejulu and Bassel, "Whose Crisis Counts?"; Bassel and Emejulu, "Struggles for Institutional Space in France and the United Kingdom."

19. On the United States see Chun, Lipsitz, and Shin, "Intersectionality as a Social Movement Strategy." On the United Kingdom and France see Bassel and Emejulu, *Minority Women and Austerity*.
20. For Canada an exception is Srivastava, "Tears, Fears and Careers"; Srivastava, "'You're Calling Me a Racist?'" See also Tungohan, "Intersectionality and Social Justice." For Germany, El-Tayeb, *European Others*, provides a first analysis of the emergence of Black feminism in the 1980s and 1990s.
21. See Bacchetta, "Co-formations"; Vergès, *Le ventre des femmes*. In France, prominent Black feminist activists and collectives are also producing their own histories and analyses; see the Mwasi website https://mwasicollectif.com/, Amandine Gay's 2016 movie, *Ouvrir la voix*, and her blog https://badassafrofem.wordpress.com/. See also the blog of Afro-feminist Many Chroniques, https://manychroniques.wordpress.com/.
22. Anzaldúa and Moraga, *This Bridge Called My Back*; Lorde, *Sister Outsider*; Nelson, *Women of Color and the Reproductive Rights Movement*; Roth, *Separate Roads to Feminism*; Springer, *Living for the Revolution*; Beltrán, *The Trouble with Unity*; Hancock, *Intersectionality*.
23. Roth, *Separate Roads to Feminism*, 9.
24. Springer, *Living for the Revolution*, 138.
25. Bacchetta, "Co-formations"; Paris, "Un féminisme anti-colonial"; Vergès, *Le ventre des femmes*.
26. Ricci, "Un féminisme inclusif?"; Ricci, "Contesting the Nation(s)."
27. Kymlicka, *Finding Our Way*, especially chap. 3. Since the 1980s especially, multiculturalism has meant a rejection of cultural assimilation and the valorization of cultural diversity and immigration—although Quebec has not fully adopted the Canadian narrative following which the diversity of the "Canadian mosaic" has become synonymous with Canadian national identity itself.
28. Bloemraad, *Becoming a Citizen*; Ku, "Multicultural Politics and the Paradox of Being Special."
29. Chapman and Frader, *Race in France*.
30. Silverman, *Deconstructing the Nation*; Bleich, *Race Politics in Britain and France*; Keaton, Sharpley-Whiting, and Stovall, *Black France / France noire*; Simon, "The Choice of Ignorance."
31. Ku, "Multicultural Politics and the Paradox of Being Special."
32. Ethel Tungohan offers another example of this critical engagement with Canadian multiculturalism by Filipina migrant women's organizations in Ontario; see Tungohan, "Intersectionality and Social Justice."
33. Interview with a South Asian women's organization in Montreal.
34. Lesselier, "Pour une histoire des mouvements de femmes de l'immigration en France."
35. Vergès, *Le ventre des femmes*, 208. One of the Coordination founders, Gerty Dambury, analyzed the end of the organization as the result of the return of its Caribbean and African members to their home countries. Dambury, oral presentation, conference "Faire et écrire l'histoire: Féminisme et lutte de classes, de 1970 à nos jours," Paris, September 25, 2010.

36. Lesselier, "Pour une histoire des mouvements de femmes de l'immigration en France."
37. Vergès, *Le ventre des femmes*; Shepard, *The Invention of Decolonization*.
38. Authenticity that legitimizes the relationship of representation of the constituency (here immigrant women) is performed; see Luna, "Who Speaks for Whom?"
39. These discrepancies generate tensions as immigrant women activists are called upon to "represent" their community; see Ku, "Multicultural Politics and the Paradox of Being Special."
40. Springer, *Living for the Revolution*.
41. Crenshaw, "Mapping the Margins."
42. The veiled girl appears as the exact negative opposite of the well-assimilated *beurette* described in Guénif-Souilamas and Macé, *Les féministes et le garçon arabe*. See also Scott, *The Politics of the Veil*.
43. Scott, *The Politics of the Veil*.
44. Vergès here follows Antonio Gramsci's analysis. See Vergès, *Le ventre des femmes*, 15.
45. Reger, "Micro-cohorts."
46. Reger, "Micro-cohorts."
47. Reger, "Micro-cohorts," 52.
48. On how these differences play out in Quebec, see Laperrière and Lépinard, "Intersectionality as a Tool for Social Movements."
49. Lépinard, "Doing Intersectionality."
50. Bacchetta, "Co-formations."
51. Allen, *The Politics of Our Selves*.
52. Butler, *Giving an Account of Oneself*, 17.
53. See Paola Bacchetta's analysis of the group in "Co-formations," as well as Groupe du 6 novembre, *Warriors/Guerrières*.
54. See Fassa, Lépinard, and Roca i Escoda, "Introduction."
55. Perreau, *Queer Theory*.
56. Pereira, *Les grammaires de la contestation*.
57. A finding corroborated in Britain by Bassel and Emejulu, *Minority Women and Austerity*. See also Maiguashca, Dean, and Keith, "Pulling Together in a Crisis?"
58. Laugier, "Voice as Form of Life."
59. Laugier, "Voice as Form of Life," 73.
60. Gay, *Ouvrir la voix*.
61. Molinier, *Le care monde*, chap. 3.
62. A claim that typically invisibilizes women at the intersectional of race and gender. See Crenshaw, "Demarginalizing the Intersection of Race and Sex."
63. Trudel, "L'engagement des femmes en politique au Québec."
64. Until the Quiet Revolution in the 1960s and 1970s (la Révolution tranquille), being anglophone was a prerequisite to access positions of power within the administration of the government or private business. English was compulsory in many workplaces. The rise of the nationalist party and its victory in Quebecois politics opened the way in the 1970s and 1980s to a political promotion of the French language, the most emblematic being the law making it compulsory for children of nonfrancophone immigrants to attend francophone public schools (Bill 101, 1977).

65. Vergès, *Le ventre des femmes*, chap. 5.
66. Bentouhami-Molino, *Race, cultures, identités*, 103; Fanon, *Peau noire, masques blancs*; Michel, "Quand les mots et les images blessent."
67. Michel, "Equality and Postcolonical Claims."
68. Michel, "Quand les mots et les images blessent."
69. This famous political song from the French second wave, "Debout!," considered the hymn of the MLF, compares women to slaves: "Levons-nous femmes esclaves, brisons nos entraves" (Let's rise, women slaves, and break our chains), https://www.youtube.com/watch?v=lIE9HtFv0fc. See also this critique in Vergès, *Le ventre des femmes*.
70. See Mercier, "Sexualité et respectabilité des femmes." See also Reger, "Micro-cohorts"; Reger, "The Story of a Slut Walk."
71. Sibertin-Blanc, "Deleuze et les minorités," 55.
72. Bacchetta, "Co-formations."
73. Brown, *States of Injury*.
74. Zerilli, *Feminism and the Abyss of Freedom*. On how love must constitute the basis of feminist transracial alliances, see also Rowe, *Power Lines*.
75. Nussbaum, *Political Emotions*.
76. Marchetti, "Resentment at the Heart of Europe."
77. Michel, "Equality and Postcolonical Claims"; Michel, "Quand les mots et les images blessent."
78. Michel, "Equality and Postcolonical Claims"; Butler, *Giving an Account of Oneself*; Butler, *Excitable Speech*.
79. Butler, *Giving an Account of Oneself*, 5.
80. Butler, *Giving an Account of Oneself*, 7.
81. Deleuze and Guattari, *Mille plateaux*, 134.
82. I agree here with Bruno Perreau's argument that "minorities do not have the luxury of disavowing, once and for all, their sense of belonging"; see *Queer Theory*, 15.
83. Laugier, "Voice as Form of Life," 64.
84. Of course, this understanding of language is diametrically opposed to that of Deleuze and Guattari, who conceive of language not as a form of life (as do Laugier, Wittgenstein, and Cavell) but as a way to "give orders to life" and to submit individuals to social rules; see Deleuze and Guattari, *Mille plateaux*, 95–96.
85. Cornell, "What Is Ethical Feminism?," 85.

Chapter 6

1. Butler, "Contingent Foundations," 1995, 48.
2. Farris, *In the Name of Women's Rights*.
3. Zerilli, *Feminism and the Abyss of Freedom*, 144.
4. I discuss this claim further in the conclusion of this book.
5. See, for example, Butler, *Gender Trouble*; Butler and Scott, *Feminists Theorize the Political*; Mouffe, "Feminism."
6. Allen, "Emancipation without Utopia."

7. Allen, "Feminism, Modernity and Critical Theory."
8. Reagon, "Coalition Politics," 357.
9. Reagon, "Coalition Politics," 361.
10. hooks, *Feminist Theory*; Butler, *Gender Trouble*; Mouffe, "Feminism."
11. Lugones, "Purity, Impurity," 463.
12. Young, *Inclusion and Democracy*, 41–50; Beltrán, *The Trouble with Unity*, chap. 2.
13. Chun, Lipsitz, and Shin, "Intersectionality as a Social Movement Strategy"; Carastathis, "Identity Categories as Potential Coalitions," 945.
14. Lyshaug, "Solidarity without 'Sisterhood'?"
15. On this point see Crenshaw, "Mapping the Margins," 1299; Cole, "Coalitions as a Model for Intersectionality."
16. "Manifestation du 8 mars à Belleville," Paris-luttes.info, March 5, 2015, https://paris-luttes.info/manifestation-du-8-mars-a-2731, accessed March 19, 2018.
17. Cole, "Coalitions as a Model for Intersectionality."
18. Weldon, "Inclusion, Solidarity, and Social Movements."
19. This is also evident in the feminist literature: racialized feminists have often reflected on the conditions for coalition work; see, for example, Ange-Marie Hancock's account in *Intersectionality*, 69–71.
20. Beltrán, *The Trouble with Unity*, chap. 2; Luna, "'Truly a Women of Color Organization.'"
21. Zerilli, *Feminism and the Abyss of Freedom*, 117.
22. Lugones, "On Complex Communication."
23. Lyshaug, "Solidarity without 'Sisterhood'?"
24. Benhabib, *Situating the Self*.
25. Lyshaug, "Solidarity without 'Sisterhood'?," 84.
26. Lyshaug, "Solidarity without 'Sisterhood'?," 86.
27. Lugones, "On Complex Communication."
28. Lyshaug, "Solidarity without 'Sisterhood'?," 95.
29. Lyshaug, "Solidarity without 'Sisterhood'?," 97.
30. Beltrán, *The Trouble with Unity*; Carastathis, "Identity Categories as Potential Coalitions."
31. Ahmad, "Not Yet beyond the Veil."
32. Ahmad, "Not Yet beyond the Veil"; Barras, "Travelogue of Secularism."
33. Zerilli, *Feminism and the Abyss of Freedom*.
34. Zerilli, *Feminism and the Abyss of Freedom*, 17.
35. Zerilli, *Feminism and the Abyss of Freedom*, 19.
36. Zerilli, *Feminism and the Abyss of Freedom*, 22.
37. Zerilli, *Feminism and the Abyss of Freedom*, 140–45.
38. Zerilli, *Feminism and the Abyss of Freedom*, 172.
39. Zerilli, *Feminism and the Abyss of Freedom*, 145.
40. Zerilli, *Feminism and the Abyss of Freedom*, 104–5.
41. Zerilli, *Feminism and the Abyss of Freedom*, 144.
42. Zerilli, *Feminism and the Abyss of Freedom*, 171.
43. Perreau, *Queer Theory*, 15.

44. Young, "Asymmetrical Reciprocity," 349.
45. Young, "Asymmetrical Reciprocity," 349.
46. Young, "Asymmetrical Reciprocity," 346.
47. Young, "Asymmetrical Reciprocity," 360.
48. Young, "Asymmetrical Reciprocity," 349.
49. Young, "Asymmetrical Reciprocity," 352.
50. Young, *Inclusion and Democracy*, 57.
51. Young, *Inclusion and Democracy*, 68.
52. Young, *Inclusion and Democracy*, 119.
53. Young, *Inclusion and Democracy*, 115.
54. Young, "Asymmetrical Reciprocity," 351.
55. Harris, "Whiteness as Property."
56. Hoagland, "Denying Relationality," 96.
57. Hoagland, "Denying Relationality," 98.
58. Butler, *Giving an Account of Oneself*, 5.
59. Butler, *Giving an Account of Oneself*, 6.
60. Molinier, *Le care monde*, 31.
61. Molinier, *Le care monde*, 34.
62. Das, *Life and Words*.
63. Tronto, *Moral Boundaries*.
64. Of course, a relational account of human life also has implications for how we think about values such as equality or autonomy. Mackenzie and Stoljar, *Relational Autonomy*; Nedelsky, *Law's Relations*. Judith Butler also places vulnerability and the precariousness of life as a fundamental experience of interdependency, which may lead to the political formation of coalition through copresence in the public space. However, her analysis does not consider the moral dimensions of the condition of precariousness, but rather how precariousness and structural differentials in vulnerability affect the constitution of possible political subjects. While she does suggest that power may lead to a denial of vulnerability, a proposal that echoes Tronto's idea that the powerful can be irresponsible, Butler does not investigate further how precariousness can sustain moral relations; rather she sees the body, and the copresence of bodies, as the site where political coalitions may be forged. See Butler, "Vulnerability, Precarity, Coalition"; Butler, *Precarious Life*.
65. Laugier, "Voice as Form of Life," 64.
66. Laugier, "Voice as Form of Life," 64.
67. On the contextual nature of moral reasoning, see Tronto, *Moral Boundaries*, 27.
68. Tronto, *Moral Boundaries*, 14.
69. Das, "What Does Ordinary Ethics Look Like?," 108.
70. Das, "What Does Ordinary Ethics Look Like?," 58.
71. Das, "What Does Ordinary Ethics Look Like?," 95.
72. Laugier, "Voice as Form of Life," 73.
73. Tronto, *Moral Boundaries*, 5.
74. Tronto, *Moral Boundaries*, 175.
75. Tronto, *Moral Boundaries*, 160.

76. Tronto, *Moral Boundaries*, 14.
77. Tronto, *Moral Boundaries*, 174.
78. Tronto, "Partiality Based on Relational Responsibilities."
79. Young, "Responsibility and Global Justice."
80. Tronto, "Partiality Based on Relational Responsibilities," 306.
81. Young, "Responsibility and Global Justice," 126.
82. Tronto, "Partiality Based on Relational Responsibilities," 308.
83. Tronto, "Partiality Based on Relational Responsibilities."
84. See the distinction drawn by Soran Reader between groups we happen to belong to, and groups we choose; Reader, "Distance," 376.
85. I will give only one example here: the collection of essays in *This Bridge Called My Back*. Many of the essays explore and analyze the moral and affective relationship among feminists and within and across racial and sexual boundaries, and the meaning of solidarity. See Anzaldúa and Moraga, *This Bridge Called My Back*. Today discourses invigorating for example the 2017 and subsequent Women's Marches also display the complex relationship of solidarity, beyond representation, that the movement is supposed to create, with mottoes such as "We are our sisters' voices."
86. Reader, "Distance," 371.
87. de Lauretis, "Upping the Anti," 266.
88. Tronto, *Moral Boundaries*, 3.
89. Tronto, *Moral Boundaries*, 168.
90. Tronto, *Moral Boundaries*, 19.
91. Das, "What Does Ordinary Ethics Look Like?," 75.
92. Das, "What Does Ordinary Ethics Look Like?," 75.
93. This question has been explored in the political theory discussion on internal minorities. Multiculturalist feminist theorists insist that minority rights are compatible with women's rights if we ensure the participation of minority women's voices in the debate. However, they acknowledge that the exercise of making sure that minoritized and oppressed voices are appropriately represented is a difficult one. See Deveaux, *Gender and Justice in Multicultural Liberal States*; Phillips, *Multiculturalism without Culture*.
94. Mohanty, "Under Western Eyes"; Abu-Lughod, "Do Muslim Women Really Need Saving?"
95. Avramopoulou, "Crossing Distances to Meet Allies."
96. Boltanski, *La souffrance à distance*.
97. Nash, "Practicing Love," 14.
98. Iris Young makes a similar argument, asserting that public discussion cannot aim at transcending particularity but must encourage sharing the various particularities that characterize the participants; see Young, *Inclusion and Democracy*, 113. Bruno Perreau also underlines that the ethic of the privileged is oriented toward principle rather than context; see Perreau, *Queer Theory*.
99. In the context of feminist activism across class and racial divides in the US South at the end of the 1980s, Barbara Ellen Smith writes: "Every issue required analysis from the perspective of those disadvantaged by all forms of oppression, and

privileged by none. Only then would it have been possible to avoid strategies that neglected or even disadvantaged women who live at the very different intersections of race, gender, and class." This analysis clearly echoes the idea of placing the most vulnerable person's needs at the center of moral judgment and political analysis. See Smith, "Crossing the Great Divides."p.694

100. Hache, *Ce à quoi nous tenons*, 13.
101. Hache, *Ce à quoi nous tenons*.
102. Hache, *Ce à quoi nous tenons*, 44.
103. Baines, "Must Feminists Support Entrenchment of Sex Equality?"
104. Hache, *Ce à quoi nous tenons*, 54–63.
105. Young, *Inclusion and Democracy*.
106. Zerilli, *Feminism and the Abyss of Freedom*, 144.
107. Latour, *Science in Action*.
108. Saba Mahmood suggests that translation might be an important ethical practice when reflecting on the question of the relation between Western feminist theory and illiberal forms of life; see Mahmood, *Politics of Piety*, 39. See also Nicole Doerr's important reflection in *Political Translation* on translation as a social movement democratic practice and on the specific role played by translators to address differences and inequalities in sociale movements.
109. Beltrán, *The Trouble With Unity*, 73.
110. On the notion, developed by Jacques Rancière, that equality requires us to acknowledge others as interlocutors, and that politics can emerge only in a space defined by equality, see Rancière, *Disagreement*; Zerilli, *Feminism and the Abyss of Freedom*; Bassel, *Refugee Women*.

Chapter 7

1. Scott, *Sex and Secularism*.
2. Farris, *In the Name of Women's Rights*.
3. Deveaux, *Gender and Justice in Multicultural Liberal States*; Phillips, "Feminism and Liberalism Revisited"; Hirschmann, *The Subject of Liberty*; Mackenzie and Stoljar, *Relational Autonomy*.
4. Abu-Lughod, "Do Muslim Women Really Need Saving?"; Mahmood, *Politics of Piety*.
5. Lépinard, "Autonomy and the Crisis of the Feminist Subject."
6. Rinaldo, "Pious and Critical"; Bracke, "Conjugating the Modern/Religious"; Reilly, "Recasting Secular Thinking for Emancipatory Feminist Practice"; Brandt and Longman, "Working against Many Grains."
7. I borrow here Amy Allen's distinction—which she borrows from Seyla Benhabib—between explanatory-diagnostic and anticipatory-utopian moments in political theorizing. See Allen, *The Politics of Our Selves*.
8. Scott, *The Politics of the Veil*.
9. Crenshaw, "Mapping the Margins"; Crenshaw, "Postscript"; Townsend-Bell, "What Is Relevance?"; Emejulu and Bassel, "Whose Crisis Counts"; Bacchetta, "Décoloniser le féminisme."

10. Farris, *In the Name of Women's Rights*.
11. Mills, *The Racial Contract*; Sullivan and Tuana, *Race and Epistemologies of Ignorance*.
12. Wekker, *White Innocence*.
13. The debate started at the end of the 1980s, with interventions such as those of Linda Alcoff, Teresa de Lauretis, and Denise Riley. See Alcoff, "Cultural Feminism vs. Poststructuralism"; de Lauretis, "Eccentric Subjects"; Riley, *"Am I That Name?"*. Since then, this debate has continued to shape feminist theorists' understanding and reflections; see, for example, recently Weir, *Identities and Freedom*.
14. Butler, "Contingent Foundations," 1995; Butler, "What Is Critique?," 216.
15. de Lauretis, "Eccentric Subjects," 116.
16. Butler, "Contingent Foundations," 1995.
17. Zerilli, *Feminism and the Abyss of Freedom*.
18. Butler, "Contingent Foundations," 1995, 50.
19. Butler, "Contingent Foundations," 1995, 46.
20. Butler, "Vulnerability, Precarity, Coalition."
21. Allen, "Emancipation without Utopia."
22. Muñoz, *Disidentification*.
23. See Jagose, "Feminism's Queer Theory."
24. Muñoz, *Cruising Utopia*.
25. Perreau, *Queer Theory*.
26. Avramopoulou, "Crossing Distances to Meet Allies."
27. Hache, *Ce à quoi nous tenons*, 31.
28. Rancière, *Disagreement*; Hache, *Ce à quoi nous tenons*.
29. Amy Allen captures artfully this connection in "Emancipation without Utopia."
30. Reformulations of freedom and autonomy are present in feminist critical theory, multiculturalist feminism, and feminist liberal theory. See Allen, "Feminism, Modernity and Critical Theory"; Hirschmann, *The Subject of Liberty*; Deveaux, *Gender and Justice in Multicultural Liberal States*; Mackenzie and Stoljar, *Relational Autonomy*. For an analysis of the multiculturalist and proceduralist feminist accounts of autonomy and their limits for rethinking the feminist project, see Lépinard, "Autonomy and the Crisis of the Feminist Subject."
31. Ratna Kapur provides a similar critique of the liberal assumptions of human rights discourse and its failure to account for subaltern subjectivities. She argues that this failure leads to the demise of that ideal; see Kapur, "In the Aftermath of Critique."
32. Mahmood, *Politics of Piety*, 197.
33. Weir, *Identities and Freedom*.
34. Mahmood, "Feminist Theory, Embodiment, and the Docile Agent," 225.
35. Mahmood, "Feminist Theory, Embodiment, and the Docile Agent," 225.
36. Allen, "Feminism, Modernity and Critical Theory," 278.
37. Allen, "Feminism, Modernity and Critical Theory," 279.
38. Allen, "Emancipation without Utopia," 515.
39. See in particular Nedelsky, *Law's Relations*.
40. Weir, *Identities and Freedom*.
41. Lugones, "Playfulness."
42. Inckle, "Debilitating Times."

43. Zerilli, *Feminism and the Abyss of Freedom*.
44. Nash, "Practicing Love"; Molinier, *Le care monde*.

Appendix on Methodology

1. Molinier, *Le care monde*, chap. 1.
2. Molinier, *Le care monde*, chap. 2.
3. Devault, "Talking and Listening."

Bibliography

Abu-Lughod, Lila. "Do Muslim Women Really Need Saving? Anthropological Reflections on Cultural Relativism and Its Others." *American Anthropologist* 104, no. 3 (2002): 783–90.

Agustín, Lise Rolandsen. *Gender Equality, Intersectionality, and Diversity in Europe*. New York: Palgrave Macmillan, 2013.

Ahmad, Dohra. "Not Yet beyond the Veil: Muslim Women in American Popular Literature." *Social Text* 27, no. 2 (99) (June 1, 2009): 105–31.

Ahmed, Sara. *Cultural Politics of Emotion*. 2nd ed. Edinburgh: Edinburgh University Press, 2014.

Ahmed, Sara. "Declarations of Whiteness: The Non-performativity of Anti-racism." *Borderlands* 3, 2004. http://www.borderlands.net.au/vol3no2_2004/ahmed_declarations.htm.

Ahmed, Sara. "Feminist Killjoys." In *The Promise of Happiness*, 50–87. Durham, NC: Duke University Press, 2010.

Ahmed, Sara. *Living a Feminist Life*. Durham, NC: Duke University Press, 2017.

Ahmed, Sara. "The Nonperformativity of Antiracism." *Meridians: Feminism, Race, Transnationalism* 7, no. 1 (2006): 104–26.

Ahmed, Sara. "A Phenomenology of Whiteness." *Feminist Theory* 8, no. 2 (2007): 149–68.

Ahmed, Sara. *The Promise of Happiness*. Durham, NC: Duke University Press, 2010.

Ahmed, Sara. *Willful Subjects*. Durham, NC: Duke University Press, 2014.

Ahmed, Sara, Jane Kilby, Celia Lury, Maureen Mcneil, and Beverley Skeggs. "Introduction: Thinking through Feminism." In *Transformations: Thinking through Feminism*, 1–24. London: Routledge, 2000.

Alcoff, Linda Martín. "Cultural Feminism vs. Poststructuralism: The Identity Crisis in Feminist Theory." *Signs* 13, no. 3 (1988): 405–36.

Ali, Zahra. *Féminismes islamiques*. Paris: La Fabrique, 2012.

Allen, Amy. "Emancipation without Utopia: Subjection, Modernity, and the Normative Claims of Feminist Critical Theory." *Hypatia* 30, no. 3 (2015): 513–29.

Allen, Amy. "Feminism, Modernity and Critical Theory." *International Critical Thought* 3, no. 3 (September 1, 2013): 268–81.

Allen, Amy. *The Politics of Our Selves: Power, Autonomy, and Gender in Contemporary Critical Theory*. New York: Columbia University Press, 2007.

Amara, Fadela, and Sylvia Zappi. *Ni putes ni soumises*. Paris: La Découverte, 2003.

Amiraux, Valérie, and Jean-François Gaudreault-Desbiens. "Libertés fondamentales et visibilité des signes religieux en France et au Québec: Entre logiques nationales et non nationales du droit?" *Recherches sociographiques* 57, no. 2–3 (2016): 351–78.

Anderson-Bricker, Kristin. "'Triple Jeopardy': Black Women and the Growth of Feminist Consciousness in SNCC, 1964–1975." In *Still Lifting, Still Climbing: African American Women's Contemporary Activism*, edited by Kimberly Springer, 49–69. New York: New York University Press, 1999.

Andreassen, Rikke, and Doutje Lettinga. "Veiled Debates: Gender and Gender Equality in European National Narratives." In *Politics, Religion and Gender: Framing and Regulating the Veil*, edited by Sieglinde Rosenberger and Birgit Sauer, 17–36. London: Routledge, 2012.

Anzaldúa, Gloria, and Cherrie Moraga, eds. *This Bridge Called My Back: Radical Writings by Women of Color*. 2nd ed. New York: Kitchen Table, Women of Color Press, 1983.

Arendt, Hannah. *The Human Condition*. Chicago: University of Chicago Press, 1958.

Armstrong, Elizabeth A. *Forging Gay Identities: Organizing Sexuality in San Francisco, 1950–1994*. Chicago: University of Chicago Press, 2002.

Arruzza, Cinzia, Tithi Bhattacharya, and Nancy Fraser. *Feminism for the 99%*. London: Verso, 2019.

Asad, Talal. *Formations of the Secular: Christianity, Islam, Modernity*. Stanford, CA: Stanford University Press, 2003.

Asal, Houla. "Au nom de l'égalité! Mobilisations contre l'islamophobie en France. La campagne contre l'exclusion des mères voilées des sorties scolaires." In *L'Islam et la cité: Engagements musulmans dans les quartiers populaires*, edited by Julien Talpin, Julien O'Miel, and Frank Frégosi, 137–64. Villeneuve d'Ascq: Presses Universitaires du Septentrion, 2017.

Assemblée nationale du Québec. "S'opposer à l'implantation de tribunaux dits islamiques au Québec et au Canada." *Journal des débats de l'Assemblée nationale* 38, no. 156 (2005): 37e législature, 1re session. http://m.assnat.qc.ca/fr/travaux-parlementaires/assemblee-nationale/37-1/journal-debats/20050526/2773.html#_Toc104971753.

Avishai, Orit. "'Doing Religion' in a Secular World: Women in Conservative Religions and the Question of Agency." *Gender & Society* 22, no. 4 (2008): 409–33.

Avramopoulou, Eirini. "Crossing Distances to Meet Allies: On Women's Signatures, the Politics of Performativity and Dissensus." In *Thinking Collective Action with Judith Butler*, edited by Delphine Gardey and Cynthia Kraus, 78–103. Zurich: Seismo, 2016.

Bacchetta, Paola. "Co-formations: Des spatialités de résistance décoloniales chez les lesbiennes 'of color' en France." *Genre, sexualité & société* 1 (2009). http://journals.openedition.org/gss/810.

Bacchetta, Paola. "Décoloniser le féminisme: Intersectionnalité, assemblages, co-formations, coproductions." *Les cahiers du CEDREF* 20 (2015).

Baines, Beverley. "Must Feminists Identify as Secular Citizens? Lessons from Ontario." In *Gender Equality: Dimensions of Women's Equal Citizenship*, edited by Linda C. McClain and Joanna L. Grossman, 83–106. Cambridge University Press, 2009.

Baines, Beverley. "Must Feminists Support Entrenchment of Sex Equality? Lessons from Quebec." In *Constituting Equality: Gender Equality and Comparative Constitutional Law*, edited by Susan H. Williams, 137–56. Cambridge: Cambridge University Press, 2009.

Bakht, Natasha. "In Your Face: Piercing the Veil of Ignorance about Niqab-Wearing Women." *Social & Legal Studies* 24, no. 3 (2015): 419–41.

Bakht, Natasha. "Religious Arbitration in Canada: Protecting Women by Protecting Them from Religion." *Canadian Journal of Women and the Law* 19, no. 1 (2007): 119–44.

Bakht, Natasha. "Were Muslim Barbarians Really Knocking on the Gates of Ontario: The Religious Arbitration Controversy—Another Perspective." *Ottawa Law Review* 67 (2006): 67–82.

Balibar, Etienne. "Le mot race n'est pas 'de trop' dans la constitution française." *Mots: Les langages du politique* 33 (December 1992): 241–56.

Balibar, Etienne, Saïd Bouamama, Françoise Gaspard, Catherine Levy, and Pierre Tevanian. "Oui au foulard à l'école laïque." *Libération*, May 20, 2003.
Bangstad, Sindre. "Saba Mahmood and Anthropological Feminism after Virtue." *Theory, Culture & Society* 28, no. 3 (2011): 28–54.
Banting, Keith, and Stuart Soroka. "Minority Nationalism and Immigrant Integration in Canada." *Nations and Nationalism* 18, no. 1 (2012): 156–76.
Barras, Amélie. *Refashioning Secularisms in France and Turkey: The Case of the Headscarf Ban*. London: Routledge, 2014.
Barras, Amélie. "Travelogue of Secularism: Longing to Find a Place to Call Home—1350506818755415." *European Journal of Women's Studies*, February 11, 2018, 1–16.
Barras, Amélie, and Xavier Guillaume. "The Safety of Authenticity: Ali Kebab, or an Exploration in the Contemporaneity of Foreignness and the Self's Post-colonial Imaginary." *European Journal of Cultural Studies* 16, no. 3 (2013): 310–28.
Bassel, Leah. "Intersectional Politics at the Boundaries of the Nation State." *Ethnicities* 10, no. 2 (2010): 155–80.
Bassel, Leah. *Refugee Women: Beyond Gender versus Culture*. London: Routledge, 2012.
Bassel, Leah, and Akwugo Emejulu. *Minority Women and Austerity: Survival and Resistance in France and Britain*. Bristol: Policy Press, 2017.
Bassel, Leah, and Akwugo Emejulu. "Struggles for Institutional Space in France and the United Kingdom: Intersectionality and the Politics of Policy." *Politics and Gender* 6, no. 4 (December 2010): 517–44.
Baubérot, Jean. *Une laïcité interculturelle: Le Québec, avenir de la France?* La Tour-d'Aigues, France: Editions de l'Aube, 2008.
Baxandall, Rosalyn. "Re-visioning the Women's Liberation Movement's Narrative: Early Second Wave African American Feminists." *Feminist Studies* 27, no. 1 (2001): 225–45.
Beaman, Lori G. "Overdressed and Underexposed or Underdressed and Overexposed?" *Social Identities* 19, no. 6 (2013): 723–42.
Beaman, Lori G., and Lisa Smith. "'Dans leur propre intérêt': La Charte des valeurs québécoises, ou du danger de la religion pour les femmes." *Recherches sociographiques* 57, nos. 2–3 (2016): 475–504.
Beckwith, Karen. "Women's Movements at Century's End: Excavation and Advances in Political Science." *Annual Review of Political Science* 4 (2001): 371–90.
Beltrán, Cristina. *The Trouble with Unity: Latino Politics and the Creation of Identity*. Oxford: Oxford University Press, 2010.
Benani, Souad. "Faire et écrire l'histoire: Féminisme et lutte des classes." Presented at the Conference "History of the Class Struggle Trend of the Feminist Movement, Paris, September 25, 2010.
Benhabib, Seyla. *Democracy and Difference: Contesting the Boundaries of the Political*. Princeton, NJ: Princeton University Press, 1996.
Benhabib, Seyla. *Situating the Self*. New York: Routledge, n.d.
Benhabib, Seyla, Judith Butler, Drucilla Cornell, and Nancy Fraser. *Feminist Contentions: A Philosophical Exchange*. New York: Routledge, 1995.
Bentouhami-Molino, Hourya. *Race, cultures, identités: Une approche féministe et postcoloniale*. Paris: PUF, 2015.
Bereni, Laure. *La bataille de la parité: Mobilisations pour la féminisation du pouvoir*. Paris: Economica, 2015.
Berlant, Lauren. *Cruel Optimism*. Durham, NC: Duke University Press, 2011.

Bilge, Sirma. "'... Alors que nous, Québécois, nos femmes sont égales à nous et nous les aimons ainsi.'" *Sociologie et sociétés* 42, no. 1 (2010): 197–226.
Bilge, Sirma. "Mapping Quebecois Sexual Nationalism in Times of 'Crisis of Reasonable Accommodations.'" *Journal of Intercultural Studies* 33, no. 3 (2012): 303–18.
Bilge, Sirma. "Plaidoyer pour une intersectionalité critique non blanchie." In *L'intersectionnalité: Enjeux théoriques et politiques*, edited by Farinaz Fassa, Éléonore Lépinard, and Marta Roca i Escoda, 75–102. Paris: La Dispute, 2016.
Blee, Kathleen M. *Women of the Klan: Racism and Gender in the 1920s.* Berkeley: University of California Press, 1991.
Bleich, Erik. *Race Politics in Britain and France: Ideas and Policymaking since the 1960s.* Cambridge: Cambridge University Press, 2003.
Bloemraad, Irene. *Becoming a Citizen: Incorporating Immigrants and Refugees in the United States and Canada.* Berkeley: University of California Press, 2006.
Boggio Éwanjé-Épée, Félix, and Stella Magliani-Belkacem. *Les féministes blanches et l'empire.* Paris: Edition La Fabrique, 2012.
Boltanski, Luc. *La souffrance à distance: Morale humanitaire, médias et politique.* Paris: Métailié, 1993.
Bosset, Pierre. "Les fondements juridiques et l'évolution de l'obligation d'accommodement raisonnable." In *Les accomodements raisonnables: Quoi, comment, jusqu'où?*, 3–28. Montreal: Editions Yvon Blais, 2007.
Bouchard, Gérard, and Charles Taylor. *Building the Future: A Time for Reconciliation. Report of the Consultation Commission on Accommodation Practices Related to Cultural Differences.* Quebec: Government of Quebec, 2008.
Boumediene-Thiery, Alima, Dounia Bouzar, Christine Delphy, Françoise Gaspard, Éric Fassin, Madeleine Rebérioux, and Nicole Savy. "Un voile sur la discrimination." *Le Monde*, December 17, 2003.
Bouteldja, Houria. "De la cérémonie du dévoilement à Alger (1958) à Ni putes ni soumises: L'instrumentalisation coloniale et néo-coloniale de la cause des femmes." *Oumma* (blog), October 13, 2004. https://oumma.com/de-la-ceremonie-du-devoilement-a-alger-1958-a-ni-putes-ni-soumises-linstrumentalisation-coloniale-et-neo-coloniale-de-la-causedes femmes/.
Bouyahia, Malek, and Karima Ramdani. "D'un voile à l'autre." In *La polysémie du voile: Politiques et mobilisations postcoloniales*, edited by Maria Leonora Sanna and Malek Bouyahia, 117–34. Paris: Editions des archives contemporaines, 2013.
Bouyahia, Malek, and Maria Eleonora Sanna, eds. *La polysémie du voile: Politiques et mobilisations postcoloniales.* Paris: Editions des archives contemporaines, 2013.
Bowen, John R. "How the French State Justifies Controlling Muslim Bodies: From Harm-Based to Values-Based Reasoning." *Social Research* 78, no. 2 (2011): 325–48.
Bowen, John R. *Why the French Don't Like Headscarves: Islam, the State, and Public Space.* Princeton, NJ: Princeton University Press, 2007.
Bracke, Sarah. "Conjugating the Modern/Religious, Conceptualizing Female Religious Agency: Contours of a Post-secular Conjuncture." *Theory, Culture & Society* 25, no. 6 (2008): 51–67.
Braidotti, Rosi. "In Spite of the Times: The Postsecular Turn in Feminism." *Theory, Culture & Society* 25, no. 6 (2008): 1–24.
Braidotti, Rosi. *Nomadic Theory: The Portable Rosi Braidotti.* New York: Columbia University Press, 2011.

Brandt, Nella Van Den, and Chia Longman. "Working against Many Grains: Rethinking Difference, Emancipation and Agency in the Counter-discourse of an Ethnic Minority Women's Organisation in Belgium." *Social Compass* 64, no. 4 (December 1, 2017): 512–29.
Brems, Eva. *The Experiences of Face Veil Wearers in Europe and the Law.* Cambridge: Cambridge University Press, 2014.
Brown, Wendy. *States of Injury: Power and Freedom in Late Modernity.* Princeton, NJ: Princeton University Press, 1995. http://press.princeton.edu/titles/5715.html.
Brudholm, Thomas. *Resentment's Virtue: Jean Améry and the Refusal to Forgive.* Philadelphia: Temple University Press, 2008.
Brudholm, Thomas. "Revisiting Resentments: Jean Améry and the Dark Side of Forgiveness and Reconciliation." *Journal of Human Rights* 5, no. 1 (2006): 7–26.
Butler, Judith. "Contingent Foundations." In *Feminist Contentions: A Philosophical Exchange*, by Seyla Benhabib, Judith Butler, Drucilla Cornell, and Nancy Fraser, 35–58. New York: Routledge, 1995.
Butler, Judith. "Contingent Foundations: Feminism and the Question of 'Postmodernism.'" In *The Postmodern Turn: New Perspectives on Social Theory*, edited by Steven Seidman, 153–70. Cambridge: Cambridge University Press, 1994.
Butler, Judith. *Excitable Speech: A Politics of the Performative.* New York: Routledge, 1997.
Butler, Judith. *Gender Trouble: Feminism and the Subversion of Identity.* New York: Routledge, 1990.
Butler, Judith. *Giving an Account of Oneself.* New York: Fordham University Press, 2005.
Butler, Judith. *Precarious Life: The Powers of Mourning and Violence.* New York: Verso, 2004.
Butler, Judith. *The Psychic Life of Power: Theories in Subjection.* Stanford, CA: Stanford University Press, 1997.
Butler, Judith. "Vulnerability, Precarity, Coalition." In *Politics of Coalition: Thinking Collective Action with Judith Butler*, edited by Delphine Gardey and Cynthia Kraus, 250–71. Zurich: Seismo, 2016.
Butler, Judith. "What Is Critique? An Essay on Foucault's Virtue." In *The Political: Readings in Continental Philosophy*, edited by David Ingram, 212–26. London: Blackwell, 2002.
Butler, Judith, and Joan W. Scott, eds. *Feminists Theorize the Political.* New York: Routledge, 1992.
Butler, Judith, Joan W. Scott, and Kirstie McClure. "The Issue of Foundations: Scientized Politics, Politicized Science, and Feminist Critical Practice." In *Feminists Theorize the Political*, edited by Judith Butler and Joan W. Scott, 341–68. New York: Routledge, 1992.
Carastathis, Anna. "Identity Categories as Potential Coalitions." *Signs* 38, no. 4 (2013): 941–65.
Carbin, Maria, and Sara Edenheim. "The Intersectional Turn in Feminist Theory: A Dream of a Common Language?" *European Journal of Women's Studies* 20, no. 3 (2013): 233–48.
Carroll, Tamar. "Unlikely Allies: Forging a Multiracial, Class-Based Women's Movement in 1970s Brooklyn." In *Feminist Coalitions: Historical Perspectives on Second-Wave Feminism in the United States*, edited by Stephanie Gilmore, 196–224. Urbana: University Illinois Press, 2008.
Cervulle, Maxime. "La conscience dominante: Rapports sociaux de race et subjectivation." *Cahiers du genre* 53, no. 2 (2012): 37–54.
Chapman, Herrick, and Laura L. Frader. *Race in France: Interdisciplinary Perspectives on the Politics of Difference.* New York: Berghahn Books, 2004.

Chetcuti-Osorovitz, Natacha. "Féminismes contemporains et controverse du pacte laïque en France: D'un modèle d'émancipation unique à sa confrontation plurielle." *L'homme et la société* 4, no. 198 (2015): 51–72.
Cho, Sumi, Kimberlé Williams Crenshaw, and Leslie McCall. "Toward a Field of Intersectionality Studies: Theory, Applications, and Praxis." *Signs* 38, no. 4 (2013): 785–810.
Chun, Jennifer Jihye, George Lipsitz, and Young Shin. "Intersectionality as a Social Movement Strategy: Asian Immigrant Women Advocates." *Signs* 38, no. 4 (2013): 917–40.
Cobble, Dorothy Sue. *The Other Women's Movement: Workplace Justice and Social Rights in Modern America*. Princeton, NJ: Princeton University Press, 2005.
Cohen, Joshua, Matthew Howard, and Martha C. Nussbaum, eds. *Is Multiculturalism Bad for Women?* Princeton, NJ: Princeton University Press, 1999. https://www.jstor.org/stable/j.ctt7sxzs.
Cole, Elizabeth R. "Coalitions as a Model for Intersectionality: From Practice to Theory." *Sex Roles* 59, nos. 5–6 (2008): 443–53.
Cole, Elizabeth R., and Zakiya Luna. "Making Coalitions Work: Solidarity across Difference within US Feminism." *Feminist Studies* 36, no. 1 (2010): 71–98.
Collectif des féministes pour l'égalité. "Pour les droits des femmes, contre les exclusions, pour un monde plus solidaire." *Les mots sont importants*, May 6, 2015. http://lmsi.net/Pour-les-droits-des-femmes-contre.
Collectif national pour les droits des femmes. *De nouveaux défis pour le féminisme: Forum du Collectif national pour les droits des femmes*. Paris: Le Temps des Cerises, 2003.
Collectif national pour les droits des femmes. *En avant toutes! Les assises nationales pour les droits des femmes*. Paris: Le Temps des Cerises, 2003.
Collectif une école pour tou-te-s. "Communiqué du collectif Une école pour tou-te-s: Contre les lois d'exclusion." *Les mots sont importants*, January 23, 2004. http://lmsi.net/Communique-du-Collectif-Une-ecole.
Collins, Patricia Hill. *Black Feminist Thought: Knowledge, Consciousness, and the Politics of Empowerment*. Boston: Unwin Hyman, 1990.
Commission des droits de la personne et des droits la jeunesse. "Le pluralisme religieux au Québec, un défi d'éthique sociale." Government of Quebec, Cat. 7.113-2.1.1., 1995.
Conseil du statut de la femme. *Affirmer la laïcité: Un pas de plus vers l'égalité réelle entre les femmes et les hommes*. Quebec: Government of Quebec, 2011.
Conseil du statut de la Femme. *Avis: Droit à l'égalité entre les femmes et les hommes et liberté religieuse*. Quebec: Government of Quebec, 2007.
Cornell, Drucilla. "What Is Ethical Feminism?" In *Feminist Contentions: A Philosophical Exchange*, by Seyla Benhabib, Judith Butler, Drucilla Cornell, and Nancy Fraser, 75–106. New York: Routledge, 1995.
Corral, Benito Aláez. "Some Constitutional Thoughts about the Islamic Full Veil Ban in Europe." *Vienna Journal of International Constitutional Law* 7, no. 3 (2013): 275–307.
Cott, Nancy F. *The Grounding of Modern Feminism*. New Haven, CT: Yale University Press, 1987.
Crenshaw, Kimberlé. "Demarginalizing the Intersection of Race and Sex: A Black Feminist Critique of Antidiscrimination Doctrine, Feminist Theory and Antiracist Politics." *University of Chicago Legal Forum* 139 (1989): 139–68.

Crenshaw, Kimberlé. "Mapping the Margins: Intersectionality, Identity Politics, and Violence against Women of Color." *Stanford Law Review* 43, no. 6 (1991): 1241–99.
Crenshaw, Kimberlé. "Postscript." In *Framing Intersectionality: The Feminist Imagination—Europe and Beyond*, edited by Helma Lutz and M. T. Herrera Vivar, 221–33. Farnham, UK: Ashgate, 2011.
Dalpé, Samuel, and David Koussens. "Les discours sur la laïcité pendant le débat sur la 'Charte des valeurs de la laïcité': Une analyse lexicométrique de la presse francophone québécoise." *Recherches sociographiques* 57, nos. 2–3 (2016): 455–74.
Das, Veena. *Life and Words: Violence and the Descent into the Ordinary*. Berkeley: University of California Press, 2006.
Das, Veena. "What Does Ordinary Ethics Look Like?" In *Four Lectures on Ethics: Anthropological Perspectives*, by Michael Lambek, Veena Das, Didier Fassin, and Webb Keane, 53–126. Chicago: HAU Books, 2015.
Davis, Angela Y. *Women, Race, & Class*. New York: Vintage, 1983.
Davis, Kathy. "Avoiding the 'R-Word': Racism in Feminist Collectives." In *Secrecy and Silence in the Research Process: Feminist Reflections*, edited by Róisín Ryan-Flood and Rosalind Gill, 147–60. New York: Routledge, 2010.
Davis, Kathy. "Intersectionality as Buzzword: A Sociology of Science Perspective on What Makes a Feminist Theory Successful." *Feminist Theory* 9, no. 1 (2008): 67–85.
De Galembert, Claire. "La fabrique du droit entre le juge administratif et le législateur." In *La fonction politique de la justice*, edited by Jacques Commaille and Martine Kaluszynski, 95–118. Paris: La Découverte, 2007.
de Lauretis, Teresa. "Eccentric Subjects: Feminist Theory and Historical Consciousness." *Feminist Studies* 16, no. 1 (1990): 115–50.
de Lauretis, Teresa. "Upping the Anti in Feminist Theory." In *Conflicts in Feminism*, edited by Marianne Hirsch and Evelyn Fox Keller, 255–70. New York: Routledge, 1990.
Dean, Jonathan, and Kristin Aune. "Feminism Resurgent? Mapping Contemporary Feminist Activisms in Europe." *Social Movement Studies* 14, no. 4 (2015): 375–95.
Debono, Emmanuel. *Aux origines de l'antiracisme: La LICA (1927–1940)*. Paris: CNRS, 2012.
Deleuze, Gilles. "Philosophie et minorité." *Critique* 369 February (1978): 154–55.
Deleuze, Gilles, and Félix Guattari. *Mille plateaux*. Vol. 2 of *Capitalisme et schizophrénie*. Les Éditions de Minuit. Paris, 1980.
Della Sudda, Magali. "Par-delà le bien et le mal, la morale sexuelle en question chez les femmes catholiques." *Nouvelles questions féministes* 35, no. 1 (2016): 82–101.
Delphy, Christine. "The Invention of French Feminism: An Essential Move." *Yale French Studies* 87 (1995): 190–221.
Delphy, Christine, Natalie Benelli, Jules Falquet, Christelle Hamel, Ellen Hertz, and Patricia Roux. "Sexisme et racisme: Le cas français." *Nouvelles questions féministes* 25, no. 1 (2006).
Delphy, Christine, Natalie Benelli, Jules Falquet, Christelle Hamel, Ellen Hertz, and Patricia Roux. "Sexisme, racisme et postcolonialisme." *Nouvelles questions féministes* 25, no. 3 (2006).
Deveaux, Monique. *Gender and Justice in Multicultural Liberal States*. Oxford: Oxford University Press, 2007.
Dewey, John. *The Public and Its Problems: An Essay in Political Inquiry*. Edited by Melvin L. Rogers. Philadelphia: Pennsylvania State University Press, 2012.

Doerr, Nicole. *Political Translation: How Social Movement Democracies Survive.* Cambridge: Cambridge University Press, 2018.
Dot-Pouillard, Nicolas. "Les recompositions politiques du mouvement féministe français au regard du hijab." *Sociologies*, October 31, 2007. Online.
Eid, Paul, Pierre Bosset, Micheline Milot, and Sébastien Lebel-Grenier, eds. *Appartenances religieuses, appartenance citoyenne: Un équilibre en tension.* Quebec: Presses Université Laval, 2009.
Eloit, Ilana. "Lesbian Trouble: Feminism, Heterosexuality and the French Nation (1970–1981)." PhD diss., London School of Economics, 2018.
El-Tayeb, Fatima. *European Others: Queering Ethnicity in Postnational Europe.* Minneapolis: University of Minnesota Press, 2011.
Elver, Hilal. *The Headscarf Controversy: Secularism and Freedom of Religion.* New York: Oxford University Press, 2012.
Emejulu, Akwugo, and Leah Bassel. "Minority Women, Austerity and Activism." *Race & Class* 57, no. 2 (October 1, 2015): 86–95.
Emejulu, Akwugo, and Leah Bassel. "Whose Crisis Counts? Minority Women, Austerity and Activism in France and Britain." In *Gender and the Economic Crisis in Europe. Politics, Institutions and Intersectionality*, edited by Johanna Kantolo and Emanuela Lombardo, 185–208. New York: Palgrave Macmillan, 2017.
Equy, Laure. "Ni putes ni soumises manifeste en burqa devant le siège du PS." *Libération*, January 25, 2010. http://www.liberation.fr/france/2010/01/25/ni-putes-ni-soumisesmanifeste-en-burqa-devant-le-siege-du-ps_606252.
Evans, Elizabeth. "Intersectionality as Feminist Praxis in the UK." *Women's Studies International Forum* 59 (2016): 67–75.
Evans, Elizabeth. *The Politics of Third Wave Feminisms: Neoliberalism, Intersectionality, and the State in Britain and the US.* New York: Palgrave Macmillan, 2015.
Evans, Elizabeth, and Éléonore Lépinard. *Intersectionality in Feminist and Queer Movements: Confronting Privileges.* Routledge, 2019.
Ewing, Katherine Pratt. *Stolen Honor: Stigmatizing Muslim Men in Berlin.* Stanford, CA: Stanford University Press, 2008.
Fadil, Nadia. "Not-/Unveiling as an Ethical Practice." *Feminist Review* 98, no. 1 (2011): 83–109.
Fanon, Frantz. *Peau noire, masques blancs.* Paris: Éditions du Seuil, 1952.
Farris, Sara R. "Femonationalism and the 'Regular' Army of Labor Called Migrant Women." *History of the Present* 2, no. 2 (2012): 184–99.
Farris, Sara R. *In the Name of Women's Rights: The Rise of Femonationalism.* Durham, NC: Duke University Press, 2017.
Fassa, Farinaz, Éléonore Lépinard, and Marta Roca i Escoda. "Introduction: L'intersection alité pour une pensée contre-hégémonique." In *L'intersectionnalité: Enjeux théoriques et politiques.* Paris: La Dispute, 2016.
Fassa, Farinaz, Éléonore Lépinard, and Marta Roca i Escoda, eds. *L'intersectionnalité: Enjeux théoriques et politiques.* Paris: La Dispute, 2016.
Fassin, Didier. "On Resentment and Ressentiment: The Politics and Ethics of Moral Emotions." *Current Anthropology* 54, no. 3 (2013): 249–67.
Fassin, Didier. "Troubled Waters: At the Confluence of Ethics and Politics." In *Four Lectures on Ethics: Anthropological Perspectives*, by Michael Lambek, Veena Das, Didier Fassin, and Webb Keane, 175–210. Chicago: HAU Books, 2015.

Fassin, Didier, and Éric Fassin. *De la question sociale à la question raciale? Représenter la société française*. Paris: Découverte, 2006.
Fassin, Éric. "Sexual Democracy and the New Racialization of Europe." *Journal of Civil Society* 8, no. 3 (2012): 285–88.
Favell, Adrian. *Philosophies of Integration: Immigration and the Idea of Citizenship in France and Britain*. New York: Palgrave Macmillan, 1998.
Fédération des femmes du Québec. "Débat sur la laïcité et le port de signes religieux ostentatoires dans la fonction et les services publics québécois." 2009. Proposal from the Board for the Special General Assembly of May 9, 2009, n.d.
Fédération des femmes du Québec. "La laïcité: Un moyen de lutter contre les fondamentalismes religieux. Mythes et réalités à propos de la FFQ et la laïcité." *L'R des centres de femmes du Québec*, 2013. http://www.rcentres.qc.ca/public/la-laicite-un-moyen-de-lutter-contre-lesfondamentalismesreligieux.html.
Fédération des femmes du Québec. "Mémoire présenté par la Fédération des femmes du Québec à la Commission de consultation sur les pratiques d'accommodements reliées aux différences culturelle. L'égalité entre les femmes et les hommes: Une valeur fondamentale de la société québécoise." October 19, 2007.
Fédération des femmes du Québec. "Résister construire transformer. Congrès d'orientation, 27 Au 29 Mars 2015." March 29, 2015. www.ffq.qc.ca/wp-content/uploads/2015/04/Cahier-de-propositions-Amandées.pdf.
Fernando, Mayanthi L. "Exceptional Citizens: Secular Muslim Women and the Politics of Difference in France." *Social Anthropology* 17, no. 4 (2009): 379–92.
Fernando, Mayanthi L. *The Republic Unsettled: Muslim French and the Contradictions of Secularism*. Durham, NC: Duke University Press, 2014.
Ferrari, Alessandro, and Sabrina Pastorelli, eds. *The Burqa Affair across Europe: Between Public and Private Space*. London: Routledge, 2013.
Ferree, Myra Marx. *Varieties of Feminism: German Gender Politics in Global Perspective*. Stanford, CA: Stanford University Press, 2012.
Ferree, Myra Marx, and Silke Roth. "Gender, Class, and the Interaction between Social Movements: A Strike of West Berlin Day Care Workers." *Gender & Society* 12, no. 6 (1998): 626–48.
Fornerod, Anne. "The Burqa Affair in France." In *The Burqa Affair across Europe: Between Public and Private Space*, edited by Alessandro Ferrari and Sabrina Pastorelli, 59–76. New York: Ashgate, 2013.
Foucault, Michel. *The Use of Pleasure*. Vol. 2 of *The History of Sexuality*. Translated by Robert Hurley. New York: Vintage Books, 1990.
Fournier, Pascale. "Headscarf and Burqa Controversies at the Crossroad of Politics, Society and Law." *Social Identities* 19, no. 6 (2013): 689–703.
Frankenberg, Ruth. "Growing Up White: Feminism, Racism and the Social Geography of Childhood." *Feminist Review* 45, no. 1 (1993): 51–84.
Frankenberg, Ruth. *White Women, Race Matters: The Social Construction of Whiteness*. Minneapolis: University of Minnesota Press, 1993.
Fraser, Nancy. "Mapping the Feminist Imagination: From Redistribution to Recognition to Representation." *Constellations* 12, no. 3 (2005): 295–307.
Fraser, Nancy. "Multiculturalism and Gender Equity: The US 'Difference' Debates Revisited." *Constellations* 3, no. 1 (1996): 61–72.
Friedman, Marilyn. *Autonomy, Gender, Politics*. New York: Oxford University Press, 2003.

Frye, Marilyn. *The Politics of Reality: Essays in Feminist Theory*. New York: Crossing Press, 1983.
Gagnon, Jeanne. "Ma rupture avec la Fédération des femmes du Québec." *L'aut'journal*, January 16, 2014. http://lautjournal.info/20140116/ma-rupture-avec-laf%C3%A9d%C3%A9ration-des-femmes-du-qu%C3%A9bec.
Galonnier, Juliette. "The Racialization of Muslims in France and the United States: Some Insights from White Converts to Islam." *Social Compass* 62, no. 4 (December 1, 2015): 570–83.
Garcia, Marie-Carmen. "Des féminismes aux prises avec l'"intersectionnalité': Le mouvement Ni putes ni soumises et le Collectif féministe du mouvement des indigènes de la République." *Cahiers du genre* 52, no. 1 (2012): 145–65.
Gardey, Delphine. "From Hospitality to Coalition." In *Politics of Coalition: Thinking Collective Action with Judith Butler*, edited by Delphine Gardey and Cynthia Kraus, 34–53. Zurich: Seismo, 2016.
Gay, Amandine. *Ouvrir la voix*. Bras de Fer Production et Distribution, 2016.
Giraud, Isabelle. "Intégrer la diversité des oppressions dans la Marche mondiale des femmes." *L'homme et la société* 4 (2015): 95–112.
Giraud, Isabelle, and Pascale Dufour. *Dix ans de solidarité planétaire: Perspectives sociologiques sur la Marche mondiale des femmes*. Montreal: Éditions du Remue-ménage, 2010.
Grewal, Kiran. "'Va t'faire intégrer': The Appel des Féministes Indigènes and the Challenge to Republican Values in Postcolonial France." *Contemporary French Civilization* 33, no. 2 (2009): 105–33.
Griffin, Gabrielle, and Rosi Braidotti. "Whiteness and European Situatedness." In *Thinking Differently: A Reader in European Women's Studies*, edited by Gabrielle Griffin and Rosi Braidotti, 221–37. London: Zed Books, 2002.
Groupe du 6 novembre. *Warriors/Guerrières*. Paris: Nomades' langues, 2001.
Guénif-Souilamas, Nacira. "The Other French Exception: Virtuous Racism and the War of the Sexes in Postcolonial France." *French Politics, Culture & Society* 24, no. 3 (2006): 23–41.
Guénif-Souilamas, Nacira. *La République mise à nu par son immigration*. Paris: Editions La Fabrique, 2006.
Guénif-Souilamas, Nacira, and Éric Macé. *Les féministes et le garçon arabe*. La Tour-d'Aigues: Editions de l'Aube, 2006.
Habermas, Jürgen, Tony Blair, and Régis Debray. "Secularism's Crisis of Faith: Notes on Post-secular Society." *New Perspectives Quarterly* 25, no. 4 (2008): 17–29.
Hache, Émilie. *Ce à quoi nous tenons*. Paris: La Découverte, 2014.
Hadj Abdou, Leila. "'Gender Nationalism': The New (Old) Politics of Belonging." *OZP: Austrian Journal of Political Science* 46, no. 1 (n.d.): 84–88.
Hajjat, Abdellali. *Les frontières de l'"identité nationale': L'injonction à l'assimilation en France métropolitaine et coloniale*. Paris: La Découverte, 2012.
Hamrouni, Naïma, and Chantal Maillé, eds. *Le sujet du féminisme est-il blanc? Femmes racisées et recherche féministe*. Montreal: Les editions du remue-ménage, 2015.
Hancock, Ange-Marie. *Intersectionality: An Intellectual History*. Oxford: Oxford University Press, 2016.
Hancock, Ange-Marie. "When Multiplication Doesn't Equal Quick Addition: Examining Intersectionality as a Research Paradigm." *Perspectives on Politics* 5, no. 1 (2007): 63–79.

Harding, Sandra. "Rethinking Standpoint Epistemology: What Is 'Strong Objectivity'?" In *Feminist Epistemologies*, edited by Linda Martín Alcoff and Elizabeth Potter, 49–82. New York: Routledge, 1993.
Harris, Cheryl I. "Whiteness as Property." *Harvard Law Review* 106, no. 8 (1993): 1707–91.
Hemmings, Clare. "Telling Feminists Stories." *Feminist Theory* 6, no. 2 (2005): 115–39.
Hennette-Vauchez, Stéphanie. "Derrière la burqa, les rapports entre droit et laïcité: La subversion de l'état de droit?" In *Quand la burqa passe à l'ouest: Enjeux éthiques, politiques et juridiques*, edited by David Koussens and Olivier Roy, 159–76. Rennes: Presses universitaires de Rennes, 2013.
Hercus, Cheryl. "Identity, Emotion, and Feminist Collective Action." *Gender & Society* 13, no. 1 (1999): 34–55.
Hesford, Victoria. *Feeling Women's Liberation*. Durham, NC: Duke University Press, 2013.
Hirschmann, Nancy J. *The Subject of Liberty: Toward a Feminist Theory of Freedom*. Princeton, NJ: Princeton University Press, 2003.
Hoagland, Sarah Lucia. "Denying Relationality. Epistemology and Ethics and Ignorance." In *Race and Epistemologies of Ignorance*, edited by Shannon Sullivan and Nancy Tuana, 95–118. Albany: State University of New York Press, 2007.
Honnig, Bonnie. "My Culture Made Me Do It." In Okin, Susan, et al. *Is Multiculturalism Bad for Women?*, edited by Joshua Cohen et al., 35–40. Princeton, NJ: Princeton University Press, 1999.
hooks, bell. *Feminist Theory: From Margin to Center*. Boston: South End Press, 1984.
Host, Jerôme. *Un racisme à peine voilé*. La Flèche production, 2004.
Hughey, Matthew W. "The (Dis)similarities of White Racial Identities: The Conceptual Framework of 'Hegemonic Whiteness.'" *Ethnic and Racial Studies* 33, no. 8 (2010): 1289–309.
Hull, Gloria T., Patricia Bell-Scott, and Barbara Smith, eds. *But Some Of Us Are Brave: All the Women Are White, All the Blacks Are Men. Black Women's Studies*. Old Westbury, NY: Feminist Press at CUNY, 1982.
Hurtado, Aída. *The Color of Privilege: Three Blasphemies on Race and Feminism*. Ann Arbor: University of Michigan Press, 1996.
Inckle, Kay. "Debilitating Times: Compulsory Ablebodiedness and White Privilege in Theory and Practice." *Feminist Review* 111, no. 1 (2015): 42–58.
Jagose, Annamarie. "Feminism's Queer Theory." *Feminism & Psychology* 19, no. 2 (2009): 157–74.
Java. "La marche de toutes les femmes?" *Les mots sont importants*, August 3, 2004. http://lmsi.net/La-Marche-de-toutes-les-femmes.
Jayawardena, Kumari. *Feminism and Nationalism in the Third World*. London: Verso Books, 2016.
Jenkins, Fiona. "Sensate Democracy and Grievable Life." In *Butler and Ethics*, edited by Mona Lloyd, 118–40. Edinburgh: Edinburgh University Press, 2015.
Joppke, Christian. "Beyond National Models: Civic Integration Policies for Immigrants in Western Europe." *West European Politics* 30, no. 1 (2007): 1–22.
Joppke, Christian. "State Neutrality and Islamic Headscarf Laws in France and Germany." *Theory and Society* 36, no. 4 (2007): 313–42.
Kapur, Ratna. "In the Aftermath of Critique We Are Not in Epistemic Free Fall: Human Rights, the Subaltern Subject, and Non-liberal Search for Freedom and Happiness." *Law and Critique* 25, no. 1 (2014): 25–45.

Kassir, Alexandra, and Jeffrey G. Reitz. "Protesting Headscarf Ban: A Path to Becoming More French? A Case Study of 'Mamans Toutes Egales' and 'Sorties Scolaires Avec Nous.'" *Ethnic and Racial Studies* 39, no. 15 (2016): 2683–700.

Keaton, Trica Danielle. *Muslim Girls and the Other France: Race, Identity Politics, & Social Exclusion*. Bloomington: Indiana University Press, 2006.

Keaton, Trica Danielle, T. Denean Sharpley-Whiting, and Tyler Stovall, eds. *Black France / France Noire: The History and Politics of Blackness*. Durham, NC: Duke University Press, 2012.

Kian, Azadeh. "Le voile islamique et la question de l'identité nationale en France." In *La polysémie du voile: Politiques et mobilisations postcoloniales*, edited by Maria Eleonora Sanna and Malek Bouyahia, 15–32. Paris: Editions des archives contemporaines, 2013.

Kılıç, Sevgi, Sawitri Saharso, and Birgit Sauer. "Introduction: The Veil: Debating Citizenship, Gender and Religious Diversity." *Social Politics: International Studies in Gender, State & Society* 15, no. 4 (December 1, 2008): 397–410.

Korteweg, Anna C. "The Sharia Debate in Ontario: Gender, Islam, and Representations of Muslim Women's Agency." *Gender & Society* 22, no. 4 (2008): 434–54.

Korteweg, Anna C., and Jennifer A. Selby, eds. *Debating Sharia: Islam, Gender Politics, and Family Law Arbitration*. Toronto: University of Toronto Press, 2012.

Korteweg, Anna C., and Gökçe Yurdakul. *The Headscarf Debates: Conflicts of National Belonging*. Stanford, CA: Stanford University Press, 2014.

Koussens, David. "Neutrality of the State and Regulation of Religious Symbols in Schools in Québec and France." *Social Compass* 56, no. 2 (2009): 202–13.

Koussens, David. "Sous l'affaire de la Burqa . . . Quel visage de la laïcité française?" *Sociologie et sociétés* 41, no. 2 (2009): 327–47.

Koussens, David. "Symboles et rituels catholiques dans les institutions publiques québécoises: Aspects juridiques débats politiques et enjeux laïques." *Annuaire droit et religions* 6, no. 1 (2012): 161–72.

Koussens, David. "Une mise en scène nationaliste de la laïcité en porte-à-faux avec la réalité des aménagements laïques canadiens: Éléments du débat québécois." *Revue de droit de l'Université de Sherbrooke* 43 (2013): 183–204.

Kramer, Sina. *Constitutive Exclusion*. New York: Oxford University Press, 2017.

Ku, Jane S. C. "Multicultural Politics and the Paradox of Being Special: Interrogating Immigrant Women's Activism and the Voice of Difference." *Journal of International Women's Studies* 10, no. 4 (2009): 65–84.

Kymlicka, Will. *Finding Our Way: Rethinking Ethnocultural Relations in Canada*. Oxford: Oxford University Press, 1998.

Laacher, Smaïn. *L'institution scolaire et ses miracles*. Paris: La Dispute, 2005.

Laborde, Cécile. *Critical Republicanism: The Hijab Controversy and Political Philosophy*. Oxford: Oxford University Press, 2008.

Laborde, Cécile. "On Republican Toleration." *Constellations* 9, no. 2 (2002): 167–83.

Lamoureux, Diane. *L'amère patrie: Féminisme et nationalisme dans le Québec contemporain*. Montreal: Editions Remue ménage, 2001.

Laperrière, Marie, and Éléonore Lépinard. "Intersectionality as a Tool for Social Movements: Strategies of Inclusion and Representation in the Québécois Women's Movement." *Politics* 36, no. 4 (2016): 374–82.

Larcher, Silyane. *L'autre citoyen: L'idéal républicain et Les Antilles après l'esclavage*. Paris: Armand Colin, 2014.

Larcher, Silyane. "Troubles dans la 'race': De quelques fractures et points aveugles de l'antiracisme français contemporain." *l'homme et la société* 4 (2015): 213–29.
Latour, Bruno. *Science in Action: How to Follow Scientists and Engineers through Society.* Cambridge, MA: Harvard University Press, 1987.
Laugier, Sandra. "Voice as Form of Life and Life Form." *Nordic Wittgenstein Review* 4, no. 0 (October 6, 2015): 63–82.
Laxer, Emily, Rachael Dianne Carson, and Anna C. Korteweg. "Articulating Minority Nationhood: Cultural and Political Dimensions in Québec's Reasonable Accommodation Debate." *Nations and Nationalism* 20, no. 1 (2014): 133–53.
Lefebvre, Solange, and Lori G. Beaman. "Protecting Gender Relations: The Bouchard Taylor Commission and the Equality of Women." *Revue canadienne de recherche sociale / Canadian Journal for Social Research* 2, no. 1 (2012): 95–104.
Lépinard, Éléonore. "Autonomy and the Crisis of the Feminist Subject: Revisiting Okin's Dilemma." *Constellations* 18, no. 2 (2011): 205–21.
Lépinard, Éléonore. "The Contentious Subject of Feminism: Defining Women in France from the Second Wave to Parity." *Signs* 32, no. 2 (2007): 375–403.
Lépinard, Éléonore. "Doing Intersectionality: Repertoires of Feminist Practices in France and Canada." *Gender & Society* 28, no. 6 (2014): 877–903.
Lépinard, Éléonore. "Writing the Law and the Regulation of Minority Religions in Frane and Canada." *Revue française de science politique* 64, no. 4 (2014): 669–88.
Lépinard, Éléonore. *L'égalité introuvable: La parité, les féministes et la République.* Paris: Presses de Sciences Po, 2007.
Lépinard, Éléonore. "For Women Only? Gender Quotas and Intersectionality in France." *Politics & Gender* 9, no. 3 (September 2013): 276–98.
Lépinard, Éléonore. "From Immigrants to Muslims: Shifting Categories of the French Model of Integration." In *Identity Politics in the Public Realm: Bringing Institutions Back In*, edited by Avigail Eisenberg and Will Kymlicka, 190–214. Vancouver: University of British Columbia Press, 2011.
Lépinard, Éléonore. "In the Name of Equality? The Missing Intersection in Canadian Feminists' Legal Mobilization against Multiculturalism." *American Behavioral Scientist* 53, no. 12 (2010): 1763–87.
Lépinard, Éléonore. "Migrating Concepts: Immigrant Integration and the Regulation of Religious Dress in France and Canada." *Ethnicities* 15, no. 5 (2015): 611–32.
Lépinard, Éléonore. "Writing the Law and the Regulation of Minority Religions in France and Canada." Translated by Vicki Whittaker. *Revue française de science politique* 64, no. 4 (2014): 669–88.
Les invités de Mediapart. "Lettre ouverte aux maires à l'origine des arrêtés anti-burkini *Club de Mediapart*, August 26, 2016. https://blogs.mediapart.fr/edition/les-invites-demediapart/article/260816/lettre-ouverte-aux-maires-l-origine-des-arretes-anti-burkini.
Les invités de Mediapart. "Pour en finir avec le contrôle politique du corps des femmes." April 6, 2016. Club de Mediapart. https://blogs.mediapart.fr/edition/les-invites-demediapart/article/060416/pour-en-finir-avec-le-controle-politique-du-corps-des-femmes.
Lesselier, Claudie. "Pour une histoire des mouvements de femmes de l'immigration en France." In *Les cahiers de critique communiste: Femmes, genre, féminisme*, 85–104. Paris: Syllepse, 2007.
Lettinga, Doutje, and Sawitri Saharso. "The Political Debates on the Veil in France and the Netherlands: Reflecting National Integration Models?" *Comparative European Politics* 10, no. 3 (2012): 319–36.

Lloyd, Mona. "The Ethics and Politics of Vulnerable Bodies." In *Butler and Ethics*, edited by Mona Lloyd, 167–92. Edinburgh: Edinburgh University Press, 2015.
Lorcerie, Françoise. "La 'loi sur le voile': Une entreprise politique." *Droit et société* 68, no. 1 (2008): 53–74.
Lorcerie, Françoise, ed. *La politisation du voile en France, en Europe et dans le monde arabe*. Paris: L'Harmattan, 2005.
Lorde, Audre. *Sister Outsider: Essays and Speeches*. New York: Crossing Press, 1984.
Lozano, Alberto Arribas, Aurora Álvarez Veinguer, and Nayra García-González. "Intersectionality and the Discourses of Women's Social Movement Organizations Across Europe." In *Negotiating Gender and Diversity in an Emergent European Public Sphere*, edited by Birte Siim and Monika Mokre, 43–59. London: Palgrave Macmillan, 2013.
Lugones, María. "On Complex Communication." *Hypatia* 21, no. 3 (August 1, 2006): 75–85.
Lugones, María. "Playfulness, 'World'-Travelling, and Loving Perception." *Hypatia* 2, no. 2 (1987): 3–19.
Lugones, María. "Purity, Impurity, and Separation." *Signs* 19, no. 2 (1994): 458–79.
Luna, Zakiya. "'Truly a Women of Color Organization': Negotiating Sameness and Difference in Pursuit of Intersectionality." *Gender & Society* 30, no. 5 (October 1, 2016): 769–90.
Lyshaug, Brenda. "Solidarity without 'Sisterhood'? Feminism and the Ethics of Coalition Building." *Politics & Gender* 2 (2006): 77–100.
Mackenzie, Catriona, and Natalie Stoljar, eds. *Relational Autonomy: Feminist Perspectives on Autonomy, Agency, and the Social Self*. New York: Oxford University Press, 2000.
Mahmood, Saba. "Feminism, Democracy, and Empire: Islam and the War of Terror." In *Women's Studies on the Edge*, edited by Joan W. Scott, 81–114. Durham, NC: Duke University Press, 2008.
Mahmood, Saba. "Feminist Theory, Embodiment, and the Docile Agent: Some Reflections on the Egyptian Islamic Revival." *Cultural Anthropology* 16, no. 2 (November 11, 2012): 202–36.
Mahmood, Saba. *Politics of Piety: The Islamic Revival and the Feminist Subject*. Princeton, NJ: Princeton University Press, 2005.
Maiguashca, Bice, Jonathan Dean, and Dan Keith. "Pulling Together in a Crisis? Anarchism, Feminism and the Limits of Left-Wing Convergence in Austerity Britain." *Capital & Class* 40, no. 1 (2016): 37–57.
Malik, Maleiha. "Complex Equality: Muslim Women and the 'Headscarf.'" *Droit et société* 1, no. 68 (2008): 127–52.
Mane, Rebecca L. "Transmuting Grammars of Whiteness in Third-Wave Feminism: Interrogating Postrace Histories, Postmodern Abstraction, and the Proliferation of Difference in Third-Wave Texts." *Signs* 38, no. 1 (2012): 71–98.
Marchetti, Sabrina. "Resentment at the Heart of Europe: Narratives by Afro-Surinamese Postcolonial Migrant Women in the Netherlands." In *Postcolonial Transitions in Europe: Context, Practices and Politics*, edited by Sandra Ponzanesi and Gianmaria Colpani, 135–50. Lanham, MD: Rowman & Littlefield, 2015.
Masclet, Camille. "Sociologie des féministes des années 1970 : Analyse localisée, incidences biographiques et transmission familiale d'un engagement pour la cause des femmes en France." PhD diss., Université Paris 8 and Université de Lausanne, 2017.

Mazouz, Sarah. *La république et ses autres: Politiques de la discrimination et pratiques de naturalisation dans la France des années 2000.* Lyon: ENS édition, 2017.
McBride, Dorothy E., and Amy G. Mazur. "Women's Movements, Feminism, and Feminist Movements." In *Politics, Gender and Concepts: Theory and Methodology*, edited by Gary Goertz and Amy G. Mazur, 219-43. Cambridge: Cambridge University Press, 2008.
McGoldrick, Dominic. *Human Rights and Religion: The Islamic Headscarf Debate in Europe.* Oxford: Hart Publishing, 2006.
McRobbie, Angela. *The Aftermath of Feminism: Gender, Culture and Social Change.* London: Sage, 2008.
McWhorter, Ladelle. "Where Do White People Come From? A Foucaultian Critique of Whiteness Studies." *Philosophy & Social Criticism* 31, nos. 5-6 (2005): 533-56.
Mepschen, Paul, Jan Willem Duyvendak, and Evelien H. Tonkens. "Sexual Politics, Orientalism and Multicultural Citizenship in the Netherlands." *Sociology* 44, no. 5 (2010): 962-79.
Mercier, Élisabeth. "Sexualité et respectabilité des femmes: La slutwalk et autres (re)configurations morales, éthiques et politiques." *Nouvelles Questions Féministes* 35, no. 1 (2016): 16-31.
Meret, Susi, and Birte Siim. "Gender, Populism and Politics of Belonging: Discourses of Right-Wing Populist Parties in Denmark, Norway and Austria." In *Negotiating Gender and Diversity in an Emergent European Public Sphere*, edited by Birte Siim and Monika Mokre, 78-96. New York: Palgrave Macmillan, 2013.
Michel, Noémi Vanessa. "Equality and Postcolonial Claims of Discursive Injury." *Swiss Political Science Review* 19, no. 4 (2013): 447-71.
Michel, Noémi Vanessa. "Quand les mots et les images blessent: Postcolonialité, égalité et politique des actes de discours en Suisse et en France." Université de Genève, 2014.
Michel, Noémi Vanessa. "Sheepology: The Postcolonial Politics of Raceless Racism in Switzerland." *Postcolonial Studies* 18, no. 4 (2015): 410-26.
Mills, Charles W. *The Racial Contract.* Ithaca, NY: Cornell University Press, 1997.
Mills, Charles W. "White Ignorance." In *Race and Epistemologies of Ignorance*, edited by Shannon Sullivan and Nancy Tuana, 13-38. Albany: State University of New York Press, 2007.
Ministère de l'immigration et des communautés culturelles. *Pour enrichir le Québec: Affirmer les valeurs communes de la société québécoise.* Mesures pour renforcer l'action du Québec en matière d'intégration des immigrants. Quebec: Government of Quebec, 2008.
Mohammed, Marwan, and Abdellali Hajjat. *Islamophobie: Comment les élites françaises fabriquent le "problème musulman."* Paris: La Découverte, 2013.
Mohanty, Chandra Talpade. *Feminism without Borders: Decolonizing Theory, Practicing Solidarity.* Durham, NC: Duke University Press, 2003.
Mohanty, Chandra Talpade. "Under Western Eyes: Feminist Scholarship and Colonial Discourses." *Boundary 2* 12, no. 2 (1984): 333-58.
Mohanty, Chandra Talpade, and Biddy Martin. "What's Home Got to Do with It." In *Feminism without Borders: Decolonizing Theory, Practicing Solidarity*, by Chandra Talpade Mohanty, 85-105. Durham, NC: Duke University Press, 2003.
Molinier, Pascale. *Le care monde.* Lyon: ENS editions, 2018.
Molinier, Pascale. "Des féministes et de leurs femmes de ménage: Entre réciprocité du care et souhait de dépersonnalisation." *Multitudes* 37-38, nos. 2-3 (2009): 113-21.
Montesquieu, Charles-Louis de Secondat de. *Esprit des lois.* Libr. de F. Didot Frères, 1867.

Moore, Henrietta L. *A Passion for Difference: Essays in Anthropology and Gender.* Bloomington: Indiana University Press, 1994.
Möser, Cornelia. *Féminismes en traductions: Théories voyageuses et traductions culturelles.* Paris: Editions des Archives Contemporaines, 2013.
Mouffe, Chantal. "Feminism, Citizenship, and Radical Democratic Politics." In *Feminists Theorize the Political*, edited by Judith Butler and Joan W. Scott, 369–84. New York: Routledge, 1992.
Moujoud, Nasima. "Femmes sans-papiers et exilées dans des mobilisations féministes: Les limites de la solidarité formelle." In *Le genre au coeur des migrations*, edited by Claire Cossée, Adelina Miranda, Nouria Ouali, and Djaouida Séhili, 255–70. Paris: Petra, 2012.
Mueller, Jennifer C. "Producing Colorblindness: Everyday Mechanisms of White Ignorance." *Social Problems* 64 (2017): 219–38.
Muñoz, José Esteban. *Cruising Utopia: The Then and There of Queer Futurity.* New York: NYU Press, 2009.
Muñoz, José Esteban. *Disidentifications: Queers of Color and the Performance of Politics.* Minneapolis: University of Minnesota Press, 1999.
Narayan, Uma. "Essence of Culture and a Sense of History: A Feminist Critique of Cultural Essentialism." In *Decentering the Center: Philosophy for a Multicultural, Postcolonial, and Feminist World*, edited by Sandra Harding and Uma Narayan, 80–100. Bloomington: Indiana University Press, 2000.
Nash, Jennifer C. "Re-thinking Intersectionality." *Feminist Review* 89: 1–15, 2008.
Nash, Jennifer C. "Practicing Love: Black Feminism, Love-Politics, and Post-intersectionality." *Meridians: Feminism, Race, Transnationalism* 11, no. 2 (2013): 1–24.
Nash, Jennifer C. "Re-thinking Intersectionality." *Feminist Review* 89 (2008): 1–15.
Nedelsky, Jennifer. *Law's Relations: A Relational Theory of Self, Autonomy, and Law.* Oxford: Oxford University Press, 2011.
Nelson, Jennifer. *Women of Color and the Reproductive Rights Movement.* New York: New York University Press, 2003.
Ngai, Sianne. *Ugly Feelings.* Cambridge, MA: Harvard University Press, 2005.
No One Is Illegal–Montréal. "Statement on the Racist Quebec Debate about 'Reasonable Accommodation.'" *No One Is Illegal–MONTRÉAL* (blog), May 2, 2007. http://nooneisillegal-montreal.blogspot.com/2007/02/statement-on-racist-quebec-debateabout.html.
Nordmann, Charlotte, ed. *Le foulard islamique en questions. multitudes.* Paris: Editions Amsterdam, 2004.
Nussbaum, Martha C. *Political Emotions.* Cambridge, MA: Harvard University Press, 2013.
Okin, Susan Moller. "Feminism and Multiculturalism: Some Tensions." *Ethics* 108, no. 4 (1998): 661–84.
Okin, Susan Moller. "Is Multiculturalism Bad for Women? When Minority Cultures Win Group Rights, Women Lose Out." *Boston Review* 22 (1997): 2–28.
Ortega, Mariana. "Being Lovingly, Knowingly Ignorant: White Feminism and Women of Color." *Hypatia* 21, no. 3 (August 1, 2006): 56–74.
Ouali, Nouria. "Les rapports de domination au sein du mouvement des femmes à Bruxelles: Critiques et résistances des féministes minoritaires." *Nouvelles questions féministes* 34, no. 1 (2015): 14–34.

Pagé, Geneviève. "'Est-ce qu'on peut être racisées nous aussi?' Les féministes blanches et le désir de racisation." In *Le sujet du féminisme est-il blanc? Femmes racisées et recherche féministe*, edited by Naïma Hamrouni and Chantal Maillé, 133–54. Montreal: Les éditions du remue-ménage, 2015.

Paperman, Patricia, and Pascale Molinier. "Présentation: Désenclaver le care?" In *Contre l'indifférence des privilégiés*, by Carol Gilligan, Arlie Hochschild, and Joan C. Tronto, 7–34. Paris: Payot, 2013.

Paris, Myriam. "Un féminisme anti-colonial: L'union des femmes de la réunion (1946–1981)." *Mouvements* 91 (2017): 141–49.

Paye, Ndella. "Stop! Mon corps ne vous appartient pas!" *Les mots sont importants*, March 28, 2015. http://lmsi.net/Stop-Mon-corps-ne-vous-appartient.

Pereira, Irène. *Les grammaires de la contestation: Un guide de la gauche radicale*. Paris: La découverte, 2010.

Perreau, Bruno. *Queer Theory: The French Response*. Stanford, CA: Stanford University Press, 2016.

Perreau, Bruno, and Joan W. Scott. *Les défis de la République: Genre, territoires, citoyenneté*. Paris: Les Presses de Sciences Po, 2017.

"Pétition: Nous sommes toutes des femmes voilées." Change.org. April 23, 2013. https://www.change.org/p/nous-sommes-toutes-des-femmes-voilées.

Phillips, Anne. "Feminism and Liberalism Revisited: Has Martha Nussbaum Got It Right?" *Constellations* 8, no. 2 (2001): 249–66.

Phillips, Anne. *Multiculturalism without Culture*. Princeton, NJ: Princeton University Press, 2007.

Phillips, Anne, and Sawitri Saharso. "Guest Editorial: The Rights of Women and the Crisis of Multiculturalism." *Ethnicities* 8 (2008): 291–301.

Phoenix, Ann, and Pamela Pattynama. "Intersectionality." *European Journal of Women's Studies* 13, no. 3 (2006): 187–92.

Picq, Françoise. *Libération des femmes: Les années-mouvement*. Paris: Seuil, 1993.

Polletta, Francesca, and James M. Jasper. "Collective Identity and Social Movements." *Annual Review of Sociology* 27, no. 1 (2001): 283–305.

Pollock, Griselda. "Is Feminism a Trauma, a Bad Memory, or a Virtual Future?" *Differences* 27, no. 2 (2016): 27–61.

Pratt, Minnie Bruce. "Identity: Skin Blood Heart." *Women's Studies Quarterly* 11, no. 3 (1983): 16.

Predelli, Line Nyhagen, and Beatrice Halsaa. *Majority-Minority Relations in Contemporary Women's Movements: Strategic Sisterhood*. Houndmills, Basingstoke: Palgrave Macmillan, 2012.

Puar, Jasbir K. *Terrorist Assemblages: Homonationalism in Queer Times*. Durham, NC: Duke University Press, 2007.

Rancière, Jacques. *Disagreement: Politics and Philosophy*. Translated by Julie Rose. Minneapolis: University of Minnesota Press, 1999.

Ray, Raka. *Fields of Protest: Women's Movements in India*. Minneapolis: University of Minnesota Press, 1999.

Razack, Sherene H. *Casting Out: The Eviction of Muslims from Western Law and Politics*. Toronto: University of Toronto Press, 2008.

Razack, Sherene H. "The 'Sharia Law Debate' in Ontario: The Modernity/Premodernity Distinction in Legal Efforts to Protect Women from Culture." *Feminist Legal Studies* 15, no. 1 (2007): 3–32.

Reader, Soran. "Distance, Relationship and Moral Obligation." *The Monist* 86, no. 3 (2003): 367–81.
Reagon, Bernice Johnson. "Coalition Politics: Turning the Century." In *Home Girls: A Black Feminist Anthology*, edited by Barbara Smith, 356–69. New York: Kitchen Table, Women of Color Press, 1983.
"Le référendum s'en vient." *Le féminisme en bref* 5, no. 2 (1994).
Reger, Jo. *Everywhere and Nowhere: Contemporary Feminism in the United States*. New York: Oxford University Press, 2012.
Reger, Jo. "Micro-cohorts, Feminist Discourse, and the Emergence of the Toronto SlutWalk." *Feminist Formations* 26, no. 1 (2014): 49–69.
Reger, Jo. "Organizational Dynamics and the Construction of Multiple Feminist Identities in the National Organization for Women." *Gender & Society* 16, no. 5 (2002): 710–27.
Reger, Jo. "Organizational 'Emotion Work' through Consciousness-Raising: An Analysis of a Feminist Organization." *Qualitative Sociology* 27, no. 2 (2004): 205–22.
Reger, Jo. "The Story of a Slut Walk: Sexuality, Race, and Generational Divisions in Contemporary Feminist Activism." *Journal of Contemporary Ethnography* 44, no. 1 (2015): 84–112.
Reilly, Niamh. "Recasting Secular Thinking for Emancipatory Feminist Practice." *Social Compass* 64, no. 4 (December 1, 2017): 481–94.
Ricci, Amanda. "Contesting the Nation(s): Haitian and Mohawk Women's Activism in Montreal." In *Women's Activism and "Second Wave" Feminism: Transnational Histories*, edited by Barbara Molony and Jennifer Nelson, 273–94. London: Bloomsbury Academic, 2017.
Ricci, Amanda. "Un féminisme inclusif? La Fédération des femmes du Québec et les femmes immigrantes ou racisées, 1966–1992." *Bulletin d'histoire politique* 25, no. 3 (2017): 102–23.
Riley, Denise. *"Am I That Name?": Feminism and the Category of "Women" in History*. New York: Springer, 1988.
Riley, Denise. "A Short History of Some Preoccupations." In *Feminists Theorize the Political*, edited by Judith Butler and Joan W. Scott, 121–29. New York: Routledge, 1992.
Rinaldo, Rachel. "Pious and Critical: Muslim Women Activists and the Question of Agency." *Gender & Society* 28, no. 6 (December 1, 2014): 824–46.
Ringelheim, Julie. "The Roma Minority and the Utility of Human Rights." *International Journal on Minority and Group Rights* 16, no. 1 (2009): 157–63.
Rochefort, Florence. "Foulard, genre et laïcité en 1989." *Vingtième siècle: Revue d'histoire* 75, no. 3 (2002): 145–56.
Rochefort, Florence. *Le pouvoir du genre: Laïcités et religions, 1905–2005*. Toulouse, France: Presses Universitaires du Mirail, 2007.
Rojtman, Suzy, Maya Surduts, and Josette Trat. "On ne peut taire les critiques à l'égard du voile au nom de la solidarité avec les jeunes des quartiers populaires: Contre le racisme et pour les femmes." *Libération*, January 27, 2004.
Rorive, Isabelle. "Religious Symbols in the Public Space: In Search of a European Answer." *Cardozo Law Review* 30, no. 6 (2009): 2669–98.
Rosenberger, Sieglinde, and Birgit Sauer. *Politics, Religion and Gender: Framing and Regulating the Veil*. London: Routledge, 2012.
Roth, Benita. *Separate Roads to Feminism: Black, Chicana, and White Feminist Movements in America's Second Wave*. Cambridge: Cambridge University Press, 2004.
Rousseau, Louis. "Le travail obscur de la mémoire identitaire dans les débats nés d'une nouvelle diversité religieuse au Québec." *Recherches sociographiques* 57, nos. 2–3 (2016): 289–310.

Rowe, Aimee Carrillo. "Locating Feminism's Subject: The Paradox of White Femininity and the Struggle to Forge Feminist Alliances." *Communication Theory* 10, no. 1 (2000): 64–80.

Rowe, Aimee Carrillo. *Power Lines: On the Subject of Feminist Alliances*. Durham, NC: Duke University Press, 2008.

Rushing, Sara. "Butler's Ethical Appeal: Being, Feeling and Acting Responsible." In *Butler and Ethics*, edited by Mona Lloyd, 65–90. Edinburgh: Edinburgh University Press, 2015.

Saada, Emmanuelle. "The Empire of Law: Dignity, Prestige, and Domination in the 'Colonial Situation.'" *French Politics, Culture & Society* 20, no. 2 (2002): 98–120.

Sabbagh, Daniel, and Shanny Peer. "French Color Blindness in Perspective: The Controversy over 'Statistiques Ethniques.'" *French Politics, Culture & Society* 26, no. 1 (2008): 1–6.

Schippers, Birgit. "Violence, Affect and Ethics." In *Butler and Ethics*, edited by Mona Lloyd, 91–117. Edinburgh: Edinburgh University Press, 2015.

Schuster, Julia. "Intersectional Expectations: Young Feminists' Perceived Failure at Dealing with Differences and Their Retreat to Individualism." *Women's Studies International Forum* 58 (September 1, 2016): 1–8.

Scott, Joan W. "Experience." In *Feminists Theorize the Political*, edited by Judith Butler and Joan W. Scott, 22–40. New York: Routledge, 1992.

Scott, Joan W. *Only Paradoxes to Offer: French Feminists and the Rights of Man*. Cambridge, MA: Harvard University Press, 2009.

Scott, Joan W. *The Politics of the Veil*. Princeton, NJ: Princeton University Press, 2007.

Scott, Joan W. *Sex and Secularism*. Princeton, NJ: Princeton University Press, 2018.

Scott, Joan W. "Sexularism: On Secularism and Gender Equality." In *The Fantasy of Feminist History*, edited by Scott, Joan W, 91–116. Durham, NC: Duke University Press, 2011.

Selby, Jennifer A. "French Secularism as a 'Guarantor' of Women's Rights? Muslim Women and Gender Politics in a Parisian Banlieue." *Culture and Religion* 12, no. 4 (2011): 441–62.

Selby, Jennifer A. "Hijab Debates in Europe." In *The Oxford Handbook of European Islam*, edited by Jocelyne Cesari, 701–41. New York: Oxford University Press, 2014.

Selby, Jennifer A. *Questioning French Secularism: Gender Politics and Islam in a Parisian Suburb*. New York: Palgrave Macmillan, 2012.

Selby, Jennifer A. "Un/veiling Women's Bodies: Secularism and Sexuality in Full-Face Veil Prohibitions in France and Québec." *Studies in Religion / Sciences Religieuses* 43, no. 3 (2014): 439–66.

Shepard, Todd. *The Invention of Decolonization: The Algerian War and the Remaking of France*. Ithaca, NY: Cornell University Press, 2008.

Sibertin-Blanc, Guillaume. "Deleuze et les minorités: Quelle 'politique'?" *Cités* 4, no. 40 (2009): 39–57.

Siim, Birte. "How Institutional Context Shapes Headscarf Debates across Scandinavia: The Impact of Institutions on Perceptions and Boundaries." In *European States and Their Muslim Citizens: The Impact of Institutions on Perceptions and Boundaries*, edited by John R. Bowen, Christophe Bertossi, Jan Willem Duyvendak, and Mona Lena Krook, 216–34. Cambridge: Cambridge University Press, 2014.

Siim, Birte, and Monika Mokre, eds. *Negotiating Gender and Diversity in an Emergent European Public Sphere*. New York: Palgrave Macmillan, 2013.

Silverman, Maxim. *Deconstructing the Nation: Immigration, Racism and Citizenship*. London: Routledge, 1992.

Simon, Patrick. "The Choice of Ignorance: The Debate on Ethnic and Racial Statistics in France." *French Politics, Culture & Society* 26, no. 1 (2008): 7–31.
Simonin, Anne. *Le déshonneur dans la république*. Paris: Grasset, 2008.
Singh, Jakeet. "Religious Agency and the Limits of Intersectionality." *Hypatia* 30, no. 4 (2015): 657–74.
Smith, Barbara Ellen. "Crossing the Great Divides: Race, Class, and Gender in Southern Women's Organizing, 1979–1991." *Gender & Society* 9, no. 6 (1995): 680–96.
Spelman, Elizabeth V. *Inessential Woman: Problems of Exclusion in Feminist Thought*. Boston: Beacon Press, 1988.
Spivak, Gayatri Chakravorty. "Can the Subaltern Speak?" In *Can the Subaltern Speak? Reflections on the History of an Idea*, 21–78. New York: Columbia University Press, 1988.
Springer, Kimberly. *Living for the Revolution: Black Feminist Organizations, 1968–1980*. Durham, NC: Duke University Press, 2005.
Srivastava, Sarita. "Tears, Fears and Careers: Anti-racism and Emotion in Social Movement Organizations." *Canadian Journal of Sociology* 31, no. 1 (2006): 55–90.
Srivastava, Sarita. "'You're Calling Me a Racist?' The Moral and Emotional Regulation of Antiracism and Feminism." *Signs* 31, no. 1 (2005): 29–62.
Stark, Heidi Kiiwetinepinesiik. "Criminal Empire: The Making of the Savage in a Lawless Land." *Theory & Event* 19, no. 4 (2016). https://muse.jhu.edu/journal/191.
Stetson, Dorothy M., and Dorothy E. McBride. *Women's Rights in France*. Westport, CT: Greenwood Press, 1987.
Stoler, Ann Laura. "Colonial Aphasia: Race and Disabled Histories in France." *Public Culture* 23, no. 1 (2011): 121–56.
Strolovitch, Dara Z. *Affirmative Advocacy: Race, Class, and Gender in Interest Group Politics*. Chicago: University of Chicago Press, 2007.
Sullivan, Shannon, and Nancy Tuana, eds. *Race and Epistemologies of Ignorance*. Albany: State University of New York Press, 2007.
Tamzali, Wassyla. "Féministes, je vous écris d'Alger." *Libération*, January 14, 2004. http://www.liberation.fr/tribune/2004/01/14/feministes-je-vous-ecris-d-alger_465226.
Taylor, Charles. "Interculturalism or Multiculturalism?" *Philosophy & Social Criticism* 38, nos. 4–5 (May 1, 2012): 413–23.
Taylor, Verta, and Nancy Whittier. "Collective Identity in Social Movement Communities: Lesbian Feminist Mobilization." In *Frontiers in Social Movement Theory*, edited by Aldon D. Morris and Carol M. Mueller, 104–29. New Haven, CT: Yale University Press, 1992.
Tevanian, Pierre. "Une loi antilaïque, antiféministe et antisociale." *Le monde diplomatique*, February 1, 2004.
Tevanian, Pierre. *Le voile médiatique: Un faux débat. "L'affaire du foulard islamique"*. Paris: Raisons d'Agir Éd., 2005.
Thomas, Elaine R. "Keeping Identity at a Distance: Explaining France's New Legal Restrictions on the Islamic Headscarf." *Ethnic and Racial Studies* 29, no. 2 (2006): 237–59.
Tissot, Sylvie. "Excluding Muslim Women: From Hijab to Niqab, from School to Public Space." *Public Culture* 23, no. 1 (2011): 39–46.
Tocqueville, Alexis de. *De la démocratie en Amérique*. Vol. 2. Paris: Gallimard, 1986.
Tomlinson, Barbara. "To Tell the Truth and Not Get Trapped: Desire, Distance, and Intersectionality at the Scene of Argument." *Signs* 38, no. 4 (2013): 993–1017.

Townsend-Bell, Erica E. "Intersectional Advances? Inclusionary and Intersectional State Action in Uruguay." In *Situating Intersectionality: Politics, Policy, and Power*, edited by Angelia R. Wilson, 43–61. New York: Springer, 2013.
Townsend-Bell, Erica E. "What Is Relevance? Defining Intersectional Praxis in Uruguay." *Political Research Quarterly* 64, no. 1 (2011): 187–99.
Townsend-Bell, Erica E. "Writing the Way to Feminism." *Signs* 38, no. 1 (2012): 127–52.
Trat, Josette. "Les féministes blanches et l'empire ou le récit d'un complot féministe fantasmé." *Europe solidaire sans frontières*, April 12, 2012. https://www.europesolidaire.org/spip.php?article27144.
Trat, Josette. "Non à une loi contre le voile intégral." *L'hebdomadaire du NPA, tout est à nous* 34 (January 23, 2010). https://npa2009.org/content/non-%C3%A0-une-loi-contre-le-voile-int%C3%A9gral.
Tronto, Joan C. *Moral Boundaries: A Political Argument for an Ethic of Care*. New York: Routledge, 1993.
Tronto, Joan C. "Partiality Based on Relational Responsibilities: Another Approach to Global Ethics." *Ethics and Social Welfare* 6, no. 3 (2012): 303–16.
Trudel, Flavie. "L'engagement des femmes en politique au Québec: Histoire de la Fédération des femmes du Québec de 1966 à nos jours." Université du Québec à Montréal, 2009.
Tungohan, Ethel. "Intersectionality and Social Justice: Assessing Activists' Use of Intersectionality through Grassroots Migrants' Organizations in Canada." *Politics, Groups, and Identities* 4, no. 3 (2016): 347–62.
Vakulenko, Anastasia. *Islamic Veiling in Legal Discourse*. London: Routledge, 2012.
Vance, Carole S., ed. *Pleasure and Danger: Exploring Female Sexuality*. New York: Routledge & Kegan Paul, 1984.
Vauchez, Stéphanie Hennette, and Vincent Valentin. *L'affaire Baby Loup ou la nouvelle laïcité*. Vol. 1. Issy-les-Moulineaux: L.G.D.J., Lextenso éditions, 2014.
Vergès, Françoise. *Le ventre des femmes: Capitalisme, racialisation, féminisme*. Paris: Albin Michel, 2017.
Vigerie, Anne, and Anne Zelensky. "'Laïcardes,' puisque féministes." *Le Monde*, May 29, 2003.
"Le voile et ce qu'il dévoile." *Les mots sont importants*. http://lmsi.net/-Le-voile-et-ce-qu-il-devoile.
Walby, Sylvia. *The Future of Feminism*. Cambridge: Polity, 2011.
Walker, Margaret Urban. *Moral Repair: Reconstructing Moral Relations after Wrongdoing*. Cambridge: Cambridge University Press, 2006.
Wayland, Sarah V. "Religious Expression in Public Schools: Kirpans in Canada, Hijab in France." *Ethnic and Racial Studies* 20, no. 3 (1997): 545–61.
Whittier, Nancy. *Feminist Generations: The Persistence of the Radical Women's Movement*. Philadelphia: Temple University Press, 1995.
Whittier, Nancy. "Political Generations, Micro-cohorts, and the Transformation of Social Movements." *American Sociological Review* 62, no. 5 (1997): 760–78.
Weir, Alison. *Identities and Freedom: Feminist Theory Between Power and Connection*. New York: Oxford University Press, 2013.
Wekker, Gloria. *White Innocence: Paradoxes of Colonialism and Race*. Durham, NC: Duke University Press, 2016.
Weldon, S. Laurel. "Inclusion, Solidarity, and Social Movements: The Global Movement against Gender Violence." *Perspectives on Politics* 4, no. 1 (2006): 55–74.

Yancy, George. *Look, a White! Philosophical Essays on Whiteness*. Philadelphia, PA: Temple University Press, 2012.
Young, Iris Marion. "Asymmetrical Reciprocity: On Moral Respect, Wonder, and Enlarged Thought." *Constellations* 3, no. 3 (January 1, 1997): 340–63.
Young, Iris Marion. *Inclusion and Democracy*. Oxford: Oxford University Press, 2000.
Young, Iris Marion. "Responsibility and Global Justice: A Social Connection Model." *Social Philosophy & Policy* 23, no. 1 (2006): 102–30.
Yuval-Davis, Nira. *Gender and Nation*. London: Sage, 1997.
Yuval-Davis, Nira. "Intersectionality and Feminist Politics." *European Journal of Women's Studies* 13, no. 3 (2006): 193–209.
Yuval-Davis, Nira. *The Politics of Belonging: Intersectional Contestations*. New York: Sage, 2011.
Zajicek, Anna M. "Race Discourses and Antiracist Practices in a Local Women's Movement." *Gender & Society* 16, no. 2 (2002): 155–74.
Zerilli, Linda M. G. *Feminism and the Abyss of Freedom*. Chicago: University of Chicago Press, 2005.

Index

For the benefit of digital users, indexed terms that span two pages (e.g., 52–53) may, on occasion, appear on only one of those pages.

abortion rights, 75–76
academia, 73–74, 155–56
Adorno, 176–77, 206–7
affective politics, 35–36, 43, 224
affective turn, 41
Afro-feminism, 114, 155–58, 167–68
agency
   debate over, 21–22
   ethical, 6–7
   feminist, 6, 7, 8–9, 243–46
   of religious women, 5–8, 50
   and power, 6–7, 246–47
Ahmed, Naima Atef, 55
Ahmed, Sara, 24–25, 234
   feminist killjoy, 129–30
   feminist whiteness, 111
   identity, 36–37, 41
   nonperformativity of antiracism, 67–68
   relationships, 33, 34–35, 267n98
   solidarity, 179
Algeria, 92–94, 146, 149–50
Allen, Amy, 151–52, 182–83, 241, 244–46
Amara, Fadela, 70
ambivalence, 108, 109, 117
Améry, Jean, 130
anger
   against colonialism, 146
   and exclusion, 173–74
   white feminist, 112, 113, 115–16, 117, 124
anticipatory-utopian moment, 236–37, 240, 241
antiracism, 38–39, 49, 59–60
   lack of institutionalization of, 76–78, 79
   nonperformativity of, 67–68
anti-Semitism, 282n43

Arendt, Hannah
   freedom, 27–28, 104–6
   plurality, 28–29
   political community, 216
   promises, 190, 196–97
   relations, 20–21
   resentment, 170–71
   theory of judgment, 183, 197–98
Armstrong, Elizabeth, 264n48
Aune, Kristin, 42
autonomy, 5–7, 244–46, 247
Avramopoulou, Eirini, 221, 242–43
axes of domination, 30, 34–35

Baby-Loup, 72–73, 269n20
Bacchetta, Paola, 89, 129, 151–52, 169–70, 267–68n105
Bangstad, Sindre, 259n33
bargaining, 5–6
Bartky, Sandra, 193–94
Bassel, Leah, 265n66
Beauvoir, Simone de, 152–53
becoming feminist, 37–38
   See also feminist political subjectivation
Beltrán, Cristina, 116, 231–32, 266n84
benevolent care, 106, 124, 138, 218
Benhabib, Djemila, 124–25
Benhabib, Seyla, 193
Black feminism, 31, 43, 131–32, 224
Black Women's Coordination, 135
bodily autonomy, 73
Boggio Éwanjé-Épée, Félix, 73–74
Bouchard, Gérard, 54–55
Bouchard-Taylor Commission, 54–55, 57, 58–59
Bourdieu, Pierre, 253

Bouteldja, Houria, 71–72
Braidotti, Rosi, 5
Bread and Roses March, 63–64
Brown, Wendy, 129–30
Brudholm, Thomas, 130
burqa, 277n130
burkini, 3–4, 68, 73
Butler, Judith, 12
  agency, 6–7
  critique, 239–40
  ethical turn, 28, 206–7, 259–60n40, 260n47–48
  exclusion, 179
  morality, 176–77
  subject question, 25, 26, 40, 81, 151–52

Canada, 52–53
Canadian Charter of Rights, 53, 58
Canadian Supreme Court, 55–56
care, 13–14
  deserving of, 34–35
  for distant others, 43, 154, 218–19
  feminist, 144–45, 220–25
  for other feminists, 159, 214–18, 219, 248, 249
  theories of, 20–21
  women as object of, 105–6
  See also benevolent care, ethics of care
Casgrain, Thérèse, 63
categorization, 16
Catholic Church, 50, 58, 74–75, 118, 119–20
Cavell, Stanley, 156, 177, 208
Charest, Jean, 54–55
Charte de la laïcité, 56, 124–25
Charte des valeurs, 56, 158, 174–75, 227, 272n61
Chirac, Jacques, 69
Cho, Sumi, 268n5
choice, 106–7, 123, 124, 137, 142–43, 144–45, 151
Christian extremism, 120
Christian religious symbols, 56
Circulaire Chatel, 72–73
class, 88, 91, 95, 147, 161
Coalition for Abortion and Contraception Rights (CADAC), 75–76

coalitions
  desire for, 192, 194–95
  emotional dimension, 188
  and identity, 183–85
  moral bonds of, 183, 189–91
  politics of, 61–62
  possibility for, 31–32
  and power asymmetry, 185–86, 187–89
  as a promise, 191–92
  among racialized women's organizations, 189–90
Cole, Elizabeth, 273n78
Collectif féministe pour l'égalité (CFPE), 71–72, 73–74
Collectif national pour les droits des femmes (CNDF), 69–71, 75–79, 273n77
colonial aphasia, 71–72, 73–74, 92
colonialism
  erasure of, 71–72, 135
  in feminism, 71–72, 119–20
  politicization of, 140–41, 171–72
  and race, 89, 92–93, 168
  and secularism, 49
  settler, 51, 65–66, 134–35
coloniality of power, 148–49
color-blindness, 51, 86, 91, 95
Commission Debré, 69
Commission Gérin, 277n130
communicative ethics, 201–4, 228–29
Communist Party, 70, 124
Conradi, Alexa, 63–64
Conseil du statut de la femme (CSF), 57, 58–59, 71–72
Cornell, Drucilla, 26, 177–78
Crenshaw, Kimberlé, 30, 142, 268n5
critical theory, 14–15
culture, 97–98, 135–39
  See also difference: cultural, Western culture

Das, Veena, 208–9, 217–18
David, Françoise, 63–64
Davis, Kathy, 26–27
Dean, Jonathan, 42
Debono, Emmanuel, 282n43
Debout!, 288n70
de Lauretis, Teresa, 12, 14, 26, 41, 42–43, 215–16, 239–40

Deleuze, Gilles, 20, 128–29, 176–78
Delphy, Christine, 71–72
Derrida, Jacques, 26
Deveaux, Monique, 5–6
difference
　in coalitions, 183–84, 193
　cultural, 97–98, 99, 107, 136–40
　as divisive, 59–60
　between feminists, 24
　in feminist theory, 7–8, 18, 24–27, 237
　hierarchy of, 45
　in judgments, 32–33
　and plurality, 197–98
　politics of emotion, 39
　religious, 33–34, 108
　universal, 119–20
distance, 88, 89–90, 91, 110, 111,
　　219, 253–54
diversity, 86, 90, 97
divorce, 107, 136–37
Doerr, Nicole, 292n109
Dot-Pouillard, Nicolas, 275n101
double oppression, 31, 47

El-Tayeb, Fatima, 48
emancipation
　and agency, 244–46
　collective, 32
　of feminist subjects, 8–9, 12
　and gender equality, 234–35
　as political project, 15, 38
　and public schools, 71
　questioning of, 150–51
　and religion, 50, 121
　Western conception of, 73
emotions
　and care, 219, 224
　and identification with others, 193
　as moral demands, 169–70
　political, 20, 37
　and subjectivation, 37–39, 41, 43
　of whiteness, 83–84
enlarged mentality, 193, 196–200,
　　209–10, 217
enlarged sympathy, 192–96
enlarged thought, 201–5, 228–29
equality, 28, 248
　See also gender equality

ethic of care, 13–14, 28, 208, 210
　See also benevolent care, care
ethical disposition. *See* moral disposition
ethical violence, 153–54, 156–57, 173–74,
　　176–77, 206–7
ethics, 6–7, 12–15, 253
Europe, 45, 47–48, 49–50, 79
exclusion
　from deliberation, 202–3
　from feminist subject, 115–16, 173–74,
　　179–80, 207–8, 237–38
　from public school, 94–95
　through secularism, 126
　social, 88
　by white feminists, 194–95
experience, 35–37, 39

false consciousness, 113–14
Farris, Sara, 2, 23, 258n17
Fassin, Didier, 14–15, 37–38, 40–41
fear, 117
Fédération des femmes du Québec
　　(FFQ), 95–96
　Comité des femmes des communautés
　　culturelles, 66–67
　historical legacy, 62–68
　inclusion of racialized women, 103–4,
　　186, 217
　intersectionality, 59–60, 99, 172–73
　racialized feminists' demands, 163–64
　racism, 58–59, 60
　and regulation of Islamic veiling, 57,
　　174–75, 221–22
　and religious arbitration, 54
female genital mutilation, 115–16
feminism
　as an activity, 180–81
　foundationalist, 220
　Islamic, 123, 129, 158, 168, 188–89
　located in the past, 116
　as a moral project, 11–14, 181
　multiculturalist, 5–6
　as a political project, 11–15, 20–21,
　　83–84, 104–6, 112
　postcolonial, 5–6, 26–27, 34, 47,
　　113–14, 219, 258n13, 261–62n10
　and racism, 4–5
　secularist, 70

feminism (cont.)
  as a set of dispositions, 24–25
  as a social project, 83–84, 104–6, 112, 117
  See also Afro-feminism, Black feminism, feminist political community, feminist subject, feminist theory, liberal feminism, second-wave feminism, third-wave feminism
feminist activists, 3, 9, 16
feminist collective subject, 25, 32, 40, 105–6, 113
  and difference, 197–98
  enrollment in, 110
  exclusion from, 115–16, 173–74
  and representation, 214
Feminist Dare, 87–88, 120, 283n63
feminist ethic of responsibility, 14, 20–21, 210–18, 231
  and compassion, 216
  and exclusion, 183
  and others, 244–46
  and political community, 12–13, 218, 220–25
  and pragmatism, 225–33
  in relationships, 244, 248
feminist imagination, 2, 7, 242–43
feminist intervention, 106–7, 109, 110, 117, 137
feminist movements, 16, 50–51
  See also second-wave feminism, third-wave feminism
feminist political community, 242–43
  boundaries of, 13–14, 28–29
  care for, 214–18
  creation of, 24, 43, 180–81, 182
  and emotions, 37–38
  exclusion from, 203
  and feminist ethics, 197–98
  inclusion in, 199–200, 220–21, 249
  and representation, 213–14
feminist political subjectivation, 24, 39–44, 236–37
  and coalitions, 188
  and exclusion, 194–95
  through feminist intervention, 110, 111
  identity building, 184–85, 231

  and political community, 214
  of racialized feminists, 152–58, 159
  through resistance to power, 169–70
  as shaped by emotions, 37
feminist praxis, 9–10, 19–20, 33, 162–63
feminist relationships, 20–21, 43, 82
  abandonment, 221–23
  equal, 27, 112, 117
  ethical, 13–14, 40–41
  in fieldwork, 254
  free, 104–5, 197
  and identity, 35–36
  moral, 181–82, 189–91
  and moral dispositions, 125
  and power asymmetries, 32, 100, 201
  and responsibility, 211–13, 244
  transformative, 247
feminist subject
  boundaries of, 13–14, 42, 81, 113–14, 117, 125, 150, 169, 181, 182
  construction of, 179–80
  emancipated, 3–5, 8–9, 93, 235–36
  "good" or "bad", 16, 33–35, 38–39, 46–47, 111–12, 118, 150–51, 194–95, 207–8
  as lost, 116
  moral dimension, 12, 28, 34–35
  nonwhite women as, 104, 110, 111–12, 188–89
  passive, 108, 109
  in question, 11–12, 14, 25, 26–27
  recognition as, 215–16
  as white, 90, 91, 95
  See also feminist collective subject
feminist theory, 42–43, 235–36
  difference in, 7–8, 18
  ethics in, 10
  intersectionality in, 47
  postcolonial, 26–27, 258n13
  poststructuralist, 26
  subject question in, 26, 196–97
feminist values, 40–41, 151, 161–64, 226–28, 234, 242–43, 247–48
feminist whiteness, 19–20, 81
  boundaries of, 102, 180
  challenges to, 119–20, 151–52, 160–65, 176
  denial of relationality, 205–8

and education, 101–2
as feminist subject, 109
moral dispositions, 104, 117
and nationalism, 84–85, 118, 124–25
and privilege, 167
production of, 36–37, 82–83, 91, 104
repertoires of, 94–95, 96, 103–4
and secularism, 122
as universal, 162–63
femonationalism, 2
challenges to, 67–68, 248–49
in feminist organizations, 45–46, 75
and feminist whiteness, 19, 84, 124–25, 238
rise of, 23, 68–69, 235
and secularism, 49–50, 118
femoresistance, 249–50
fetishization, of nonwhite bodies, 167–68
Finestone, Sheila, 65
Foucault, Michel, 6–7, 40, 152, 246–47
France, 3–4, 266n81
assimilation, 147
color-blind approach, 51
femonationalism, 45–46
fieldwork in, 85, 251–53
headscarf debates, 68–69, 74–75
history of race, 89
intersectionality, study of, 268–69n8
religion, 49–50
See also republican universalism
Frankenberg, Ruth, 81–82, 86–87, 95, 104
freedom, 5, 6, 27–28, 104–5, 197, 244–46
Freud, Sigmund, 26
Friedman, Marylin, 5–6
Front de Libération des Femmes (FLF), 64–65

Gay, Amandine, 157–58, 286n21
gender equality
and cultural difference, 47–48, 107
and national identity, 49–50, 54–55
as primary value, 7–8, 9, 119–20, 138–39
as secular, 2, 45–46, 55
as specific to Western culture, 2, 9–10
gender parity, 119–20
generational gap, 95, 102, 114–16, 153–54
Giraud, Isabelle, 273n78
Girls on the Rise, 90, 121

Grosz, Elizabeth, 21–22
Groult, Benoîte, 152–53
Groupe du 6 novembre, 155
Guénif-Souilamas, Nacira, 49

Habchi, Sihem, 124, 277n130
Habermas, Jürgen, 246
Hache, Emilie, 226–28, 243
Hancock, Ange-Marie, 265n66, 268n5
headscarf debates, 4–5, 18–19, 32, 36–37, 47–48, 49–50, 68–70
hierarchy of struggle, 142, 154
hijab, 53, 72–73, 143–44, 174–75
Hill, Anita, 204
Hoagland, Sarah Lucia, 206
Hollande, François, 72–73
homonationalism, 2, 15
hooks, bell, 129–30
hospitality, 33
Houda-Pepin, Fatima, 54, 124–25

identity, 20–21
construction of, 35–37, 184–85, 195–96
depoliticization of, 199
and exclusion, 220
as multiple, 193–94
identity/freedom paradox, 5
identity politics, 27, 30–33, 34–35, 59–60
ignorance
and anger, 115–16
epistemology of, 81–82, 84, 167, 206, 223
and ethical violence, 176–77
as privilege, 93, 235
and universalism, 89–90
whiteness as, 19–20, 81–83, 118, 122, 238
in women's organizations, 78, 79
immigrant integration, 47–48, 51, 58, 91, 96, 97–98
inclusion, 47
in coalitions, 185, 186
desire for, 86, 150
and difference, 193–94, 202, 203–4
as feminist priority, 100, 229–30, 238–39
and intersectionality, 96–97
and religion, 49–50

inclusion (cont.)
  in women's organizations, 65, 66, 154, 163–64, 172, 231
indignation, 112, 113
indigenous women, 65–66, 71–72, 113–14, 132
  ties with migrant women's organizations, 134–35, 141, 189–90
integration. See immigrant integration
interculturalism, 52–53, 58, 96–99, 103–4, 132–33
International Women's Day, 71–72, 79, 112–13, 160, 163–64, 186, 189
intersectionality, 18–19, 24, 26–27, 29–35, 59–60
  adoption by women's organizations, 61–62, 67–68, 99–102, 172, 238–39
  diffusion in France, 155
  foundations of, 25–26, 131–32
  and emotions, 35–36, 37
  and politics, 30, 34–35, 135–36
  and representation, 151–52, 161
  resistance to, 95, 101–2, 172–73
  structural, 30, 47–48
  as tool for inclusion, 96
  as tool for self-criticism, 99, 101–2
intersectional identities, 135–36
Iran, 92–93
Islam, 1–2, 46–47, 48
  and national identity, 118
  and race, 49–50, 84–85, 87
  and racialized feminists, 135–36
  See also Muslim men, Muslim women
Islamic veiling
  as a choice, 123, 124, 142–43
  criticism of, by racialized women, 145–46, 147–48
  and feminism, 34–35
  and feminists, 78–79
  meanings of, 69–70, 71–72, 110–11
  regulation of, 2, 3–4, 49–50, 52–53, 55–56, 72–73, 87, 144–48
  and republican values, 70
  in women's organizations, 34, 107–8, 110, 225–26
  See also burqa, burkini, headscarf debates, hijab, niqab
Islamophobia
  and bans on veiling, 3–4, 50–51, 71–72

racialization of, 87
and secularism, 71–72, 121–22
and women's organizations, 60, 78, 148

Jews, 65, 94, 271n46, 273n67

Kandel, Liliane, 70
Kapur, Ratna, 293n31
Kateb, George, 193–94

Laborde, Cécile, 121, 258n20
laïcité, 59–60, 95, 119–21
  See also Charte de la laïcité
language, 156–57, 166, 169–70, 174, 177, 208, 254–55
Latour, Bruno, 229–30
Laugier, Sandra, 156, 177, 208, 209–10
leftists, 64–65, 71, 76, 91–92
  radical, 89–90, 95–96, 113–14, 156
lesbians, 141, 154, 155–56, 157, 160
Les Mots Sont Importants, 258–59n21, 275n101
Les Yvettes, 172
Levinas, Emmanuel, 259–60n40, 260n48
LGBT movement, 154–55, 160, 221, 264n48
liberal feminism, 4–8, 9–10
liberalism, 4–6, 38–39, 244–46
Liberal Party, 55–56, 57, 63
Ligue Communiste Révolutionnaire, 76, 152–53
Lloyd, Moya, 259–60n40
Lorde, Audre, 129–30, 268–69n8
love, 170–71, 224, 249
L'R des femmes, 161–62
Lugones, María, 193–94, 247
Lyshaug, Brenda, 192–97

Magliani-Belkacem, Stella, 73–74
Mahmood, Saba, 6–8, 244–46, 292n109
March 8 for all, 112–13, 114
  See also International Women's Day
Martin, Biddy, 35–36
Marxism, 152–53, 156
Masclet, Camille, 270n27
McCall, Leslie, 268n5
melancholy, 112, 113, 116
Michel, Noémi, 173–74

micro-cohort, 149–50, 152–53, 155–56, 158
migrant women, 33–34, 76–78, 98–99, 100, 132
See also racialized women
migrant women's organizations, 65–67, 76–77, 134–35
minority cultures 1–2
minority position, 20, 128–29, 169–70, 175–78
minority women, 266n77, 280n18
modernity, 234–35, 246
Mohanty, Chandra, 35–36, 267n96
Molinier, Pascale, 207–8, 253–54, 261n65
Montesquieu, 266n81
Moraga, Cherríe, 37
moral bonds, 182–83
moral demands, 170
moral dispositions, 10, 12, 14, 18, 19–20
   boundaries of, 199–200
   and care, 218–19
   and coalitions, 188, 193–94
   and emotions, 37–39, 43
   and feminists, 40–41, 104
   of Muslim women, 109
   and power, 41–42
   of racialized feminists, 128
   of whiteness, 83–84, 117
   See also ambivalence, anger, benevolent care, fear, indignation, love, melancholy, resentment, self-righteousness
morality, 13, 34–35, 208–11, 214–15
moral judgment, 112–13, 114
moral position, 16–17
moral pragmatism, 150–51
moral values, 226–28
mosque movement, the, 6–7
Mouvement des libération des femmes (MLF), 152–53, 288n70
multiculturalism, 26–27
   Canadian, 51, 52–53, 58, 132–33
   in Quebec, 95–97, 103–4, 280n18
   in women's organizations, 134–35, 138, 143
   See also interculturalism
Muñoz, José Esteban, 41, 241–42
Muslim men, 49

Muslim women
   agency of, 109
   care for, 225–26
   experiences of, 228
   and feminist responsibility, 222–23
   as feminist subject, 123, 148
   invisibilization of, 88, 89
   as subject of public debates, 47–48
   as victims, 124–25, 168, 195
   in women's organizations, 101–2, 145–46

Narayan, Uma, 5–6
Nash, Jennifer, 43, 224, 265n66
Nasreen, Taslima, 70
National Front, 72–73
national identity
   debates about, 55
   feminism in, 19
   feminist whiteness as, 84, 118
   as secular, 46–47, 49–50, 56, 121–22
nationalism
   challenges to, 28, 165–67
   and instrumentalization of gender equality, 2
   instrumental use of, 74–75
   resistance to, 15
   and women's rights, 118
   See also femonationalism, homonationalism, Quebec: nationalism
Ni putes ni soumises (NPNS), 70, 71–73, 124
niqab, 59–60, 72–73, 143–44, 221–22
nonwhite women. *See* racialized women
Nouveau Parti Anticapitaliste, 76

Okin, Susan Moller, 26–27, 257n3
Ontario, 53–54
Ortega, Mariana, 93
other, the, 13–14, 20–21, 26–27
   care for, 218–19, 222
   moral relation to, 94–95, 208–9
   in the political community, 220–21
   and white feminists, 43

Pagé, Geneviève, 283n60
Paris, Myriam, 281n35
Pelchat, Christiane, 57

Perreau, Bruno, 200, 241–42, 288n83, 291–92n99
plurality, 28–29, 197–98, 203
political community, 1–2, 12–13, 24, 27–28, 56, 241–42
   See also feminist political community
political context, 13, 40
political passions, 37–38, 129–30
political subjectivation, 14–15, 16–17, 18, 19, 38, 41
   See also feminist political subjectivation
political subjectivity, 5, 40–41
politics of location, 35–36
populism, right-wing, 51, 79
positionality, 16–17, 253–54
postcolonialism
   in feminist movements, 34, 47, 68–69, 71–72, 113–14, 135–36
   in feminist theory, 2, 4–6, 26–27, 219
   guilt, 71
   and race, 167, 168
   racialized discursive injuries, 173–74
   representation of the other, 219
   and resentment, 171
   See also colonialism, feminism: postcolonial
postcolonial melancholia, 83
postsecularism, 5, 33–34
power, 6–7, 8–9, 14–15, 16
   erasure of, 98
   in feminist practices, 33
   hierarchies of, 40–41
   and identity politics, 30–32
   and moral dispositions, 38–39, 41–42
   structural relations of, 47–48
   in women's organizations, 111
power asymmetries, 23–24, 30, 32, 100, 201–2, 203–4
   in coalitions, 61–62, 187–89
   in political community, 199
   reflection on, 219
   and responsibility, 204, 210–13, 223
pragmatism, 226
privilege, 81–83, 84, 92, 110, 212
projects, the, 88, 90, 133–34
Proletarian Left, 92
promises, 11–12, 174–75, 214–16
Puar, Jasbir, 2

Quebec, 74–75
   feminist coalition, 45–46, 61–62
   fieldwork in, 85, 251–53, 254
   francophone identity, 65, 165–67, 283n60, 284n84
   immigrant integration, 51, 58
   nationalism, 52–53, 58, 63, 65–66, 95–96, 134–35, 165–66, 167
   regulation of Islamic veiling, 53, 54–56
   religion, 50
   secularism, 119
   women's movements, 57
Quebecois Party, 55–56, 58–59
queer theory, 241–42, 262n14, 262n20
Quiet Revolution, the, 58, 63, 288n65

race
   depoliticization of, 95, 96, 125, 138
   and feminists, 83, 101–2
   and immigration, 84–85, 115–16
   and others, 81–82
   outside the national borders, 92–93, 94–95
   politicization of, 62–63, 67–68, 92, 103–4, 140–42, 150
   and religion, 124–25, 142–43
race cognizance, 86–87, 91, 96, 103–4
racialization
   of religious identity, 47–48, 49–50, 56
   politics of, 34–35
   process of, 34, 46–47
racialized feminists, 20, 140, 148–49, 155–56
   criticism of mainstream women's organizations, 127–28, 136–38, 238–39
   emotions, 37, 169–70
   and Islamic veiling, 142–43, 145–46, 147–48
   political subjectivation, 150, 152–58
   social movements, 131–32
   relation with white feminists, 128–29, 158, 170, 187–88
   visibility, 158, 159–60
   See also self-organizing
racialized women, 47–48
   exclusion of, 77
   as feminist subjects, 106, 113, 115–16, 117

and integration, 96
  as object of feminist care, 104, 106, 117
  and secularism, 124
  self-organizing, 45–46, 61–62, 90, 95–96, 98–99, 102–3
  social distance, 88, 89–90, 91, 111
  terminology, 103–4, 141
  in mainstream women's organizations, 98–99, 100–1, 111–12
  See also indigenous women, migrant women, Muslim women, self-organizing
racialized women's organizations, 61, 79, 252
  See also migrant women's organizations
racism
  evasion of, 114
  in the feminist movement, 37, 60, 253–54
  in headscarf debates, 71
  institutional, 88–89
  and Islam, 50–51
  in Quebec, 59
  virtuous, 49
  See also antiracism
Rancière, Jacques, 243
Reader, Soran, 214–15, 291n85
Reagon, Bernice Johnson, 184
reasonable accommodation, 53, 56, 143
Reger, Jo, 16
relationality, 190–91, 208–10, 231
  affective dimension, 242
  denial of, 211–13, 238
  and moral values, 226–28
relationships, 33, 34–35, 37–38
  See also feminist relationships
religion
  and agency, 6–7, 50
  discrimination, 53
  as inherently oppressive to women, 90, 94–95, 120–21, 123, 124, 149–50
  and race, 48, 50–51, 142–43
religious accommodation, 47–48, 54–55, 58, 60
  See also reasonable accommodation
religious arbitration, 53–54
religious discrimination, 69
representation, 213–14

representation, descriptive, 66–68, 186
republicanism, 70, 71, 258n20
republican universalism, 91, 95, 119–20, 133–34, 148–49
resentment, 129–30, 170–72, 174, 177–78, 238–39
responsibility, 10, 12–13, 210–14, 222–23, 224–25
  See also feminist ethic of responsibility
Ricci, Amanda, 65
Riley, Denise, 179
Roth, Benita, 31, 64–65, 89–90, 131–32
Rowe, Aimee Carrillo, 266n68

Sadou, Zazi, 70
Sarkozy, Nicolas, 69, 72–73
Scott, Joan, 36–37, 45–46
second-wave feminism, 64–65, 115–16
  autonomist trend, 70
  class-struggle trend, 70, 73, 75–76, 91–92, 112–13
  and race, 91–92
  and secularism, 120
  US, 37, 86, 128–29, 268–69n8
  See also Black feminism
secularism, 49
  as ally of women's rights, 45–46, 57, 70, 148
  and feminist whiteness, 118–26
  instrumental use of, 74–75
  and national identity, 46–47, 49–51, 56
  and Quebec, 58
  and republicanism, 70, 121
self-organizing
  to challenge feminist whiteness, 163–64
  and coalitions, 185
  and cultural difference, 137–38
  history of, 131–35, 157–58
  to self-represent, 158
  on shared experience, 138–39
self-representation, 158–60
self-righteousness, 114, 117
sexual freedom, 49
sexualarism debates, 45–46, 51–52, 55, 57, 74–75, 119–20, 122, 235–36
Sikhs, 271n46, 273n67
Simonin, Anne, 266n82
Sisters Unite, 92–93

Smith, Barbara Ellen, 265–66n67, 292n100
social location, 84, 149–50, 153–54
social movements, 38, 131
solidarity, 9, 35–36, 154, 179, 247–48
South-Asian Women's Center of Montreal (SAWC), 57, 59–60
Springer, Kimberly, 131–32, 142
Stasi, Bernard, 69
Stewart, Maria, 25–26
Stoler, Ann Laura, 264n52, 277n123
subject, 11–12, 41
   See also feminist subject
subjectivation, 6–7, 12–13, 37–38, 40
   See also feminist political subjectivation, political subjectivation
subjectivity, 30, 197–98, 217
   See also political subjectivity

Tamzali, Wassyla, 70
Taylor, Charles, 54–55
third-wave feminism, 86
Third World women, 26–27
Tocqueville, Alexis de, 266n81
Trat, Josette, 277n137, 278n149
triple jeopardy, 31, 47
Tronto, Joan, 13–14, 17, 40–41, 208–9, 210–13, 216–17, 221–22
Truth, Sojourner, 25–26
Tunisia, 278n149

umbrella organizations, 45–46, 60, 69, 70
Une école pour tou-te-s, contre les lois d'exclusion, 71–72
universalism, 31
   French, 87–91
   of gender oppression, 102–3, 138–39, 195–96, 206–7
   and secularism, 74–75, 121
   as strategic, 89–90
   as violence, 176–77
   of whiteness, 82, 162–63
   See also republican universalism

values, 20–21, 28–29, 54–55, 119–20, 121–22
   See also feminist values
veiled women. *See* Muslim women
veiling. *See* Islamic veiling

Vergès, Françoise, 94–95, 120, 135, 148–49, 264n52, 278n149, 281n35
Vigerie, Anne, 70
violence against women, 138–39
violence, ethical. *See* ethical violence
voice, 156, 159, 177, 197, 198–99, 208, 209–10
vulnerability, 240–41

We Care about One Another, 221
Weir, Allison, 5, 244–46, 247–48
Wekker, Gloria, 104
Weldon, Laurel, 185, 273n78
Western culture, 1–2, 49, 51
Western gaze, 26–27
white feminists
   and care, 93
   and international solidarity, 87, 92–93
   as knowledgeable, 97–98, 115–16, 123
   moral identity, 13, 38–39, 108
   and nationalism, 65
   and others, 43, 82, 83
   political subjectivation of, 82–83, 113–14
   and power, 171, 173–74
   race cognizance, 86–87, 96
   resistance to antiracism, 59–60
   and universalism, 64–65, 87, 89–90
   as victims, 166–67, 274n87
whiteness, 19, 81–82, 84–85
   and autonomy, 259n38
   desire for diversity, 86, 90
   and emotions, 104
   and ignorance, 81–83, 206
   as invisible, 81–82
   as universal, 31
   See also feminist whiteness
Wittgenstein, Ludwig, 26, 208, 209–10
Women Mediators, 139
women of color, 141
   See also migrant women, Muslim women, racialized women
Women's Health, 106–7
women's movements, 30, 31–32, 128, 131–32
   See also second-wave feminism, third-wave feminism

women's organizations
  advocacy-oriented, 140, 164
  funding of, 132–34, 140, 188
  and immigrant integration, 99
  inclusion of men, 161–62
  Muslim, 53–54
  power relations, 61–62
  representing racialized women, 34
  service-oriented, 95–96, 97–98, 106–7, 136–38
  See also migrant women's organizations, racialized women's organizations
women's rights, 55
  See also gender equality
Women's Rights Collective, 88–89, 91–92
women's rights organizations
  inclusion of racialized women, 97
  language in, 165–66
  and nationalism, 2
  and national values, 54–55, 119–20
  and sexularism debates, 45–46
world-building, 27–28, 104–5, 196–97, 249
World March of Women, 59–60, 63–64, 66–67, 164, 273n78, 279n152

Young, Iris, 14–15, 201–5, 210–12, 228–29, 247–48, 291–92n99
Yuval-Davis, Nira, 259n38

Zélensky, Anne, 70
Zerilli, Linda
  on difference, 28–29
  enlarged mentality, 196–200, 201
  feminism as a political project, 104–6, 180–81
  feminist subject, 25
  freedom, 32–33, 239–40
  judgment, 228–29
  political community, 27–28, 204, 209–10, 216
  promises, 190
  resentment, 170–71

www.ingramcontent.com/pod-product-compliance
Ingram Content Group UK Ltd.
Pitfield, Milton Keynes, MK11 3LW, UK
UKHW021317180426
11947UKWH00015B/1277